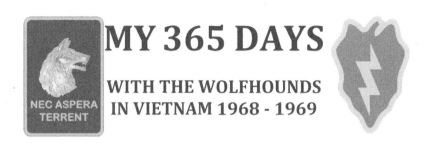

MY 365 DAYS

WITH THE WOLFHOUNDS
IN VIETNAM 1968 - 1969

NEC ASPERA TERRENT

A COMBAT VETERAN'S JOURNEY

John Quintrell

Foreword by LTG Claude "Mick" Kicklighter Army (Ret)

ACKNOWLEDGMENT

Thanks to my wife Laura Anne, who married a Vietnam Vet not knowing what she was getting into. She has stood by me through thick and thin. She has supported all things Wolfhounds and tirelessly worked on reunions and the Wolfhound Facebook page. She has always loved me just as I am, not how I should have been. Thank you, Ray Bourgeois and Russ Bruns, who were my best friends in Vietnam, and my best friends in life, and who helped me survive Vietnam. We made it against all odds.

Thank you, Christine King, MSc, PsyD, LMFT, LCPC, for helping me through very tough emotional times. Thank you for helping me understand and learn how to cope with the horrors of war.

Thank you, Dr. Katy Smith, Montana VA for dedicating your life to serving Veterans and giving them a better quality of life. Caring does not end at 4:30 pm.

Thank you, Dr. Rick Florette, D.C., for keeping me walking on the straight and narrow.

Thanks also to Jerry Lehman, my cherished friend, who for years sat for hours listening to the stories written in this book. You were one of the earliest supporters who gave your time and treasure to further the work of the Wolfhounds.

Thank you, Karen Gessaman, CPA, for making our nonprofit corporation become a reality.

Thank you, Diane Carlson Evans, for volunteering to be a Vietnam nurse. You and your sister nurses were responsible for getting so many of us home alive. We can never thank you enough. Your job exposed you and your sisters to horrors no person can conceive.

"The true soldier fights not because he hates what is in front of him, but because he loves what is behind him."

— G.K. Chesterton

Copyright 2022

My 365 Days with the Wolfhounds in Vietnam 1968-1969

Published by

BOOKMARKETEERS

www.wolfhounds2nd27th.org

Cover Design by MPrintUSA

ISBN: 978-1-649-70329-3

BOOKMARKETEERS

Email: **myvietnam365@gmail.com**

www.wolfhounds2nd27th.org

Printed in the United States of America

Thank you, Diane, for introducing me to school teachers who would allow me to share the Vietnam experience in their classrooms.

Thanks to all the teachers that had me come back year after year to speak to new generations of America's brightest young Americans.

Thank you, Jim Irby, Ph.D., for incorporating the veteran's interviews into your teaching curriculum and having the students interact with the veterans.

Thank you, Tommy Milner, our guardian angel, for sponsoring our fishing trips and for believing in my vision to interview all the living heroes that I served with. Without your support, none of that would have been possible.

Bless the many men that I served with who made the ultimate sacrifice. As you look down upon us, I hope you all approve of my attempt to tell our story the way it was; the good the bad, and the ugly. To all the guys still living, I say you are the bravest of the brave, you are my heroes. You have inspired me by your tenaciousness to live the best lives you can.

Thank you, Tommy Clack for gently pushing me to the finish line. Your life and integrity have inspired me and your dedication to veterans is remarkable.

Heartfelt thanks to Sarah Hord, houndette, events coordinator extraordinaire, whose tireless efforts have produced the best reunions we could ever hope for.

A debt of gratitude to Dick Glover whose wisdom and example in the field of battle taught so many of us how to survive Vietnam. Your life continues to be an inspiration to us all.

To the Cobra pilots Greg Bucy, Bob Segers and Chuck Moore and those pilots that gave their lives to bail us out of overwhelming situations and allowed us to make it home alive.

We would not be here if it wasn't for your bravery and courage. To all the helicopter pilots and medevac pilots who risked their lives so that we could perform our missions.

Thanks, Jim Brandau, for pinning on my sergeant stripes and being my co-partner in organizing our Wolfhound reunions.

Thank you, Bob "Moose" Mollenhauer, for organizing and putting on the Minnesota fishing trips for the guys in the platoon; they were amazing.

Thanks to all of Moose's buddies for serving us at these wonderful trips. Never forget you are all Honorary Wolfhounds. Those days spent together will be cherished by us all.

Thank you, Patty Mollenhauer, for organizing the special outing to Duluth that created many cherished memories for our wives.

Thank you, Mary Wiebush, for lovingly creating our Wolfhound casket cover. You have made it possible for us to honor our deceased brothers at the highest level.

Thank you to all the volunteers that help make our reunions beyond special.

Thank you to my sister Joanne and brother-in-law Dick Pirch for keeping the money straight and the camera in focus. No stronger bonds have been created than those bonds between combat buddies.

Thank you, Percy Allen, Arthur Anderson, Jack Atchison, Robert Bailey, Joel Baker, Jim Bartlett, William Bass, Jr. James Bentley, Jr., Dale Berg, James Bergman, Keith Bickel, Calvin Bigger, Arthur Blackwood, Ronnie Blair, Joe Bogar, Wardell Borders, Ray "Rick O Shay" Bourgeois, John Boyle, Jim Brandau, Charles Bridgewater, Randall Brockway, Scott Brockway, David Brogan, Barton Brooks, David Brown, Joel Brown, Russell Bruns, Donald Buchanan, Richard Buchanan, Sr., Greg Bucy, Ron

Burrow, James Burton, Bill "Alabama" Butler, Dale Butler, James Calvert, Jr., Donald Cartland, Dale Cathorall, J. Tommy Clack, Philip Clifton, Ed Clennon, Robert Cohen, Bobby Connell, John "John Boy" Cook, John Cooper, Robert E. Corbett, Don Cornett, Leroy Crabtree, Cy Creveling, Dale "Bruiser" Cutler, Larry Dasher, Preston Davis, Jr., Ronnie Dawley, Rudy Deanda, Bruce Deisinger, Jim Dotson, Mike "Soda man" Deline, John "Doc" Dellagarino, Dan Deitz, Larry Dobesh, Melvin Dowdy, Dave Duininck, Gerald "Dixie" Dykstra, Diane Carlson Evans, Willis Estes, James Fell, Patrick Fitzgerald, David "Doc" Flores, Gary Flowers, Ed Frey, Rick Galli, Conrad Garcia, Dale Glenn, Richard Glover, Thomas Gorman, Jerry Granger, Keith Gregory, David "Grimm Reaper" Grimm, William "Chief" Gritts, Charlie Hacker, Craig Hacker, Fred Hannah, Mack Henderson, Arnie Hendry, Earl Herndon, Matias Herrera, Howard Hibbard, Frank Higgins, Arie Hill, Doug Holston, Robert Howell, Vladimer Honchar, Gary Hunt, Bill Hurley, Donald Ide, Harry Ikner, Phil Iserino, Ernest Jackson, Roosevelt Jackson, Jerry Jazwieck, Little Joe, Cal Johnson, Robert Jones, John Kavanaugh, Lee Keith, Dave "Teach" Kelley, Ken Kelly, Lee Ketchum, Ron King, Steve Klaus, Fred "Rabbi" Kramer, George "MF" Kush, Larry Lamb, Larry Lamere, Terry Lane, Bruce Laugaunet, Jim Langley, Allen "Claymore" Larsen, Wayne Lee, Joe Leibel, George Leidy, David Lininger, Dennis "Sneaker" Lorenzini, Stout Leblanc, Mike "The Kid" Lozon, Greg Mannarelli, Gonzalez Marquez, Jim Marshall, Bill McCure, Mike Mehelich, Mack Mitchell, Eugene Mollberg, Robert "Moose" Mollenhauer, Chuck Moore, Robert C. Mora, Wayne Morris, Jack Morrison, Paul Naso, Wayne Neal, Bob Noel, Bob Nowaki, Herb Nye, Jamie O'Brien, Opey, George Parounagian, James Pelipesky, Tony Pieroni, Sam Praw, Ed Rambo, Steve Randock, Gerard Rattelade, George Reinwald, Gary Richardson, Harold Riney, Rickey Robinson, David C. Rodgers, Rodriquez, Sgt. Romero, Lanny Ross, Dale Rundquist, Sylvester Salono, Bob Segers, Dave "Smokes" Schimmoeller, Richard Schultz, Michael Scott, Charles "Bill" Scott, Jack Slovey, Michael Smith, Spurill,

David Stansbury, Larry Stanzyk, Kenneth Steinhebel, Gilbert Stogsdill, Coy Strobel, Steve "Doc" Swartz, DeWayne "Sugarbear" Taylor, Robert Taylor, Jerry Tempesta, William Tennent, Thacker, Steve Thorpe, Clement Todd, Thomas Tomsic, Maurice Tubbs, Doc Turner, Charles "Hedgy" VanArk, Trung "Pete" Van Than, Bill Vaught, Les Waggoner, George Walton, Forrest Ward, Joe "Big Joe" Waskom, Michael Waterloo, James Weaver, Cyrus Weisner, Willy Williams, George Weldon, Jerry White, Doc Wolff, George "Woody" Woodman III, Tom Wooten, Michael K.Wonderlich, Dean Wooten, Lloyd Yost, Ricardo Zamora, Johnny Zanders.

To my children, Tim, Tom, Tammy, and Laura Louise, who were too young to understand what I was going through when they were young. I hope this book answers the questions I never adequately answered back then.

My daughter Laura Louise inspired me to write my story several years ago when she bought me a book on "How to write your life story." It took years, but you never gave up encouraging me.

In particular, I thank my son, Timothy, who has always believed in me and my vision for the Wolfhounds. He has dedicated himself to honoring the veterans in this book. Without his expertise, our reunions and interviews would have been mediocre at best. Tim loves the veterans with all his heart, and they love him.

In closing, I want to express my deepest appreciation and abiding love to my wife, Laura. She has supported me through the rough times of reliving the horrors of Vietnam. She sat in the background listening to all the stories the Wolfhounds would tell me. She cried along with me as memories of the war were shared by the men in this book. She was and will always be my hero.

Thank you, Laura Anne, for your unconditional love to me and my children, grandchildren, and great grandchildren. You will always be their beloved Nana.

FOREWORD

Sergeant Quintrell's 365 Days is an unvarnished, unfiltered, and unapologetic memoir of one of the bloodiest years of this painful and complex war in Vietnam. His account practically oozes grit and authenticity. Quintrell calls it like he sees it.

His story serves as a powerful reminder of the incredible sacrifices that were made on behalf of a divided and ambivalent nation. Instead of gratitude for dutifully answering the nation's call, so many members of the US Army, Marines, Navy, Air Force, and Coast Guard were not only unappreciated, but scorned for their efforts. This Book reminds us that it is never too late to say to a Vietnam Veteran, "Thank You for Your Service."

I am glad I read this Book, it brought back many memories.

Claude M. (Mick) Kicklighter
Lieutenant General, US Army (Retired)

Commissioned as a Regular Army officer in 1955, at Mercer University, Macon, Georgia, Mr. Kicklighter is a longtime public servant who has been recognized for devoting more than 50 years of combined military and public service to his country.

Mr. Kicklighter served two tours of duty in the Vietnam War, first with the 1st Logistics Command and then with the 101 Airborne Airmobile Division.

Mr. Kicklighter went on to serve as the commander of the 1st Battalion, 21st Field Artillery, 4th Infantry Division at Fort Carson, 1972-1973; Director for support for Vietnam and Cambodia, J 4 Joint Chiefs of Staff, 1974-1975; Army Representative on a Defense Assessment team Iran, 1975-1976; Commander, Division Artillery and Assistant Division Commander, 24th Infantry Division, 1976-1979; Assistant Chief of Staff, Logistics, Allied Forces Central Europe, The

12

Netherlands, 1979-1981; Commander of the Army Security Assistance Command and Chief of Staff of the US Army Materiel Development and Readiness Command, Alexandria, Virginia, 1981-1984; Commanding General, 25th Infantry Division, Schofield Barracks, Hawaii 1984-1986.

Mr. Kicklighter served as Director of the Army Staff from 1987-1989. His last assignment before retiring from active duty was Commanding General, US Army Western Command and then Commanding General, US Army Pacific, 1989-1991. His rank at retirement was Lieutenant General.

After retiring from the US Army, Mr. Kicklighter was selected to lead our nation's effort to commemorate the 50th Anniversary of World War Two, 1991-1995. He then became the Deputy Under Secretary of the Army for International Affairs, 1995-1998.

Mr. Kicklighter was then appointed by the President and confirmed by the Senate to serve as the Assistant Secretary for Policy and Planning, Department of Veterans Affairs, which became the Office of Policy, Planning and Preparedness after the terrorist attacks of September 11, 2001, and he then served as Chief of Staff of the Department of Veterans Affairs, 1999-2005.

In 2003, Mr. Kicklighter was chosen by the Secretary of Defense as Director of the Department of Defense's Iraq Transition Team that planned the deactivation of the Coalition Provisional Authority and the establishment of the US Mission Baghdad during ongoing combat operations.

In 2005, he was selected to establish and direct the Iraq/Afghanistan Joint Transition Planning Group, a joint Department of State and Department of Defense team that provided analysis and recommendations for coordinating efforts to address transition challenges in Iraq and Afghanistan.

In April 2007, following Senate confirmation, General Kicklighter was sworn in as the sixth Inspector General of the Department of Defense.

Mr. Kicklighter then served as Director of the Center for Critical Infrastructure Protection and Homeland Security, Scalia School of Law, George Mason University, Arlington, Virginia, 2008-2015. During this same period, he served as head of the Department of Defense Office of Commemorations, 2012-2014; and coordinating the Nation's "50th Anniversary" Commemoration of the End of the Vietnam War. The office was still coordinating the same for World War II and the Korean War.

Mr. Kicklighter was very active with Habitat for Humanity International. He chaired the nonprofit organization between 1998 and 2001, and served on the board of directors from 1996 to 2001. He served on the Board of Trustees, Mercer University, 2012-2017.

During his tenure at Mercer, he co-directed the establishment of the Mercer University Center for Leadership and Ethics. His special passion today is his service on the board of Rescue: Freedom International, which has the mission of rescuing and restoring young women and children who have been sold into sex slavery.

The recipient of multiple awards for his military service, Mr. Kicklighter notably received a Distinguished Service Medal with Two Bronze Oak Leaf Clusters, Defense Superior Service Medal, Legion of Merit with Three Bronze Oak Leaf Clusters, and a Bronze Star Medal. As a civilian, he was awarded the Department of Defense Medal for Distinguished Public Service (Gold Palm), and was awarded the Presidential Citizens Medal, presented by The President at a ceremony in the White House.

He was awarded the Eisenhower Liberation Medal by the United States Holocaust Memorial Council at a ceremony in the US Capitol Rotunda.

Mr. Kicklighter earned a Bachelor of Arts from Mercer University and a Master's degree from the School of Business, George Washington University.

Mr. Kicklighter is proud to have been made an Honorary Member of the Sisseton-Wahpeton Sioux Tribe of South Dakota in 1984.

REVIEWS

"John Quintrell writes a devastatingly personal memoir. His recalling the chilling nature of guerrilla and helicopter warfare and its effect on the men who fight in it chronicles their cold fear. Ground with precision, John evokes the foot soldier's daily life. Its raw language brings a shocking and gritty portrait of horror and pain with its immediate emotional impact of shame and guilt – recalled even 50 years after his one heartrending year in Vietnam. Not all soldiers were honorable. Judging by his clarity in the narrative, he has yet to forget those years and its moral confusion.

With intense sketches of fellow soldiers, hedgerows and villages, bloodied bodies and land scarred by bullets and napalm the author never lets up with the gore and agony and loss of yet another brother-in-arms, enemy, child or innocent civilian. As an Army Nurse in South Vietnam, I saw the results of war every day. Soldiers like John handed his men off to our hospitals or to the angels. Read this book to grasp that profound bravery, self-sacrifice and heroism in the Vietnam generation is undeniable. John lived to tell his story and he tells it well."

Diane Carlson Evans, Captain, Army Nurse Corps, Vietnam 1968-69.
Author of Healing Wounds, A Vietnam War Combat Nurses' 10-year
Fight to Win Women a Place of Honor in Washington, DC and Founder,
Vietnam Women's Memorial

"It was the best of times; it was the worst of times. John looks back into the military experiences of the young men he served with trying to survive during the Vietnam War."

Russell Bruns – Wolfhound Veteran

This is a story about the men who served with "Big John" in the second platoon Wolfhounds. Our story began in August 1968 and ended in August 1969. John's memories of Basic and

Advanced Infantry training are remarkable and anyone who went through these experiences will relive those challenging times. The story covers the trials and tribulations of the grunts that served in the platoon, as well as the lighter moments and gallows humor that prevailed as a way to help us cope with the insanity of war.

I am extremely proud of John's accurate accounts of the battles we fought together. John is my friend and cherished brother Wolfhound, who has written a book that, will allow all Vietnam Vets to take pride in their service.

Ray Bourgeois – 2nd Platoon 2nd 27th Inf. August 1968-August 1969

For those who enjoy reading a book that makes you feel like you are actually viewing the scene as written and want to turn the page to learn what transpired, then My 365 Days with the Wolfhounds in Vietnam is a must read.

Through the eyes of a typical young American man, who is thrust into the reality of the Vietnam War and survives a complete tour of one year, the reader lives through all the human feelings that exist in this environment.

You feel the emotions of fear, anguish, sorrow, joy, relief and want this young man to survive and go home in one piece. You get to see the bond that develops between young men, from every segment of the American society.

You are present as a member of the writer's unit; and, when his 365 days of a roller coaster ride of life and death are over, you are relieved that you too have made your DEROS. This story is a must-read to open the door of the reality of an Army infantryman's fight to survive 365 days in the Vietnam War.

As a combat-wounded Army soldier, I, and every "ground pounder" who served in S. Vietnam, experienced the story played out in this most unique book! You will not put it down once you start reading.

If those surviving veterans of the Vietnam War can bear to revisit their half-century-old memories at all, most cannot bring themselves to speak of their loss of innocence and the horrors they experienced. "Big John" Quintrell, who should have stayed in college instead of becoming the squad leader of an infantry unit, has been able to do both in this rare memoir. The often-raw specificity he provides belies a brilliant mind that could have been the top-notch doctor, lawyer or a senator as his family envisioned.

It reminds us of how careful we need to be when we decide to wage war, committing our youth to causes they do not fully understand and depriving our society of their talents. As Quintrell takes us through the incredible 365-day journey he managed to survive, one grieves the loss of the precious young men and women, who did not make it back, but also of those who did, because their lives were irreparably altered.

If he could bring himself to go on with the telling of his story, the devastation of war and the effects of post-traumatic stress would be revealed in his and the lives of his wives and children. The hope is we will listen to these veterans, who are able and willing to speak to us of the miseries of war. It is they, who are the authoritative scholars on the subject. This work is far more than the equivalent of the college thesis Quintrell would have produced in academia. If we are to ensure veterans' lives matter, please read it. Few accounts like this have or probably ever will be written.

Christine King MSc, PsyD, LMFT, LCPC

My 365 Days with the Wolfhounds in Vietnam is the accurate accounting of one Vietnam veteran's life from being a carefree, 1968 California teenager, being transformed into a 1969 battle-hardened Vietnam veteran questioning his own survival, mourning the loss of those left behind and asking the question: "What the hell just happened to me?"

your blood. We were America's best and brightest exposed to the lethal chemical known as Agent Orange.

Our war included officers whose tour of duty in the field only lasted for six months; leaving the field when they just started to be proficient at their jobs. The stories in this book are true; keeping in mind that in combat everyone in attendance has their own point of view. Ten guys in a firefight have ten different stories based on what they saw and experienced.

Some of the names have been changed. I believe that the Vietnam Veterans should be proud of their service. The US Army in Vietnam never lost a major battle and, in the end, the war came to an end with a negotiated peace. Our stories are important and need to be preserved for generations to come. For those who protested the war, I would say, it is ok to hate the war but please don't hate the warriors.

We were sent to a faraway place to fight communism and protect America's freedoms. We fought and gave everything we had; some making the ultimate sacrifice. Read this story about the heroes I served with and the families and loved ones that were the real victims of the Vietnam War.

John "Big John" Quintrell August 2020

Fort Ord, U.S. Army Training Center

August 21, 1968 - August 21, 1969
My 365 Days with the Wolfhounds in Vietnam
My journey as a combat soldier

PROLOGUE

I will never forget the day that I left Vietnam. It was a hot and muggy afternoon when I reached Long Binh Air Force Base. I stood in line for what seemed like hours before I finally got to the front of the line. The Sgt. standing there asked to see my DEROS (date estimated returning from overseas) orders. All I could think of was whether or not he would check my duffel bag and see the war trophies that I was trying to sneak home. Back in Cu Chi they had warned us that if we were caught with any contraband, we would have to stay in Vietnam for an extended period of time.

There were two lines of GIs getting ready to board the freedom birds. One line went to a United Airlines flight, the other flight was a military transport plane. I was in the left line and my buddy Ray Bourgeois was in the right line. As luck would have it, my line went to the United Airlines flight and Ray's line went to the government transport plane. I later found out that the transport plane had web seats and an airman that handed out bag lunches and bottles of water.

When I boarded the United Airlines flight, I was greeted by beautiful round-eyed stewardesses. They all had big smiles on their faces and told each of us, as we reached the top of the stairs, "welcome aboard." The Captain and co-pilot were standing beside them to shake our hands. There were no seating assignments so we were able to pick any seat we wanted. As I boarded the plane to get seated, everybody on board appeared to be very quiet.

Everyone was thinking the same thing; am I really going to get out of Vietnam? Is this plane really going to get off the ground? Am I really going to be going home to see my mom, my dad and my sister? The tension got worse as the plane taxied down to the end of the runway. The pilot got on the intercom and said, "make sure your seat belts are buckled guys; we're getting ready to take this freedom bird home!" The roar of the engines was a sweet song to our ears as the plane slowly but surely started to make its way down the runway.

Each man looking out the window wondered if he would see Charlie standing on the edge of the runway holding RPG rocket launchers. Two days before, a Tiger Airlines flight had the front wheel blown out from underneath it on takeoff by a Viet Cong mortar. Our Captain used the entire runway to get the plane off the ground because it was loaded to the gills with all the men and equipment.

The minute the wheels lifted off of the runway, every man on that plane started to shout for joy. Guys were throwing their hats up in the air and as I looked around, I saw several guys with tears in their eyes. A booney hat landed in my lap and I turned the headband inside out and saw it belonged to Roosevelt Jackson. It seemed like I had finally made it. The Captain pulled up sharply with throttles wide open to get us out of the combat zone as quickly as he could.

It was not uncommon for the NVA to send planes on their way with a few 51 caliber machine gun bullets. After the shouting settled down, the stewardesses came down the aisle and shook every man's hand and said they were going home. Several of the guys, including myself, took the opportunity to kiss the young lady's hand. The clean smell that each of the ladies had been almost intoxicating and we all started thinking about our sweethearts at home.

23

There were several other thoughts running through my mind at the time. What were my guys doing that day? I had left the field while we were doing seven-day sweeps along the Cambodian border. Our Kit Carson Scout Pete had stepped on a booby trap the morning I left. I had severe feelings of guilt leaving the guys behind. I can still see their faces as they looked up at me as the helicopter lifted off the ground taking me back to Cu Chi. Mike "THE KID" was standing brushing his teeth, and he saluted me as the helicopter faded into the distance

I had no idea at the time how that would affect me for years to come. The stewardesses gave us just about anything we wanted, including steak sandwiches, any kind of pop or beer we asked for, plus they threw in a pillow fight once in a while just for fun. About an hour into the flight, the Captain walked down the aisle and shook every man's hand again and said thank you for your service. He told us he had flown Navy phantoms in Vietnam in 1965 and 1966.

After returning home, he decided to become a commercial airline pilot and volunteered to fly the Vietnam route. During the flight home, I tried to close my eyes and sleep, but I couldn't get my mind to stop thinking about my last 12 months in Vietnam. When the United flight landed at Travis Air Force Base, we were marched into a hanger just off the tarmac. I remember looking at my watch and it was 4 o'clock in the afternoon on a Friday. The Army personnel in the hangar told us that they were responsible for signing us in but said they would skip the orientation speech and allow us to sign a roster and then we would be free to go.

They also suggested not wearing our Army uniforms when we left the base. They said that there were Vietnam War protesters standing outside the gate and they could be very abusive to returning GIs. My goal at that time was to get a taxi and go to the nearest Greyhound bus station and get a ticket to Fullerton, California, where my sister Joanne lived.

There were indeed protesters waiting for us at the gate. They were shouting at us and calling us baby killers and many of them spit on us as we tried to get in the cabs. To say I was confused was an understatement. I had just spent 12 months fighting for my country, in a God-forsaken jungle called Vietnam. I asked the cab driver what the hell was going on, and he said, "you're lucky you didn't get hit with rotten tomatoes." My only reply was, "take me to the nearest Greyhound bus station."

When I got there, I called my mother and told her that I was back in the United States, and that I was going to Joanne's house, and that I would be seeing her the following day. Upon arriving at my sister's house, I was greeted by not only my sister Joanne but also her roommate Marie. There were plenty of hugs and kisses to go around, but I felt no joy or good feelings. That night I slept on my sister's floor, and I woke up in a cold sweat, having just had a flashback of an ambush we popped in early September.

The following day my sister Joanne drove me to San Diego to see my mother. My mother had requested that I wear my uniform to her house so she could take a picture with me wearing my dress greens. I was getting my duffel bag out of the trunk of the car, when Mr. Reed who lived across the street, came out of his house and started walking towards me. This was the neighborhood where I was born and raised. Mr. Reed had always been a hero to me growing up. He worked for the phone company and his job included climbing telephone poles.

Every so often, when the neighborhood boys would be playing in the street together, he would climb the telephone pole in front of my house just to show us how it was done. I had just closed the trunk expecting Mr. Reed to welcome me home or give me a hug, but instead, he got in my face and said, "you should be ashamed of yourself!" I was stunned, my throat closed up, and I didn't know what to say.

He went on to tell me how I had killed innocent babies and women in Vietnam and how wrong the war was. Something happened within me that day that would change my life forever. I decided right then and there that I would not tell anybody that I was a Vietnam veteran. That promise would last for 30 years.

Mr. Reed turned on his heels, headed back towards his house, shaking his head and as I started walking towards the front steps of mom's house, she came out with a huge smile on her face and with her arms opened wide. She stood next to the American flag she had flown for the 365 days I was in Nam. She was crying and as she tried to talk, it just came out as gibberish. We embraced and mom told me to come in the house and we could sit down and talk. She told me she was cooking a big dinner in my honor that night, and that she was going to invite some family members.

Mom put on a fantastic feed of turkey with all the trimmings. My mother's boyfriend Bill said grace and, in his prayer, he thanked God that I had returned home safely. The next words that were spoken came from me; "will someone please pass the fuckin butter?" There was dead silence at the table and there was a look of shock on everyone's face but mine. I did not know that I'd said anything wrong, that's just the way we talked in Vietnam. But I'm getting way ahead of myself in the story, because the beginning of the story started 16 months earlier, in March 1968.

John and Bango Just Before Draft

John & Dad 1968

John's Dad and Mom

Quintrell Wins Heroism Awards

Sgt. John F. Quintrell, son of Mr. and Mrs. John E. Quintrell of Cody, was awarded the Bronze Star and Purple Heart medals for action in Vietnam.

Quintrell entered the Army in 1968 and plans to be home from Vietnam in September. He attended San Diego Junior College.

The citation for the Bronze Star follows:

For heroism in connection with military operations against a hostile force: Private First Class Quintrell distinguished himself by heroic actions on 9 December 1968, while serving as a rifleman with Company C, 2d Battalion, 27th Infantry in the Republic of Vietnam. While acting as a blocking element, Company C came under an intense hostile attack. During the ensuing battle a squad that *was* isolated from the rest of Private Quintrell's platoon by a river came under immense hostile pressure. In an attempt to reinforce the beleaguered position, a four-man boat overturned. An RTO heavily ladened with equipment began to flonder in the water. With complete disregard for his own safety, Private Quintrell exposed himself to the hostile fire a s he ran through the kill z o n e and jumped into the river to aid his beleaguered comrade. His actions were directly responsible for getting the RTO to safety. Private Quintrell's personal bravery, aggressiveness, and devotion to duty are in keeping with the highest traditions of the military service and reflect great credit upon himself, his un it, the 25th Infantry Division, and the United States Army."

SGT. JOHN QUINTRELL, who was awarded the Bronze Star and Purple Heart for heroism while serving with Company C, 2nd Battalion, 27 Infantry during an engagement with the enemy December 9, 1968. Quintrell is the son of Mr. and Mrs. John E. Quintrell of 1126 Alger Ave.

TABLE OF CONTENTS

Chapter One
NOT SO SMART

Growing up as a kid in San Diego, California, offered me many opportunities to experience life that many guys only dreamed of. I grew up close to the Pacific Ocean and I spent my summers there enjoying what the beach had to offer. I especially remember the sunburns, the surfing, and hanging around the surf shops located at Pacific Beach.

Hobart "Hobie" Alter was getting his surfboard business up and running at Dana Point in Mission Bay. It was not uncommon to join a family around a bonfire on the beach and enjoy eating hot dogs that were being cooked on metal un-bent clothes hangers over an open fire. It didn't matter whether you knew the family or not, everyone seemed to be welcome.

My dad worked for the University of California at San Diego, located at La Jolla Beach. During the summer when I was 11 years old, my dad would take me to work with him every day and I would spend the day at the beach fishing off of the La Jolla pier, snorkeling, and spearing various kinds of fish. I also joined the junior oceanographers club at the Scripps Aquarium and supplied them with fresh fish to feed the sharks they had on display.

It was always fun to go behind the scenes and see how the aquarium was run from behind the tanks. Some of my fondest memories from those years were when my dad and I would go to the food vendor in front of the aquarium and get cheeseburgers for lunch.

During my high school years, my dad and I lived outside of San Diego in a place called Rancho Bernardo. We lived out in the county where we had no electricity and we relied on a well for our water. Our indoor lights and refrigerator operated on propane gas. Dad bought a generator that he hooked up to the electrical box that supplied us with electricity to watch TV or listen to the radio at night.

I studied Morse code with a school buddy named Larry and was able to pass the test to become a ham radio operator. My dad and I set up a 40-foot dipole antenna that allowed me to communicate with people all over the world. I had a dog named Rusty, an Irish setter, and two horses: Bango and Cloud. Being alone out in the country didn't seem to bother me much because I always found projects to work on and things to do.

One of my more interesting hobbies was beekeeping. When I was 15 years old, I went to the Safeway store in Rancho Bernardo and asked the manager if he needed any help. He said he was looking for a box boy and said he would give me an application. I filled out the application and indicated I was 16 years old, which was the minimum age a kid could work in those days. I fibbed on the application and said I was 16. I worked part-time there during the school year and full-time during the summer.

Life was good except my dad would not let me get my driver's license. It had something to do with the increased cost of insurance. At 17 years old, my mother went down and signed for me and I was on my way to cruising Southern California's highways. When I was in ninth grade, Pres. Kennedy was coming to San Diego and his motorcade was going to travel down El Cajon Blvd right past our school. The school let the kids out so that we could go lineup along the street and see the President as he drove by in his limousine. I will never forget that day as long as I live, I was within 15 feet of the man my parents said was the greatest President of all times.

The day I graduated from high school was a banner day for me. I had looked forward to this day for what seemed like my whole life. After graduation, my dad and I moved to a little town called Poway, California. It was there that my dad and I discussed my future. The first thing he did was inform me that I would be paying him $50 a month rent, and I would be responsible for my own car insurance. He told me that was the cost for being an adult and that he would no longer ask me when I would be getting home at night.

I was the first kid on my block to have an eight-track stereo in my car with a big speaker mounted in the back seat. Later, I would add a reverb unit to the mix. My manager at Safeway informed me that the store in Oceanside was looking for someone to come in and work on the revamp crew. This was when the store completely changed the interior of the store and rearranges all the aisles and the space that each vendor receives.

This all had to be done after hours, as the store manager was not willing to shut down completely to do this task. It would mean I would get a promotion to retail clerk and quite a bit more money per hour. I drove to Oceanside to interview and after about 15 minutes, I had the job. Revamping the store was a brutal job, including a lot of heavy lifting. We got the entire job done in three weeks and the manager asked me if I wanted to stay on as a retail clerk. Oceanside was only 20 miles away from Poway and driving on the interstate only took me 20 minutes to get to work.

I advanced very quickly in that store, and within one year, I had already been put in charge of the frozen food section and the dairy department. In August 1966, my dad asked me if I was going to sign up for college. He had always told me that he wanted me to get a college education, something he never did. There was a community college in Claremont, California, that was only 25 minutes from our house.

It wasn't in my heart to go to college, but I signed up anyway to satisfy my dad. Safeway in Solano Beach was looking for someone to run their night stocking crew. My manager told me it would be a great way to move up in the company. He said I would be promoted to assistant manager. I immediately accepted the job. That decision forced me to juggle a lot of balls at the same time. I worked at night and went to school during the day. After one semester of college, I quit school without saying anything to my dad.

The most important thing in my life at that time was making money and chasing girls. A buddy of mine, Tom Packman and I would cruise the streets of Escondido on Friday nights trying to pick up any girls that would fall for our tricks. Eventually, my dad found out I was no longer in college and told me how disappointed he was. The one thing I never counted on was that the college was legally bound to inform the selective service of my dropping out of school.

As long as I was in college, I was given a draft deferment which kept me out of the Army. I lost that deferment when I dropped out. Sometime in February 1968, my dad handed me a letter that came in the mail with a return address of selective service. It did not even occur to me that for the next two years, my life would not be my own.

When I opened the letter, it started out with: Greetings, your President wants you to show up at the selective service office in

San Diego in two weeks. I remember standing there feeling numb and trying to figure out how I could get back into college and avoid the draft. When I called the college, they told me regrettably that there was no opportunity for me to get back into college since I had received a draft letter. The realization hit me, "Not So Smart!"

John and Bango

John and his Irish Setter Rusty

Chapter Two
I'M IN THE ARMY NOW

W hen I showed my dad the letter, it was one of the first times I saw my Dad at a loss for words. I was so involved in my own life that I never knew anything about the Vietnam War that was going on at that time. The only time I ever heard about Vietnam was when one of my best friends from high school called me and told me about Eddie Tesla.

Eddie was a good friend and was killed in Vietnam after only being there for two weeks. Apparently, his Marine unit had been walking through a jungle and a sniper shot Eddie between the eyes, killing him instantly. His identical twin brother Benny was devastated. Of course, I was shocked, but my grief only lasted a short time. I was too involved in making money and chasing girls.

On March 26, 1968, my dad dropped me off at the selective service office in downtown San Diego on the appointed date and time and I stood in a room with a bunch of guys and raised my right hand and pledged allegiance to the United States Army. I was given some papers to sign, and the guy with Sgt. stripes on his shirt came over and handed me a piece of paper that gave me a time and date to show up for my induction physical.

The Army rented Greyhound buses and they took us to Los Angeles, where hundreds of guys lined up to go in and get their Army physical. The physical turned out to be a joke. I had to piss in a cup, some doctor stuck his fingers in my nuts and told me to cough, and they stuck me for a blood sample and that was it. I was told that I would be receiving a letter from the Army within the next couple of days telling me what I would be doing next. When I got off the Greyhound bus that night, the realization that I was going to be in the Army hit me hard.

I never had a chance to even consider whether I would want to serve in the Army. When I got home that night my dad was very sullen and didn't have much to say. He mentioned that one of his co-worker's son dodged the draft and went to Canada. He was not suggesting for me to do the same. In three days, I got a letter from the Army congratulating me on passing the physical and telling me that I would be reporting for basic training at Fort Ord, California.

Transportation instructions were included, and it looked as though I was going to be taking another Greyhound bus ride. My mother was heartbroken when I told her the news. She didn't even know I dropped out of college and said she was worried about me going into the Army. My sister, who was starting her own career at the Telephone Company, didn't have much to say one way or the other.

Looking back, it seems really weird that I never had a chance to say goodbye to so many of my relatives and my friends. My grandfather, who was a highly decorated Navy Veteran, said the Army was going to make a man out of me. He had served 35 years as a chief warrant boatswain and fought in two wars but did not have any advice for me before I left.

The thought of going to Canada crossed my mind. I did, however, get a chance to meet with some of the neighborhood

40

boys that I had grown up with that were all currently enrolled in college and they gave me a going-away party. None of them had a clue what the Vietnam War was all about, nor did they have any interest in knowing about it. My dad, mom, and sister drove me down to the bus station and they all hugged me and had tears in their eyes as they told me to take care of myself.

The bus ride to Northern California seemed like it took forever. We had left early in the morning and traveled down Highway 101 all the way up the Pacific coastline. I kept staring out the window, watching the surf coming in, remembering how it seemed like only yesterday I had been playing in the surf without a care in the world. They handed out bag lunches and they only stopped three times for us to use the bathroom. Everybody's ass was aching by the time we got to the front gate at Fort Ord.

I clearly remember driving through the front gate and winding around many streets filled with barracks until we reached the reception area. When the driver opened the door, a drill sergeant wearing a Smokey bear hat jumped on board with a megaphone in his hand and started yelling at us to grab our gear and get off the bus. He told us to line up information. I don't think a single man on that bus had any idea what a formation was, but we would soon find out.

The guys that exited that bus were a mix of long-haired hippie types, bad asses from LA and a few jocks like me. There were three buses unloading about 120 men that included 30 guys from Guam. I thought it was a good idea to get my hair cut short before going to basic training because I'd heard about the haircut ceremony.

There were four drill Sergeants waiting for us and they all seemed very angry and threatening. One of the drill Sergeants brought a garbage can and placed it in front of our half-assed formation. He told us that we had one chance and one chance only to get rid of any items that were not allowed into basic training. He started listing these items as guns, knives, dope, needles, weed, hemp, ganja, pills, any sharp objects that were not designed for shaving and anything else that could be used as a weapon.

I stood in disbelief as several guys went forward and I saw two guys who looked like Mexican gang members drop handguns and ammunition into the trash can. There must've been at least 20 guys that went forward and dropped knives in the can.

There was one guy who pulled out a 12-inch hunting knife and he regrettably tossed it into the trash can. When everyone was back in formation, one of the drill Sergeants went over and looked in the can and said, "I know that some of you turds have not given up your stuff. I will be doing a strip search and emptying out all your bags and if I find anything, you'll wish you were dead." He said, "I'm going to give you assholes one more chance to bring your guns, knives, pills, and dope and put them in this can."

Again, in disbelief, I stood there and watched several guys go forward and dump out many items that the drill Sergeant had mentioned. When they were done, the trash can was almost full. The drill Sergeant told us to do a right face and about a third of the guys turned left and the drill Sergeants pounced on those guys turning them around and yelling in their ears. They marched us into the barracks and assigned us our bunks and told us to put our bags on the floor in front of us.

The drill Sergeants started to go and grab bags, open them, and empty the contents out onto the floor. If the drill Sergeant found any contraband, they would have the owner of that bag stripped down to their underpants. This went on for an hour straight; some guys looked very nervous about having the drill Sergeant go through their bags. After this brutal assault on our persons was over, we were told to put our stuff back in our bags.

We were then instructed to put the sheet and blanket onto the bed and stuff the pillow into the pillowcase and prepare ourselves for an inspection. After everyone had accomplished this task, the drill Sergeants went bed by bed, tearing up the blankets and sheets and throwing the mattresses onto the floor yelling at each man, "Didn't your mommy teach you how to make a bed?" The atmosphere within the barracks was nerve-racking with a constant cacophony of yelling and screaming.

One of the drill instructors told us to gather around one of the bunks and he would show us the proper way to make a military bed. This training included the art of making hospital corners and stretching the blanket so tight that you could bounce a quarter off of it. The drill Sergeant said we had one more chance to make it right and those that didn't get it right would be punished severely. That punishment would turn out to be pushups, and lots of them. By the time 9 p.m. rolled around, everybody in the barracks was exhausted.

We were told to go to bed and get some sleep and that we would be woken in the morning and marched over to the chow hall for breakfast. At 4 o'clock in the morning, we were all suddenly startled by the sounds of trash cans rolling down the middle of the bay being hit by DIs with nightsticks. We were told to get dressed, stand in front of our bunks and prepare to go to breakfast. That was the rudest awakening I have ever experienced in my life.

The drill instructors lined us up in front of the barracks in single file and we marched about two blocks to the mess hall. The whole time we were marching, the drill instructors kept pulling guys out of line and making them drop and do 10 pushups for reasons beyond anybody's understanding. It was a never-ending drawl of verbal abuse and a couple of the guys made the mistake of yelling back at the DIs.

The guy in front of me said under his breath, "I don't think these DIs have the right to treat us like this." Little did we know our lives were no longer our own. Uncle Sam owned us lock, stock and barrel. I remember being really hungry that morning and when we got to the mess hall, we picked up a metal tray, silverware and a melmac coffee cup. We got in line that moved quite swiftly as cooks' helpers put what seemed like a small amount of food on each man's tray. They told us to find a seat at one of the long tables set up in the mess hall and to sit there and eat our breakfast and keep our mouths shut.

I immediately thought that sounded kind of funny since how can you eat your breakfast with your mouth shut! Even before we were through eating breakfast, the DIs started yelling at us again and made us get up and empty our trays into the trash can next to the door as we were leaving. Some guys had not been able to eat half their breakfast. This was just a sign of things to come. They loaded us on buses again and drove us to an area that looked like a warehouse complex. We got off the bus and were marched into the building and I realized we were in a clothing and equipment warehouse.

You started in line, and at each station, you were issued a different piece of clothing or equipment. The first thing they gave you was a duffel bag and told you this is what would be used to carry our gear. There was civilian personnel at each station that looked you up and down and guessed what size you were and threw clothing at you and told you to try it on and put it in your bag. The only piece of clothing they did check for accuracy was the combat boots that you were issued.

Everything you would need for the next eight weeks was being put in that bag. Four pairs of underpants, four T-shirts, four pairs of olive drab green socks, two fatigue shirts, two fatigue pants, one pair of combat boots (Korean war era), one poncho, two tent poles, four tent stakes, one helmet liner, one helmet, one cunt cap (their description of dress hat), one dress green uniform, two poplin shirts, two pairs of black socks, backpack, one set of suspenders, one pair of shiny black dress shoes, one belt, one brass belt buckle, one fatigue jacket, one fatigue jacket liner, and last but not least one pair of wool gloves.

When we were marched out of the warehouse, the buses were nowhere to be found. We were lined up and told that we were going to be marching back to our reception station building that was about a mile and a half away. We all slung our duffel bags over our shoulders and began our first forced march, but it would certainly not be the last.

Third Platoon 1968

Big John in Basic

Chapter Three
ORIENTATION

fter we retrieved our personal belongings in the barracks, the DIs told us to throw our duffel bags in the back of the truck and climb up in the back and take a seat. They told us we were heading to our permanent area, which we were told was Delta Company. When the trucks pulled up in front of the company barracks, we were ordered to dismount the trucks and line up information. Looking back, we did the best we could, but I'm sure at the time, we looked like a bunch of sorry asses.

The Captain of Delta Company came out and stood on the top steps and introduced himself. He then introduced us to our First Sgt. He said we were to be divided in four separate platoons and that a Drill Sergeant would be assigned to each platoon. Then the Captain turned it over to First Sergeant Franks and did an about- face and went back into the building. The First Sgt. looked at his clipboard and said, "all of you assholes from Guam step out of the formation and line up to the left."

There was a Puerto Rican drill sergeant named Gomez waiting for them and he immediately started barking orders at them in Spanish. From the looks of things, he was going to be dealing with a bunch of unruly knot heads. The First Sgt. then started calling out names and when our name was called, we were to move to the right. I was in the second group which turned out to be the third platoon. Our Drill Sergeant's name was Sergeant Columbus. He looked to me like he was only about 20 years old and was in good enough shape to be a marathon runner.

To all of our dismay, we found out he was indeed a marathon runner! Our platoon living quarters were located on the second floor of the barracks. We were marched up the stairs and entered from the end of the barracks. There were only two exits in that building, the way we came in and a fire escape at the opposite end of the barracks. The huge room was full of bunk beds and they told us to choose a bunk and put our duffel bag at the foot. Figuring out who would sleep on top or who would sleep on the bottom was up to the guys sleeping there. There were footlockers located at each end of the bunks that would hold our toiletries and clothing. The rest of our gear would be stored in our duffel bag.

The first thing we were told to do was to get out of our civilian clothes, put them in our duffel bag and change into our new military uniforms. The first lesson that we were given that day was how to properly fold and store our military clothing. Items like tent poles, ponchos, backpacks could stay in our duffel bags which would be stowed underneath the bunk. Sgt. Columbus told us that he was not a DI by job description but rather a "shake and bake" Sgt. that was given the opportunity to teach basic trainees and in return, would not have to go to Vietnam.

He told us he did not want to be a hard ass but that we had to listen and obey all his orders, or he would have no choice but to punish us. After Sgt. Columbus showed us the proper way to fold our clothes and arrange them in our footlockers it was time to go get our hair cut. There were a number of different hairstyles in our platoon. We had guys with greasy, dirty hair that hung below their shoulders and guys with afros with different kinds of dreadlocks.

There were hippies whose hair was dyed in multi-colored hues and a few guys like me that had the sense to get a short haircut before showing up for basic. There was even one guy who had an outrageous Mohawk greased into a peak resembling a shark's fin.

We lined up outside the barbershop and three guys at a time went in and experienced a humiliating affront to their very person. The barbers were grinning and laughing, asking guys what style they preferred. The guy with the Mohawk said, "take a little off the top, please." The barber said, "yes, sir," and proceeded to scalp the hair off his head. I believe the clippers had a balder attachment on them.

When those guys with freaky hair exited the shop, several were crying, and the DI picked out several and told them to go to sick call the following morning to have the puss-filled scabs on their scalps treated. There was a mess hall located at the end of the company building that we would eat at for the next eight weeks. Outside the mess hall door was a set of monkey bars that we had to do hand over hand before entering the mess hall.

It turned out to be a living hell for someone like me who was overweight and had no experience with that exercise. My hands got blisters on them in the first week. It was almost impossible for them to heal because we had to do that exercise at least twice a day. Many times, for lunch, when we were out in the field, the mess truck would come out and dump out cases of C rations and a couple of mermite cans filled with cold cartons of milk.

After our first day was coming to an end, drill Sgt. Columbus came into the bay and asked if any of us had attended college. He said, "if you've attended college, step out into the center of the bay." Out of the 40 guys in my platoon, there were six of us that stepped out. He told us six to come down to the end of the bay where his living quarters were located and wait for him to call our name.

When it was my turn to go into his room, he said, "come in and close the door." He asked me several questions about where I was from and if I was in high school athletics. I told him I played football and baseball and that I enjoyed them very much.

We had some small talk that I can't remember and at the end of our talk he handed me a black arm band that had a corporal insignia sewn onto it. The armband had two snaps on it to hold it in place so that when you wrapped it around your upper arm, the Chevron would show the corporal's rank. He told me that I was going to be a squad leader and I would have 10 men under my supervision. He also said that he would find someone else to do it if I couldn't hack it.

One of the perks of being a squad leader was that I got a private room at the end of the bay with one of the other squad leaders. Little did I know that in the beginning, the men would look at us as dreaded scofflaws or guys that kissed the DI's asses.

Our job was to make sure everyone we were responsible for made it to the formation on time and give extra help to the guys that had trouble learning how to march or clean their weapon. It turned out that I had a bunch of nice guys in my squad and I only had to help a couple of them from time to time. When it was time to go to bed, Sgt. Columbus called out one of the guys' names and told him that he was going to stand fireguard.

The position of fireguard was as old as the Continental Army. Being located on the second floor with only one fire escape created a problem for the soldiers in case of fire. If there was a fire in the barracks, the fire guard's job was to wake everybody up and get them down the fire escape. Each fireguard stood two-hour shifts and then woke the next guy on the duty roster, handing him a flashlight, special helmet liner, and a nightstick. Did I mention that another perk of being a squad leader was I didn't have to take a turn walking around in the darkness listening to guys fart and snore and call out their girlfriend's names in their sleep!

Basic Training

The first day of basic training, they loaded us up into two and a half-ton trucks again and hauled us over to a building where they told us we would be tested to determine our MOS, which stood for Military Occupational Specialties. In other words, what job you would qualify for. They started out with pretty easy math tests and gradually, they got harder.

After a round of testing, the instructor would give us a break and score the tests. Depending on the score, you were either asked to stay or asked to leave. There were 5 batteries of tests and after the fourth test, there were only a handful of guys left, including myself. The last test was to see if the trainee could learn Morse code and be able to send and receive it after a short while. When I heard that I about jumped out of my seat. I was a ham radio operator for Christ's sake.

The last time I was on the air, I was sending and receiving 40 words a minute. As we went through the testing, I knew I had maxed the test. After they scored the tests, an NCO (Noncommissioned officer) came out and took each of us aside for MOS (military occupation specialty) counseling. I was told I scored very high in all tests and got 100% on the code test. Because of this, the NCO said the Army was offering me a chance to go to OCS (Officer Candidate School) and become an officer.

My mind was spinning, what did he just say? He said I had to decide now. I asked what I would be doing as an officer and if it added time to my military commitment. He said when I was at OCS, they would do further testing and he assured me because of my high code scores, I'd wind up commanding a radio facility somewhere in Germany.

He then told me it would add another 2 years to my commitment. That statement hit me right between the eyes. My goal was to do my 2 years and get out of the Army, so I could get back to the good life I had before I got drafted. With an apologetic voice, I told him thanks, but I would pass. He said ok and good luck and assured me I'd wind up in a radio MOS.

Every morning at 5 o'clock, we were woken up by the shouting of our DIs. Most of the time, they would yell, "ok ladies drop your cocks and grab your socks." We had about 20 minutes to perform the three S's: shit, shower and shave. I was always envious of the baby-faced guys that didn't have to shave. The bathroom wall was lined with toilets that were about 18 inches apart with no divider between them and the same number of sinks on the opposite wall.

The mirrors were shiny sheets of aluminum that were indestructible. They referred to the bathroom as a latrine. The showers were in a separate area that included 15 shower heads and nothing else. The first 15 guys to hit the showers were the lucky few to feel hot water. The rest of the platoon was forced to take cold showers.

There was no privacy and I believe this was the Army's intention. They were going to break us down until we understood we were all equally worthless. Within those 20 minutes, we had to square our bunk and footlocker away. We never knew when we would have a surprise inspection. We all

51

ran down the stairs and stood in formation and the Captain would come out and give us the orders of the day.

We were then marched to the parade ground, where we participated in PT. The NCOIC (sergeant in charge of the PT grounds) was a specimen of physical fitness and health. This guy could do 300 pushups, 300 sit-ups, 100 leg risers, limitless jumping jacks, and 100 squat thrusts without breaking a sweat. We, however, were poor souls that cried after 10 pushups. We were a sorry bunch for sure.

As the days went by, we were transformed into men that could do 50 pushups, 100 sit-ups and perform the low crawl according to Army specifications. After an hour of PT, we were marched to the mess hall to eat breakfast. The morning meal usually consisted of bacon or sausage links, scrambled eggs, fruit, sometimes oatmeal and a piece of toast. One morning we were introduced to SOS or as the DIs called it: shit on a shingle. It was ground hamburger drowning in white gravy on top of a biscuit cut in half. After loading it down with salt and pepper, it wasn't too bad.

After breakfast, we returned to the barracks and spit-shined our boots, cleaned the barracks, and cleaned the latrine until it was clean enough that the Virgin Mary herself would be honored to take a dump there. One of the guys sneaked a can of Glo Coat into his bag and instead of giving his boots a genuine spit shine, he just took a cotton ball and swiped it across the toe of the boot with the liquid from the can. Voila, instant shine, or so he thought.

He charged several guys 2 bucks per application. What these sad sacks didn't realize was the Glo Coat would crack, leaving the toe of the boot looking horrible. The guys that participated in the get shine quick scheme were punished severely. They were told they had character flaws and were lazy asses. We were informed that our barracks would be inspected daily and if there were any deficiencies, we would be on our hands and knees cleaning the toilets with our toothbrushes.

The same went for the barracks. Our floor had to have a mirror shine so that you could see your face in it. It didn't take us long to figure out that every man had to remove their boots before entering the bay, so scuff marks didn't ruin the finish. The platoon that got the highest scores on the weekly inspections received a half-hour off to enjoy a sheet cake provided by the mess hall. My platoon enjoyed more sheet cakes than the other platoons combined. I don't believe the boys from Guam ever won a cake.

The first segment of our training was military codes of conduct and military justice. There was never a mention of rules of engagement but that is a story later told. Hygiene was another segment of training I will never get out of my mind. They stressed the importance of brushing your teeth. We were shown a 20-minute movie of GIs sitting in the dentist chair with their jaws propped open and the dentist looking at the worst cases of gingivitis, pyorrhea, rotten teeth, broken off teeth and gums that had separated from the teeth themselves.

The instructor told us that if we didn't care for our teeth, the teeth might be ok, but our gums would fall out! To a man, every swinging richard in that classroom was disgusted and disturbed after watching that film.

Next, we were taught about sexually transmitted diseases. Another 20-minute movie titled the "horny swabby" was put up on the screen. This little vignette started out showing a bunch of sailors standing around talking about girls and telling bullshit stories about their exploits in the sex dept. Pretty soon, a couple of street hookers walked by and batted their pretty eyes and said, "any of you boys want to have a good time?"

A couple of the swabs took them up on their offer and followed them down the street. Cut to the next scene where the swabby was in bed with the hooker. Our only regret was that Army training films never contained any X-rated footage. Cut to the next scene, our sea-going swabby is standing in a shower washing himself from head to toe.

A soft voice in the background was saying, "oh I wish I hadn't done that. I feel so dirty and so ashamed and I may have just picked up a case of the clap or worse." To end the film, a strong voice said, "remember you will never be able to wash off those feelings of dirtiness and shame!"

When the lights came on you could look around and see guys snickering under their breath. The instructor proceeded to list off the sexually transmitted diseases in Vietnam. They included the clap, chlamydia, gonorrhea and a new strain of VD called brand X. This strain was the worst because there was no known cure for it. The Army decided they could not risk this VD entering the USA so if a man caught it, they shipped him off to a remote island to live out the short rest of his life.

They would record the man as MIA and send his family the notice. Being raised a catholic, I knew about VD and that after shots of penicillin, a patient could recover but this brand X had me in serious doubt. So much so, that the whole time I was in Vietnam, I never partook in any monkey business with the boom-boom girls. After several days in the classroom, we were given tests to see if we comprehended what we were taught. Guys that flunked would be required to attend remedial classes on Saturdays until they passed. Next was Drill and Ceremony.

We would find out this was serious business to the Army. A soldier had to know how to march, how to go through all the drills with his rifle and do it with precision. Training took place on the parade field. Our instructor was Sgt. Columbus. We still had guys that didn't know their right from their left and those guys got humiliated ruthlessly.

Forward march, column right march, column left march, to the rear march, oblique march. Then there were order arms, present arms, and fall in, fall out, rest and port arms. There was so much to learn and so much to remember. By the time we graduated, my platoon was standing tall and looking good, we should have been in Hollywood!

I still remember the cadence songs we would sing. The prettiest girl I ever saw was sipping bourbon up through a straw etc. Oh, the memories. You would think as much time as the Army put into teaching us all this stuff, it would be part of our military life. The truth is I never used any of this training the day after I graduated basic.

In Vietnam, there was an entirely different way of commanding soldiers. "Keep your distance, one round could kill you all." "Hey assholes, get over here and help me get out of this mud." We never saluted an officer in the field and there was no real respect for rank among the enlisted men. If a specialist four was experienced and could keep his guys alive we would never put a sergeant in charge just because of their rank.

After being in Nam for four months, I was a squad leader, just after receiving my spec four rank. Basic Training also included field training like first aid, basic rifle marksmanship, overnight bivouacking and constant training for the PT test that we would take at the end of our seventh week. I could see the light at the end of the tunnel and couldn't wait to graduate and go to my next training post as a radio operator.

Most of the time, we got Saturdays and Sundays off and could hang around and sleep. We were not allowed to leave the company area because we were being quarantined due to an outbreak of spinal meningitis. There were several trainees that had died from it in the past year. We were only allowed to have visitors twice during our eight-week training. On my fourth week in Basic Training, I received a note from the day room ordering me to report ASAP to the Company Commander's office.

I could not imagine what I had done wrong to stand tall before the man. When I walked into his office, he locked my heels in front of his desk and asked me why I thought I was more privileged than the rest of the guys in my platoon. I had no response. I didn't know where he was going with this. He asked me what the rules were for visitation and I told him we were allowed two visits during our training cycle. He waved a paper in the air and said, "then what in the Sam Hill is this?"

I was speechless. He said the Post Commander was requesting time off for me to have a picnic with my sister tomorrow afternoon. It seems she was coming to Ft Ord to visit one of her girlfriends who was married to a Colonel currently living at the fort. My sister's friend asked her husband to see if he could pull some strings and make me available.

Now I knew why my goose was cooked or should I say my fried chicken. The CO was not happy but approved the request with the understanding I would pull KP duty for the entire day Sunday. My sister did show up and we had a nice picnic and spent the afternoon talking about things going on at home. I told her about the training and let her know I was going to radio school. I spent the entire day Sunday peeling potatoes and washing pots and pans.

The old lifer mess sergeant was a very kind man that didn't raise his voice at us once. He let us eat anything we wanted in the kitchen and we got as many bowls of dessert cobbler that we wanted. Before leaving he thanked us for our good work, and I asked him where I could sign up for more KP! On Saturday in the sixth week Sgt. Columbus told our platoon that because we didn't win the inspection for the week, we were going on a 10-mile run.

He said to get ready and form up in front of the company area. I'll never forget the looks on the guy's faces. Everybody was pissing and moaning, and one guy said he was not going to do it.

After talking to him for a few minutes, he decided the alternative I was offering him wasn't worth it, so he joined the rest of us. We marched in formation for about half a mile then changed to double time. By this time, most of the guys could jog for miles so it was no big deal. We changed directions after two miles and headed towards an area with tall trees. As we approached the tree line, we could see a few of our cooks unloading mermite cans from the back of the mess trucks.

When we reached them, Sgt. Columbus sat us in a circle around the cans and told us that he was proud of all of us for the good work we had done in the past weeks. He opened a mermite can and started throwing cold beer and cokes to all the guys. We were all speechless. The sound of pop-tops popping was almost deafening. We spent the next 3 hours drinking as much beer and soda as we could hold.

Needless to say, we did not run back to the company area. A casual observer would have seen a bunch of guys trying to walk in a straight line, trying to keep in some semblance of order. That day was a turning point in all our lives. We went from totally worthless to totally gung ho. Our next two weeks were much easier, and the DIs treated us like young men who had earned some respect.

First Sergeant Franks gathered the company around and read off what MOS we were being assigned on the last day of basic training. This is where I would be told where I'd go for radio school training. Most of the guys were receiving the MOS of 11B Infantry.

When my name was called, First Sergeant Franks said 11B Infantry. My ears heard but my mind did not comprehend. I thought I had mistakenly heard him say 11B. I waited until the last name was called and the group dismissed, and I approached First Sgt. Franks and asked him to re-look my name and MOS. He went down the list and came to my name and said 11B.

There must be a mistake I said, I was told I was going to radio school. He asked me if I'd been told that at the testing facility and I said, yes. He asked, did they offer you OCS? I said yes and I turned it down. First Sergeant Franks got a sad look on his face and said, "That's why you are going infantry."

I suddenly felt my hands get clammy and my forehead broke out in sweat. Franks, an old Vietnam vet, told me, "good luck soldier and keep your head down."

My dad came up for my graduation and we had the weekend together before I had to check-in for Advanced Infantry Training right there at Ft. Ord. He said, "I thought you were going to radio school?" The first place we went was Poor Boys Smorgasbord, where I tried to eat myself into imbecility. The weekend went way too fast and on Monday, I showed up at the AIT reception station to join up with a new bunch of guys to enter into phase two: Advanced Infantry Training.

Chapter Four
ADVANCED INFANTRY TRAINING

When I checked in at the reception station, I was given my orders to report to the Charlie Company area and check-in with First Sergeant Conrad. The company area looked older and the buildings were wooden structures. The first Sergeant looked at his clipboard and told me to go to building 102 and report to drill Sgt. Kalis. When I walked into the barracks, I noticed the layout of the barracks was the same as basic training. The latrines were the same and I no longer cared that there were no partitions between the toilets.

I saw Sgt. Kalis sitting in a folding chair at the end of the barracks. I approached him and stood at attention, and he said, "at ease, take a seat." He took my orders and had a pile of folders sitting on the floor next to him and he thumbed through the files until he found mine. He looked briefly through the file and said, "I see you were a squad leader in Basic." I told him I was, and he handed me an armband and said, "you will be my second squad leader."

The armband had a private first-class emblem on it. He said if you don't screw up at the end of AIT, you will be promoted to Private first class ahead of the rest of the platoon. Again, squad leaders had their own rooms at the end of the barracks, and I went there and unloaded my gear.

I couldn't help but notice that there was a cane standing up against the wall behind Sgt. Kalis. I also noticed he had a CIB patch on his shirt. I had heard about the CIB and knew only combat soldiers who had seen action were eligible to wear them. That's about all I knew about that.

AIT was similar to Basic Training. We had footlockers, latrines that had to shine at all times, a bay floor that you could see your face in and weekly inspections. The difference was we did not have DIs harassing us and making us do pushups all the time. Throughout the day, guys came into the barracks and checked in with the DI.

I was surprised that none of the guys showing up weren't in my basic training unit. Most of these guys came from other forts around the country. We had an opportunity that first day, to introduce ourselves and find out where each of us took basic and where everybody's hometown was. That first evening, Sgt. Kalis formed us up out in front of the barracks and marched us to the mess hall. We went at a slow pace because Sgt. Kalis was using a cane. I could tell his leg was messed up.

The mess hall in AIT was the same as it was in basic training. The only difference was if you wanted more food put on your tray, all you had to do was ask. As I recall, the first meal I had in AIT was roast beef, mashed potatoes and mixed vegetables. There was dessert available at the end of the line. Since being in the Army, there was chocolate milk available at the milk station for the first time. Things were surely looking up.

The next morning, we stood in formation and were greeted by the commanding officer of Charlie Company. He told us what his expectations were, and he assured us that we would receive the best training that the Army had to offer. He also told us, unlike basic training, we would be allowed to leave the company area after training to go to the PX and buy incidentals that we might need, including having a beer or two and buying junk food. If we didn't want to eat at the mess hall, we could go to the PX and have greasy cheeseburgers, greasy French fries, and a milkshake.

Since I didn't have a lot of extra money, I usually opted for the mess hall. After the Company Commander had finished, he turned us over to our drill Sergeant and wished us good luck. Sgt. Kalis informed us that we were going to march to the supply building, where we would be picking up all the gear we would need to go through AIT. This would include being issued an M-14 rifle. I asked Sgt. Kalis why we were being issued M-14 rifles when the soldiers in Vietnam were using M-16s. He told me that the Army had not yet gotten enough supplies of M-16s but was hoping to have them before our AIT cycle ended.

It didn't make a lot of sense to me to go to Vietnam without knowing how to fire the weapon you were going to be issued. As luck would have it, the M-16 rifles showed up at Fort Ord at the beginning of our third week. We turned in our M-14 rifles and were issued a brand-new M-16. They had to rearrange training so that we would have time to learn how the M-16 operated and that we had time to practice live-fire shooting.

This new weapon was definitely different than the M-14 and was more complicated to tear down and clean. The coolest thing was that it fired fully automatic! Sgt. Kalis told us the secret to keeping your weapon firing in Vietnam was to have it clean at all times. They gave us a small plastic bottle of white grease called LSA. Plenty of LSA would keep the weapon from jamming up during a firefight. At that time, none of us could even imagine what a firefight was. We all suspected; however, it was not a good thing.

Drill Sergeants Revelation

In the third week of training on a Friday night after lights out, sergeant Kalis opened his door and light came beaming out of his room into the bay. Sgt. Kalis came out of his room wearing only his boxer shorts and Smokey bear hat. On his feet was a pair of shower shoes. You could see the deep scars running up and down his leg. It was very disconcerting to see a wound this serious. He was carrying a bottle of whiskey and seemed a little shaky on his cane. He came to the middle of the bay and sat down on one of the foot lockers.

Someone turned on the lights and we all got out of bed and sat on the floor in a semicircle around him. Right away you could tell that he had been drinking. I suspected it helped him deal with the pain in his leg. He looked around at us and said in a loud voice, "listen up, people."

He said he wanted to tell us about Vietnam. He also said every single one of us was going to wind up in Vietnam in an infantry unit. He said the rumors of units going to Germany were bullshit. He told us about his experiences, starting with his basic training and his AIT training.

When he got to Vietnam, he was assigned to the Big Red One that was located in the central highlands. He started out as a grunt and experienced six months of heavy combat. He said he was very lucky that he had never stepped on a booby trap or been shot. He told us he was scared from the first day he arrived till the day he left Vietnam. He said anybody that is not scared is either crazy or lying. As he was talking to us, he would take a pull off of the whiskey bottle right from the neck. You could tell that he was getting more emotional as his story went on. He told us that many of his friends had been wounded or killed and that we would experience the same thing.

After he had been in the field for six months, he volunteered to be a door gunner in an aviation unit. The crew chief told him he would not need any training because he had already been in the field for six months and experienced many firefights.

On his first day on the job, he was assigned to a Huey helicopter unit that was used to transport troops in and out of landing zones. He told us his job as a door gunner was to lay down machine-gun fire into the hedgerows (hedges consisting of bamboo and other brush-like vegetation, sometimes 20 feet tall) as the helicopter was coming in for a landing.

The Army figured that all that shooting would keep the gooks heads down and allow the grunts a chance to bale off the aircraft without the helicopter being shot down. One of the dumb asses in our group asked Sgt. Kalis what a hedgerow was. Kalis said it's where Charlie hides his tunnel entrances and plants beaucoup booby traps. It was made up of bamboo plants and scrub brush.

On several occasions, his helicopter was assigned to bring in fresh troops in the middle of the battle and load up the dead and wounded and take them back to the field hospital. He said those were some of the scariest days of his life. He said during those missions, the gooks always tried to shoot the helicopters down. AK rounds would pepper the side of the helicopter, making a distinct ting sound.

He told us during these times, his asshole would be tighter than a bull's ass at fly time. A few of the guys could be heard laughing under their breath when he said that. We were about to find out being a door gunner in Vietnam was no laughing matter.

One afternoon while sitting at the fire support base, three of the helicopters in his unit were scrambled to perform an emergency extraction of two gunship pilots shot down by an

NVA 51 cal. Machine gun. Before going down, the pilots had radioed their location and sent a Mayday. The second gunship stayed there, keeping the NVA at bay until help could arrive. Sgt. Kalis said when his helicopter arrived, they could see the gunship's tail section was on fire. It was apparent that the pilot and copilot and crew were all dead.

As his helicopter banked to the left, he could see NVA soldiers coming out of the hedgerow. He continued shooting and saw that he had hit five NVA soldiers. He told us that was one of the last things he remembered because his helicopter was suddenly shot out of the air. He remembers the helicopter spinning around as it fell to the ground and he saw the ground coming up fast and that he was thrown from the helicopter as it rolled over on its side. He saw the rotor blades break off and go through the bubble windshield, killing both pilot and copilot. He had no idea what happened to the other door gunner.

The other two helicopters in his unit stayed on station as long as they could, keeping the NVA back in the hedgerows. He told us that he knew he was hurt bad and that his leg caused him excruciating pain. He had landed flat on his stomach and knew there was nothing he could do but lay there and play dead. He was praying that somehow one of the helicopters could get down and pull him out of there. He remembers laying there for over half an hour as his leg and other injuries continued to bleed out. He said he went in and out of consciousness and was close enough to the hedgerow that he could hear the NVA soldiers yelling orders back and forth to each other.

At this point in the story, tears started running down the Sergeant's face. The two helicopters above were running low on fuel and he suddenly realized they were flying away. Kalis broke down and started crying out loud and said, "I was sure this was going to be the end of my life." I looked around and saw that many of the men had tears in their eyes as well, including me.

The Sgt.'s story was having a huge impact on every man sitting there that night.

He said he knew his only hope was to lay there and play dead and hope that a rescue team was on the way. The NVA soldiers ran out of the hedgerow and swarmed the downed gunship. They were pulling the pilot and copilot out of their seats and were busy removing as much of the electronic equipment as they could. Two NVA soldiers came over to where he was lying and started removing his boots and his belt. He told us his whole body was numb and that if he opened his eyes, they would surely kill him.

After stripping the ship, the NVA disappeared back into the hedgerow. It seemed like an eternity as he lay there smelling the burning jet fuel and looking at the dead pilots lying on the ground only a few meters away. He told us that he had accepted the fact that he was going to die and said a prayer that God would forgive him of all the sins that he committed in his life. He said he thought of his mother and his brother and sister back home. He wondered how they were going to react when they received a telegram from Uncle Sam telling them of his death. He recalled how dry his mouth and throat were and figured he was dying.

As he laid there with his face on the ground, he said he started dreaming about things that happened in his past. He said he could see his mom and dad and that they were smiling at him, telling him everything was going to be all right. In this dream, he heard helicopters in the distance.

After that, he passed out from loss of blood and the next thing he remembered, there were doctors and nurses hovering over him, asking him if he could hear them. The helicopters that he heard in the distance were a rescue team that came and extracted him and the dead pilots. His fellow door gunner's body was never accounted for.

The doctors told him that his leg was broken in several places and would require several special surgeries in order to save his leg. He was sent to Japan, where he was in recovery for 60 days before being sent back to the states with a pocket full of pain killers. Because he had volunteered for the Army, he still had two years of commitment to fulfill. He was able to get around with the aid of a cane and he contemplated what he would be doing for the next two years. His next assignment would be at Ft. Ord.

Because of his experience in combat, he would be teaching AIT as a Drill Sergeant. He told us he had regular nightmares and that whiskey was his way of coping with the nightmares and forgetting about the horror. He lowered his head and said, "my biggest fear is that you men are going to go to Vietnam and experience the horror that I went through." He took one last pull from the black label booze, stood up and wobbled back to his room, and we all sat there looking at each other, not saying a word. The stark look on everybody's face told the story of what we had just heard.

In our hearts, we all knew that we would be going into a war where guys were getting killed and wounded every single day. We all knew that each of us, in our own way, would be faced with the same horror that Sgt. Kalis had experienced.

Serious Training

After Sgt. Kalis shared his story with us, we were all much more serious about paying attention at the training classes. Several of the instructors, who were returning Vietnam vets, would warn us about paying attention and learn everything we could before being sent to Vietnam. The classes included booby trap detection and disarming, escape and evasion, M-60 machine gun live-fire course, M-79 live-fire course, throwing live hand grenades, practicing squad size assaults, simulated night ambush patrols, and of course, the gas chamber.

The gas chamber was one of the more interesting classes because it included going through a gas chamber and being exposed to CS gas. The instructors told us that we would have to learn how to put our gas masks on quickly and correctly. The one thing they did not tell us, however, was that CS gas is the type that will penetrate into your pores, blind your eyes, and burn your lungs.

Our instructor was a short E-4 that seemed to be overly cocky. One of the guys mumbled that he looked like Popeye. He told us when we marched into the chamber, he would be with us to instruct us what to do. He said when he yelled the word gas, we would have 30 seconds to put on our masks before the gas grenades went off. He said for those guys that did it correctly, they would experience no problems.

For the guys that could not get their mask on correctly, he said they would be in a world of hurt. We practiced removing our gas masks from their holders and putting them on our faces. We did this several times until the instructor was satisfied that all of us would be able to do this within the 30 seconds allotted time. He lined us all up outside the chamber door and said that he would be taking ten of us at a time into the chamber.

When we were finished, we would leave from the opposite side of the chamber. The chamber would be cleared of all gas and the next ten guys would take their turn. I was one of the first ten guys in line and was marched into the chamber when suddenly I heard the metal door slam behind us. There was a distinct smell in the chamber that was the remnants of CS gas.

There was one small light bulb hanging from the top of the ceiling and our instructor was explaining one more time how the drill was going to go.

I noticed that our instructor was not carrying a gas mask and thought that perhaps he would leave the chamber just before the gas started. Little did I know that this little version of Popeye was one tough little dude. He said, "I'm going to count three and you will then have 30 seconds to get your masks on." At the count of three, the light went off and there was mass confusion in the chamber.

All I could think of was that I had 30 seconds to get that mask on before the gas started. Eight out of the ten of us were able to do it before CS gas permeated the chamber. The guys that did not put their masks on fell to the floor screaming, writhing, and begging to be let out.

I felt pretty good but noticed my hands and neck were starting to burn like crazy. I mean, they were really burning bad. Suddenly out of nowhere, the instructor walked by us one by one, tearing our masks off our faces. As long as I live, I will never forget the first breath that I took after my mask was off. There was a horrible burning sensation in my eyes, on my face, and my lungs felt like they were on fire. It took me just seconds to figure out that rubbing my eyes made it much worse.

All of us fell to our knees and tried crawling towards the end of the chamber, hoping Popeye would let us out. He didn't, and he waited a full minute after we'd hit the floor before opening the door. We all crawled out on our hands and knees, followed by a rush of CS gas. It took several minutes for us to recover from this horrible experience. While we were sitting in the bleachers, we watched the rest of the platoon marched into the chamber and gassed just like we were.

When all the men had completed the exercise, the instructor stood in front of us and began to tell us that having our gas masks near us at all times could be the difference between life and death. All of us were amazed that this little Popeye was able to go through that chamber with no gas mask. He was one tough SOB. One of the guys behind me yelled, "what the hell is wrong with you, Popeye." This whole experience would serve me well in Vietnam, but that story comes later.

Night vision class was one of the less strenuous activities. We were marched out to a field where there was a large building with no windows. We were marched into the building and we sat in the bleachers waiting for our instructor to start the class. The instructor told us that night vision was one of the most important things we had when fighting Charlie out in the bush at night. We learned that the rods and cones in our eyes would adapt to the darkness and allow us to partially see in the darkness. To illustrate this, all the lights in the building were shut off and it was pitch dark. He told us it took about five minutes for our eyes to adjust and that soon he would ask us to identify different objects in the room.

Pretty soon, we could see small red pinpricks of light moving around the building. He explained that a sudden burst of light like an illumination flare or the light from the muzzle of a gun could ruin our night vision. As a matter of fact, he said that kind of light could keep us from seeing for up to a minute or two. Without warning, a strobe light suddenly went off and all I could see was red. I could not make out anything in the room and I suddenly realized I was temporarily blinded.

After that exercise, the lights were turned on and the instructor told us just how important night vision could be in Vietnam. He told us that Charlie liked to walk around at night smoking his dope and telling jokes. He also told us that our hearing would be hypersensitive in the dark. On a quiet night, we would be able to hear noises from far away. He said we would be able to see the glow from a burning joint up to a half-mile away. He told us we would be going outside after dark and that there was a night vision course we would be walking to where we would experience night hearing and night vision.

When we got to the course, it was very dark outside and again, we were instructed to sit in the bleachers. He told us that there were soldiers out in front of us at different distances and that we were to listen and see if we could locate any of them. In a minute or two, we could hear what sounded like a rifle bolt being opened and closed. He asked one of the trainees which direction he thought the sound came from. The trainee pointed out to the left and the instructor said, good job. We went through this hearing exercise several more times with many different sounds, including coughing, talking and rustling through the bushes.

It was amazing how we were able to hear the sounds even though they were 50 yards away. The night vision exercise was equally as impressive. As we sat there staring out into the darkness suddenly, you could see a match light. After that, a cigarette was lighted which also illuminated the man's face.

The instructor told us how important it was when we were out at night in Vietnam, we should be as quiet and as vigilant as possible. He also said that under no circumstances should any man smoke or light up a cigarette. He said one man smoking a cigarette or joint with a slight breeze would carry the smell well over 100 yards. He told us that when he was in Vietnam, his ambush patrol could smell marijuana well before Charlie walked into the ambush on several occasions.

That class gave all of us a lot to think about, especially the part about going out on ambush patrols at night. It would become apparent later in Vietnam that some of the guys assigned to my platoon had not paid attention to this class; that story will come later.

Weekend Passes

In the fourth week of AIT, there was a three-day weekend coming up. My buddy Don and I decided it would be fun to hitchhike up to San Francisco and see what the free love movement was all about. Each of us packed an overnight bag and had $100 in our pocket. It was amazing how easy it was to hitchhike during the 1960s. After hooking a few rides, we found ourselves on the streets of San Francisco. I'm not sure what our preconceived notions were but San Francisco was nothing like we thought it would be.

We headed towards Haight Asbury Park, where we were told there were concerts going on and lots of hippie girls looking for love. Never in my life have I been more disappointed. As we got closer to the park, we were being bum-rushed by hippies panhandling and asking us if we had any cigarettes or change. Everywhere we looked, there were people sitting up against buildings, their heads bowed and many of them lying down stoned out of their minds.

Guys were pissing on the sides of buildings and the closer we got to the park, the worse the smell got. When we arrived at the park, it looked like a freak show. There was a bandshell at one end of the park and a guy playing a guitar singing folk songs. He had a microphone, amplifier and one speaker.

We looked completely out of place with our short hair and our nerdy civilian clothes. Guys would come up to us and say, "Hey man, it's all cool." It didn't take us long to figure out that the advertisement of free love was just a myth. Both of us agreed that this was not where we wanted to spend our weekend. It was getting late and we talked about getting a motel room for the night.

When we found out the cost, we decided to look for a car lot and sleep in the back of a used car. We found a Chevy station wagon unlocked and flipped a coin to see who got the back cargo area. As luck would have it, I won and slept in the back. The next morning, we got up and started to look for a place to get breakfast. I ordered a traditional breakfast of bacon and eggs and hash browns with whole wheat toast and Don decided on ham and pancakes. He was a huge fan of maple syrup.

As we sat there eating, we started to talk about what we would do for the next two days of our leave. Don said that he had heard about a place called Santa Cruz where there was a huge amusement park and Boardwalk. Since our objective was to try to find girls to hook up with, we figured an amusement park would be a great place to connect. Besides, it was only a hop skip and a jump from where we were.

We hitchhiked up to Santa Cruz and within 20 minutes of our arrival, we found ourselves walking up and down the boardwalk located right next to the amusement park. We tried out several come-on lines with the single girls we spotted sitting on benches or just walking by us on the boardwalk. We would ask them if they wanted us to buy them a Coke or ice cream cone, and if that didn't work, we would ask them if they wanted to go to the amusement park and try out some of the rides.

After striking out several times, we decided to go find a hot dog stand and buy some lunch. As I was standing there getting ready to pay for my lunch, I noticed two girls standing just to my right. They were a couple of cute girls that looked in their late teens. They were ordering lunch and giggling about what I have no idea. I quickly scooted over and asked them if it was okay if I bought their lunch for them.

Without hesitation, they giggled and said sure, and then I asked them their names. Don and I escorted the two girls to the nearest bench and started a small conversation. The girl I was sitting next to told me her name was Linda and that the other girl was her cousin Sarah. We sat there chatting and eating our lunch for about half an hour and then decided all of us would go to the amusement park. The girls seemed to be a little naive and immature in many ways. We told them we were soldiers on leave from Fort Ord. Linda told me that her home was located in Northern California in a small town not far from the Oregon border.

Sarah lived north of San Francisco and the two girls had come to Santa Cruz to spend the weekend together. We also learned that Sarah had a car and was willing to drive us around Santa Cruz. About 6 p.m., Don and I took the girls to McDonald's and bought them a Big Mac, fries and a chocolate shake. Sarah drove us to a scenic overlook, and we parked and ate our dinner. Sarah and Don were sitting in the front seat and Linda and I were sitting in the back. I had noticed that Don had scooted over and was sitting right next to Sarah.

I think Sarah must've been a little promiscuous because they started making out even before they finished their shakes. Linda looked at them for a few minutes, turned to me and smiled and scooted across the seat until she was practically sitting in my lap. Without a word, she closed her eyes, puckered her lips, and waited for me to make the first move. During our make-out session, there was light petting and I occasionally tried to cop a feel. Overall, our mission to hook up with girls was a success.

Occasionally, we would come up for air and look towards the front seat, where we saw Don removing Sarah's blouse. We had no idea where this was going to lead but decided to continue what we were doing in the back seat. It must've been about two hours later when suddenly Sarah declared that she had told her mother that she and her cousin would be home by 9 o'clock. We asked them if they would drive us to San Francisco, where we could continue to hitchhike back to Fort Ord.

On our drive back to San Francisco, Linda and I cuddled in the back seat and we noticed that Don was still sitting right next to Sarah. It must've looked weird to anyone looking to see a guy riding bitch next to a girl who could barely see over the steering wheel. When I teased Don about it later, he chuckled and said, "you didn't see what I was doing with my hands." Enough said. When we reached San Francisco, we exchanged addresses with one another and promised to keep in touch. At that point, Don and I never expected to see either one of the girls again. We got back to the post at about 11 o'clock and had plenty of time to get ready for the next day's training and get a good night's sleep.

Awesome Display of Power

Monday morning found us standing in formation listening to Sgt. Kalis telling us what the day's training was going to be. He said we would be loading up on trucks and transported to a live-fire demonstration range. He said we were going to enjoy this because we would witness the firepower the Army could bring to a battle. He said we would be seeing most of the ordinance currently being used in Vietnam. It was hard to imagine what this was going to look like, but we were all anxious to find out.

When we got to the demonstration range, we were seated in the bleachers and our Company Commander took the podium to explain to us that what we were about to see would convince us that we would be serving with the strongest military force on earth. With that, he turned over the microphone to the NCOIC (non-commissioned officer in charge), who told us they would begin with the smallest ordinance and work up to the largest.

Out in the field in front of us were several vehicles and a couple of old tanks located at different distances from where we were sitting.

There were also several groups of silhouette targets resembling Viet Cong in black pajamas. The first weapon to be demonstrated was the M-16 rifle. The rifleman stood about 25 meters from a group of VC silhouettes and opened up on full automatic and totally destroyed the five silhouettes. We were told that the M-16 was one of the most effective weapons of its kind. What they failed to tell us was that this weapon had several problems.

It had an open three-pronged flash suppressor that would catch on vegetation and would plug up when coming in contact with mud or dirt, resulting in the rifle blowing up in a soldier's face when fired. Another problem was it jammed in the middle of a firefight. The next weapon to be demonstrated was the M-79 grenade launcher, otherwise known as a duper. It got its nickname from the sound the weapon made when the M-79 round exited the end of the tube. The duper man stepped up to the firing line, took aim and shot at one of the trucks about 75 yards away. The round was a direct hit and there was a fiery explosion producing fire and smoke. The truck did not move but we could see that the round had put a hole in the driver's door.

The soldiers took several more shots, including buckshot, parachute flares and smoke grenades. The demonstration was truly impressive. Up next, we would see what damage could be caused by an M-72 LAWS Rocket. The LAWS rocket was designed as a light anti-tank weapon. It is a portable one-shot 66 mm unguided antitank weapon fired from the shoulder. I didn't realize it at the time, but this would become one of my favorite weapons while serving in Vietnam. A soldier approached the firing line, extended the tube which cocked the weapon, and aimed it at one of the 2 ½ ton trucks about 100 yards away. He held the tube on his shoulder while looking through a vertical site and squeezed the trigger.

The first thing we saw was a blast coming out the rear the tube. Then we saw the rocket hitting the truck and the impact was so great it blew the driver's door and the hood completely off the truck. All the guys in the bleachers started cheering. Slowly but surely, we were beginning to see just how well armed the Army was and that we would have these weapons at our disposal. Next, we noticed three soldiers approaching the firing line with an 81 mm mortar. It took the three men only a couple of minutes to set the tube on the base plate and make firing adjustments.

We were told that the mortar team would place a round as close to the tank as possible and then adjust fire until they made a direct hit. The first round dropped short, approximately 50 feet in front of one of the tanks. You could see one of the soldiers making adjustments on the angle of the tube and a second round was dropped, resulting in a direct hit on the tank. It was a loud explosion that resulted in real damage to the turret. Again, the bleachers broke out in a cacophony of hoots and hollers. At that point, we were given a 15-minute break and the NCOIC told us, "smoke 'em if you got 'em, bum 'em if you don't!"

When our 15-minute break was about over, you could see guys field stripping what was left of their cigarette. Field stripping included tearing the paper on the cigarette so that the remaining tobacco could fall on the ground. If it was a filtered cigarette, you removed the filter and put it in your pocket. The remaining white paper was also put in your pocket. The reasoning behind this is if GIs throw their cigarette butts on the ground in Vietnam, the Viet Cong will follow them like breadcrumbs. More than one platoon had been ambushed as a result of not field stripping cigarettes.

When we returned to the bleachers, we noticed two soldiers were standing on the firing line. One held a map and the other was wearing a radio. The instructor told us the officer on the left was a forward artillery observer and the man on the right was his RTO (radio telephone operator). We were told that we would be witnessing 105 mm artillery fire that would be called in and adjusted by the FO (forward observer) in front of us.

Since none of us could see any artillery pieces, we had no idea where the round would be coming from. The FO held the radio handset and, in a loud voice, said, "fire mission." He then called out coordinates and asked for one Willy Peter (white phosphorous) round at a height of burst of 300 ft. We waited about one minute and heard a faint booming noise in the distance to our left.

Within seconds you could hear the round coming in and then an explosion out in front of us about 200 meters. When the round went off, it was about 300 feet off the ground and produced a white cloud-like substance that hung like a cloud above the ground. The round had gone off over an old WW2 Sherman tank. The FO barked orders into the handset and said, "1 HE (high explosive) on the deck fire for effect."

We heard another boom in the distance and again, within seconds, the round hit about 50 meters from the front of the tank. The explosion was loud and produced fire and tremendous amounts of dirt and dust. The FO gave one last command and said, "add 50 fire for effect."

When the artillery came in it hit the tank directly, causing an indescribable sound and momentary fire and smoke. As the smoke settled, the tank was lying on its side and you could see the twisted metal where the round had hit. This was one of the most impressive displays of firepower any of us had ever seen. The last weapon that we would see that afternoon was a UH-1

Huey gunship. We could hear the helicopter flying in from a distance and when it arrived, it hovered directly over the bleachers. The instructors asked us to look up and observe the rocket pods and the miniguns that were attached under the helicopter. The helicopter rose and banked to the left and prepared to make an assault run through the demonstration field.

When the helicopter was close to the field, all hell broke loose. Rockets were directed at both vehicles and silhouettes alike. The miniguns that resembled Gatling guns also started firing at the silhouettes. Within seconds the helicopter had destroyed two trucks and several of the remaining silhouettes. It was simply unbelievable, and the guys were standing and cheering throughout the whole demonstration. We resembled an uncontrolled mob demanding someone's execution. The helicopter continued through the demonstration area and disappeared to our rear.

At this point, the instructor told us we would be witnessing the grand finale. He said we would be witnessing all the weaponry being used in concert. It took only a few minutes for the soldiers to reappear at the firing line and prepare for what the Army called "a mad minute." When the signal was given, all the soldiers in front of us opened up and started firing at the targets in front of them. It was deafening and the amount of explosions was indescribable. Without warning 105 mm artillery shells started raining down, hitting trucks and tanks alike.

After a short time, there was a cease-fire called to close out the artillery demonstration. Two UH-1 Hueys came flying in about 20 feet off the ground, hosing down the entire demonstration field. It took my breath away thinking about how much destruction we had seen in a mere minute or two. The two helicopters finished and flew off into the distance behind us.

Everybody in the bleachers was wound up tighter than an eight-day clock. It took about 10 minutes for the DIs to get us back to some semblance of order.

There was no doubt in anyone's military mind that we were going to be a force to be reckoned with in Vietnam. The demonstration took up most of the afternoon and the Company Commander decided to take us back to the barracks and give us the rest of the day off. We used this time to sit around the barracks talking about what we had just observed. It gave all of us a huge sense of confidence, knowing that the Army had the ability to destroy our enemies.

Unfortunately, we were all caught up in the day's demonstration and none of us were thinking about what was going to be like in the jungles of Vietnam. When it came to guerrilla warfare, the fight was still done by soldiers on the ground, going head-to-head and toe to toe fighting for their lives.

Surprise Visitor

The following day was Tuesday and at mail call, I could not believe there was a letter addressed to me from Linda in San Francisco. Linda told me how much fun she had meeting me and hoped we could see each other again soon. She told me she would be staying with Sarah another two weeks and that she could come down to Fort Ord and meet me the following weekend.

This whole proposal caught me completely off guard. I never really expected to see Linda again but thought to myself, I'm going to Vietnam, so what the heck. She gave me a phone number to call her and said she would be waiting for my reply. I called her and told her that I would be available the upcoming weekend and that she could come down and we could hang out on Saturday. She asked me if my friend Don would be available because Sarah was going to drive her down and wanted to see him again.

I told her Don had nowhere else to go and we would meet both of them at the front gate at nine in the morning. As the week ground on, I received a letter from Linda every day. She expressed how excited she was to see me again and hoped that I was excited too. As each letter arrived, I became more confused about what Linda's intentions were.

We had only been together a day and already she was making it sound like we would be spending the rest of our lives together! Oh well, I figured I'd be going to Vietnam and would never see or hear from her again. Little did I know how wrong I would be. Saturday finally came and the girls met us at the front gate at 0900 hrs. sharp. Don and Sarah decided to go to Monterey, which was not far from Fort Ord and Linda and I decided to spend the day on the base. I called a cab and told the driver to take us to the enlisted man's club.

The club was basically a bar and grill with a couple of TVs, pool tables and some pinball machines. We played a few games of pool and afterward, we had lunch and sat around for a while telling each other about ourselves. Linda came from a large family with several brothers and sisters. Her father was a heavy equipment operator and poker player and her mother was a bartender at the local bar. I told her about my mom and dad and how I had lived on a ranch with horses and of course, told her about my Irish setter Rusty. I asked Linda if she would like to see the post and she said yes, so I called a cab and proceeded to give her a tour of Fort Ord. In the afternoon, I had the cab driver drop us off at a park. with some secluded areas.

We spent the rest of the afternoon lying in the grass, making out and groping each other. At times it got pretty hot and bothered but nothing too serious happened. Before leaving that afternoon, Linda wrote down her home address and phone number and asked me to consider coming up to meet her parents and family. I told her sure but had no intention of following through with it. During the last few weeks of training, Sgt. Kalis told us that we were, "Born Again Hard," and he was proud of us for the soldiers that we had become. He continued to have heartfelt talks with us at night in the barracks and continued to tell us he prayed none of us would get hurt or killed in Vietnam.

My parents came up for graduation and after the ceremony, we returned to our barracks for the last time to receive our orders and say goodbye and good luck to the men that we had just spent the last eight weeks with. I would never see or hear from any of these men again, with one exception. I did run into Byron, a friend from AIT, in the PX in Cu Chi fire support base in November 1968. He told me he was serving with Americal Division and that his unit had seen plenty of shit around the Michelin rubber plantation.

After graduation, I would never see Don again. I often thought of him and wondered if he made it home alive. The ride home to San Diego seemed like it took an eternity. The Army gave me a 30 day leave before I shipped off to Vietnam. What does a guy do for 30 days, knowing that he is about to enter a shit storm? I spent some time riding Bango, my four-year-old chestnut gelding and I returned to the Safeway store in Solano Beach to shoot the breeze with the guys that I had worked with only four months ago. They all seemed glad to see me but were somewhat detached since I didn't work there anymore.

One of my best friends, Jim, however, took me out to lunch a couple of times and wanted to know what it was like going through basic and AIT. I drove over to Pacific Beach and my best friend Fred and I spent a few days hanging out. We reminisced

81

about all the fun we had during our high school years fishing in a small boat at the bait barge in San Diego Bay and shooting guns at my house in Rancho Bernardo. We never discussed Vietnam, but I knew it weighed heavy on his mind. He had started dating a girl named Kathy from La Jolla and said it might turn into something serious.

I went back to my old neighborhood, visited with some of the neighbor boys I'd grown up with, and told them I might be seeing them after returning from Vietnam. All my friends were in college and had not been subjected to the draft. They all wished me luck and Big Mike told me not to get killed. I spent a week with my mother, and we made the rounds visiting with the grandparents and other relatives.

I just couldn't get excited about seeing all these people because I had so much more on my mind. I went camping with my dad and we went fishing at one of his favorite lakes and took a long drive in our Jeep through the Cuyamaca and the Laguna Mountains. We took my dad's 30-06 hunting rifle and my .303 British infield rifle and spent one afternoon shooting at targets about 50 yards away.

He was truly impressed with my improved shooting skills. I think we were trying to re-live years passed in just a few short days. My dad seemed to be somewhat melancholy at times and we didn't crack many jokes like we had done so many times before. There was an unspoken feeling between us, I was going to Vietnam as an infantry soldier and might come home in a coffin.

When my 30-day leave was up, my parents and sister drove me to the airport in San Diego, where I would catch a plane that would take me to Oakland, California, to the processing center and go to Vietnam. As I was walking down the boarding ramp, I turned around and saw my parents and sister standing together, tears running down their faces. It was one thing to see my mother or sister cry, but it really shook me up when I saw my dad crying. It was only the second time in my life I had ever seen him do that. I fought back my own tears, turned around, and boarded the aircraft.

John in AIT

John and Dad

AIT Formation

Chapter Five
HURRY UP AND WAIT

The flight from San Diego to Oakland only took about 50 minutes but it seemed like a lifetime to me. My mind kept jumping from one thing to another. I kept remembering my high school days when I was pitching against our cross-town rival and kicking their butts. Then I was thrown back to the horror of dealing with CS gas in training. I just couldn't keep a thought straight in my mind.

I was shocked out of my thoughts by a stewardess asking me if I would like a drink or snack. I was dreading landing in Oakland, getting off the plane, and reporting into the reception station at Oakland Replacement Personnel Center. I had heard from other guys that some soldiers had to wait a week before heading to Vietnam. I wanted to get to Vietnam and get it over with. I thought to myself, I'd be bored to tears and go out of my mind.

When I got to the reception center, I reported at the incoming window and handed the clerk my orders and in return he handed me an instruction sheet and a coupon good for one free steak dinner. The instruction sheet told me where I was going to stay while waiting for my orders to Vietnam. They also included information about where to eat our meals and where to go to find out when we would be getting on the plane to Vietnam.

There was a huge cafeteria where we would eat our meals and get our free steak dinner. I had to laugh to myself when I thought they usually give a steak dinner to prisoners preparing to go to the electric chair. Sadly, it wasn't that far off from being the truth. My first day at the center as a newbie replacement turned out to be a very lonely experience. I found myself in a sea of other replacements, most of whom didn't know each other.

The war in Vietnam was going strong and I was called to replace those wounded or killed as an infantryman. Barracks life in a transient station is chaotic at best and zoo-like at its worst. The transient billets were equipped with bunks only; no lockers. About the only way to secure your gear was to tie it to a bunk rail and hope it would be there when you got back.

There were two or three formations in the large parking lot out behind the long row of concrete barracks buildings every day. At these formations, they would read names off of the list. Those names that were read off were manifested on a flight. At that time, those manifested would get their gear and be marched away to a holding area pending transit to Travis Air Force Base to get on a flight to Vietnam. If your name wasn't read for the latest flight manifest, cadre would come through the remaining transient personnel looking for people to put on various details around the base.

It didn't take me long to figure out that the back of the formation was the best place to be, since the cadre took their victims from the front ranks. Those not chosen for some chicken shit details were dismissed and could melt away and do whatever they wanted to until the next formation. It was in one of these formations that I met a replacement who was carrying around a clipboard. I asked him what that was for, and he told

85

me he used it as a prop to avoid work details. If he was selected in ranks for a detail, he would tell the cadre member that he was already on a detail for the "post engineers."

After the formations were over, he would wander around the post with his clipboard. If anyone stopped him and asked him what he was doing, he would flash the clipboard and tell that he was checking for broken windows or burned-out light bulbs for the post engineers. It seemed like it was working for him.

There were certain practical and psychological limitations that were in practice at Oakland Army Base for dealing with transient personnel. After reporting in for overseas movement, replacement personnel were restricted to the base. Apparently, it was felt that some people might disappear at this late stage in their deployment to Vietnam in a kind of last-minute change of heart or mind. No photography was permitted in the replacement center.

My guess about this was they used the old story about matters concerning troop movements being secret, when in fact what they were concerned about was the negative impact on morale that might occur if such photos got out. There was also the problem with the media getting a hold of such pictures during those turbulent times when military involvement in Vietnam was controversial. Through this very portal quite a few men would pass that never came back alive. Once started off on such a journey, no one knows how it's going to turn out. It's kind of depressing, but for those who didn't make it back, this was the last they saw of their homeland.

Finally, on the third day they read my name from the list. From there I was manifested on a flight. At that time, those who were manifested would get their gear and be marched away to a holding area pending transit to Travis Air Force Base to get on a flight to Vietnam. It was finally happening; I was really going to Vietnam to face my manifest destiny. The Army used buses to transport us to Travis Air Force Base. Once again, our orders were checked, and we were told which holding area to go to.

Upon arrival at the holding area, we were given tags and black magic markers. We printed our name and service number on the tags and attached them to our duffel bag. We were told to put our bags on a long flatbed trailer sitting out on the tarmac when we finished that. After I threw my bag onto the trailer, I looked up and saw a large United Airlines passenger plane sitting not too far from where I was standing.

The ground crew was wheeling a set of stairs over to the plane and positioning them at the front door. An airman came up to our group and said, "form yourselves up in line." From there we were marched to the base of the stairs where each of us took our turn boarding the aircraft. There was a Salvation Army lady greeting us and giving us a small tote bag that contained toiletries, candy and a pocket bible. She told us good luck and God bless you.

Leaving On a Jet Plane
Don't Know When I'll Be Back Again
Peter, Paul, and Mary

As I ascended the stairs, I thought to myself isn't it strange that there was only one Salvation Army volunteer there to see us off. At this point, I felt very alone and thought to myself I wish I would've stayed in college. As I entered the plane, there was a stewardess standing there waiting to greet me, and she told me I could sit wherever I wanted to.

The first thing I noticed was there were no first-class seats in this aircraft! There were several guys on the plane ahead of me, so the first seats available were in the middle of the aircraft. I slipped into a seat next to the window and looked out and saw the line of soldiers still boarding the plane.

When everyone was boarded and the door closed, the stewardess came on the intercom and welcomed us aboard. She said our flight would last for about 23 hours including stops at Guam and Kyoto, Japan. The jet started taxing out to the end of the runway and the pilot came on the intercom and told us we were second in line for takeoff. As I looked around, I saw mostly serious-looking faces.

Ordinarily when you get a bunch of GIs together there's a lot of poking and joking, but not this time. The stewardess came back on the intercom and gave us the safety talk and that there were flotation devices under our seats in case of an unexpected emergency water landing. Great, that's all I needed, to go down in the middle of the ocean somewhere and find myself floating around with 140 other GIs.

The last thing the stewardess said was that after takeoff they would be serving refreshments and snacks. She also said we would be served dinner consisting of steak, baked potatoes, vegetables and a side salad with our choice of dressing. Wow, sounded just like home! After the plane had reached 35,000 feet the seat belt sign went off and we were told we could move about the cabin. I would soon find out that after sitting in an airplane seat for hours moving around the cabin became a necessity.

One of the things I noticed about the stewardesses was that they were all older women. Usually when flying on commercial airlines the stewardesses are young very attractive chicks that you would give your right arm to have a date with. I found out that the entire crew on this aircraft volunteered to take us to Vietnam. It seemed like it was only the old-timers who had that sense of patriotism that allowed them to take the risk of being shot down over Vietnam or blown up while the aircraft sat on the ground. I suddenly had a deeper appreciation for those seasoned airline employees that volunteered for this mission. I would find out in about 23 hours how serious the risk was in hauling soldiers into a war zone.

After we had been in the air for about 12 hours the captain came on the intercom and told us we would be making a stop in Guam. The commercial airlines haul mail for the U.S. government that includes Guam and Japan. As I looked out my window, I could see in the distance what looked like a very small island out in the middle of the ocean. The water was the prettiest colors I'd ever seen. Blues and blue-green colors mixed themselves circling around the circumference of the island. It was a breath-taking view.

Looking at the island and the beautiful water took me back to my high school days when I would spend endless days riding waves and snorkeling at La Jolla. Man, what I wouldn't do to be back there right now riding my Hobie surfboard and eating burgers and fries at the local eatery with the local gremmies (novice surfers).

As the airplane descended, I kept thinking to myself that we were about halfway to Vietnam. My ass was killing me, and my neck felt like somebody had been standing on it. There is absolutely no way to get comfortable when you're riding in an airliner for 12 hours. I think I remembered from my history class in high school that Guam was an unincorporated and organized territory of the United States located in Micronesia in the West Pacific Ocean.

The governor of the island was a naval officer appointed by the President of the United States. The island itself is 30 miles long and 10 miles wide. Guam serves the United States as a strategic military base used to harbor nuclear subs, long-range bombers, stockpiles of nuclear weapons, and other conventional weapons. Guam was also the taking-off place for B-52 bombers that supported troops in Vietnam (soon to be my new best friends).

As we approached the island, the Captain came on the intercom and told everyone to buckle their seat belts and prepare for landing. The stewardesses took their seats and within five minutes our wheels touched the runway and we were taxiing to a small building midway down the runway.

When the aircraft came to a complete stop, the stewardess told us we could get off the plane and stretch our legs or go into the small building that housed a gift shop and junk food of all kinds. She also said we would be re-boarding in about an hour and that no one should leave the area.

As I descended the stairs, I noticed a technician exiting a fuel truck hooking up the fuel hose underneath the airplane's wing. There were small open trailers filled with boxes and bags of mail pulled by what looked like golf carts. They pulled in front of us and stopped at the cargo door. Mail from the United States was unloaded and mail from Guam loaded back on to the plane.

There was also a food and beverage truck with a scissor lift bed that backed up to the back door of the plane. They would remove all the trash that had accumulated during the flight and restock meals and sodas. They also sucked out the holding tanks where all the human waste collected from the bathrooms.

The small building or I guess you could call it a visitor center wasn't big enough to hold all 140 soldiers at one time. We lined up outside the door and as one soldier came out one soldier went in. Since the airline was supplying all the sodas and candy we could eat, I decided I would go in and pick up some postcards that I could send home as soon as I got to Vietnam. The guy sitting next to me on the plane told me that this was his second tour in Vietnam and the mail sent home by soldiers was postage-free.

After about 45 minutes we were told it was time to re-board the plane. When everyone had securely fastened themselves in their seats, the plane taxied to the end of the runway and what seemed like only a minute or two, we were back in the air headed to Japan. The captain came on the intercom and said the flight to Yakota Air Force Base in Japan would only take about four hours. I thought to myself that's just about the right amount of time for me to close my eyes and get some rest. I must've gone to sleep because I was suddenly awakened by the captain's voice on the intercom telling us that we were passing Mount Fuji.

Fuji is the tallest active volcano in Japan. It towers 12,889 ft. above the sea. We only had 319 miles to go until we reached Yakota. While making our approach to Yakota Air Force Base the pilot said it was raining hard and the temperature was 99 degrees. We were stopping there to top off the fuel tanks and unload more mail and load mail that was either heading to Vietnam or back to the United States. Unlike Guam there was a military BX located close to where we would be parking. The stewardess told us again that we would only be on the ground for about an hour and that no one should leave the immediate area.

When the door to the airplane opened, there was a sudden shock to everyone's system that simply sucked the air out of our lungs. In an instant everyone's clothes were soaking wet from the high heat and humidity. When I entered the BX, I noticed it was much more than a convenience store. You could buy all sorts of stuff like clothing, knives, electronics, all kinds of food goods and of course postcards to send home after getting to Vietnam. The time went by too quickly and we were told we had to re-board the plane again.

Once again, we found ourselves lifting off the runway, engines roaring, climbing to 35,000 feet. The captain came on the intercom and told us we were on the last leg of our flight and that we would be touching down at Long Binh Air Force Base in Vietnam. It suddenly came to me that I would be leaving this plane for the last time and step foot in the People's Republic of Vietnam in five short hours.

What was ahead of me I had no idea and it didn't help that the guy sitting next to me told me the first time he landed in Vietnam the Viet Cong were mortaring the airfield. I suddenly thought back to the reason pilots and stewardesses volunteered for this duty. It was surely high risk, but they all had the guts to do it. After we had been in the air about two hours, the stewardesses came down the aisles pushing their carts and handed out our last main meal of the trip.

I remember it reminded me of Thanksgiving because the meal consisted of sliced turkey, mashed potatoes and gravy, stuffing and a small bowl of cranberry sauce. Little did I know this exact same kind of meal would completely debilitate my platoon while patrolling the Cambodian border. But that's another story. A stewardess following the cart had a big basket full of rolls and butter and she said we could have as many as we liked. Another stewardess followed handing out pumpkin pie with whipped cream on top. As I was stuffing my face the thought occurred to me again, with a smile on my face, that this was like a man on death row eating his last meal.

After the meal was done the stewardesses collected all the trays and the Captain came on the intercom and said we would be landing at Long Binh Air Force Base in approximately two hours and 15 minutes. Then something unusual happened. The stewardesses came down the aisle holding beach balls. They spread out throughout the cabin and started throwing the beach balls at the guys, aiming at their heads.

92

They had smiles on their faces and before long the balls were ricocheting around the cabin by guys hitting them just like you would see at a Beach Boys rock concert. Pillows were added to the list of projectiles. It was though the stewardesses wanted everyone to be happy before we touched down in Vietnam. That simple act of kindness would be the most memorable part of my trip.

After about 30 minutes of riotous behavior, the stewardesses collected the balls and pillows and said they would be bringing the beverage carts around for the last time. I stared out the window looking at the ground wondering what Vietnam would look like from the air. I imagined it would consist of triple canopy jungles and rice paddies.

I would later find out that I wasn't too far off. About a half an hour before we landed at Long Binh Air Force Base, the captain came on the intercom and said he wanted to explain the procedures that were in effect when we landed. He said, "as you are aware Vietnam is a war zone." Several of the guys started laughing at his comment and almost as if he knew this was going to happen, he waited a minute before continuing his speech.

He went on to tell us that a Flying Tiger airliner after landing yesterday had the front wheel assembly destroyed by an explosion caused by a VC mortar. He went on to tell us that no one on board was injured and that all the occupants of the airplane got off safely. He said there was no way of telling when the VC would do this again but that the base had incoming mortars almost every day. After the plane landed the Captain said he would taxi to the tarmac.

When our plane came to a complete stop, stairs would be wheeled towards the plane. The stairs would be pushed up to the front door and that we were to disembark in an orderly manner and that there would be Army personnel waiting for us to take us to the reception station. He told us as soon as the last soldier was on the ground soldiers going home would start boarding.

The stewardesses made their last trip up the aisle to make sure all of our seat belts were fastened, the tray tables were up, and our seats were in the upright position. I'll never forget the sound of the wheel hatch covers opening and the wheels locking themselves in place for the landing. I looked out the window and saw the ground coming up fast.

We were coming in hot, real hot. The last thing I remember when the plane touched down is that I thought to myself, "Lord I am not worthy that you should come under my roof, say but the word and my soul shall be healed." This was a Bible verse that the nuns had taught us in catholic school to say if we ever found ourselves faced with imminent danger. I figured landing in Vietnam certainly qualified for that.

John Helps Bruns Go Under Wire

CuChi Base Camp

Mess Sgt. Arie Hill

Lt. Cy Creveling

Lt. Cy Creveling Outside Crockett FSB

Chapter Six
GRAB YOUR GEAR AND LOAD
UP ON THE BUSES

t was August 21 when I stepped foot into Vietnam. In five days, I would turn 20 yrs. old. I remember it was 1400 hrs. on the dot. After everyone had gotten off the plane, our duffel bags were unloaded onto a couple of trucks, and no sooner had we boarded the bus, we could see the plane being boarded by soldiers that had completed their time in Nam and were returning home. I would later learn that this plane was referred to as the freedom bird back to the world. These soldiers going home looked tired and worn out.

None of them had smiles on their faces and none of them were laughing or joking. I wondered why they weren't more excited about getting on the plane. By the time I got to the processing station I noticed the airliner screaming down the runway lifting off and gaining altitude as fast as it could. It didn't take long for it to disappear into the low-hanging clouds heading back to Japan. I imagined that the crew probably breathed a sigh of relief knowing they had gotten in and out without incident one more time.

When we got off the bus at the processing center, I couldn't help but notice a terrible smell in the air. I would find out soon enough that the Vietnamese working for the Army burned the garbage and human feces every day and the smell hung in the air like an invisible fog. My first stop would be the incoming personnel center. I stood in a long line waiting to turn in my orders and see where I was going to go.

After giving the private first class my orders he told me that for the next couple of days I would be waiting for further orders on where I would be assigned. He pointed to a long building, referring to it as hooch and said I could go in and pick any cot. He told me to stow my gear under the bunk and suggested I always keep a lock on it. He then pointed to another area and told me this was where the mess hall was located. Three hot meals a day are served there including breakfast lunch and dinner. And finally, he told me the most important part of his instructions were to show up every morning at 0800 hrs. in the bleachers to see if my orders had arrived yet.

He told me that I had to be at the bleachers twice a day: 0800 hrs. and 1300 hrs. He said we were finished and that I could head over to where the cots were located. When I entered the hooch, I noticed that there were about 100 military cots lined up from one end of the building to the other. It appeared that over 75 of the cots were already taken. I located one and put my duffel bag on the floor and sat down to think about what I would do next.

The guy sitting about three cots away from me said, "welcome to Vietnam." He asked me where I had taken basic and AIT and I told him Fort Ord, California. He said he had done his basic and AIT at Fort Lewis Washington. He told me he had been in Nam for two days and that on the first day the Viet Cong had dropped three mortar rounds that hit near the ammo dump. I would find out later that the Army hires hundreds of local Vietnamese to do odd jobs around the base.

These jobs include cleaning buildings, helping in the mess hall, barbers, and of course those unfortunates that got stuck burning the shit barrels. I also learned that most of these civilians were VC sympathizers and would report to the VC on a daily basis, letting them know what was going on at the base. On one occasion they caught a mama-san stepping off the distance from the chow hall to the ammo dump. It soon became apparent that the mama-san was reporting accurate coordinates to the VC when she would go home at night. This would not be the last time I would witness this same activity.

This covert activity was going on at Cu Chi and other fire support bases around Vietnam. At 1700 hrs., I walked over and got in line at the mess hall. When I got my tray and started through the food line, I realized that this was the same food they served us in basic and AIT. Oh well, at least it was hot food and I was about to learn a very important lesson in Vietnam: beggars can't be choosers.

Little did I know that where I was going hot meals were few and far between. My first night in Vietnam would be the beginning of my indoctrination into war, VC style. Shortly after dark as I was lying on my cot, I could hear explosions in the distance caused by an artillery unit supporting some grunt unit in trouble. There was no way I was going to be able to go to sleep tonight. At about 0300 hrs., there were explosions overhead that turned out to be illumination flares.

Apparently, this was done on a nightly basis to illuminate the runways and make sure Charlie wasn't planting some kind of explosive devices. Somewhere between 0300 hrs. and 0600 hrs. I must have fallen asleep. The screeching of wheels awakened me as an airliner touched down bringing in a plane load of new replacements. I got up, put my boots on and headed for the mess hall. Some things never change in the Army. The breakfast they were serving included burnt bacon swimming in grease, scrambled eggs with a slight green tinge, watery oatmeal, and burnt toast.

The coffee still had a bitter taste to it as well. It wasn't too bad after if I added a couple of packets of sugar and some milk. GIs through history have figured out ways to doctor up unappetizing army food. After breakfast, I grabbed my duffel bag, headed to the bleacher area, and waited for an NCO to read out the names of the men assigned to different units in Vietnam. I heard units like the 25th, Big Red One, 101 Airborne, and Americal.

I had no idea where these units were operating, and I knew less about what they did. My name wasn't called so I headed back to the hooch where my cot was placed. I sat down on the cot, opened my duffel bag and retrieved a plastic bag that contained some envelopes, paper, and a few pens. I thought this would be a great time to write a letter home and let them know that I arrived in Vietnam in one piece. I would also send the post cards I purchased in Guam and Japan.

There was no need to bring any stamps because all outgoing mail sent by soldiers in Vietnam were postage-free. I wasn't sure whether the post office was being good to the GIs or if the military paid for the mail on the back end. In my letter, I told them that I had not been assigned yet and that I did not have an address for them to send mail to me. I finished the letter, put it in an envelope, licked it and went looking for a mailbox. On my way back from mailing the letter a soldier approached me and asked me if I would like to have my picture taken to send back to the folks at home. He had an M-16 rifle and said for five bucks he would pose me with the rifle and capture my first picture in Vietnam.

Years later, I found out that guy made a fortune from taking pictures of the new replacements. Almost every guy in my unit sent home the same picture of themselves holding that M-16 rifle! On the way back to the hooch I saw a sergeant that had an electric strawberry-looking patch on his sleeve. I asked him what unit he was in and he said the 25th Infantry. I asked him what I could expect in the field and he said that an infantry soldier had an average lifespan in Vietnam of about 3 months. I had a sick feeling in my stomach. I was 11-B infantry. He told me that Long Binh was regularly mortared and rocketed and the bunker lines were tested by the VC almost every night.

He told me in case of an attack I could stay in my hooch or I could go into the bunker that was located outside the hooch. That night all hell broke loose. Incoming rockets hit in front of the runway and small arms fire was heard on the perimeter. It was the first time I'd ever heard an AK-47 and I will never forget that sound as long as I live. Illumination flares burst overhead, and I remember looking out of the bunker hoping and praying Charlie wouldn't get in. I had no way to defend myself.

The next morning at 0600 hrs., I found myself in the chow line again, but this time I was standing behind some sergeant that was dirty from head to toe. He was covered in red dust. I tapped him on the shoulder, and he jerked around suddenly and said, "what the fuck do you want?" I told him I was curious about what was happening out in the field. He looked at me with blank eyes and said, "fuck it," and turned back around and never said another word.

I thought to myself, I guessed I'd find out soon enough and continued through the chow line. A special forces Sgt. that overheard our conversation said, "your job is to kill gooks and protect yourself and your buddies."

I kept thinking about what the Sgt. said about killing gooks. I had never really thought about that before, I was thinking more about protecting myself. I was actually getting scared and hoped my name would be miraculously lost and I would spend my year in the bleachers. When I got back to the hooch area, I approached a Sergeant and complained about not having a weapon. The Sgt. said, "shit new guy, we give you a rifle and you're liable to shoot someone. Be patient you'll have plenty of time to kill gooks."

That afternoon I returned to the bleacher area with my duffel bag on my shoulder to find out if it was my turn to receive an assignment. After a couple of dozen names were read the NCO called out John Quintrell, 25th Wolfhounds, and directed me to an area where a deuce and a half truck was waiting to take me and other newbies to our new base camp named Cu Chi.

As I turned to leave, I heard him say, "Wolfhounds: I feel sorry for you man.," I wondered why he said that. I didn't have much time to think about that as I walked down a dusty path where I would load up and officially begin my first day as a so-called Wolfhound.

Wolfhounds No Fear on Earth

When I arrived at the truck there were a half a dozen guys loading their duffel bags getting ready to leave. I would soon find out that two of them were assigned to the same unit as me. I looked at my orders again and it said I was assigned to Charlie Company 2/27 Inf. I also noticed that there was an M-60 machine gun mounted on the roof of the truck. In 10 minutes, the driver and his co-driver arrived and told us to get in the back of the truck and get ready to leave. He started the truck, got back out and came around to the back and said, "if we get ambushed on the way to Cu Chi, one of you guys get on that M-60 and rock and roll."

We all looked at each other and one of the guys said, "what the hell was that all about?" Our convoy consisted of one Jeep with an M-60 machine gun mounted in the back and two trucks: one loaded with replacements, the other loaded with supplies. We were embarking on a trip about 30 miles long that went through many small villages along the way. The roads we were driving on consisted of a red dirt called laterite.

All of the guys I was riding with including myself complained that we did not have any weapons besides the M-60 machine gun to defend ourselves with if we got involved in a firefight. It was very unnerving and made us all feel defenseless.

We were told we would be issued weapons when we got to Cu Chi. The trucks averaged about 25 miles per hour, and the road was full of potholes filled with water from the monsoon rains. It was a horrible ride to say the least made much worse by the fact we had to sit on wooden seats in the back of the truck. I found out that this convoy was a regular event.

Every day, soldiers that were going home and outgoing mail were driven from Cu Chi to Long Binh. Every village we went through was lined with little kids waving and holding up their hands hoping that we would throw them candy or other edible items. Since none of us had any of these items at our disposal, the kids were out of luck.

Some of the kids gave us the finger. It seemed like we had been riding for hours but eventually we found ourselves driving through the main gate at Cu Chi. There was a sign outside the gate that said, Home of the Wolfhounds Nec Aspera Terrent. The truck pulled up and stopped in front of the Charlie Company area. The driver said anybody assigned to Charlie Company get off the truck now. He said wait here and someone would come and tell us where to go.

Not far from where we were standing was a Quonset building with a sign out front that read, Charlie Company Home of the Wolfhounds. We asked the driver when we would be issued weapons. He started laughing and said, "shit new guy, we give you a rifle and you're liable to shoot someone. Be patient, you'll have plenty of time to kill gooks."

After standing in the hot sun and humidity for about 15 minutes we saw a guy holding a clip board come out of the Quonset and walk directly towards us. The man introduced himself as Sergeant Kelley, who was the company clerk. He said he preferred to be called Teach, as this was his nickname since he joined the second platoon.

Before coming to Vietnam, Kelley was a teacher back in the world. He gave each of us a Zippo lighter with the Wolfhound crest and 25th ID logo on it. It was engraved with C company 2/27 Wolfhounds 25th ID on the side. Teach's Dad had them made and sent 500 of them to Teach to give to the guys in the Company. Then he told us the story of getting gored on the Hoc Mon Bridge.

Incident On HOC Mon Bridge

While serving in the second platoon Teach suffered a terrible accident when the platoon was guarding the Hoc Mon Bridge. One afternoon while crossing the bridge, Teach was attacked by a water buffalo being led across the bridge by a 10-year-old boy. Water Buffalo attacks had already accounted for several GI deaths. The buffalo looked straight into Teach's eyes and lowered its head and drove him into the railing along the edge of the bridge. Teach grabbed the horns, but one still gored him in the stomach.

As Teach lay under the 2000 lb. beast he figured he was done. Higgins, Deline and Fitzgerald stood in disbelief as their buddy fought to draw air into his lungs. SSGT Glover was the first to arrive and knelt down to see how teach was doing. There was a lot of screaming and yelling going on and Willy, Cal and Dobesh shot the water buffalo several times. One of the bullets went through the buffalo and went into Teach's leg.

Seeing the 2000 lb. water buffalo lying on top of Teach crushing him almost to death was quite a sight. Glover immediately knew they had to get the buffalo off of Teach. He commandeered a Jeep and it pulled the buffalo off of the beleaguered Wolfhound. He had been lying under the buffalo for 30 minutes.

Teach immediately gasped for air and a couple of guys carried him to a sleeping position under the bridge. Higgins said he would stay with Teach that night. About 2400 hrs., Teach felt something wet on his legs. When he pulled the poncho off, he saw both his legs drenched with blood.

The blood was coming from the 2-inch hole in his stomach caused when the buffalo horn gored him. Glover tried to get a medevac but there was none available until morning. At 0900 hrs., a medevac landed on top of the bridge and waited to load up Teach. Two of the guys carried Teach to the center of the bridge and after Teach was loaded up, it took off to Cu Chi.

When Teach was examined at the field hospital, the doctors discovered that in addition to the hole in his stomach, he had three broken ribs on his left side and two broken ribs on his right side. If that wasn't enough his left foot was broken and he had an M-16 round embedded in his knee.

After the chopper lifted off, an old papa san ran up to the lieutenant and demanded that the Army pay for his dead animal through an interpreter.

The Lieutenant tried to calm the old gentleman down and assure him the Army would compensate him for his loss. As was the Army's custom, if any GI killed a water buffalo either accidentally or on purpose, the Army would give the owner a cash payment of $500. The Lieutenant got on the radio to Battalion and told them they needed to send someone out to pay the old man.

A group of villagers had gathered around during this whole debacle and were yelling obscenities and shaking their fists at the guys still waiting on the bridge. Little did I know that this scene of water buffaloes being killed would play itself out many times during my tour in Vietnam.

After Teach finished the story, he directed us to the supply/armory building where we would be issued our field gear and be issued a weapon. When we entered the supply building SSGT Jim Calvert pointed to a pile of gear and said take what you want. The first web belt I grabbed had a bullet hole in it and dried blood covered the inside. I tossed it back and scavenged through the pile until I found gear with no holes and no blood stains. I was issued a brand-new M-16 and 3 empty magazines and was told we would be given ammo when we got to fire support base Crockett.

Then SSGT Calvert showed us where we would spend the night and said dinner would be served in the mess hall at 1700 hrs. I didn't realize it at the time but the two guys I had arrived with would turn out to be my best friends in Nam and my best friends for life. Their names were Ray and Russ. Ray was from Barstow, California and Russ was from Peoria, Illinois.

Our first night in Cu Chi proved to be very unnerving. Throughout the night we could hear explosions in the distance and automatic weapons fire not far from our perimeter. This went on most of the night. In time we would eventually learn how to sleep through the noise of bombs being dropped. In fact, the rumbling of B-52 strikes would be music to our ears. Better you than me sucker. Artillery being shot nearby and illumination flares being dropped overhead would become a nightly event.

The next morning, we went to the shower area and performed the three S's (shit, shower and shave). None of us would have guessed that this would be the last running water we would see until we returned to Cu Chi three months later. After breakfast we reported to the Company Quonset and Teach told us we would be attending a three-day jungle warfare school in Cu Chi. He said the school was affectionately known as charm school.

The first day of class was mostly sitting in the bleachers listening to a Spec 4 tell us about the various kinds of booby traps and land mines being used in Vietnam. He showed us many pictures which included soda can grenade traps, punji stick traps, bouncing bettys and various ways the VC hid tripwires and claymore mines set up along ox cart trails. He told us we would be going through a simulated jungle course and that there would be several booby traps planted along the trail that we were supposed to find and disarm.

Unfortunately for us, we didn't know that there were some sadists teaching in that school. On the second day of class, they split us up into groups of three and sent us down a heavily vegetated trail. The bamboo was so thick, that we had to keep pushing it aside to make our way down the trail.

It was all but impossible to look down and in front of us at the same time to try to see any tripwires. We were down the trail about 50 feet when there was a sudden loud explosion just off the right side of the trail. Apparently, the instructors had planted concussion grenades throughout the course, and they were manually setting them off as we worked our way down the trail.

Needless to say, it scared the holy ba-Jesus out of all of us. Our ears were ringing, and I had a feeling this was only one of many to come. The bamboo finally opened up to an open area which gave us an opportunity to locate tripwires that were cleverly camouflaged crossing the trail. My group found every tripwire stretched across the trail. What we didn't see was the monofilament line stretched across the trail about 5 feet off the ground. One of the guys walked into it and another concussion grenade went off and the instructor jumped out and said we had all been wiped out by a Claymore mine hanging in the brush to our right.

It taught us all that Charlie would rig booby traps in many different ways to maim or kill as many GIs as possible. On the third day the instructors had us crawling through tunnels that were camouflaged with covers made out of vegetation and bamboo.

The only thing they gave us to take down in the tunnel was a flashlight. After uncovering the opening, I saw that the tunnel went straight down for about 6 feet then turned 90° to the left and went another 30 feet. I went into the hole head first and it looked like I was running into a dead end. The tunnel smelled of mold and damp earth. There were several spider webs crisscrossing across the top and when I got to the end of the tunnel it dropped down another 6 feet which led to an underground room large enough to be a living space. I noticed there was a vent pipe in the ceiling that led to the surface that supplied air to the occupants of the tunnel.

As I was about to leave, there was a sudden scream behind me. One of the instructors was hiding behind a piece of dirty canvas hanging from the ceiling. I actually thought I was having a heart attack as my chest suddenly had a pain in it from the jolt of adrenaline that hit me like a freight train. The instructor started laughing and told us to get our sorry asses out of his tunnel.

I couldn't believe that people could actually live under these conditions. We all graduated from charm school (no one ever flunked) and returned to the Charlie Company area. Teach told us that we would be joining the second platoon located at Crockett Fire Support Base. Teach told us to ask for SSGT Glover when we arrived and he would tell us what to do and where to go.

We were to assemble in front of the supply building at 1300 hrs. and load up on the re-supply truck and ride out to join the second platoon. We stood in the hot sun for 30 minutes before the truck arrived. We helped load cases of C rations, ammo boxes, cases of canned food for the mess hall, cases of beer and coca-cola and of course a mail bag that contained letters and care packages from home. The ride to Crockett was dusty and hot but eventually we arrived at a perimeter set up next to a graveyard. There were multiple strands of concertina wire stretched between metal fence posts.

The first thing we noticed was that bunkers were being built inside the wire and the three 105 mm howitzer emplacements. There was also a mortar pit located on the far side of the perimeter. The mortar pit contained 81 mm mortars and 4.2-inch mortars as well. We unloaded and walked into the perimeter and the first soldier we ran into we asked, "do you know where SSGT Glover is located?" He pointed to the far end of the perimeter and said his bunker has an American flag next to it on a fence post. We located his bunker and walked there to discover a man sitting on a sandbag in his boxer shorts writing a letter.

I asked the man if he was SSGT Glover and he looked up at me and said, "you must be the new replacements." He pointed at Russ and me and said, "you two go over to the perimeter by the graveyard and set up that half-round culvert and fill sandbags to cover it." That half-round culvert would turn out to be our home as long as we were at Crockett. He told Ray to go to the bunker next to the culvert and ask for Big Joe. That would be Ray's home. Russ and I spent the rest of the day filling sandbags and positioning them around and on top of the metal culvert.

The sandbags were meant to protect us from incoming mortars and flying shrapnel. Filling sandbags was not part of basic training or AIT. I'm assuming the army didn't want to have guys skip to Canada after that exercise. We would end up filling many hundreds of sandbags during our time in Nam. We also noticed several potholes full of water within the perimeter.

This was evidence that we were indeed in the middle of the monsoon season. Big Joe told us Glover was from South Dakota and he thought he was an Indian and that he could see in the dark. At 1600 hrs., we met at SSGT Glover's bunker and I noticed there were only 11 guys including us 3 new guys. Glover told us that in the next week we would be receiving several more replacements.

Until that time, we would be assigned perimeter security and the job of building bunkers and fighting positions. That meant that we would spend most of the day filling sandbags in the scorching heat. At 1700 hrs., we lined up in the chow line to hear Mess Sgt. Arie Hill announce what was on the menu. You would've thought we were eating at a four-star restaurant! It was our first meal out in the field, and they were serving sliced beef that had a greenish-purple tint to it, mashed potatoes and gravy and boiled sliced carrots.

There were buns at the end of the line, and I noticed the cooks gave their buddies an extra helping of meat. Good to know. That first day at Crockett went by pretty fast and before we knew it the sun was going down and it started to get dark. A guy we had never seen before came by and said that the second platoon would be staying at Crockett tonight and we would be responsible for perimeter duty.

This was exactly what SSGT Glover had told us earlier in the day. This consisted of having one guy in each position awake and looking outside the wire in case the Viet Cong tried to attack the base. A soldier named Ketchum came by with some bandoleers of M-16 magazines filled with ammo and told us if we had to shoot, it was best if we used semiautomatic. Ketchum was an interesting fellow that had been sent to Vietnam by a Judge. The Justice gave Ketchum two choices: join the Army and go to Vietnam or go to the penitentiary. Seems that Ketchum was mixed up in an attempted murder case with drug dealers.

Since we were right next to Ray's bunker, we decided one guy could cover the area in front of the bunker and the half-round. Russ and I spread our ponchos out on the dirt floor of our corrugated metal fort, crawled in and tried to get some shut-eye. No one woke us that first night to stand guard duty, but we were awakened to the sound of torrential rain hitting the ground around us.

It was daylight outside and suddenly Russ and I discovered we were laying in 4 inches of water that had flooded in the front of our half round. I remember feeling very cold and I was shivering as I crawled out on my hands and knees into the mud. There were four or five guys standing there laughing their asses off. It didn't take long to figure out that they were in our platoon and they knew the two new guys wouldn't have sense enough not to sleep in the mud.

As it turned out it was kind of a new guy initiation that all new replacements suffered in one form or another. Big Joe told me the way to solve the problem was to go to the artillery guys and get some empty wooden ammo boxes that the artillery shells came in and put them on the ground inside our half round.

We could sleep on top of those and stay out of the water. Our location was not the only one flooded that night.

Most of the bunkers on the perimeter were half-full water as well. I thought to myself, I don't think I'm going to like this place very much! After breakfast, the second platoon gathered around SSGT Glover's bunker to get the orders of the day. I found out that day the second platoon had been in heavy contact two weeks before and many of the guys were killed or wounded. Was I hearing this right? We were the first replacements to fill those slots.

The names of the men killed in 1968 were written on a piece of wood and hung next to SSGT Glover's bunker. The names included James Bentley, Calvin Bigger, Wardell Borders, Barton Brooks, James Burton, Robert Cohen, John Cooper, Patrick Fitzgerald, William Gritts, Jack Morrison, George Parounagian, Gary Richardson, Coy Strobel and Forest Ward. I got a sick feeling in my stomach when I realized all these men had served in this platoon during the six months prior to my arrival. Glover had everyone introduce themselves including us three new guys. The first thing they wanted to know is where our hometown was.

The first man to introduce himself was Glover's RTO. He said his name was Paul Naso, but everyone called him Nase. Nase was from New York. Next was Big Joe Waskom from Oden, Indiana, Willie Williams hailed from Yuma, Arizona, Buck Buchanan from Icard, North Carolina, Sugar Bear Taylor from Birmingham, Alabama, Tommy Kemp from Waycross, Georgia and Ed Rambo from Ohio. Another new guy that came in that morning was a guy named Galli from New York.

Over the next week there would be 10 more replacements join our platoon, including a medic named John Barkley. He was a young guy who grew up in Michigan and seemed nervous in his first assignment. He only lasted two weeks when he tripped a booby trap and blew his foot off. I will never forget the sound of him screaming. He was replaced by Doc Wolf who was sent over from the battalion aid station. Wolf was a great medic who was with us for 3 months and ended up going on R&R and never returning.

Glover told us that we would be going out on an ambush patrol that night and that we needed to prepare ourselves with a minimum of 20 magazines of M-16 ammo, a claymore mine, a minimum of three hand grenades and a purple smoke grenade. This was in addition to all the normal gear we wore including backpack, two canteens full of water, a knife and a few snacks. Some of us would be asked to carry 200 rounds of M-60 machine gun ammo.

It turned out that this would be a standard practice for all patrols. Glover reminded us to clean our weapons and meet at his bunker after dinner. Russ and I returned to our half-round and started to prepare for that night's mission. Big Joe was sitting on top of the bunker next to us with a monkey on his shoulder. He said her name was Sheila and for 5 bucks he would take a picture of her on my shoulder that I could send home to the folks. I thought that would be clever and gave him the 5 bucks for a Polaroid picture.

Next, he said he had something very important to talk to me about. He said make sure you bring your M-16 with you. During the next 15 minutes Big Joe sold me on the idea of trading his M-79 grenade launcher including 80 rounds in a rucksack in exchange for my new M-16 rifle. He said he would throw in a .45 cal. pistol to sweeten the deal.

As it turned out the 45 became more of a liability than an asset. I regretted that decision for the next couple of months until another new guy came into the platoon and I talked him into trading his M-16 rifle for my M-79 and worthless 45 cal. pistol. Thank you, Bob Mollenhauer. Before returning to my position, Big Joe asked me what they called me back in the neighborhood. I told him all the guys just called me Big John. Joe said, "from now on that's what we're going to call you." That nickname stuck with me for my entire tour and years to come.

First Ambush Patrol

When we showed up at Glover's bunker at 1700 hrs., he explained to us where we were going on the ambush patrol. He said, "we would be going to a place called the laterite pits." It was a rock quarry that was located just outside of a nearby Vietnamese village. He told us that the village had several Viet Cong living there, including the village chief, a card-carrying communist. Our job was to catch them in the open when they came walking out of the village.

He also explained that we would each take turns putting out our Claymore mines after getting set up in our ambush site. His last words on that subject were "make damn sure you have the thing pointed away from us and towards the village." Before leaving, he assigned each one of us new guys to one of the more experienced men.

The guy that I was assigned to stay with was named Buck. He was a short curly haired guy who grew up in North Carolina. He kept telling me the most important thing on an ambush patrol is to not go to sleep. He seemed paranoid about this and was convinced we would get our throats cut if one of us went to sleep on guard.

Buck seemed really high strung and later I would find out it was because he was taking Benny's (Benzedrine) to keep himself awake. He handed me a bottle of Benny's and told me to take one when we left the wire, one when we got to the ambush site, and then another if I felt myself nodding off. My decision to try these pills turned out to be a disaster.

The first night I followed his prescription. By daylight, my heart was pounding so hard I thought it was going to come out of my chest. As I remember, I couldn't sleep for the next two days. That was the first and the last time I ever used pills to stay awake. Glover told us when we arrived at the ambush site, he would place each one of us in our position. When we left the wire, it was getting dark and I remember it was a clear night. SSGT Glover walked point followed by Willy and Big Joe, and the rest of the platoon followed. We walked about a half a klick and when we arrived at the ambush site SSGT Glover placed each man about 6 feet apart with the quarry to our backs.

Buck whispered to me to go set my Claymore out and I remember how I fumbled getting the Claymore out of the bag. My hands were shaking, and I felt nervous as hell. I pulled out the wire with a blasting cap attached and the handheld magneto detonating device. I crawled out into the darkness until I reached the end of the detonating wire. I set the little legs up on the Claymore and positioned it so that the curved side was pointing towards the village. I placed the blasting cap into the top of the Claymore with a shaky hand, turned around, and followed the wire back to our position.

When I returned, Buck said that he was going to set his Claymore and I watched him disappear in the darkness. When he returned, he showed me how to place my bag of M-79 rounds in front of me so that they would be easily accessed in the middle of a firefight. Even though it was a clear night it was difficult to see across the open field to where the village was located.

I remember seeing shadows that I thought might be VC walking out in the open field to our front; I didn't realize that SSGT Glover had a starlight scope and that he and the guys in his position would take turns keeping an eye on the area in front of us. If we were going to pop an ambush it would be after he started shooting. It was a strange feeling laying there on the ground waiting for some VC to walk by.

As luck would have it, nothing happened on that first ambush patrol and just before daylight we crawled out and retrieved our Claymores and saddled up and started marching back towards Crockett. When we got back to our positions on the perimeter, Big Joe walked by and said, "good job boys that was an easy one." We would replay that scenario several times in the next month.

One memorable night it was so dark you could not see your hand in front of your face. I was partnered up with Alan Larsen who came into the platoon about the same time I did. We both knew just enough to make us dangerous. When we were set up in our ambush site, I told Larsen I was going to set my claymore out. I was scared half to death as I crawled out into the black abyss. It took me a few minutes using the Braille method, but I finally got my claymore set up.

When I got back, I told Larsen to go and set his claymore. I could not see him out in front of us and hoped he didn't crawl over my claymore. He finally returned and whispered how dark it was and that he got a little disoriented. The night passed by slowly and by daybreak it was obvious nothing was going to happen.

When there was enough daylight to see to our front, Glover yelled, "holy shit whose claymore is that?" We all looked around like dumb asses and Glover walked out in front of me and Larsen and stood next to a claymore that was only 20 feet away and pointing directly towards us. Glover said, "if we would have popped the ambush Larsen and I would have been put into body bags." We looked at each other dumbfounded. From that day forward Larsen was known as Allen "Claymore" Larsen.

115

We never set up in the same place twice, but we were always set up where we could keep an eye on the village. Ambush patrols are a funny thing; when you think something might happen it doesn't and when you don't think anything is going to happen all hell breaks loose. On one such night, shortly after setting up, we heard the distinct sound of the 90 mm recoilless firing pin click.

What followed next was a voice saying, "oh shit," and all hell broke loose. We popped our ambush on four VC walking in front of our position about 25 yards out. The sound of all the weapons firing was deafening. Most guys were just shooting out in front of themselves not able to see a definite target. I had no idea where the VC was, so I just started shooting HE (high explosive) rounds about 100 feet in front of us.

Without warning, illumination rounds went off over our heads. Our mortar platoon at Crockett had responded to Glover's radio request. As soon as the field was illuminated, I saw a VC running away off to my right. I guessed on the elevation and pointed my M-79 towards the fleeing VC and squeezed the trigger. The round hit the VC in the back of the legs, and he went ass over tea kettle into the dirt. Several of the guys that saw the VC go down started telling me that was a great shot.

I was going through several mixed feelings about what just happened. I didn't feel glad that I had hit the VC but more a feeling of shock. Eventually, the shooting stopped and the illumination ended and we were on high alert the rest of the night. Our platoon had killed 4 VC soldiers. When morning came Glover came by and told me to come with him and see where the VC had fallen.

When we got to the area where the gook had gone down, we saw lots of blood on the ground and bloody drag marks headed towards the village. Glover told me I had definitely messed the guy up and that someone from the village had snuck out there and drug the man's body back into the village. I would soon learn that this was a tactic that the VC and the NVA used to minimize the number we could use as body count. Only after being in Vietnam for a month, I had experienced what war was all about. It was either kill or be killed with no other options.

When we weren't pulling ambush patrols, we were being flown by Huey Helicopters out into the countryside to walk around looking for VC or NVA. Many times, the choppers would drop us off outside a village and we would walk through it poking our heads inside the hooches, looking for any evidence that the VC or the NVA had been there recently. We were always up tight thinking that the enemy could open up on us at any time. We poked around looking for any weapons or caches of rice that the enemy could use when they came into the area.

We usually had an interpreter with us that would question the local peasants about the movements of the VC. They always said they had no idea about any movement of the enemy. It really did make me mad when an interpreter would slap around some old mama-san when she didn't tell him what he wanted to hear. I could tell that these village people were caught between the VC and the NVA and the GIs that came there to help them. On one of these patrols our new medic James "Smitty" Smith stepped on a bouncing betty land mine and was blown into the air about 10 feet. He was missing his manhood and was unconscious when we got to him.

The medevac landed within 10 minutes and we loaded him up and he was taken to the evac hospital in Cu Chi. We never heard how he made out. We were once again without a medic. A week after this incident, Alpha Company had gone back into the same village and got ambushed by local VC regulars. They had one man killed and three wounded.

The Battalion Commander was furious. He gave our CO orders to return to the village and tear the place apart. He wanted dead VC or caches of rice or any hidden weapons. When we jumped off the Hueys outside the village we all had a bad feeling. As we walked through the village, we went into the hooches, tipping over baskets and lifting mats to see if a concealed hole was underneath. Chris was with me and we walked into a hooch and found an old mama- san sitting on the floor with her arm around a 20-year-old man.

I could tell by looking at him that he was mentally retarded. Chris said, "there are no men that age that aren't VC." He grabbed the man and pulled him to his feet and started yelling at him: "You VC, You VC." The man kept trying to reach for his mother and Chris slapped the man in the face knocking him to the ground. I stepped in front of Chris and said, "what's wrong with you man?" This guy is retarded and definitely not VC. He looked at me with hate in his eyes and said, "don't you ever do that again or I will cut you." The mama-san was crying and clutching her son to her chest when we left the hooch.

I turned around and threw her a couple of cans of fruit and said, "sin loy" (I'm sorry). Before leaving we were told to torch the village. Several guys were lighting matches and throwing them on the thatched roofs of the hooches. As we walked out of the village, Russ and I turned and saw flames leaping 20 feet in the air and villagers grabbing their children and running behind us. I thought to myself, what the hell are we doing, these people never hurt us. It all seemed so senseless, but the battalion commander got his payback for Alpha's losses.

When we were not out on patrols or pulling ambushes, we would spend the day in the fire support base cleaning our weapons, reading letters from home, writing letters and playing a lot of pinochle, hearts or spades. It was during these times that I had a chance to find out about the other guys in the platoon. We were always interested in finding out where everybody's hometown was, if they were married, engaged, or just had a girlfriend. Guys from New York, Chicago and LA were considered hoods and thugs. The guys didn't always get along with each other, but everyone had each other's backs when we left the wire on a mission.

Rick Galli, Russ Bruns

Cobra Gunship

Teach, Mike Deline (Sodaman)

Mess Sgt. Arie Hill in Love

Mama-San

Big Joe and Sheila

119

John's Medal Ceremony

John in Hong Kong

Chapter Seven
INCIDENT IN THE HOBO WOODS SEPTEMBER 1968

y the time we jumped off the helicopters in the Hobo Woods the temperature had reached 100°. The Hobo Woods consisted of dense vegetation that Charlie and the NVA used as cover for their command posts and hiding companies of soldiers. We were told our mission was to find any tunnels that might be hiding VC, ammunition or supplies. It seemed to most of us that this was a major waste of time since we could barely see in front of us to make our way through the jungle. We were all uptight thinking that we would be sitting ducks for any sappers that might be in the area.

After walking about an hour in the sweltering heat, the guy walking left flank yelled that he had a prisoner. Lieutenant Creveling made his way over to where the flank man was standing and sure enough there was a VC kneeling on the ground.

The prisoner had thrown his weapon into the brush just before he was caught. The weapon was an old French MAS-36 7.5 mm 5 round bolt action rifle. These old relics were used during the French Indochina wars. This guy was definitely not a VC regular but some poor peasant forced into service by local VC leaders. On that particular day we did not have a Kit Carson Scout that could act as our interpreter so Creveling radioed back to battalion to send us out a South Vietnamese interpreter.

It only took 20 minutes before we could hear the sound of helicopter blades in the distance heading our way. The helicopter landed behind us and an ARVN Ranger jumped out and walked towards our location. I had never seen an ARVN Ranger before, and I couldn't believe how his uniform looked. His fatigues were skin tight and starched. His combat boots were spit-shined and he was wearing a red beret.

He was carrying a holstered 45 cal. pistol that had been chrome plated. The two officers saluted each other and Creveling led the way to where the prisoner was being held. By this time, the prisoner's hands were tied behind his back. When the officers approached the prisoner, the Ranger started shouting obscenities at the prisoner. Sweat was dripping off of the prisoner's face and he looked terrified.

The Ranger asked the prisoner a number of questions about where the tunnels were located and if there were any VC or NVA in the area. The prisoner kept saying no and the Ranger repeatedly slapped him across the face. Apparently, the prisoner told the Ranger he knew where there was a tunnel that contained rice. The prisoner led the Ranger a short way where there was an old tunnel entrance with no cover on it. Our lieutenant sent Stubbs our tunnel rat down the hole to see if there was anything there.

When Stubbs emerged, he was holding a dirty bag that contained a couple of pounds of rice. He told the Lieutenant it was an old tunnel and there was nothing else down there. The South Vietnamese Ranger went into a rage and threw the prisoner on the ground and kicked him in the ribs. He was shouting and screaming obscenities and threatening to kill the prisoner if he didn't come up with better information.

At one point the Ranger took out his 45-cal. pistol, stuck it in the prisoner's mouth, and cocked it, threatening to blow his brains out. The prisoner started crying and begging for his life.

It was the first time I had ever witnessed an interrogation and I was sure that this method was not approved by the U.S. Army or the Geneva Convention. We all had an eerie feeling that we were being watched and wished we could get out of the area. The Ranger marched the prisoner back to his helicopter handing him over to the crew chief and jumped up into the copilot seat.

Usually when a helicopter takes off, it gets off the ground, lowers its nose and accelerates forward gradually increasing its altitude. This pilot however, lifted the bird off the ground and just kept going straight up. The helicopter faded eastward from our position and when it was about 500 feet off the ground, we all heard a horrible scream and witnessed the prisoner falling out of the helicopter.

The whole incident was shocking, and it was like watching a movie. There was dead silence among the platoon members until Big Joe said, "He must have slipped on some transmission oil." I couldn't believe it when a few of the old-timers started laughing and said let's get the hell out of this place.

For several months I could not get the picture and sound of that prisoner falling to his death out of my mind. I guess the ARVN Ranger thought he had gotten all the information from him that he could. We never did find any tunnels or caches of weapons or food, but a couple of the guys came close to getting heat exhaustion. This would be one of many missions that we were sent on that produced no favorable outcomes.

A week later Delta Company was sent into the Hobo Woods exactly where we had been and made contact with a company-sized unit of NVA. I kept thinking back to that day we were there and how I felt like somebody was watching us. Why didn't they open up on us?

Why did they give us a pass? I would ask myself this question a hundred more times and never came up with a suitable answer. I was losing my innocence one day at a time. When we got back to Crockett, we cleaned our weapons, got ready for evening chow, and looked forward to getting a letter or care package from home. I learned not to dwell on what had happened that day but from time to time when I fell asleep, I could hear the scream as the prisoner fell to his death.

A week later we were in the Iron Triangle and we came upon a young Vietnamese man who was just sitting in the trail. Almost all men his age were drafted into the VC Army. We called for an interpreter and they sent out another ARVN officer. The interrogation went about the same as the one we had witnessed the week before.

The only difference was that the officer had the crew chief bring a field telephone over to where the prisoner was kneeling. The officer stood the prisoner up and pulled his shorts down. He connected alligator clips from the radio to the prisoner's testicles. He asked the prisoner several questions and the prisoner continued to deny any knowledge of any VC or NVA activity in the area.

The interpreter turned to his crew chief and told him to crank the ringer handle on the phone, which sent a severe voltage shock into the prisoner's testicles. As we all stood around dumbfounded, we witnessed this young man screaming and convulsing with pain. After that, the prisoner was loaded up into the helicopter and the Officer and his crew chief took off towards Cu Chi. We all looked at each other as if to say what the hell was going on here.

I believe this VC was trying to Chieu Hoi. The Chieu Hoi program allowed VC soldiers to surrender to allied troops and be reintegrated into South Vietnamese life. Many of the Chieu Hoi's would become Kit Carson scouts for the Army. Once again Big Joe came up with the logical explanation. He said, "the crew chief must have been trying to call home... collect!"

As usual several guys laughed, and I was beginning to see how these dark gallows humor had a place in Vietnam. It helped us cope with circumstances and events that we could not comprehend or wrap our brain around. In the months to come, I would become a wordsmith in sarcasm and dark humor. Little did I know that this would stay with me for the rest of my life.

In the next 10 months I would see things and do things that went against all my beliefs including my belief in God. During the month of September, it rained every single day and after a while the monsoon weather started to get on everybody's nerves. Nothing ever dried out, everything felt and smelled musty and I had a hell of a time trying to keep my feet dry. I always carried an extra pair of dry socks in my pack. When I knew we were going to be marching in the rice paddies, I would not wear socks or underwear. By doing this, my feet and crotch area dried out much faster.

During my 12 months in Vietnam, I would experience all kinds of skin rashes, toe jam, trench foot, and a very unpleasant condition we referred to as knife ass. Knife ass was caused by extreme heat and long marches. My crotch and ass cheeks would get sweaty and the constant rubbing caused the skin to inflame to the point where it felt like someone was shoving a knife up your ass. A young medic named Doc Turner joined our platoon and told us he was from Memphis, Tennessee, the home of Elvis Presley.

Doc brought two things with him to the field: his aid bag and a $10 Vietnamese 6 string guitar. First thing I told Doc was,

125

"watch out for trip wires" and from that day forward Doc always walked behind me when we went outside the wire.

USS New Jersey Fire Mission

Glover told us we were going on an ambush patrol to a new area where we had not been before. We would take an eagle flight late in the afternoon and be dropped off a half a klick from our ambush site. It was like being told you are going out in the middle of nowhere with little support for the new guys. Glover said there had been intelligence reports indicating lots of VC movement in the area.

That's about all we knew about the mission. After dinner we gathered up our gear and met at Glover's bunker. Everyone was in good spirits and several guys were making the usual wisecracks about Big Joe sleeping with a monkey. Glover went over the final plan for the mission and said, "Nobody gets hurt tonight." The eagle flight took about 45 minutes, so I knew we were getting pretty far away from Crockett.

It was still daylight when we landed and jumped off the choppers. Glover was walking point with Big Joe and Willy and the rest of the platoon followed in single file. I was remembering what Joe had said about Glover being able to see in the dark and hoped right then he wasn't pulling my leg. We walked a quarter of a klick when the sun dropped down below the horizon. It was getting dark quickly.

We continued on and kept up a good pace when suddenly our march came to a screeching halt and everyone took a knee. It took about 10 minutes for the word to work its way back to us that there was a movement to our front and Glover wanted us to come up and get on line. The hair on the back of my neck stood

126

up and the knot in my stomach tightened up. I could not see anything in the dark.

While walking toward our objective Glover spotted movement in the hedgerow we were walking towards. The hedgerow was our ambush site and it appeared that Charlie got there before us. When Glover looked through the starlight scope, he saw lots of movement to the tune of over 50 VC setting up right in front of us.

He knew we were no match to go head-to-head with them but figured we were far enough away from the hedgerow that we could call in artillery and ruin their party. Glover is one of the best at calling in accurate artillery. He was trying to get the 6-inch guns at Trang Bang to support us with a fire mission. The battery told Glover we were just out of range for them to safely shoot as we were on their gun target line and at max range.

There was too much danger of a short round hitting us. The artillery TOC suggested Glover contact another group who could fire for him. This "other group" turned out to be the Navy battleship New Jersey steaming off the coast. The New Jersey had 16- inch artillery cannons that shot a projectile weighing between 1500 and 2700 lbs. Glover was able to contact them almost immediately and they said they would be happy to serve.

Since Glover already had our ambush site plotted on the map, he did not have to refigure a firing coordinate; he knew right where we were. He gave them the coordinates and asked for 1 Willy Peter height of burst for a marking round. Glover could have called in an HE round but erred on the side of caution in case the round was off course and hit us. None of us had experienced the effects of a 16-inch round before and had no idea what to expect.

Within a minute the battleship radioed Glover and said the round was on the way. Imagine a Volkswagen bug hurling through the air at supersonic speed and that's a 16-inch shell. When the white phosphorous shell arrived and exploded it was exactly 200 ft. over the hedgerow. The place lit up like daylight and we could see VC ducking and running everywhere. Glover immediately called for HE rounds on the deck and fire for effect.

Once again, the New Jersey responded that the rounds were on the way and when they arrived and exploded in the hedgerow the ground under us shook. Having no knowledge of the exact size of the enemy force we had encountered, Glover had us quickly hat up and leave the same way we came in. We did not look back and had no desire to go back and count bodies.

Since arriving in Vietnam this was the largest show of U.S. power I had witnessed. We went to an alternate ambush site and waited out the darkness until daylight. The Little Bears came to get us at 0800 hrs., and we were back at Crockett by 0900 hrs. This was a story the guys at Crockett just wouldn't believe.

Too Close For Comfort/Drowned Rats In The Morning

An order had come down from Battalion Headquarters that they wanted us to kill a village chief, who was an NVA sympathizer. The Chief's village was located about a klick from Crockett. SSGT Glover told us that the only way we would be able to accomplish the mission was if we set up the ambush in the village and hope we could catch him walking around at night. In order to help us accomplish this mission the Army assigned another ARVN Special Forces Ranger to accompany us. Our experience in the last couple of days proved to us that these Rangers were out of their minds.

After evening chow, we gathered in front of Glover's bunker, and he explained to us that we would be entering the village from the north and he would place two men in a hooch. We would wait inside the hooch and wait for someone to walk by. Nobody told us what the village chief looked like or what to do if someone walked in front of us. It seemed like another cobbled-up mess to me.

As soon as our meeting with Glover was over, we went and got our gear and prepared to leave the base after dark. The ARVN Special Forces Ranger and Glover would be walking point. There was a lot of grumbling from the guys and Rambo said it sounded like a good way for us to get ambushed ourselves. If the Chief was a NVA sympathizer, it only made sense that there might be some NVA in the village.

That night we walked straight into the village and it was one of the scariest nights of my life. The ARVN Ranger pushed me and Bruns into a hooch and we came face to face with a mama-san and her three little children huddled in the corner.

There was a single candle sitting next to them on the floor and the dim light showed the fear on their faces. Not being able to speak Vietnamese, I used hand signs to express to her that we would not hurt them and to stay calm. I had a candy bar and I handed it to the mama-san so she could give it to her kids. Seems like chocolate is a universal symbol of kindness and she and the kids got huge smiles on their faces.

We sat at the entrance of the hooch peeking out from side to side hoping that we did not see anything. I had been thinking about what we would do if someone in the village started shooting. Would we stay where we were, would we run out to see what was happening? At this point we had no clue what we would do. Somewhere around 0300 hrs., there was a loud scream a couple of hooches down from where we were located.

It shattered the silence of the night and we grabbed our weapons and waited for something to happen. The rest of the

129

night was eerie quiet and not a single man was able to go to sleep. Around 0400 hrs., a single shot was fired from the hooch next to ours. Bruns and I were ready to shoot when someone said, "it was only a water buffalo." Galli had gotten spooked by a passing water buffalo and the poor animal got shot in the ass for being at the wrong place at the wrong time.

This whole night seemed insane. I couldn't help but wonder what this mama-san was thinking having GIs invade her home in the middle of the night. When daylight came, we assembled at the end of the village and prepared to walk back to Crockett. Glover told us that the mission had been a success and that the ARVN Special Forces Ranger had located the chief and slit his throat. I guess we were there in case there was resistance from any VC or NVA within the village. I kept thinking to myself I wish I knew more about what was going on before we left on these ambush patrols. There never seemed to be any plan except to go out in the middle of the night, set up somewhere, and hope that Charlie would accidentally walk into our ambush site.

Little did I know, but this was the plan, and we would be executing it over and over again. Apparently, the VC did not appreciate the village chief being assassinated. When we got back to Crockett there was a mortar attack that lasted for about 10 minutes. One of the shells hit a case of C rations and a sundry pack and a bag of mail full of packages sitting behind the supply truck. Now Charlie was really getting into our shit!

None of our guys were injured but a bunch of Wolfhounds were pissed off beyond belief. This was the first time since being in Vietnam that Charlie had attacked us at will. Not a good feeling. In two days, more mail and a care package were waiting for me that my mother had sent. She had sent a box full of my favorite homemade chocolate chip cookies. When I opened the box, I was disappointed to see that the cookies had been reduced back to their original ingredients.

Not to be defeated, I ate the contents of the box with a spoon. I got a letter from my dad and he kept me informed about what was happening with our horses and life in general at home. He always included a line or two about his girlfriend Wilma, whom I had no use for at all. On our next ambush patrol my mind drifted off to the days when I rode my horse Bango in the foothills outside

Poway, California. Those were some of the best days of my life and I wondered if I would ever make it out of this shit hole to ride Bango again. Suddenly, I was snapped out of my dream by someone whispering, "here's the watch, you're on guard duty." Passing the watch on guard duty was a ritual as old as the Army itself. The way it worked: each man took turns standing guard for an hour at a time. At the end of the hour, he would wake up the next man and pass him the watch.

Unfortunately for the new guys, the old-timers would turn the watch forward after standing only a half an hour before passing it to the next guy. Some of us new guys ended up standing watch for three hours a night instead of one or two. This was a trick I would remember in my later tour and the new guys coming in would be initiated in the same way. Before being drafted into the Army, Ray worked for a man named Bernie, who owned a jewelry store in Barstow, California. Ray was a salesman and Bernie treated him like a son. Bernie always hoped Ray would marry his daughter and eventually take over the business. Bernie's dream would never come true.

It is almost impossible to keep a watch from coming apart in Vietnam. Moisture would get under the lens and body sweat would eat the metal backs out. Ray and I were discussing this one day and he said Bernie sold a waterproof watch with a glow in the dark dial. It was guaranteed to stand up under the worst of conditions.

The watch brand was Caravelle and Bernie would sell them to us at his cost which was about $39. We sent Bernie the money and within a week we received our new watches. We had the watches about a week when we were told we were going on an ambush patrol. It was one of those nights that it was so dark you could not see your hand in front of your face. Each man held onto the web gear of the man in front of him to avoid getting separated from the rest of the platoon.

We were about halfway to our ambush site when suddenly someone grabbed my arm and pushed it to my side. It was SSGT Hannah and he said, "why the hell are you wearing this watch with the lighted dial?" It was lit up so brightly a gook could see it from a long-distance away. He told me to take it off and put it in my pocket. I didn't know it then, but he had just grabbed Ray's arm minutes before. Those watches lasted our entire tour of duty and many years after we came home. We simply put a piece of tape on the lens when we went out on future ambushes; problem solved.

September 19, 1968

On Thursday, September 19, we were told to prepare ourselves for an all-day mission walking through a place called Dodge City West. The helicopters picked us up at 0800 hrs. and unloaded us on the outskirts of the village. On this particular day all of Charlie Company was in attendance. Our mission was to look through the hooches and see if we could find any evidence of VC or the NVA being there. We knew beforehand that Dodge City West was a notorious NVA hang out. We were all pretty nervous and fully expected to get into contact sometime that day.

As we walked through the banana tree groves there were NVA flags hanging from the palm fronds. I pulled one down, folded it, and put it into my backpack. It felt like we were being watched by a thousand eyes and hoped whoever it was wouldn't open up on us. Halfway through the day we stopped and were told that we would be there for half an hour to eat lunch. That meant pulling out a box of C rations, having a cigarette, and thinking about what would happen the rest of the day.

I saw some ripe bananas up in a tree and used my rifle to knock a couple off the bunch. Out of nowhere, an old mama-san came running at me swinging a rice thistle broom, cursing many obscenities. At just that moment we were told to get up and get ready to move. The CO told Lt. Creveling to get his second platoon online at the head of the formation. That meant we were going to walk point for the rest of the day. We were on the edge of a peanut field and I remember walking about 100 feet into the peanut plants when suddenly the shit hit the fan.

The gooks had caught us out in the open and we had no place to go. I remember thinking this could be it as bullets snapped by our heads and kicked up the dirt in front of us and beside us. I lunged head first into a 6-inch depression used to irrigate the plants. I prayed, "God help me; please get me out of here." I looked to my right and saw Russ and I looked to my left and saw Ray and all we could do was keep our heads down and fire to our front.

Within the first minute there were guys behind us screaming for medics. I could hear Lt. Creveling directing guys to move up to the edge of the field and not shoot the guys lying in the field. Some of our guys were either wounded or killed. It wasn't until later that day we found out that Lt. Mike Wonderlich was shot in the head in the opening ambush. He was one of the most liked and well-respected officers in our Company. The sound of gunfire was deafening and suddenly I had to pee really badly.

Believe it or not, I was concerned about pissing my pants. After about five minutes of being pinned down I couldn't hold it any longer and I emptied my bladder while lying flat on my stomach. There was no time to be embarrassed or worried about what anyone would say if we got out of this alive. The CO called in artillery support and requested Cobra helicopters to come as soon as possible to support us. We lay out in the 120° sun for about a half an hour as AK bullets snapped over our heads. It seemed like the gooks were shooting at the guys behind us.

After the Cobras arrived the enemy stopped firing and as far as I could tell they had fled the area. When we thought it was safe, our platoon turned around and crawled back to the edge of the peanut field. By that time medevac helicopters were landing and picking up the dead and the wounded. Not a single person said a word to me about the wet spot in the front of my pants.

I suspect that I was not the only one that had pissed themselves during the heat of the battle. Later we found out that the local village people had contacted the VC telling them how many of us were there and the weapons we were carrying. During the time that we ate lunch the VC had plenty of time to set up their ambush. Up to this time I had never felt the kind of fear that swept over me that day.

Unfortunately, that same fear would revisit me on many occasions. When we got back to the fire support base, we cleaned our weapons and sat around sharing our stories about what happened to us that day. It's interesting that there were so many different points of view. One thing everybody did agree on was that Charlie had definitely handed us our asses and it was not a good feeling.

A couple of days later, they had a memorial service for Lt. Wonderlich and the guys who were with him were asked to attend. That memorial service affected me so badly that I promised myself I would never go to another one.

The monsoon rains were still hitting us hard and I often wondered if they would ever stop. Our new Kit Carson Scout Trung Van Than told me that the weather would improve the end of October. It was raining an average of 21 days a month and there was standing water everywhere we went.

Did I mention that our clothes never got completely dry? If that wasn't bad enough, I only had 299 days left to go.

Mosquitoes, Leeches, And Cobras

When I was in training at Fort Ord, California they never mentioned the mosquitoes, leeches, and all the different varieties of poisonous snakes that inhabited Vietnam. Besides getting a regimen of shots for every known disease on earth before coming to Vietnam, the company medic handed out two pills a day: a white one and a large orange one. The big ones were malaria pills that we were supposed to take every day.

It seems the culprit in this story is the female anopheles mosquito. She is the one that carries the virus that causes malaria. Now several of the guys refused to take the malaria pills because they said it caused them to have diarrhea. That is what the white pill was for dumbass! Depending on what I was eating, I experienced diarrhea on a regular basis, so I took the malaria pill anyway. I seriously thought it would be better to be safe than sorry.

Later on in my tour, several guys in the platoon would come down with malaria and they had to spend a couple weeks in the field hospital in Cu Chi. Malaria makes a man weaker than a rag doll. Every man was issued a shower towel that was a little bit smaller than a regular-sized Bath towel. It was OD green and proved to be our best friend seconded only to our poncho liner.

The mosquitoes were most deadly at night when we would be out on ambush patrols in a heavily vegetated area. The mosquitoes were so big they could literally bite you wherever your clothing was pressed up tightly against your skin. Their favorite spot seemed to be around the waist where my belt cinched up my pants.

There were many mornings I woke up and I would have multiple mosquito bites and welts all along my beltline front and back. The Army-issued towel served multiple purposes. Whenever we left the wire, either on a day sweep or on night ambush patrols we would wear our towel around our neck.

It served to wipe the sweat off our faces and neck as well as dunking it in water and placing it over our heads to cool off. When folded and draped over the shoulder, the towel acted as a cushion that kept M-60 machine gun ammo belts from cutting into our shoulder. That same towel was placed over our face and head at night to keep the mosquitoes from eating our faces off.

On one of these nights in the Iron Triangle, I swear I felt the corner of my towel being lifted off my face by two mosquitoes with wing spans of about 6 inches. There was no way we were going to survive against this kind of mosquito fire power. We also noticed we were sleeping in a substance dropped the day before to kill the jungle. The obvious purpose of the towel was when we were in the fire support base taking a shower.

Our shower consisted of a canvas bag with the shower head attached to the bottom that was filled with water and raised up so we could stand underneath it. The shower lasted as long as the water held out. Of course, there was no such thing as modesty or privacy and when all was said and done, we were all just soldiers trying to survive and go home.

I mentioned earlier that each soldier was issued a poncho liner. Its purpose was to be tied inside a regular poncho so a soldier could keep warm if they were out in the middle of the monsoon rain. Very early on, most of the guys figured out that a poncho liner was the soldier's best friend. We took it everywhere we went and used it to cover ourselves up when it got cold at night.

Now you may be wondering how Vietnam could ever be cold when the average temperature is 100°. For six months out of the year the temperatures skyrockets to 120°.

When we would go out on night ambush patrols and it started raining everyone would be soaked to the bone. As soon as the rain stopped there was usually a wind that would blow causing the water to evaporate off our bodies creating a chilling effect. Many nights I sat huddled under my poncho shaking like a leaf and my teeth chattering because it felt like I was freezing to death. I fondly compare our poncho liners to Linus's blanket in the Peanuts cartoon.

I remember one such night when SSGT Glover and Lt. Creveling took us out on an ambush patrol in the pouring rain. We were supposed to set our ambush parallel to highway 1 and catch VC crossing the road headed to a nearby village. The platoon was split up in two groups. Creveling was in charge of one group and Glover the other group.

By the time we were approaching the ambush site the rain turned into a maelstrom. It was almost impossible to see and Creveling ended up leading us away from the rest of the platoon by mistake.

When he realized what had happened, he stopped and had us kneel in place. This is a horrible situation because our own men could open up on us thinking we were gooks. Creveling was just getting ready to go look for Glover's group when a lightning bolt broke overhead and lit up the sky.

Creveling was able to make out the shape of steel pots sitting upon the heads of our other platoon members. Glover had stopped and was setting up the ambush and we were told to stay where we were. The only thing we could do was sit on our helmets to keep our asses out of the water and huddle under our ponchos.

On this particular night I was so cold and discouraged I broke down and cried in despair. No self-respecting gook would be wandering around in the rice paddies on a night like this. When I thought things couldn't get worse there was a sudden bright light shining in our faces. It was two tanks outfitted with arc lights pointing out into the field looking for gooks.

Our position was compromised, and Glover got on the radio to tell the tanks not to blow us away. It turned out that the Army did not coordinate the tank mission with our company commander. The tanks were there to discourage the VC from burying mines in the highway. This was just another SNAFU moment in the life of a Vietnam grunt.

Unfortunately, for the Vietnam soldier, the United States was still using surplus items held over from World War II and Korean War. Most of the C rations and equipment we got were post-war surplus. The fatigues they issued us were okay, but they couldn't keep the leeches from crawling up our legs and feasting on our tender flesh. The combat boots that were issued in 1965 were Korean

War surplus; the same held true for the ponchos and back packs. The fatigues tore easily and getting new ones was difficult. Some of the M-16 rifles we were issued were battle-worn and many of the mechanisms were worn out. It didn't take long before we learned that the M-16 was famous for jamming.

This was one of the reasons the leaders continued to harp on us daily to keep our weapons clean and greased with LSA (lubricant small arms).

I personally never had my M-16 jam. One of the most discouraging things that faced Combat Soldiers in Vietnam is that when we walked around in wet rice paddies there were leeches trying to crawl up your legs and suck your blood. There is one particular day that I remember our platoon was on an all-day march through the rice paddies located about two klicks from our fire support base. The outside temperature in the sun was 120° and the water temperature was about 100°.

We all were asking the question: what in the hell were we looking for out here? Most guys carry two canteens of water and a bottle of iodine pills that Doc gave us in case we had to drink rice paddy water. Most of the guys ran out of water by noon and we were in serious danger of having a bunch of guys having heatstroke and dehydration.

I remember vividly taking my canteen, removing the top, putting the opening under the surface of the water and watching as my canteen filled up with several insects and small twisting wormlike creatures that undoubtedly would give a person a tapeworm. As soon as the canteen was full, I took an iodine tablet, dropped it in the top, put the cap on, and shook it vigorously for 30 seconds. The instructions on the iodine bottle said that in order to be effective the tablet needed to sit in the water for no less than one hour.

When a person is dying of thirst and you know you're not going to be getting out of the rice paddies anytime soon, the last thing on your mind is whether or not the iodine tablet will be effective or not. All you can do is hope for the best. Speaking of tapeworms, the Vietnamese people and children were full of tapeworms. This is one of the reasons the population was so skinny, and their lifespan is much shorter than the average

American. By the way, drinking 100-degree rice paddy water is disgusting.

As the day progressed, we finally came upon a village directly to our front. We were told that this was going to be our exit point and that choppers would pick us up within the hour. The first thing I did when I got out of the water was to check for leeches. When I raised my pant leg, I saw 6 leeches stuck to my leg. I squirted insect repellent on the leeches, and they let loose and fell off. The right leg was the same. Doc gave me some antibiotic cream and told me to smear it on the bite sites so they wouldn't get infected. In another five minutes we could hear the helicopters coming in the distance to pick us up.

It was a short ride back to Crockett and everyone was beat. This incident happened in October and I determined that it was one of the worst days I had spent in Vietnam. A lot of the guys were feeling very weak and Doc came around and gave us salt tablets and told us to drink lots of water. Most of us didn't feel like eating the evening meal. That evening we did not play cards. Another danger that we faced were the many venomous snakes that inhabited Vietnam.

There were 37 different varieties that included Asian cobras, King cobras, coral snakes, Kraits, vipers and pit vipers. The most venomous snake however was the two-step snake (multi-banded krait). If a person was bitten by one of these snakes, they are more than likely to be dead after taking two steps. On one occasion when we were performing seven-day riffs, Sergeant Garcia had a cobra crawl up next to him while he was sleeping and bit him in the arm. Garcia was medevacked out and was seriously ill for over a week. Welcome to Vietnam!

Fire In The Hole

About this time, we got a couple of replacements by the name of John Cook and Bob Mollenhauer. They had gone to Basic and AIT together and wound up in the same unit in Nam. What were the chances? Mollenhauer was from Minnesota and Cook was from Missouri. Both of these guys were stout and looked like they could go bear hunting with a switch. I asked Bob if he had a hobby, and he said he liked hunting a lot and loved to shoot moose. Well, Bob, from now on your nickname will be Moose! I already had the handle of Big John, so we called Cook "John Boy."

The first night we were sitting around shooting the breeze, Moose told us a story about something that had happened in Long Binh at the processing center. He and Cook were grabbed for extra duty and told to burn the shit cans near the admin buildings. The SOP to accomplish this was to pour diesel fuel into the shit can and stir it up, then light it and keep it stirred up until the contents burned to ash. The two guys were having trouble getting the diesel to light, so Moose went to a nearby fuel locker and grabbed a 5 gallon can of JP4 jet fuel.

He doused the shit cans liberally and walked back and returned the fuel can to the locker. Upon his return, he and Cook decided to take a 5-minute break. As they were sitting there chewing the fat, they saw a First Sergeant walking towards the latrine. Cook said they better slide one of the cans back under a seat so the old top could do his business. The closer the Sergeant got they could see he was smoking a cigar blunt. They didn't think anything of it and decided to walk over and sit in the shade of a palm tree about 100 feet from the latrine.

The old sergeant walked into the latrine and sat down over the only can under the seats. He removed the cigar from his mouth and tossed it between his legs into the can beneath him.

Cook and Moose were blown over when the shithouse blew up. The latrine left the ground like a rocket leaving the old Top laying on the ground in the fetal position with second and third-degree burns on his ass and balls.

The cigar had touched off the jet fuel and blew shit all over the place. Cook said the smell was awful and when the MPs arrived the two men came up with the story that it must have been a mortar round that hit the outhouse. The MPs wrote the report up and the old First Sergeant was put in for a Purple Heart. All is well that ends well. Everybody listening to the story busted a gut laughing. It took me five minutes to get my laughing under control. My ribs were aching, and Moose swore it was the truth if he ever told it!

When we were working up by the Cambodian border our lieutenant told us that we would be going out on an ambush patrol that night. That evening just before dark, we lined up and headed due north to our designated ambush site approximately a half a klick away. We had been walking for about half an hour when the sun had almost completely disappeared over the horizon. Suddenly a shot rang out in front of us where Moose was walking point.

Everybody dropped and tried to determine what the hell was going on. About five minutes later the platoon sergeant passed the word back that Moose had shot a giant Python. We resumed our march and every man had to step over this huge snake that measured over 30 feet. The ambush that night went without incident and just before daylight we gathered our gear and proceeded to walk back to the fire support base. When we arrived at the spot where the Python had been shot it was still moving.

O'Grady told a bunch of us to pick up the snake and carry it back to the fire support base. His plan was to skin it, salt it down and send it home. Over the years I've often wondered what his

142

mother thought when she opened the box, smelled the contents, and discovered it was a skinned out giant Python.

Wolfhound Territory Flag

Prisoner Falling out of Chopper

Paul Naso - SSGT Richard Glover

Joanne, John, Dad

Chapter Eight
THE DECIMATION OF THE 101ST AIRBORNE OCTOBER 10, 1968

ctober turned out to be another rough month for the Wolfhounds. We had barely gotten over the battle at Dodge City West when we were told we were going to be going back there and act as a blocking force for the 101st Airborne. The 101st was going to assume the role that we had played back in September. They were going to sweep through the village and see if they could find some of the VC that had ambushed us. They would eventually set up an ambush on the main road leading out of the village.

The only difference was, Charlie Company would be on the opposite side of the village, waiting out in the rice paddies to kill any of the VC trying to escape. In preparation for this operation, the day before we arrived, helicopters dropped thousands of leaflets telling the villagers that soldiers would be coming in and that anyone left in the village would be considered VC and subject to be killed. The Army gave them 24 hours to evacuate. The 101st was permitted to shoot anything that moved.

As we prepared for another helicopter ride, we split ourselves up into groups of six and spread out, leaving 25 meters between each group. The 10 helicopters would come in from the north and land next to us and we would jump on board as quickly as we could. It was my habit to be the last one to get on the helicopter so I could sit in the doorway with my feet touching the skids.

This all started when I was carrying the M-79 with a rucksack full of ammunition. The rucksack weighed about 40 pounds and it was difficult to get inside the helicopter and get into a seat. It was easier just to jump up with the rucksack resting on the floor, enabling me to get the weight of the straps off my shoulders.

Many of the guys were spooky about being near the door opening because they thought they would be an easy target if we landed in a hot LZ (Landing zone). I got a rush every time the helicopter lifted off and another rush just before landing. Whenever we went on an eagle flight, we knew that we were going into an area where there was known VC or NVA activity. They would always pick a landing site about 50 meters from our objective. It was usually in a rice paddy where we were exposed to any enemy hiding in the hedgerows or on the edge of the village.

There was always a chance that Charlie would wait until the helicopters were landing before opening up on us. Our job was to dismount the helicopter and get into a firing position as soon as possible.

Many times, if we landed in a hot LZ, the helicopters would not land on the ground, but we had to jump from 10 feet. This could be dicey if you hit a mud hole and sunk up to your waist. It was almost impossible to get out of the mud without help.

As the choppers started to descend, thoughts of the last time we were in Dodge City West played heavy on my mind. The sickening feeling of being stuck out in the peanut field with AK rounds popping over our heads and the shrill sound of guys yelling for medics. I could still see the look on Lt. Creveling's face as he knelt next to his friend Lt. Wonderlich and stared into his lifeless eyes.

None of us knew that the next day, Wonderlich was scheduled to go on R&R to Hawaii to reunite with his new bride Janie. No one knew she was at home packing her suitcases getting ready to spend a week with her husband. Her sister Jan was there to take her to the airport and see her off. Who could know the horror of being visited by an Army Captain the morning she was leaving for Hawaii and being told Mike had been killed? This war was destroying so many lives and I forgot what it was I was doing in Vietnam. I came to Vietnam to fight communism but now I wasn't so sure.

Since arriving in Nam, I hadn't met any communists. I was brought back to the present by the crew chief yelling at me to bail out. We were lucky that day that there was no one shooting at us as we jumped out. SSGT Glover started telling us where he wanted us to take up our positions behind an unusually high rice paddy dike. Our position stretched from the East end of the village to the west end about 300 yards. Each man was separated from the other by 20 feet.

It was getting dark and several guys were eating C rations and smoking cigarettes. We didn't know if the 101st airborne had started their sweep through the village and we took the silence as good news. In order to stay dry, we were all sitting on top of the berms hoping maybe the NVA had left the day before. About 10 minutes after dusk, the hedgerow in front of us came alive with small arms fire. The bullets were hitting the water in front of us and the earthen berm we were sitting on. It took only seconds for guys to roll off into the water.

We started returning fire and as soon as the shooting started, the sound of the AKs stopped. Guys were yelling up and down the line asking if anyone saw the gooks that were shooting at us. We found ourselves lying in shoulder-deep rice paddy water. I knew it was going to be a long night and I knew that we would get cold in a quick hurry. A couple of guys to my right tried laying on top of the berm to get out of the water and were immediately shot at by snipers that had remained in the hedgerows in front of us.

It occurred to all of us that we were pinned down and had to stay in the water. There was still no shooting going on in the village. We knew that the 101st airborne had to be in the middle of the village and wondered why they had not made any contact. Just as that thought crossed my mind, all hell broke out in the village. You could hear both M-16 and AK-47s firing nonstop for about 10 minutes. You could also hear the distinct sound of hand grenades exploding and RPGs being fired every few minutes.

All of us behind the berm were straining our eyes to see if any gooks were coming out of the hedgerows. Without warning, illumination flares popped over the village. SSGT Glover had radioed the artillery unit back at the fire support base, requesting illumination support. There was a huge gunfight going on in the village, but we couldn't tell who was winning. SSGT Glover, Willie, and Naso were on our far-left flank in the middle of a junction where four rice paddies came together and they were the last of our positions before the 101st, who had set up on the roadway leaving the village.

As I looked down to the left, I could see women and children running down an oxcart trail exiting the village right in front of Glover's position. The women and children were being pushed by a large number of NVA soldiers trying to escape the onslaught of the 101st Airborne's withering fire. We were later told that Glover told Willie and Naso he believed they might not make it out of this fight. He told Naso to lie on the ground and Willy would lie on top of him and Glover would fall on top of them both.

Glover said he hoped the NVA running past them would not notice them or think they were dead. Glover refused to shoot into the women and children and at the last minute, just before running over the top of Glover's position, the NVA peeled off to the right and started running across the rice paddy dikes towards the road.

At the same time, this was happening, two Cobra helicopters arrived on station and were shooting their miniguns into the hedgerows in front of us. At one point one of the Cobras flew over our left flank strafing our guys almost hitting Glover's position.

Under the illumination flares, I could see Glover standing on top of the berm with the radio handset to his ear, yelling at the Cobra pilot to cease-fire. The whole incident took no more than 20 minutes, but it seemed like an eternity. As the chaos continued, none of us knew that Ronnie Blair had been killed during the firefight. Three others in the company had been wounded as well. A medevac helicopter came in and picked up Blair and the wounded soldiers.

Next, three Huey helicopters from the 101st airborne landed on the oxcart trail next to Glover's position. Several soldiers jumped out of the choppers and ran into the village where the NVA had exited. Within half an hour, they were loading dead GIs onto these choppers.

After the dead were brought out, the wounded followed, and all three choppers were filled and taken off towards Cu Chi. We realized the 101st airborne had just been decimated. Once again, Dodge City West claimed more American lives and one more time, I thought to myself, "God, what the hell am I doing here, and how could you let this happen?"

Ambush Or Suicide Mission

After the gunfight at Dodge City West, we returned to Fire Support Base Crockett. We were given a few days to re-group, read our mail, write letters and pull perimeter guard duty at night. Everything seemed to be going okay until SSGT Glover told the second platoon he wanted to meet with us in half an hour at his bunker. There were 24 guys in the platoon at that time and everyone stood around wondering what Glover had to say.

He told us that Captain Sherwood had given us a mission to go back into Dodge City West at night and pull an ambush patrol. Several guys looked at each other in utter disbelief and Ed Rambo chimed in and said, "you've got to be shitting me." We all knew that this was not an ambush patrol but a suicide mission. Guys were literally speechless, and Glover knew we were visibly shaken.

Our company commander was anxious to get a body count and enhance his military career. Lamere was standing in the back and said, "let's refuse to go out." Glover said, "stand down back there and listen to the plan that I've come up with." He told us that the location we were supposed to set up in was almost in the middle of the village. He knew damn well there was no way we could get in there without a gunfight.

Glover was all about not getting any of us hurt or killed. He was not about to knowingly lead our platoon into a losing situation. He told us he knew of a place where we could go and set up in a safer location. He told us that since Dodge City West was an NVA stronghold, there would no doubt be lots of activity going on at night. He also told us that we would be completely outgunned and that we would avoid making contact at all cost.

Glover knew of an alternate site more out of harm's way that would be better to defend. He went on to say that he would place us in our positions and that no one should go to sleep and no one should shoot even if the gooks were right in front of us. All of us trusted Glover, but none of us wanted to go into Dodge City that night. Before leaving that night, Glover went and talked to the artillery officer and showed him where we would be setting up. He also marked a couple pre-fire locations in case we got in trouble.

For the next three hours, the guys sat around cleaning their weapons and bitching and moaning about how the Army wanted to get all of us killed. Many wrote what might be their last letter home. As we entered the outskirts of Dodge City that night, all of us had a feeling of dread and knew that this would be a bad night. Many of the guys had made peace with God, if there was a God.

After walking for about 30 minutes, we halted, and Glover started placing us in our positions parallel to an oxcart trail. We were far enough off the trail that we could conceal ourselves in the tall grass and still be able to see out in front of us. No one would set up their claymore mines tonight.

It was an uneventful night until about 0200 hrs. when we heard the sound of voices talking and laughing in the distance. The voices grew louder as they approached our position. Then there was the distinct smell of marijuana wafting through the air coming from the direction of the voices. It turned out that an NVA platoon was walking down the trail and would soon be right in front of us. I could still hear Glover's warning: "nobody goes to sleep; nobody shoots even if they walk right in front of us."

151

All of us lay silently like a bunch of corpses watching as 40 NVA soldiers marched past our position. I suddenly felt sick to my stomach and fought back the urge to vomit. Fear had once again overtaken my mind and my body. God, why am I here? I breathed a sigh of relief when the last NVA soldier in the group was well past our position. About 30 minutes before dawn, we all stood up and prepared to march out of Dodge City West.

When we approached the fire support base, the CO was waiting for us and he walked up to SSGT Glover and got in his face and said, "I sent you in there to make contact, what the hell happened?" In a very calm voice, Glover said, "we didn't see anything sir," and kept walking towards our bunkers. I heard Glover mumble under his breath, "you son of a bitch." The rest of the day was spent cleaning our weapons, playing cards and talking about the events of the previous night.

We were all in agreement that the company commander intentionally sent us on a suicide mission. It was becoming clear that the CO was trying to get his ticket punched for body count no matter what it cost. I couldn't get out of my mind the sound of the NVA soldiers marching by us as they talked, laughed, and smoked their marijuana joints. They truly thought they owned Dodge City and the night. Guys were talking about "fragging" the CO.

Assault On Line November/ December

The next two months were business as usual. Several of the old guys got off line and new guys replaced them. I really missed the old guys. I felt safe with them. I kept thinking, "what is going to happen if Glover gets wounded or killed?" We would all be up shits creek. Little did we know but orders were being cut to send Glover back to Battalion Headquarters to take over operations and intelligence. He stayed in the field with Charlie Company but as a liaison to plan operations.

One day they loaded up the entire company and took us to a place called Dodge City East. Our mission was to assault through the village like the 101st airborne had done in Dodge City West. What were they thinking? Didn't the Army realize that tactic got a lot of guys killed and wounded? The 25th aviation guys dropped leaflets the day before, warning the villagers of our coming. Anything that moved was considered enemy and would be shot on sight. I told Russ I had a sick feeling about this, and he said he didn't feel good about it either. It would take the Little Bears two trips to get the entire company to the village.

When everyone had arrived, the CO had all three platoons lined up parallel to the hedgerow surrounding the village. I suddenly got a déjà vu feeling that we were going to get slaughtered. Upon his command, we started walking straight into the hedgerow and vegetation behind it. Russ was on my right and Ray was on my left.

When a company assaults on line, each soldier takes two steps and fires around directly to his front. We had walked about 25 yards when we began taking fire from our front. AK bullets were flying past our heads and we could not see where they were coming from. Within a minute, the whole company was under attack. The company commander's RTO had been shot in the stomach and someone was yelling for a medic. The three amigos Russ, Ray and Big John continued moving forward, blasting away as we went. We had assumed the entire company was moving with us.

After about five minutes, we started taking fire from behind us as well as our front. The entire company, including our platoon, had retreated back to the rice paddy surrounding the village. Our own guys were shooting into the hedgerow, not realizing we were still in there. The three of us laid flat on the ground and I told Ray I was going to pop smoke and we should crawl back to the hedgerow. I was praying our guys would see the smoke and cease firing. When we got close to the hedgerow, we started waving our hands over our heads and yelling, don't shoot, we are GIs. We carefully pushed through the bamboo and I heard Big Joe yelling that he saw us out in front of the platoon.

We got to our feet, bent at the waist and ran as fast as we could and dove over the berm to safety. The firefight lasted for another half an hour and Glover told us Phantom Jets were on the way to cook the village down. A GI was killed by his own men on the left flank as he tried to crawl out of the hedgerow just like we had done earlier. This poor bastard was waving his hand over his head when they cut him down. Thank God Big Joe was always there to look out for us. When the Phantoms arrived, they dropped their napalm canisters directly to our front.

The heat was so intense that it turned our faces red like we had been sunburned. It felt like the air was being sucked out of our lungs. The napalm attack continued for the better part of an hour. Surely nothing or no one could survive this inferno. After the fires had died down, they sent us back into the village to tabulate the body count.

The only thing we saw were spider holes with their covers opened up with no one in them. As God as my witness, there was not a single dead VC anywhere to be found. In summary, the Army had spent hundreds of thousands of dollars on napalm and artillery rounds and got one GI killed and another seriously injured, and we came up with nothing. This was par for the course and we were beginning to think either Charlie was really smart or the Army was really dumb.

We would take Eagle flights around our area of operation and land during the following days, walking through a village or double canopy jungle looking for an elusive enemy. On one such

154

mission, they dropped us off at a place called the Sugar Mill. This sugar mill was built in 1955 and was owned by Mrs. Diem, the wife of Ngo Diem. Ngo Diem was the president of the Republic of Vietnam, until his assassination in November 1963. This particular sugar mill south of the Vam Co Dong River processed 15 million tons of sugar cane a year.

When processed, the plants produced bagasse that was used to fuel electro-generation plants. These plants helped to offset the shortage of electricity in the South. The sugar mill we were walking past had been abandoned and overgrown with jungle vegetation and vines and I could feel the spirits of the workers that labored there for a dollar a day. The jungle birds that inhabited this area were Rails, Crakes, Coots and Gallinules.

You could hear them whistling or making strange sounds but rarely saw them. They did make a good early warning system when we were on ambush patrols. If anyone came walking down a trail, the silence was broken by the birds' chirping out. The second day we were there, three of us walked into the jungle and proceeded down a trail keeping an eye out for tripwires.

This area had been abandoned for years, but the VC and NVA would occasionally use the area for stand-downs, including bringing prostitutes in from Saigon. We ran into an abandoned electro-generating plant that had been swallowed up by the jungle. Some of the writing on the huge generators looked like it was in German. Could the Germans have been selling Vietnam these power plants in the '50s? They used the byproduct bagasse to fuel the steam-driven turbines.

It was a perfect setup. This plant was built right next to a river! The biggest fight we had at the sugar mill was with the mosquitoes. We put up a valiant fight, but the dirty little bastards always seemed to win. When we left there, I had welts around my waist and my face took lots of hits as well. If the

Japanese, French and Chinese had not been able to defeat Vietnam, why did we think America could get the job done. I just wasn't seeing it.

Dave "Smokes" Schimmoeller,
Tommy Kemp, Buck Buchanan

Big Joe Waskom

SSGT Fred Hannah

USS New Jersey

156

Chapter Nine
PICTURE PERFECT AMBUSH
OCTOBER 4, 1968

s I sat on top of the bunker cleaning my rifle, I noticed Ed Rambo writing a letter. Ed never said anything about having a girlfriend, so I assumed he was writing home to his mom or dad. Some of the guys were playing cards, others were sleeping, and other guys were reading mail that they had received the day before. It was about 1400 hrs. in the afternoon when SSGT Hannah came around and told us that we would be having a meeting at his bunker at 1600 hrs.

Hannah was one of the old-timers that I looked up to for advice on how to survive Vietnam. Hannah was a shake and bake Sgt. who had distinguished himself in many firefights. He was promoted to E-6 the month before I arrived in the platoon. He had just returned from his R&R in Australia and was about to get off line. He had the most time in the field of any soldier in the second platoon. He often spoke of going home and spending time with his 9 sisters in Kentucky.

Hannah was the youngest boy out of the 10 children. We didn't have a platoon leader at that time, so Hannah ended up running the platoon. Hannah had seen more than his share of combat and had several confirmed kills. Some of the guys were

157

congratulating him for making it the full tour. Hannah would reply, "I'll believe it when I'm on the freedom bird going back to the world." Ray said it might be time to start a short timer's calendar.

I thought it was a little early for that and told him I was going to wait until we were down to six months. As I sat there pondering my situation, I realized I had 10 months to go. The supply truck from Cu Chi had just arrived, so I finished cleaning my weapon and headed over to the CP to see what I could grab out of the sundry pack and get my two free sodas and two free beers. The sundry pack that we received contained all kinds of items from cigarettes to toiletries and included such things as gum, stationery, envelopes, and too many things to mention. The Army had a policy of giving every combat infantryman two beers and two Coca-Colas per day.

Our only problem was that there was no ice to cool the cans down, so we just had to get used to drinking warm beer and soda. Ed Rambo was always anxious to trade me his cokes for my beers. The supply truck also brought mail that was sorted out by platoon and distributed to the guys by the platoon sergeant. There were always a lot of smartass remarks made and lots of laughter when the platoon sergeant would smell an envelope and say, "it smells like pussy to me!"

Some of the guys even bragged that their girlfriends would send them a lock of hair from their pubic area. Other guys proudly passed around photographs of their girlfriends in semi-nude or completely nude poses. These photos always acted as a good supplement to the monthly Playboy magazines that were sent to the soldiers in our platoon. By the time I got back to the platoon area, it was time to meet up with the guys at Hannah's bunker. We were told that we were going on an ambush patrol that evening. Deuce and half trucks would haul us down the LBJ highway and dump us off close to our ambush site.

After the meeting, we returned to our bunkers and got ready to go to the mess tent for dinner. Sgt. Arie Hill yelled at us to get in line for some #1 chop-chop. I remember on this particular day, the dinner menu consisted of fried chicken, mashed potatoes and gravy, green beans, and chocolate chip cookies for dessert. There were also coffee and small cartons of Foremost milk located at the end of the food line.

On this day, there were even some chocolate milk cartons mixed in with the white ones. Sgt. Hill tried to get as much chocolate milk as he could, but it was scarce. After we were through eating, we would put our trays and utensils in the large garbage can containing an immersion heater and hot water located at the end of the food line. Back at the bunker, we started discussing the upcoming ambush patrol. It had been pretty quiet for the last week so none of us were too nervous.

Our conversation was fairly jovial until Sugar Bear Taylor told us that his bunker buddy had received a Dear John letter in today's mail. Big Joe looked up and said, "that poor bastard, better him than me."

Everybody knew that receiving that kind of letter could really mess up a man's head and affect his concentration when out on maneuvers. Sugar Bear assured us he would keep an eye on the guy. At 5 o'clock, our platoon gathered at SSGT Hannah's bunker. We walked up to the CP, loaded up on the trucks, drove out of the fire support base, and headed for the LBJ highway.

Many of the guys wondered why the road was named after the President and we later found out that Johnson was balls deep into the Halliburton Corporation that had been given all the contracts for building roads and buildings in South Vietnam. Johnson pocketed millions of dollars off of his relationship with Halliburton. It got really quiet once we hit the highway and we all faced outward, keeping an eye out for any snipers or potential ambushes. It was very common for Charlie to hide off the roads and take potshots at convoys going up and down the highway.

We drove for about 20 minutes and I figured we were pretty close to the village we had walked through the day before. It was still daylight when the trucks stopped and we unloaded ourselves and all of our gear. I helped Russ unload his 90 mm recoilless and helped him load it with an HE round. Hannah yelled at us to spread out and get ready to head out.

We waited there for what seemed like an eternity until it got dark. The longer we were there, the more nervous I got. Being close to the village meant we had a hundred eyes on us at all times. Hannah gave the order to march in two files keeping a distance behind the guy in front of you. He would always say, "remember ladies, one round could get you all." We headed north in the open field for about 20 minutes.

I remember thinking, "I wonder where in the hell are we going?" I turned around and whispered, "Ray, are you there?" He said, "I'm here, you dirty bastard." After walking for about 10 more minutes, we turned right and walked parallel to a long hedgerow. The two columns came to a halt and everyone knelt down, waiting to see what we were going to do next.

One by one, Hannah positioned each man next to the hedgerow. We were facing the open field that we had just walked through. I could not believe how much noise we were making getting set up. I heard the distinct sounds of rucksacks filled with M-79 ammo hitting the ground and the clanking of M-60 machine gun belts being snapped together. These sounds could be heard a mile away on a still night.

I was lying next to Ray and Chris, fighting off the mosquitoes that had just started eating us for their evening meal. Hannah was down a way to our right and we discussed who was going to be on guard first. It's a weird experience staring out into the distance at night. Your night vision kicks in and you can see things you would not ordinarily see.

When you are tired, this can work to your disadvantage. On many occasions, I would see shadows moving in the distance and my mind would play tricks on me. The guy with the starlight scope had a definite advantage. Night vision scopes were a remarkable invention. If there was starlight or moonlight, the scope would magnify and project the light providing accurate images that were out in front of you.

One thing that spooked me about the scope was when you turned it on it made a high-pitched whining sound. I always wondered if Charlie could hear that sound. The starlight scope cost the government beaucoup dollars each and we were told if we lost one, we would be responsible for the cost to replace it. Let's see on a private's monthly salary of $95 bucks a month... well you see what I'm getting at. All was quiet until about 0300 hrs. Guys started passing the word that 6 gooks were walking directly towards our location.

No one would open up until Hannah started shooting, then it was all hands-on rock and roll. I asked Ray if he could see anything and he said, "hell I can't see the end of my machine gun barrel." The next five minutes were total agony because nobody could see and nobody knew when the shit would hit the fan.

When Hannah let go on fully automatic, the hedgerow erupted in a deafening sound of 20 weapons going off all at once. You would think, with that much firepower, nothing or no one could survive the onslaught. This, however was not the case. The six gooks returned fire immediately and green tracers were zinging between us and over our heads. Ray's machine gun had gone through 300 rounds of the 500 rounds hooked up to his gun. I looked at the barrel and could see it had turned cherry red and I could see the rounds going through it.

I yelled at him to stop shooting and he told me he had taken his finger off the trigger a minute ago. The rounds were cooking off in the super-heated chamber. I grabbed the belt of ammo and twisted it until it broke apart. Ray's gun was officially out of business after the last round left the end of the barrel.

By the time Ray's machine gun had quit firing, a burst of light exploded directly over our head. It was an illumination flare shot from our mortar platoon located at Crockett. Initially, everybody's night vision went to hell. It took a minute to refocus and I realized the gooks were only 50 feet in front of us. I was squinting and I thought I saw movement out in front.

Another illumination flare went off and I saw a gook lift his head behind his AK-47. Without thinking I squeezed the trigger on my M-16 and a red tracer left my weapon and lit up the gooks face as the round went right between his eyes. Lying beside me Chris said, "Whoa that's the neatest thing I've ever seen."

Ray had burned his hand trying to replace the burned-out barrel on his M-60 and he was cussing up a storm about what a piece of shit it was. Hannah shouted cease-fire and as soon as the shooting stopped, the last of the illumination flares broke apart overhead, leaving us in complete darkness. The only sounds I heard were guys complaining that there was no illumination. This was a really spooky couple of minutes.

We didn't know if the gooks were alive, dead or wounded. There is nothing more dangerous than a wounded VC. Within a minute or so another illumination flare popped overhead. Hannah told me and a couple of other guys to go out and drag the dead bodies over to a spot next to our right flank. I couldn't believe I was about to stand up and walk out into the open field looking for the gook that I had just killed.

My hands were shaking and my knees felt weak as I made my way out into the field. I kept thinking any minute the gook would jump up and open up on me. I knew I had seen the tracer go through the man's head, but now I wasn't so sure. With each step that I took, I became more fearful. I was filled with so many mixed emotions and the adrenaline was causing my heart to pound rapidly in my chest. Other guys to my right had located the dead gooks and were dragging them towards the hedgerow. I suddenly saw what I thought was an AK-47 laying on the ground in front of the body of a North Vietnamese soldier.

When I got to the man I had killed, I saw that the back of his head was missing and there were pieces of his brain scattered down his back. I dropped to my knees and suddenly became sick to my stomach and I fought back the urge to vomit. The smell was like nothing I had ever experienced before. It was a mixture of rust and shit. I picked up the AK-47, slung it across my shoulder, and got up and grabbed the dead man's feet and started dragging his corpse to where Hannah was having the bodies stacked in a pile. It was then that I saw that the gook had shit his pants.

There was a total of five NVA soldiers killed that night. The soldier that I had killed was much larger than the other four. The shape of his face revealed that he was Chinese and was an advisor embedded with the NVA. We took several paper documents off the bodies and Hannah told Ketchum to put a trip flare under the top body on the pile in case their friends came back to retrieve their bodies. The platoon moved 200 feet down the hedgerow away from the bodies and prepared to be there for the rest of the night.

Everybody was wound up tighter than an eight-day clock. There was enough adrenaline flowing to raise the dead. I could not get the image of the gook's brain splattered on his back and the ragged hole that was minutes before the back of the man's head. I felt numb and could not believe I'd actually killed this guy. This was the second time since being in Nam I experienced this sick feeling. No one got a minute's sleep the rest of that night and when morning came, we started to pick up our gear and get ready to march back to the highway to be picked up. It was really strange that nobody wanted to go down and look at the dead bodies.

Someone from Cu Chi radioed O'Grady and said there was a Major flying out to our position to inspect the bodies. Hannah told a couple of guys to go lay the bodies out in a row. I saw Doc squatting there looking at the dead NVA. One of the guys grabbed the leg of the guy on top of the pile and pulled him off instantly, setting off the trip flare. The white phosphorous flare produced intense heat on top of the bodies and blood that had coagulated started running freely down the outside of the pile. It was the most horrendous thing I had ever seen in my 20 years of life. One of the guys grabbed a bamboo stick and pushed the flare off the bodies onto the ground.

Without further ado, they lined the bodies up in a row face up as we waited for the helicopter to arrive from Cu Chi. After getting our gear together we, all moved down and stood around looking at these dead soldiers lying in the morning sun. The faint sound of rotor blades came from the direction of Cu Chi and we were told to get information.

Everybody stood around looking like, "what the hell did he just say?" We had just gone through the worst night of our lives and now we were asked to get information? You've got to be shitting me. No one made a move and the lieutenant raised his voice and said, "if you can't form up at least get in a straight line."

Most of us moved very slowly and got into a raggedy-ass form of a line. The helicopter landed 50 feet in front of us, exactly where we had killed the five gooks. A Major exited the helicopter and did not realize that he was walking across the kill zone. The photographer exited the helicopter after the Major and followed

164

behind him about five paces. I noticed there were pieces of brain matter stuck to the bottom of the Major's boot.

The Major approached our lieutenant and salutes were exchanged. I couldn't hear exactly what was being said but the lieutenant led the Major over to where the bodies were lined up. The Major knelt on one knee in front of the bodies and the photographer took several pictures from different angles. The major told the lieutenant to get him an M-16 from one of the men. When the lieutenant gave the major the weapon, he knelt down in front of the bodies and held the weapon in front of his chest and had the photographer take several more pictures. Everybody knew what this was all about.

The son of a bitch was going to send those pictures home and tell his family how he'd single-handedly killed these NVA soldiers. I wondered if any of the people looking at those pictures would notice his newly starched fatigues and his spit-shined boots.

After completing the photoshoot, the Major came and stood in front of us and said that he would like to say a few words. He didn't get the first complete sentence out of his mouth when Doc marched forward, stood at attention, locked his heels and saluted. He held out his closed fist and said, "Sir, on behalf of the second platoon, I would like to present you this award."

The major held out his open palm and Doc dropped two ears into his hand. The major looked at the ears, looked around and closed his palm and put the ears into his pocket. He then, without a word, did an about-face and walked back to the helicopter where he and his photographer mounted up and left the area. Not a single word was said to Doc by anyone present. Hannah said, "saddle up," and we began our march back to the LBJ highway.

We carried the dead bodies over our shoulders and the blood that was on the bodies transferred itself to our fatigues. The heat of the day was beginning to bloat the bodies and the smell was awful. We loaded the bodies onto the bed of a deuce and a half truck and headed towards the nearby village.

When we got to the center of the village, several women and children were waiting in anticipation of our arrival. Communication through the grapevine in Vietnam is super-fast. We unloaded the bodies and lined them up on the ground. Chris and Sugar Bear took ace of spades playing cards and placed them on their chests and then stomped a Wolfhound crest into their foreheads. The Wolfhounds calling cards let the villagers know what happens to VC and NVA that mess with the Wolfhounds.

The old women with betel nut-stained mouths were cussing at us and waving their arms in anger. Maybe that's why there was a bounty on the heads of the Wolfhounds. There were even wanted posters hanging around with the likeness of SSGT Glover on them. The reward at that time was $500 dead or alive. I was still confused about what Doc had done back at the ambush site. I had never seen or heard of ears being cut off dead bodies although there were rumors that guys in the central highlands cut gook ears off, strung them on leather thongs, and wore them around their necks as trophies.

What was the major going to do with the ears he was given? I was beginning to think Doc may have some issues. When he came into our platoon, he had been in Vietnam for eight months. Fifty-three days of those eight months were spent in Long Binh jail.

The way Doc told the story, he was a medic for a mechanized unit in the 1/5 Bobcats. They made Doc drive the medical personnel carrier and he had dodged several RPG rounds since being there. Doc was convinced the Bobcats were trying to get him killed. The Bobcats had been in a lot of action and Doc had seen more death and dismemberment than he could handle. His unit was overrun by a large VC company that killed several men and wounded many more.

When Doc carried the last wounded Bobcat to the medevac, he begged the crew chief to let him jump onboard and get out of there. The crew chief said, "negatory Doc only dead and wounded on this flight." Doc thought for an instant and then held the barrel of his M-16 on his little toe and pulled the trigger. He looked at the crew chief and said, "I'm wounded, man!" The crew chief said, "get in Doc we're taking off."

The medevac took the wounded men to a field hospital and the men were treated for their injuries. Ten men from Doc's unit were lying in hospital beds in the medical ward when a full bird Colonel came by to visit his troops and pin a Purple Heart onto their pillows.

When the Colonel reached Doc's bed, Doc said, "I don't deserve that medal." The Colonel smiled and said that a lot of guys feel that way, but true courage needed to be recognized and awarded. Doc said, "You don't understand, I shot myself in the foot." The Colonel turned to the attending physician and asked, "what is the meaning of this?"

The doctor said Doc had been treated for a gunshot wound that blew his little toe off. The Colonel became incensed and reached for the Purple Heart medal tearing it off the pillowcase along with a piece of linen. He turned to his attaché officer and told him to have the MPs come and arrest this traitor. The next thing Doc knew, he was sitting in Long Binh jail waiting for his court-martial hearing.

After Doc had been there for 50 days, some prisoners set the jail on fire, burning it to the ground. Shortly after that, Doc was called in for a case review. The JAG officer must have been sympathetic to Doc's plight because he offered Doc a chance to work in graves and registration, putting toe tags on dead soldiers brought in from the field. Doc took that offer and spent a couple of months in that position.

One day an officer came into the graves and registration building asking if there were any medics working there. The officer in charge said we only have Turner back there. The officer told Doc that if he would serve out his remaining time in the Wolfhounds, he would not have to do two years at Ft. Leavenworth and he would be eligible for an honorable discharge. Doc said, "where do I sign up!" Doc knew nothing about the Wolfhounds but guessed it was something to do with scout dogs.

When Doc came into the platoon, he brought his medical bag and a $10 Vietnamese guitar. Doc also had an interesting childhood. He was born and raised in Memphis, Tennessee, the hometown of Elvis Presley. As a teenager, Doc grew up in a neighborhood where the neighbor boys hung out during the summer months and contemplated their future. Two of his friends were Alex Chilton and Gary Talley. The three boys decided they wanted to learn how to play the guitar. Chilton and Talley had hand-me-down guitars that they seldom played.

Doc went to the local pawn shop and picked up an old used Conrad six-string guitar. The three boys spent endless days and nights learning basic cords and simple runs and singing country-western classics. They did most of their practicing on the car porch at Chilton's home. Doc was about 14 yrs old at the time. Living was easy during those summer months and the boys became pretty good musicians and Chilton decided to try songwriting. Just before Doc volunteered to serve in the Army, the other guys formed a band called The Box Tops.

Their first gold record was "The Letter" written by Wayne Carson. When Doc reached Vietnam, he had just celebrated his

18th birthday. Doc spent many hours entertaining us, playing "The Letter" and other Box Tops hits while hanging out at the fire support base. The guys affectionately called Doc, "the 3rd box top."

We loaded up and headed back to Crockett. When we arrived, I overheard Hannah telling O'Grady that he was sure that he had counted six gooks in the group that we had ambushed. The CO came over to our bunkers and congratulated us on a great ambush. I was sitting next to my half-round bunker, feeling numb and sick to my stomach. I couldn't get the smell of blood out of my system. I removed my bloody fatigues and soaked them in water, but I couldn't get the blood completely out. I thought to myself, "damn, clean laundry doesn't come out from Cu Chi for another 4 days." I sat for the next hour looking at the AK-47 the Chinese advisor had been trying to kill me with.

Arie Hill, the mess sergeant, was handing out C rations for lunch, but I had no appetite to eat. Ray told me he had heard we were going back out on another ambush patrol tonight to the same place we had just been. That couldn't be right; we never went out on APs two nights in a row and certainly not to the same location. That would be asking for trouble or worse: suicide.

Clement Todd, Lifer, and Alan "Claymore" Larson

Greg Bucy with Cobra

Willy, Hannah, Dasher, Cal Johnson

Eagle Flight

Doc Turner 1968 Vietnam

Kit Carson Scout Pete

Chapter Ten
THE HORRIBLE PRICE OF WAR
OCTOBER 5, 1968

t 1600 hrs., SSGT Hannah came walking around the bunker line telling us that he wanted to talk to us and we should get to his bunker double time. The minute I heard this, I had a bad feeling that what Ray had heard earlier was more than likely the truth. None of us had gotten any sleep the night before and everybody's nerves were shot. We were all waiting at Hannah's bunker when we saw him walking towards us from the CP. He was walking with his head down and you could tell there was something bothering him.

When he reached us, he said, "listen up, we're going out on an ambush tonight." You could hear the guys moaning and bitching under their breath. From the back, I heard Ketchum say, "you've got to be shitting me." Hannah said, "stand down back there, you asshole, I'm not any happier about this than you are." Hannah told us that the CO had decided to send us back where we had gone last night and get some more body count. I was a rookie, but I knew you never go to the same place twice in a row.

There was complete silence among the guys, and I looked around and saw looks of disbelief on many of the men's faces.

171

Hannah told us to be saddled up and ready to go by 1730 hrs. O'Grady said, "I'll be taking the guys out tonight," and Hannah said, "no, can't do, I've got too many new guys here that I'm responsible for, so I'll be going tonight but thanks anyway." We all felt safe with Hannah, but we knew he was a short-timer and should not go outside the wire.

When we returned to the bunker line, the guys were really complaining and a couple guys said we should refuse to go out. I kept thinking about what had happened the night before and I felt real fear to my very core. I went over and sat next to Ray and Russ and suggested that we get a spare barrel for the M-60 machine gun. I told Ray I would go over to the mess tent and see if I could get an oven mitt and look for some kind of a ramrod that we could use in the event of a cartridge jam. I told Russ he might as well leave his 90 mm recoilless back at the fire support base and take his M-16 with extra ammo.

Being stubborn, he looked at me and said, "not only am I going to take my 90 recoilless but I'm going to take my M-16 as well." Sgt. Hill gave me an oven mitt and a rod used to light the immersion heaters that would work to push out a stuck cartridge. After cleaning my weapon, I took the AK-47 that I had taken off the dead gook and wiped it off and wrapped it in a towel for safekeeping.

An AK-47 was one of the most coveted trophies in Vietnam. Air Force pilots were paying up to $150 for an AK and good money for other trophies like NVA flags or NVA officer's belts or web gear. I was trying to figure out how I could disassemble this AK and ship it home. Soldiers in the field were warned if they got caught sending home any weapons, it would be an automatic court-martial and a trip to Long Binh jail. That didn't stop a lot of guys from sending all kinds of stuff home.

My thoughts suddenly came back to the task at hand and I thought I should write my mom and dad a quick letter before going out on tonight's mission. It was always in the back of my mind that this might be my last letter home. A guy didn't want to dwell on it, but in my short time in Vietnam, I had seen a lot of guys wounded that never came back to the platoon. In the letter to my mother, I told her everything was going great and nothing much was going on.

In almost every letter I received from her she mentioned watching footage of the Vietnam War on the nightly news. She had mentioned a few times that she thought she saw me in some of the newsreels. I always assured her that I was okay and she had nothing to worry about. I sealed up the letter and wrote free where the stamp would go and dropped the letters into a mailbag that was hanging on the outside of the mess tent.

It was time to meet up at Hannah's bunker and get ready to load up on the trucks and head back down the LBJ highway. Alan "Claymore" Larson walked up to me and said he had a bad feeling about tonight. He said Todd was more negative than usual and didn't want to go. I told him I felt the same way but there wasn't a damn thing we could do about it.

As we headed out through the wire and walked towards the trucks, I noticed my hands were shaking. I put my hands together and squeezed them tight, hoping I could get the shaking to stop. What was wrong with me anyway? The trucks rumbled down the road just like we had done the night before and when we got to the drop-off point, we stopped and jumped off the trucks and spread out. Hannah told us we would form up in two files like we had done the night before. The only difference was, tonight, we would walk down the left side of the open field instead of the right side.

It wasn't quite dark when we started moving out. Hannah reminded everybody to keep their distance from the guy in front of them and keep their eyes and ears open. Hannah decided to walk towards the rear of the column in front of me, with Ray

173

walking directly behind me. We had only been walking for about five minutes when suddenly RPG rounds were raining down on top of us. One of the first rounds looked like a Roman candle coming straight towards us. There was no time to react.

The round landed 10 feet in front of Hannah and exploded. I saw Hannah fall face down on the ground and I did the same. The RPG rounds came directly from our front, so those of us towards the rear could not return fire without risking the chance of hitting our own guys. Within seconds the guys towards the front opened up and began firing into the hedgerows where the RPGs had been launched from. I heard Russ's recoilless fire with a huge bang. The round exploded in the center of the hedgerow, causing a huge explosion and starting the bamboo on fire. I was laying there, waiting for SSGT Hannah to tell us what to do. My heart was pounding out of my chest and my hands were sweating and shaking. Hannah wasn't moving and I thought maybe he was just keeping his head down to avoid the AK rounds that were snapping over our heads.

Somebody towards the front yelled medic and I could hear the screams of two or three guys that had been wounded. I crawled up to SSGT Hannah to ask him what we should do and I tapped him on the shoulder and he was unresponsive. I grabbed him by the shoulder and turned him over and immediately I heard a whistling sound coming from his chest.

From the training I had received in basic training, I immediately knew that Hannah had a sucking chest wound. I started yelling for Doc Turner and almost by instinct, I took the bandage off my Web gear, tore open the plastic wrapping and removed the bandage. I opened Hannah's fatigue jacket and I could see blood bubbling from a small hole in his chest. His eyes were wide open, looking at me and softly moaning.

I kept telling him Doc was on the way. I placed the plastic wrapper over the hole and held the compress bandage over the plastic and the whistling and bleeding stopped.

Hannah was turning his head from side to side and all I could think of was what am I'm going to do. I heard Ray behind me saying that he thought he was hit by shrapnel off of the RPG. It was dark and he couldn't see if he was bleeding but said he had several pieces hit him in the legs. Now I was really freaking out because I knew I had to stay with Hannah until Doc arrived. Illumination flares were bursting over our heads and after what seemed like forever, I saw Doc running across the field, through a barrage of tracers, directly towards our location.

Green tracers were in front of him behind him and just over his crouched-over body. He had a flashlight in his hand with a red lens and when he got to me, he said, "what have we got?" I told him Hannah had a sucking chest wound and Doc said, "turn him over." Doc took his scissors and cut Hannah's fatigue jacket up the center and when he opened up the two halves, there was a large jagged hole in the center of Hannah's back. Doc's voice was shaking as he looked at me with tears in his eyes and said, "Christ, he isn't going to make it." Doc took out a morphine syrette, stuck it in Hannah's shoulder, and pinned the needle to Hannah's fatigue jacket. I asked Doc what he wanted me to do.

He said, "turn him over, hold him and tell him everything is going to be okay and that the medevac is going to be here in just a minute." I shouted back at Ray, asking him if he was doing okay and he said he was. I told him to crawl up to my location. The intense firefight had started to slow down and I could hear the sound of helicopter blades in the distance. I was hoping and praying that this was the medevac. I kept talking to Hannah and as the medevac landed, SSGT Hannah rattled out his last breath. I couldn't believe he had just died in my arms. When the medevac landed, Ray and I picked up Hannah and carried him to the helicopter.

We slid his lifeless body onto the floor of the helicopter and the crew chief pulled him in the rest of the way. They were also loading up Claymore Larson, Clement Todd, and Rickey Fowler. I kept thinking to myself: this is really bad. AK tracer rounds were just missing the rotor blades and I wondered if we were going to get out of this alive. I was scared the gooks would fire another RPG at the helicopter and get us all.

I asked Ray where he was hit. He said that it must've been rocks and dirt that came from the RPG that hit him in the legs. I told him I was glad that he wasn't hurt. As the chopper lifted off, Ray and I looked at each other and tears ran down our faces.

We said nothing and moved forward to where the platoon was getting ready to set up a hasty ambush. We lay in the tall grass for the rest of the night expecting to be hit by RPGs at any minute. This would turn out to be one of the longest nights I had spent in Vietnam. I was beyond scared and I was beyond numb and at one point, I thought I was losing my mind. I remember asking God why he would allow somebody as good as Hannah to be killed so close to going home.

I remember thinking if experienced soldiers like Hannah could get killed, what chance would I have of making it the entire 12 months. I think this was the first time I faced the reality that I probably would not make it home alive. As it started getting daylight, we got up and marched back out to the highway and waited for the trucks to come and pick us up.

There were women and children from the nearby village watching us load up on the trucks. They probably were thinking we got what we had coming to us for killing the Vietnamese soldiers the night before. Bobby Noel came up to me and asked me if I had been wounded. I said no and he said, "why is there blood all over the front of your fatigues?" I hadn't noticed that Hannah's blood had soaked into my clothes while I was holding him waiting for the medevac.

A strange thought kept rattling around in my head. I wondered if the guy who had fired the RPG that killed Hannah was the 6th gook Hannah had seen the night before in the starlight scope. I wondered if that was the one that got away. When we got back to Crockett, SSGT Glover came around and talked to us. He saw my blood-soaked fatigues and asked me to tell him what had happened to Hannah.

A couple of the guys had already told him about Hannah dying in my arms. With tear-filled eyes, he listened as I told him about the RPG round that had landed in front of Hannah, causing a piece of shrapnel to go through his chest. This was the first time I had ever seen SSGT Glover show much emotion and it shook me to my core.

Glover and Hannah were good friends and I could see by the look on Glover's face he blamed himself for not being there that night. He asked me if Hannah had suffered and I told him I didn't think he knew what hit him. I told him he never spoke any words and I told him about Doc telling me he wasn't going to make it. I didn't realize it at the time, but as I was talking to Glover, tears were running down my face.

As Glover turned and walked away, he said, "get those fatigues off and try to get the blood out of them." Glover and I never spoke about the incident again. I removed my fatigues, walked over to the water trailer, and held them under the running water, trying to scrub the blood.

The ground underneath the spigot was turning red but I couldn't get all of the bloodstains removed. My hands were still shaking. I walked back to the bunker and laid my fatigues on top of the sandbags knowing that the 120° heat would dry them out

177

eventually. I would wear those fatigues for the rest of the week until clean fatigues came from Cu Chi. A couple of NCOs with clipboards from the command post came around and asked us about what had taken place. Several of the guys looked at them and said, "what the fuck do you think happened?"

Besides being exhausted and in shock and almost being blown away, most of us were starting to become really pissed off. A couple of guys said we should go back to the village and get some payback. Everybody was wondering why the CO would send us back out to the same place that we had been the night before. Lamere made the comment, "somebody should go shoot the son of a bitch before he gets us all killed." I was wondering what had happened to Larson and Todd and hoped that they weren't wounded too badly.

Amazingly, Fowler showed up that evening when the supply truck came from Cu Chi. Big Joe made the comment, "I thought he got Medevaced last night." I looked at Joe and said, "it don't mean nothin." Galli came by with the mail and a few care packages and told us we were getting the day off and would only be responsible for perimeter security that night.

A couple of the guys were sitting around eating C rations and writing letters home. It seemed like it was business as usual. Sergeant Hill came by with an insulated jug filled with cold lemonade and told us how sorry he was about Hannah. With tear-filled eyes he told us he knew Hannah well and had talked to him just the day before. The war had a way of affecting everyone that came in contact with it.

I was beginning to hide these horrible events in a dark room in my mind hoping to slam the door on them forever. That evening I wrote another letter home and told my mom how everything was going great and not much was happening at this time. I told her not to worry about me and asked her if she could send some more homemade chocolate chip cookies.

Crater Poisoning And Leeches

For the rest of the week, we took Eagle flights to predetermined locations and marched around in the heat looking for any signs of VC or NVA movement. Many times, we would be dropped off at an area previously bombarded by B-52 strikes. The awesome destruction we witnessed was impossible to put into words. During the monsoon season these bomb craters filled up with water and made perfect swimming holes.

One day we were sweeping through the burned-out rubble when the Lt. said we would break for lunch. Several of the guys stripped down to their boxers and combat boots and jumped into the water to cool off. A new guy, Thacker, was doing the butterfly stroke when suddenly he stopped stroking and floated face down in the water.

One of the guys pulled him to the side and we pulled him out of the water, where he proceeded to go into a seizure. The RTO called in a medevac and we all stood around wondering what had just happened. After he was dusted off a few hours later, the Lt. was told Thacker had drunk some of the crater water and gotten cordite poisoning.

When a bomb goes off, the remnants of the explosive go into the soil. When the crater filled with water, it created a poisonous cocktail. To my knowledge, the Army never told us not to drink crater water. Thacker never returned to our platoon and was never talked about again. On another day, they dropped us off in a rice paddy and we spent the rest of the day walking in waist-deep water. We were all wondering what we were supposed to be looking for and came to the conclusion that it made no sense whatsoever.

When the temperature outside is between 110° and 120°, the water temperature is usually about 95° to 100°. Walking in

179

the rice paddies is one of the most miserable things a soldier can do. We were constantly getting stuck in the mud and on several occassions, somebody would step into a hole, completely submerging themselves. Most of the time, we would laugh at the poor bastard when he came up out of the water gasping for air, looking like a drowned rat. Humor took on a completely different meaning in Vietnam.

I guess it was a survival mechanism that we acquired that kept us from living in hell all the time. After spending the day mucking around in the paddies, we finally got out on dry land and prepared to march back to the fire support base. The lieutenant told us we could take a break and have something to eat. Bruns was standing next to me and asked me if I had stepped on a punji stake. I said, "no, why do you ask?" He said, "there's blood running out the bottom of your pant leg."

I looked down and the top of my boot was crimson red. I reached down and untied the bottom pant leg string and lifted my pant leg up to my knee. I was horrified to see my leg was covered in leeches and blood was running down my leg. I felt lightheaded and abruptly sat down on the ground. Bruns looked at my leg and said, "man that's a mess." He threw me a bottle of insect repellent and I squirted it on the leeches and one by one, they started falling off my leg and onto the ground.

I took my towel, wiped the blood off my leg, lowered my pant leg, and retied the string. I undid the other pant leg string and as I pulled upward, I saw more leeches and more blood. I repeated the insect repellent procedure and when all was said and done, there were 36 leeches on my right leg and 24 leeches on my left leg.

Suddenly there was a horrible scream coming from our right flank. Bruns and I could not figure out what was going on. Everyone was shouting and asking what was going on. Within 10 minutes, we heard a helicopter approaching our location and when it landed, we saw someone being loaded onto the chopper. It wasn't until we got back to the fire support base that we found out that a leech had crawled up into Galli's penis.

When he was checking for leeches, he saw a small part of the leech sticking out the end and panicked. That's when the screaming began and the lieutenant called for a medevac. By the time we had gotten back to the fire support base, Galli had been treated at the 12th Evac hospital in Cu Chi and after a day's rest, he returned to duty. When we found out what had happened to Galli, we all agreed that was truly funny stuff. In his combat wisdom, Big Joe said, "it would have taken one helluva big leech to get into me!" Then the wisecracking began.

The following day, we had a new guy join our platoon from Oklahoma. We gave him the nickname Okie and told him he would be a rifleman in the second squad. When I asked him what he did back in the world before coming to Vietnam, he said he worked on his family's pig farm. He said he'd been doing it all of his life and considered himself to be a redneck pig farmer.

He told us that soon after his 18th birthday, he got drafted. He seemed really rough around the edges and didn't seem to be too well-educated. I saw him spitting tobacco juice out onto the ground and told him he would have to leave his plug tobacco in his pocket when we left the wire. He asked me why and I told him that every time he spit on the ground, it left a trail of tobacco juice that Charlie could use to track us down. I told him the last thing we wanted was to have Charlie sneak up behind us and shoot a couple of the guys in the back.

He said he understood, and I never saw him chew or spit outside the wire. Okie had been with us for about three weeks and was settling into the soldier's life. One afternoon a couple of boom boom girls (prostitutes) approached the wire and started to call out to the guys inside, "hey GI, you got girlfriend Vietnam? Hey, GI, I love you long time."

They would stand out there waving at the guys sitting inside the base, on top of the bunkers. Guys would often go out and partake in what the girls were selling. On one such occasion, I saw Okie go through the gate and walk over to where the girls were standing. I couldn't hear what was said but apparently, they agreed on a price and I watched as one of the girls and Okie went to a nearby berm and disappeared behind it. I was distracted when Ray asked me if I wanted to join some guys in a game of pinochle.

A few minutes later, we all heard a bloodcurdling scream from outside the wire in the direction that the girls had been standing. We all ran to the wire and saw Okie running towards the gate with his pants down around his ankles, as he held his hands over his bleeding junk.

The rube was yelling for a medic and none of us could figure out what the hell was going on. A medic met him at the gate and yelled back for someone to call for a medevac. Since Okie was screaming, we figured he was still alive, so we went back to playing pinochle. The next day Doc came up to us and told us what had happened to Okie.

Apparently, the boom-boom girl was a VC and she had some kind of a device stuffed up inside her pussy that sliced Okie's penis into four equal pieces. There had been stories going around about whores that had done this, but we all thought it was just a rumor. I did not recall the cutter in the pussy being discussed in the horny swabby film in basic training! Okie never returned to the platoon and from that day forward, we referred to him as four-prong dong. Nobody ever knew where he had ended up. He hadn't been with the platoon long enough for any of us to know what his given name was.

As I recall, no one ever mentioned his name after that incident. Ray just kept complaining that the dirty bastard had gotten away with a million-dollar wound. Big Joe, our wise sage, said, "Shit, some guys have all the luck." Ray said, "I would give anything to get a ricochet, so I could get out of here.

From that moment forward, Ray's new nickname was Rick O Shay. The new guys called him Rick and they looked at me funny when I called him Ray. The battalion was preparing to build a new fire support base east of Hwy. 22. Our company would be part of the building crew. We were told it was going to be named Reed.

November 1968

Things settled down to a dull roar for the next few weeks. We would alternate between Eagle flights and ambush patrols. If there was something I really enjoyed in Vietnam, it was riding in helicopters. During November, the Little Bears aviation company was designated as our ride when we were acting as a reactionary force.

During this time, at least two of our platoons would be dropped off into an area known to contain VC or NVA. In many instances, we were sent in to assist other units that found themselves overtaken or surrounded by a superior enemy force. On one such occasion, word came down that Bravo Company was getting their asses kicked by a Company sized unit of NVA. They had already taken six KIAs and many more wounded.

As we waited for the Little Bears to arrive, there was a buzz of conversation going around about the shit storm we were about to be dropped into. We knew this was going to be a hot LZ (landing zone) for sure.

These were the absolute worst times to be flying in a helicopter because when it came time to land, we would always start taking enemy fire. The NVA had a reputation of shooting down helicopters full of infantrymen using RPGs just before the birds would touchdown.

Because of this, the crew chiefs would tell us we had to jump out of the helicopter when it was 10 feet off the ground and still moving. This would give the helicopter and its crew at least a chance to get airborne before they were hit with hostile fire. I can't remember how many helicopters I loaded up on that had bullet holes in the sides and the tail section. Many door gunners had been killed or wounded while dropping platoons off in hot LZs.

Every man that day knew that we were going into a very dangerous situation. None of us wanted to go, but we all knew that we had to go and try to relieve our sister company. In combat, every soldier knows that the only person that has their back is another soldier. There was an unwritten rule that said, "no man gets left behind." We knew this was going to be a giant shit sandwich and there was the possibility some of our guys would get killed or hurt.

Every man silently said a prayer that he hoped it wouldn't be him. When the helicopters landed, we loaded up and I took my usual position sitting in the doorway with my feet on the skids. I had started this habit when I was carrying the M-79 grenade launcher and a rucksack full of ammo. It was too hard to try to climb up into the helicopter with the weight of the rucksack on my back. So, I simply turned my back to the door and slid inside.

I always thought that if we were being shot at when landing, I wanted to be the first guy out of the helicopter. We lifted off at 1300 hrs., and we were in the air only 20 minutes when we looked down and saw yellow smoke coming up through the jungle. I knew immediately that we were about to disembark just outside the Hobo Woods. This was a very bad place where the NVA had established their brigade headquarters and they owned this piece of real estate both day and night.

We had heard they even had tanks in there and artillery that could reach Saigon. Behind me, I saw one of the new guys crying as he covered his face with his hands. I knew how he felt, and I hated being put in these situations. I hated it with all my heart. Thoughts of home crossed my mind and I was suddenly back in high school pitching the final game of the California state championships. We won that game 10 to 4 and Kearney High, the odds-on favorite, went down in a stunning defeat. I had pitched a 3 hitter that day and it was one of the happiest days of my life. I was suddenly brought back to reality when the crew chief yelled, "It's a hot LZ and you guys are going to have to jump." All 10 ships started their steep descent towards the landing zone.

We knew that we would have to quickly form up into a wedge formation and fight our way into the jungle when we got out. The faster we got off the helicopter and the faster we got into the jungle the better off we would be. We were told that Bravo Company would be directly on our left flank and that our objective was to get behind the NVA force and execute a hammer and anvil maneuver.

In layman's terms, that meant trapping the NVA between our company and Bravo Company and killing as many of them as we could when they attempted their retreat. It always looks good on paper, but things don't always work out the way you plan. I remember my dad saying, "the best-laid plans of mice and men somehow go awry," and in this case it did. The door gunner was yelling, "get off, get off."

Bullets were hitting the tail section with a loud ting sound. The door gunner was firing on full automatic, hosing down the hedgerow to our front. Immediately after jumping out of the chopper, we were pinned down by automatic weapons fire.

Several of the helicopters had been hit and were struggling to make altitude on their departure.

A couple of them were streaming smoke from their exhaust ports. Hell was breaking loose all around us. I yelled at Big Joe and asked if anyone was hurt and he said not that he knew of. This in and of itself was a miracle. The only thing we could do from our position was shoot directly to our front into the hedgerows.

The Wolfhounds had come here for a fight today and we were getting just what we asked for. The Lt. yelled for my squad to move forward and secure the hedgerow where the heavy fire was coming from.

I yelled at Moose and told him to put as many M-79 HE rounds into the hedgerow as he could to keep their heads down. We slowly moved forward guns blazing and when we got within 10 yards of the hedgerow, we started throwing hand grenades into the thick vegetation. We must have made an impact because the firing stopped coming from our front. I thought maybe the NVA had set a trap for us and were waiting until we got close enough to blow us away. This was not the case.

When we entered the hedgerow, we saw a couple of NVA soldiers lying on the ground in grotesque stages of death. Bodies tear apart easily when hit by flying shrapnel from hand grenades or Moose's HE rounds. I counted 4 dead NVA and blood trails headed into the jungle. We had two guys wounded in the first minutes of the assault. Both were shot in the legs and Doc took care of their wounds and prepared them for the medevac. The battle, however, was just beginning for us. Lt. directed us to move online and head south towards Bravo Company, where they were fighting for their lives.

After going about 100 yards Lt. said we would stay in place and dig in and act as a blocking force. Within 10 minutes, two

Cobra helicopters came on station and started working out to our front. We had no idea how close we were to the NVA. We didn't know if they were retreating in our direction. Every man was poised and ready to bring maximum hurt to the enemy. The first NVA soldiers to emerge were in total disarray. Some wounded were being carried by their comrades.

One guy was waving an NVA flag and he was the first to be shot down. We were shooting NVA soldiers wholesale and when they realized their flank had been taken out, they turned west and disappeared into the jungle. Several of us wanted to go after them but Lt. told us to stand down. He had other ideas of his own.

Within minutes, 155 mm artillery rounds coming from Trang Bang started to sail over our heads landing where the NVA had walked into the jungle. Lt. kept walking the rounds 25 yards at a time until a grid of 100 yards had been covered. I could only imagine the devastation that occurred. Lt. said an ARVN unit would go in there later and mop up the area.

Our platoon had killed several enemies today and we only had two guys wounded. We packed up our gear, walked out the way we came, and reentered the open area where the Little Bears would extract us. The adrenaline was palpable, and guys were sweating testosterone.

Everyone was jacked up and telling each other how many gooks they killed or thought they killed. We had a confirmed body count of 8 NVA. This was the biggest battle our platoon had been in since I got here in August. One thing was learned for sure that day: the NVA were tough but could be had!

Ray Bourgeois, Sheila, Big John

Big John, Ed Rambo

Lee Ketchum

188

Chapter Eleven
BUILDING FSB REED

W hen we moved out of Crockett FSB we moved to a heavily vegetated area just east of Hwy. 22. We were sent there to serve as security for the engineers as they cleared an area right in the middle of a thick jungle area. It was so thick that the helicopters carrying D-8 Cats had to wait for us to clear small openings.

Once the dozers hit the ground the engineers began clearing a circular area about 100 yards in diameter. The dozers pushed the vegetation into huge piles that were then sprayed with diesel fuel and ignited by trip flares. The black smoke caused by the burning diesel became so heavy that visibility was reduced to 10 yards. The bamboo inferno was choking our lungs.

Our company was spread out in the jungle to provide security in case Charlie decided to attack the engineers. Even though we were surrounding the construction area, Charlie successfully used snipers to harass and interfere with the progress of clearing the area. We suspected they were popping out of spider holes. It took the engineers just two days to completely clear and level the jungle.

During this time, our platoon provided security during the day and ran ambush patrols at night. Besides the snipers, that first couple of days were relatively quiet. On the third day Chinook helicopters showed up carrying cargo nets full of sandbags, razor blade concertina wire, boxes of ammo and grenades and C rations. Next came five 105 mm artillery cannons accompanied by their respective crews. Very soon, the fire support base started taking shape.

The engineers staked out the perimeter where they wanted us to build bunkers and fighting positions. The dozers had created large piles of dirt that we could use to fill sandbags. Bravo Company was airlifted into our location shortly after noon. It was the job of our two companies to build fire support base, Reed, as quickly as possible.

Around 2 o'clock in the afternoon, another Chinook helicopter delivered our mess hall. Arie Hill, our mess Sgt. was the first person off the helicopter, and he started barking out orders to his men on where he wanted the mess hall to be set up. Our Company Commander asked Sgt. Hill how things were coming, and I heard Hill say he would try to give the guys a hot meal that evening.

I thought to myself, there's no way they can get that mess tent set up and start cooking within the next couple of hours. Charlie Company was given half the perimeter to build. The engineers were having us put up the wire and build the bunkers within 50 feet of the jungle.

It didn't feel right to me that we would not have any fields of fire in front of us and that Charlie could sneak up on us within hand grenade throwing distance. I mentioned this to Rambo, and he said the engineers were probably planning on clearing the jungle around the base another hundred yards.

For the moment, I let my concern slip from my mind and started filling sandbags with Ray and Russ. Several sorties of helicopters continued to bring in building materials, including 8 x 8 timbers that would be used as roof joists for the bunkers.

One of the guys carrying one of the timbers swung around and the end of the timber clocked Moose right in the head. Moose went down, grabbing his bleeding forehead. He got up, shook it off, and walked over to Doc and got himself patched up. On top of the timbers, we placed 12-foot-long pieces of PCP.

PCP was a heavy interlocking metal used to construct temporary runways for aircraft to land and take-off of. At 1800 hrs., one of the cooks came by and said we could go get in line for dinner. I thought it was some kind of joke and figured they would have a table set up with C rations on them. The best I could hope for was that they would have some fresh milk and peanut butter and jelly sandwiches.

Much to my surprise, when we got to the mess area, Sgt. Hill had spaghetti with meat sauce, green beans, salad and large sheet cakes for dessert. I could not believe those guys had gotten things set up in such a short period of time. Sgt. Hill had a huge smile on his face as he put a piece of cake on every man's tray. Sgt. Hill was a dedicated soldier and always did everything he could to take care of his troops.

That night we all pulled perimeter guard duty and hoped that Charlie would not try to run over the few strands of wire we had been able to put up that day. The bunkers were about half completed and we knew we would have to get them finished the following day.

The next morning all the dozers were airlifted out of the base. This meant they were not going to clear any more jungle around the perimeter. I had a very bad feeling in my gut that this would turn out to be a huge mistake.

In three days, we had constructed Reed and now we waited to find out what our mission would be from that point on. At the same time, SSGT Glover was transferred to Battalion. None of us were prepared when SSGT Glover left the platoon.

Glover was our anchor, he was our compass, and he could call in artillery and put it on a dime. His replacement was a Puerto Rican E-7 named Marquez. The new platoon sergeant gathered everyone up and introduced himself and told us in broken English that he had served two previous tours in Nam with the Big Red One. He told us he expected us to keep our shit together and he would not tolerate dirty fatigues or long hair.

Ketchum laughed under his breath and SFC Marquez looked at him and said in an angry voice, "what in da god damn hell you think you do, you sonny beach?" And now no one was laughing, but instead, we looked at each other and wondered what had just happened. He told us to have our weapons cleaned and near us at all times. As Marquez was walking away, someone said, "screw you flat dick." That would remain his nickname for the rest of my tour.

Ray looked at me and said, "he looks hard-core to me." I asked Ray if he thought this old man could keep up on the hump. We would soon find out Flat Dick was one tough son of a bitch. He was a professional soldier who joined the Army at age 17. His home had been Ft. Benning since joining the Army.

This guy was Army through and through. Flat Dick was a lifer who was no one's friend and was seriously disciplined. He told us we would be getting a new Lt. by the end of the week. The last time we had a Lt. was Creveling. We were all worried that SSGT Glover was gone.

We trusted him completely and now we had a new, unproven guy who didn't speak very good English. What the hell will happen next? We got in a routine of going on ambush patrols every other night. These patrols proved very difficult because we were always walking in thick elephant grass and bamboo.

Our ambush sites had to be very tight and we usually set up on small oxcart trails about a half a klick from Reed. On our off days, we did day sweeps a klick or so from the base. Everybody hated this place, but at least we were staying dry and not walking in rice paddies all day. Funny how you can find a positive even in the middle of a huge negative.

The following week our lieutenant arrived at Reed and his name was O'Grady. He came from a high society family in Boston, Massachusetts. He didn't have much to say and pretty much kept to himself. When O'Grady arrived, he demanded that we all salute him. The dumb shit had no idea what he was setting himself up for.

The saluting promptly ended when a sniper tried to blow his head off two days later. Although he went with us during day patrols and night ambush patrols, it seemed like Marquez was running the show. The night of O'Grady's arrival, we received a mortar attack that lasted for about five minutes.

It was impossible to tell where it was coming from and guys were diving into the nearest bunkers. Mortar attacks are very unnerving because you can hear them coming in but you have no idea where they will land. We were lucky that no one was hurt during that first attack. The biggest damage was a water trailer and a latrine that took a direct hit.

These mortar attacks became a daily event. Every day at about noon, Charlie would lob in two or three 60 mm rounds and that was it. The whole time I was at Reed, no one was ever killed by these attacks and only one bunker took a direct hit wounding four lazy assholes sunning themselves on top of the bunker.

Sir Charles was definitely getting into our heads and at noon every day, you could see guys hanging out close to the bunkers. We tried sending out patrols to see if we could locate the source of the mortars, but we were never successful. I'm sure Charlie had a tunnel that he would pop out of and drop three rounds and drop back down in his hole. Every day that went by I gained more respect for the little men that were trying to kill us.

We found out soon that the new lieutenant could not call in artillery very well and several times, he called in white phosphorous marking rounds directly over our heads. O'Grady seemed to fit perfectly into Capt. Sherwood's plans. The second platoon would continue to do the dirty work for a company commander hellbent on getting body count. We were always the vanguard platoon when we were sent into battle.

The reason it was like that was Colonel Odie knew SSGT Glover would always get the job done. After the Lt. took charge of the platoon, he decided to send two squads out on an ambush patrol. He wanted Sgt. Ketchum and Sgt. Smokes to take us out in the dense jungle after dark. This was an insane idea and the two squad leaders refused to comply with the Lt's orders. As a result, O'Grady busted both men back to Spec four ranks. Their decision saved several lives.

The men of the second platoon started looking sideways at our new Lt. During the third week at Reed, the engineers returned with their dozers and cut out a large section of the jungle on the west and of the perimeter where helicopters could land and pickup troops. The area was big enough that 10 helicopters could land at the same time.

I had a feeling we were about to get back into the eagle flight business. On Thanksgiving we were doing day sweeps up on the Cambodian border and word came down that Uncle Sam was going to feed every swinging richard a hot turkey dinner with all the fixings.

The helicopter bringing our feast didn't arrive until 1700 hrs. A couple of cooks rode out to serve us the meal. They unloaded several mermite insulated containers and set them up in a row. We lined up with our mess kits and the cooks loaded us down with turkey, mashed potatoes and gravy, dressing, mixed vegetables, shrimp with cocktail sauce, dinner rolls and butter and all the pumpkin pie we could eat. Lemonade and coffee were also served.

There was enough food for everyone to have seconds and even thirds. Guys were acting like gluttons. We were so hungry that no one paid any attention that the food was luke warm. Not a word was mentioned that the shrimp, packed in ice, was floating in luke warm water. None of us was aware that the mermite cans had been sitting out in the sun on the helicopter pad in Cu Chi since 0900 hrs.

After dinner, a helicopter came and picked up the cooks and empty mermite cans. We marched east and settled down about a klick from where we ate dinner and set up an ambush.

The next morning, we saddled up and headed towards the Angel Wing. Many guys were complaining that they had eaten so much turkey and pie that they had stomach aches. Come to think of it, I wasn't feeling so good myself. By 1500 hrs., we all had Montezuma's revenge. Guys were bent over at the waist complaining about severe cramping in their abdomens. Even Doc was sicker than a dog.

Then a shit storm hit us. Guys were shitting themselves and could not control their bowels. In a matter of an hour, every man was on the ground with dysentery. The Thanksgiving dinner we had eaten had poisoned us all. The Lt. called the CO on the radio and requested that choppers come and get us back to Cu Chi. If Charlie had attacked us, we would have been totally incapacitated. To my knowledge, I have never heard of an entire platoon being disabled on the battlefield from dysentery. This was really the shits!

When we got to Cu Chi, there were a couple of deuces and a halves waiting by the runway to take us to the battalion aid station. Crew chiefs in the helicopters were ragging on us about the smell we left in their birds. The entire platoon spent the next two days lying in the field hospital hooked up to IVs, giving us fluids to counteract the dehydration we had suffered. The only thing they gave us to eat was crackers and beef broth. I have never seen a more pitiful bunch of guys in my life. After we regained control of our bowels and were having semi-normal stools, they flew us back to Reed.

Caught In The Open With Nowhere To Go

Our first day mission after the Thanksgiving debacle was an eagle flight just south of the Boi Loi woods located 6 miles SW of Go Dau Ha. It was an open area covered with Bahia grass that grew about knee-high. Charlie Company's mission was to recon the area for a possible hard spot that the 25th INF Div was considering building there.

It was an overcast day as we began our sweep of the area. We were spread out in two files approximately 10 yards apart. Everything was going smooth until a single shot rang out and the first platoon's point man went down screaming, he had been hit in the leg.

Everyone took a knee and faced outward-looking for any kind of movement. I saw a medic running up to the wounded point man and as soon as he reached his comrade, another shot broke through the air and the medic went down. Sgt. Marquez said he had seen this before. He added that we had walked into firing lanes that the gooks had cut in the grass.

At the end of the lane, a VC was hiding in a spider hole waiting for a GI to step into his line of fire. The first GI would be wounded in the legs and everyone else that came to help him would be killed.

Everyone was ordered to stay in place and the CO radioed battalion to inform them of our situation. Within 10 minutes, the Battalion Commander was circling overhead in his loach helicopter. He was shooting his 45-cal. pistol at an unknown target. He got on his megaphone and started yelling for the Company to get online and assault. Assault where? In the meantime, first platoon got their point man and medic drug back outside the firing lane. We were caught out in the open with nowhere to go. No one was getting up and assaulting anything.

A medevac helicopter was hovering behind us, waiting to pick up the wounded. The Colonel's helicopter finally headed back to Cu Chi and the company commander ordered the Company to retreat the same way we had come in. When we were 50 yards away from where the point man was shot, artillery rounds started falling in the field to our front.

The artillery barrage lasted for 20 minutes, causing the grass to catch on fire. When the artillery stopped, the Company moved out to an area where we would be picked up and taken back to Reed. Totals for the day's work: one GI wounded another killed and hundreds of thousands of dollars, worth of artillery expended for zero body count. The Army's fuzzy math was rearing its ugly head again.

Even God Won't Forgive Us

We were working H and I (artillery term for harassment and interdiction fire) sweeps outside of Reed and I remember the potholes and craters were filled with water from the previous night's rain. Our mission was to look for signs of blood, bodies, drag marks or any indication that the previous night's artillery barrage had been successful.

The artillery Lieutenant in charge of the previous night's fire mission joined us that day to see what havoc his boys had created the night before. We were all tired because we couldn't sleep with the 155 artillery guns firing all night long. This Lt. was hell-bent on getting a body count. We swept the area for four hours without a single sign. The Lt. was getting visibly upset and I heard him say, "I'm not going to stay out here all day and go home empty-handed."

We walked by a graveyard, next to a nearby village, that had four fresh graves. It was obvious from the fresh dirt that they were recently dug. Two of the graves had little miniature ladders stuck in the dirt where a headstone would go.

The Lt. told us to hold up. He told his RTO Jimmy Langley to radio the fire support base and tell them we were checking out possible body count, weapons caches, or any sign of VC. Bruns and I were sitting on our steel pots next to the fresh graves when the Lt. yelled for us to get up. He looked at us and pointed at one of the graves and said, "Dig it up." I looked at Bruns in disbelief and turned to the Lt. and said, "it's not right to dig up a grave sir." He snarled at me and said, "dig it up, that's a direct order."

Luckily, we had brought our entrenching tools that day and we knelt down to start the excavation. Bruns said, "I'll dig, and you move the dirt." When we got the mounded dirt off, we realized it was a shallow grave. Bruns hit a wood plank that was placed over the body as a makeshift coffin lid.

The minute I pulled up the plank an unbelievable smell came billowing out from the deteriorating corpse. We both turned away and a wave of nausea rose up in my stomach. The Lt. stood over us and told us to check for weapons and ammo under the body. The body was a Vietnamese man dressed in civilian clothes and next to his head was a bowl of rice and a cup.

We rolled the body over and there was nothing under it. The Lt. then turned to Jimmy Langley his RTO and told him to call in that we had a body count.

The old women of the village stood behind us, crying and saying things to us that were obviously angry curse words. They rubbed betel nut into their nostrils which masked the horrid smell. Before we could cover the grave, the Lt. said, "dig that one up over there." We dug up two more graves with the same results; no weapons, no ammo, no documents, no nothing. The Lt. told us to dig up the last grave and Bruns and I told him we weren't going to do it.

The Lt. told us he would bust us both if we didn't follow his direct order. Russ and I were both fed up with this bullshit. Some of the guys were calling us grave robbers. We had had enough, and I said to the Lt., "you can bust me, but I'm not going to uncover this last grave. Do what you have to do." The Lt. turned to his RTO and told him to grab the entrenching tool and dig up the last grave. All the color blanched out of Langley's face as he walked over and knelt next to the grave and began digging.

When he got down to the wooden planks, he turned and bent over, vomiting on the ground. He told the Lt. he couldn't do anymore and got up and walked back to his radio. The Lt. was really pissed off and walked over and stood next to the exposed planks.

199

There was a half-inch gap between the planks and the Lt. took his bayonet and bent over the grave and shoved it down between the planks. He must have pierced the dead man's bloated belly because body fluids and gases shot up through the crack, landing on his pant legs and boots. He started cursing and the stench poured over us all. I rolled away from the grave and laid facedown, my hands covering my head. He started yelling, "let's get the fuck out of here."

We came; we desecrated 4 graves and left the mess for the mama-sans to clean up. This went against everything the nuns had taught me at catholic school. Everyone was quiet and no one was talking, no one was joking and everyone seemed to know that we were in the presence of evil. I turned to Bruns and said, "even God could not forgive us for what we have done." We left the graves uncovered and marched back to the fire support base. On the way back to the base, the Lt. told Langley to report four VC body count and no doubt received a commendation letter in his file.

Big John, Lifer the Pup

Kid with Water Buffalo

Hooch Girl

Chapter Twelve
CHRISTMAS IN CU CHI VIETNAM 1968

here were rumors that Bob Hope was going to be in Cu Chi sometime in December to put on his annual USO Christmas show.

We were stuck out in the field and had no chance of seeing Bob or the beautiful girls he brought with him. Bruns and I were still upset about the grave-digging incident and could not figure out how an officer could order such atrocities. On the morning of the 14th, Lt. told us Battalion was going to send trucks out and drive us to Cu Chi for the Bob Hope show.

Everyone thought it was some kind of a sick joke, but he said anyone not ready to go by 1000 hrs. would be left behind. He said we would be going for just the day and would return that night. Guys were scrambling to dig their cameras out of their backpacks and a few even washed the dirt and dust off their faces. It would be a short ride to Cu Chi, and we were told we would be dropped off at our Company area and we would have to turn in our weapons for the day. Everyone was excited to see the show, and no one complained about the dusty ride in the back of the deuce and a half's.

When we arrived at Cu Chi, the First Sergeant was there to greet us and explain the code of conduct during the show. No throwing objects up on the stage, no jumping up on the stage, no foul language, no pushing and shoving to get a better view and most importantly, we were to have a good time.

As it turned out, all the First Sergeant's rules could be thrown out the window. By the time we got to the show, we were several hundred feet from the stage. Shorter guys were shut out of luck as far as getting a good look at the pretty girls. Nonetheless, we were out of the field and about to see Bob Hope. For a grunt, it just doesn't get any better than that.

When the show started, a band started playing "Thanks for the Memories," and Bob Hope himself came walking out on stage wearing a fatigue jacket with a large 25th Infantry badge sewn on the front of it. He had his signature golf club with him and a ball cap with the brim turned up. The crowd in attendance went berserk. Hats were flying everywhere, and Charlie could have heard the roar all the way to Hanoi. Just as Bob was about to speak a huge explosion went off just outside the base.

There was dead silence, and everybody thought that was going to be the end of the show. Bob calmly stepped up to the microphone with a huge smile on his face and said, "I don't have time for any bombs; I'm working on my cue cards here!" The show went on and Bob did his monologue and then introduced a zany comedian named Jerry Colonna. Jerry was a bug-eyed man with a huge handlebar mustache. He had been entertaining with Bob Hope since the '40s on radio and films. He got the troops laughing from the time he got to the microphone.

After Colonna, Hope introduced the Gold Diggers, an all-female dance troupe that came out in skimpy tops and short shorts-wearing cowgirl hats. Not a single man present could tell you if they were good dancers or not because they were too busy putting their eyes and tongues back into their heads.

After the Gold Diggers, Hope introduced Joey Heatherton. She was a blonde singer/dancer/actress that was a rival to the pouty sex kitten Ann Margaret. Everyone wanted to get a gander of her gorgeous gams. She had the sex-starved jug heads swooning in their combat boots. She did a great song and dance routine and then ended the show by doing a duet song and dance with Bob Hope.

As the show drew to a close, the ensemble cast all appeared onstage and sang as the band played a silent night. The troops joined in and you could see the look of homesickness on everyone's face. After the show, Bob Hope and his entourage were taken to the officer's mess, where they were treated to a lavish Turkey dinner. Joining them was the "girl next door," Chris Noel, wearing her signature mini skirt. There were thousands of her posters hanging in bunkers throughout Vietnam. Thanks for the memories, Bob.

Trang Bang Bridge December 15, 1968

During the first part of December, we were taking Eagle flights every day out of Reed. They were dropping us off at the Michelin rubber plantation and we would walk a couple of klicks before being picked up by the Little Bears. Then they would fly five klicks northeast and drop us off outside the Hobo Woods. Our mission was to walk around looking for any tunnels or signs of recent NVA activity.

What the Company Commander really wanted was for us to make contact. We were always being told the most important thing we could do was get body count. Many times, I thought of the Mad Magazine character Alfred E Newman and his famous saying, "what me worry!" Hell, I only had 8 months to go.

Christmas was coming, and I had a feeling Santa wasn't coming to this bad place. On December 15, we got great news from the battalion that Charlie Company was being assigned to guard the Trang Bang Bridge. This was the sweetest assignment any company could get. We would sit on the bridge day and night and throw hand grenades into the water as it passed under the bridge.

The purpose of doing this was to discourage Charlie from floating up the river and using satchel charges to blow the bridge down. This was the good life indeed. We could even shoot M-79 rounds at vegetation floating down the river. We celebrated Christmas at the bridge and Ray's dad sent us a small plastic Christmas tree complete with ornaments. Guys were receiving care packages that were wrapped in Christmas paper. What do you buy a combat soldier stuck in the middle of hell?

Most of the guys asked Santa to bring them a new watch, a new Kbar knife or a couple of 30 round banana clips for an M-16. Lamere asked Santa for a can of Cherry Blend Tobacco or a can of Borgum Riff. Santa was kind to Lamere and brought him 12 of the latest science fiction books recently published. The day after Christmas, things started to change. It seemed like we were spending most days walking around the rice paddies surrounding Trang Bang.

The rumor was that O'Grady was volunteering our platoon to run security sweeps. This was some of the worst duty a platoon could do. There's nothing more miserable than mucking around in the rice paddies in 110° weather. At least one or two guys had to be medevacked out for heat exhaustion every day. I would run out of water by mid-afternoon and be forced to drink rice paddy water filled with every parasite known to man. I carried iodine tablets to purify the water but could never wait the hour it took for the tablet to be effective.

It's no wonder we had diarrhea most of the time. Malaria tablets washed down with rice paddy water made for a shitty cocktail. One night after a week of sloshing around the rice paddies, someone tossed a dud grenade into O'Grady's bunker as a warning to stop volunteering our platoon for worthless missions.

The first night we were back on bridge duty, something happened that got us kicked off the bridge forever. Every night around 2000 hrs. the battalion commander would fly over the bridge in his helicopter and would hover a hundred feet above the bridge. On this particular night, there was a burst of M-60 fire directed at the chopper. You could see what looked like a couple of tracers going right through the helicopter.

In an instant, the helicopter peeled off and returned to Cu Chi. Everybody wondered who would be crazy enough to try to shoot the battalion commander out of the sky. It only took a few minutes to confirm that it was Lamere that had perpetrated the assault.

We all know without a doubt that next morning, our shit would be flapping in the wind. At daybreak, the executive officer from Cu Chi came rolling over the bridge. He un-assed his Jeep and started interrogating guys that had been on the bridge that night. I was the second soldier he talked to and I told him from my position it looked like the rounds came from across the river from the ARVN compound. I told him there were rumors that the VC had moved into the area only a couple of days before.

The ARVNs were really nervous and shooting at anything that moved along the river. My explanation must have satisfied him because he got back in his Jeep and drove back to Cu Chi. Not another word was ever spoken about the incident but the consequences of Lamere's actions were about to come down on us like a ton of bricks. The following day we were informed that Charlie Company had been removed from Trang Bang Bridge and were being sent to Tay Ninh. Our hopes of spending more time at the bridge were doused by one burst of an M-60 machine gun.

New Year's Day 1969 Hedgy In The Hedgerow

We had just arrived at Jackson FSB base when we were told we would do an ambush patrol about 2 klicks west of the Fire Support Base. It was another one of those walk all day and ambush all night scenarios and to be honest, we were all pretty sick of that duty. I was talking to my buddy Charlie about his life in the Army and he told me he was a Michigan boy that decided since he was going to Vietnam, he might as well go as an instant NCO.

Like so many of the shake-and-bake sergeants coming into Vietnam, he was trained but not prepared for combat in Vietnam. Ray and I had taken him under our wing, and he proved to be a very good soldier. Charlie only had one bad habit to his name. When we walked by hedgerows, he would take a bamboo stick and poke around in them, looking for tripwires. We always warned him that was a good way to find one and get blown up. As a result of this continued habit, we nicknamed him Hedgy. That would be his name from that point on.

When we loaded up on the choppers that morning, Hedgy was with me, Ray, Bruns and Pete, our Kit Carson Scout. Our march took us by a village surrounded by hedgerows. Marquez told us we were going to set up our ambush inside the village that night, so we should pay attention to the lay of the land. We continued on our way and stopped around 1300 hrs. to eat lunch. I brought some extra chocolate chip cookies my mom had sent and shared them with a couple of guys while eating lunch. We had stopped in the middle of a watermelon field and the melons looked ripe enough to eat.

One of the new guys cut one in half and was about to eat the heart out of it when I said, "I wouldn't eat that if I were you." He asked why not, and I asked him if he knew what they fertilized those fields with and he got a sour look on his face and said no, what? I told him the Vietnamese farmers used human waste as their fertilizer. He dropped the melon half and we all started to laugh. I thought about the huge watermelons we would have at beach parties when I was a kid. They would put them in a washtub and cover them with ice. I could taste them now.

After marching for another 3 hours in the scorching sun, we took another break and prepared ourselves for our upcoming ambush. Setting up in villages was tricky and everyone had to be on their best game. We never knew if we would run into VC or NVA before setting up and if we did, it could be a cluster. Marquez was going to walk point and get us into the village and place us into our positions.

It was going to be a full moon tonight, so we should be able to see where we were going. We arrived outside the village right after sundown and Marquez said we would wait until 2100 hrs. before going in. We had to sit in an open field for 30 minutes before moving out. When we got up to move, Ray whispered to me, "I've got a bad feeling about this."

Marquez led the first squad through the hedgerow and Hedgy was leading the second squad close behind. As soon as Hedgy entered the hedgerow, there was a big explosion. Everyone hit the ground anxiously awaiting word on what had happened. Half the platoon was in the village and the rest of us were in the field. The RTO came up to me and said a medevac was on its way and that I had to put a strobe light down on the ground to show the pilot where to land. Great, a strobe light to give Charlie a target to shoot at.

I made my way out into the open field behind us and waited for the familiar sound of chopper blades cutting through the air in the distance.

As soon as the chopper was close, I turned on the strobe light and placed it in my helmet and put it on the ground and crawled away about 20 feet. I could see the red blinking light on top of the chopper and watched as it got brighter and brighter as it closed in on my location. It set down just behind my helmet and the blade wash pushed my helmet and strobe light along the ground about 30 feet.

A couple of guys walked quickly towards the chopper carrying a wounded soldier. As they passed by me, I saw it was Hedgy. His leg and foot were all bloody from a wound caused by a booby trap in the hedgerow. I was instantly sad that I was losing another friend I had come to trust and rely on. Now I had to go retrieve my helmet and strobe light.

Covert Operation

When we first arrived in Tay Ninh, our company was assigned to a hooch that had 50 cots set up in it. Each platoon was given a section of the hooch and it was our responsibility to keep it clean. I took my duffel bag and shoved it under one of the cots and spread my poncho liner on top. Ray located his cot to my right and Bruns was on my left.

Marquez had us meet out in front of the barracks and we walked down to the armory where we would store our weapons as long as we were in Tay Ninh. This was a point of contention with the men due to the fact that Tay Ninh had been overrun just a month before our arrival. What were we supposed to do if Charlie decided to run through Tay Ninh again? What the brass didn't know was that all of us had several hand grenades stashed in our duffel bags. Marquez was the one that told us to do this so that we would not be complete without a way to defend ourselves.

One nice thing about being in Tay Ninh was that they had a PX and a mess hall. This was the first time I had eaten in a mess hall since coming to the field in August. None of us complained about getting three hots and a cot. Nobody was sure what our assignment was going to be and SFC Marquez told us to stay in the company area.

One of the first things I did was to go to the barbershop for a haircut. Out in the field, our barber was a shammer named Percy Allen. He had been slightly wounded twice and appointed himself as the company barber so that he didn't have to go on any more missions outside the wire. When I walked into the barbershop, I was surprised to see that all the barbers were Vietnamese.

There were four barber chairs and a few chairs against the wall creating a waiting area. There were two Vietnamese kids with shoeshine kits that rushed me as soon as I entered the shop. One of the barbers waved me over to his empty chair and as soon as I sat down, the kids started shining my boots. This seemed like a waste of time to me because after being out in the bush for a day, they would go back to looking like a pair of worn-out combat boots. The barber did a nice job on my haircut and even sprinkled some bay rum on his hands and ran his fingers through my hair. I gave the barber five dollars of MPC and gave each of the shoeshine boys a dollar.

When I returned to the company area, Marquez was telling the guys that while we were in Tay Ninh, we could go to supply and exchange any worn-out fatigues or boots for new ones. He also told us that we should stock up on more socks. The three-quarter-ton mess truck pulled up in front of our hooch and unloaded two sundry packs and three washtubs full of iced cold beer and sodas. Things were looking up. Big Joe, in his infinite wisdom, said, "I hope Lamere doesn't try to shoot any helicopters down while we're here!" We were just getting settled in when Sugar Bear came by and told us that Marquez wanted the second platoon to assemble at the CP.

When we got there, Marquez informed us that the second platoon was going to meet up with a Green Beret and his Montagnard mercenaries and join them in a top-secret mission into Cambodia. He said it had to do with an underground hospital. A voice from behind me said, "what the hell?" All of us looked at each other with blank faces and wondered what this mission was all about. Finally, we were told to be at the helicopter pad at 0800 hrs.

We were also told that no one was to leave the company area and that at 0600 hrs. we were to go to the armory and draw our weapons. In addition, we were to carry three days' worth of C rations. That evening while we sat around playing cards, everybody tried to guess what we were about to get ourselves into. We never in our wildest dreams thought that we would be going into Cambodia to locate an underground hospital operated by the NVA.

Around 1900 hrs., Marquez came into the barracks and asked us all to remove our dog tags and any other form of identification that could tie us to the U.S. Army. He told us that we would be going on a clandestine mission into Cambodia and if we were captured, the U.S. government would disavow us and deny ever being there. This all had to do with President Johnson's policy of not invading Cambodia. Secretary of State Henry Kissinger had promised the Cambodians we would not bring them into the Vietnam War.

One of the newer guys asked Marquez what we should do if we were captured. Marquez snapped back, "what in da god damn hell is wrong with you, you sonny beach? You don't get captured, dumb ass." That caused an uproar of laughter and Ray said, "Yeah, you dumb ass." Marquez actually had a smile on his face when he asked if there were any questions and somebody asked, "how are we supposed to work with the Montagnards?" Marquez said the Green Beret would explain everything to us tomorrow.

The Montagnards are tribal groups. There are over 20 tribes that wander the mountains of South East Asia. Seven of the tribes are indigenous to South Vietnam. They are primarily nomadic people who hunt with crossbows. They were enlisted by the French to fight the NVA and Viet Cong. From that time on, the Vietnamese tried to exterminate the yards. The Green Berets befriended the yards in 1962 and taught them how to use modern weaponry. They fought beside the Green Berets; many giving their lives. The rest of the evening was spent packing our gear and making sure that everyone had plenty of hand grenades and ammo.

Cambodian Expedition

The next morning at 0830 hrs., we loaded up on choppers and took off in the direction of Cambodia. The door gunner told us they had not received any information about any enemy activity in the area of our landing zone. We were told we would be dropped off at a designated location about a quarter of a klick from the border and then walk into the jungle and meet up with the Green Beret.

As we got closer to our drop-off point, I could tell by the looks on everyone's faces those guys were getting very nervous. Grimm was fidgeting with the sling on his rifle while Galli kept taking his helmet off and putting it back on. Naso and Chris had their heads bowed and their eyes closed, and I assumed they were praying to their God for protection. I hadn't realized it, but I was grasping the St. Christopher medal hanging around my neck. My mother had given it to me with instructions to pray to St. Christopher if I ever found myself in danger.

Considering where I was, I should be praying 24/7. After being in Vietnam for six months, I wasn't sure that God even existed. I had said so many prayers during firefights and still, guys were wounded and killed. Lately, I had wondered if God even showed up to those gunfights.

We landed without a hitch and quickly spread out and started our march to meet up with the Green Beret. Big Joe was walking point with Tommy Kemp and Brogan following close behind. They kept up a steady pace, knowing that we had to meet up with the Green Beret at 1000 hrs. At about 0950 hrs., Big Joe spotted a bunker with fresh dirt lying in front of it. He signaled with his hand for everyone to stop and get down.

Joe crawled up as close as he could to see if there were any occupants in the bunker. He took a grenade, pulled the pin and tossed it into the bunker. Right after the explosion, Joe jumped up, raising his rifle, ready to shoot. He took four steps backward and his heel got caught in a tripwire, setting off a booby trap. Joe was blown to the ground. Kemp and Brogan yelled that they had been hit by shrapnel from the explosion.

Everybody was lying flat on the ground, wondering if we had been ambushed. Within a minute, the word came back that Big Joe had tripped a booby trap. Ray, who was standing behind me, said, "I wish I could find one of those booby traps and get my million-dollar wound." I replied, "no such luck." We moved up and formed a semicircle around our wounded buddies setting up a defensive position.

Our RTO informed us that he had just received a call from the Green Beret and that they were located a hundred yards to our front. He said they were moving to our position and telling everybody not to shoot. Doc was busy working on Joe, and a couple of the other guys were helping Kemp and Brogan. In a couple of minutes, we could see a tall figure emerging from the jungle, followed by what looked like a bunch of midgets. Doc told Joe that a medevac was on the way and congratulated him on getting a million-dollar wound.

When the Green Beret got close to our position, Big Joe looked up at him and said, "Igene, what the hell are you doing here?" The 6 ft. 7 in. Green Beret looked at Joe and said, "it's a small world, isn't it, Joe?" As it turned out, Igene Johnson was Joe's childhood friend in Oden, Indiana. They chatted with each other until the medevac arrived and Igene picked Joe up and loaded him on the chopper. I helped Kemp and Russ helped Brogan.

When Kemp saw Joe he smiled and said, "thanks, Big Joe, for tripping that booby trap and getting me out of the field." Johnson looked at Joe and said, "say hello to your mom for me the next time you write her." Joe gave him a big thumbs up and the medevac lifted off and headed back to Cu Chi. I hadn't been paying any attention but suddenly, I realized the yards (as Johnson referred to them) had disappeared.

I asked Johnson where the mercenaries had gone, and he told me they had set up a defensive perimeter around our location. He said, "Don't worry boys, from here on out, my yards are going to take good care of you." This mission was already turning out to be a giant shit show. Johnson said we were going into Cambodia to locate an underground NVA Hospital. He said it would take a day and a half to get there. He also assured us that he had complete control over the area, as it was his backyard. He and his little group of midget warriors had been working the area for three months.

Once again, he assured us it would be a walk in the park. There were now 11 of us and 12 yards that walked into Cambodia that afternoon. It appeared our mission had started out as a giant cluster. I told Ray and Russ I had a bad feeling about going into Cambodia. I didn't want to get killed or wounded in a place the Army would not come to rescue us. Hell, they would not even acknowledge we were there!

We were all nervous about the yards as well. We knew they were headhunters and got paid $50 for each pair of ears they brought back. Did GI ears count? Johnson walked point with two of his yards and it was all we could do to keep up with them. The Montagnards walked on our right and left flanks. Sometimes you would see them and sometimes, they would disappear into the jungle. I could only speak for myself, but fear started to crawl up my spine.

We were completely out of our element and not sure what to do in case we made contact. I just kept thinking of Johnson's last words, "my yards are going to take good care of you boys." I guess we would soon find out. About four hours into our trek, we stopped to take a break and eat. I was getting ready to send a couple of the guys out to guard our flanks when Johnson told me not to bother.

He said his yards would take care of our security. Just as I opened a can of beanie weenies, I could smell smoke wafting past my nose. I looked to my left and saw three of the yards cooking rice over an open fire. I thought to myself, what in the hell is going on. I didn't realize that this was how the Montagnards operated.

We carried C rations and they carried pots and pans and rice and fish heads. After half an hour, we buried our trash and got ready to head out. Smokes came up to me and asked me what I thought of the mission so far. I told him I just hoped we didn't walk into an ambush and get our shit blown away. We continued to walk until the sun went down.

Mosquito Nets And Sampans

Johnson told us that we would be spending the night near a small river and that the yards would set up our ambush site. He also told us not to wander around at night because his guys would be setting up booby traps around our location. The yards set up mosquito netting for each of us to sleep under. None of us had to stand guard and our only job that night was to get a good night's sleep.

It certainly seemed that Johnson was right when he said, "they'll take good care of you boys." I'm not sure why but I was beginning to feel like I was in a safe place. It was the first time since stepping foot in Vietnam. I was somewhere between nodding out and sleep when suddenly a single gunshot broke the eerie silence. I jumped up so quickly I got tangled up and fell down in the mosquito netting that I forgot I was sleeping under.

Before anyone could react, the calm voice of Johnson said, "Everyone, stay where you're at, everything is ok, go back to sleep." I didn't know about the rest of the guys but Bruns and I sat back-to-back with our weapons locked and loaded.

At daybreak, we watched as the yards collected the booby traps that they had set up around our location. They also came and collected the mosquito netting they had set up for us. Once again, you could smell the smoke coming from where the yards were cooking their breakfast. Johnson came walking around and told us to eat our C rations and be ready to move out in 20 minutes.

216

When we were lined up and ready to go, Johnson told us he was going to walk us by the dead gook that had been killed last night. He told us it was an old papa san who was hauling a 51-cal. machine gun down a small tributary in a sampan. As I passed the body, I noticed the yards had completely destroyed the sampan and apparently dropped the machine gun into the water.

For his trouble, the old papa-san got a bullet right between his eyes. The way he was lying in the grass, you could see the back of his skull was missing and his brains were scattered in the grass. Johnson told us he knew about the old papa-san moving weapons for the NVA and was just waiting for the chance to blow him away.

For a couple of the new guys, this was the first dead body they had seen. It brings the reality of war into perfect focus and once again, every man thought to himself, better him than me. We had been humping for about four hours when Johnson brought us to a halt and told us to take a knee and face out to our right and left.

Johnson told us the NVA usually set booby traps in areas of approach to their compounds or, in this case, their underground hospital. He had his yards take a bamboo stick about four feet long and attach three sandbags full of rocks and dirt to it. The yards then attached a rope to the stick. What happened next was as close to genius as I'd ever seen. The yards tied the rope around their waist and lined up next to each other.

They took off on a dead run pulling the bags behind them. They were trying to explode any booby traps that might be in our path. They repeated this procedure several more times, exploding five booby traps. After that, we proceeded on our way to the objective. Johnson came back and told me to grab Bruns, Ray and Rambo and follow him. He told us that we were going to go with him and see if we could find the hospital. He said he thought we were very close.

Along with three of his mercenaries, we walked due north being careful not to make any noise. We've been walking for about 15 minutes when suddenly Johnson raised his right hand and knelt down. This was our sign to stop, get down, and keep our eyes and ears open. After a minute or so, we resumed walking for another 5 minutes. It was when we came upon a large area where the jungle thinned out. He led us down into what appeared to be a large bomb crater and when we reached the bottom, we saw a large opening that led underground.

We walked through the opening and we emerged into a very large underground structure. There were electric light bulbs hanging from the ceiling and we could make out large numbers of cots and some nurses dressed in white coats attending to the wounded not a hundred feet from where we were standing.

We had just entered an emergency exit at the end of the hospital. I looked at Bruns and we both had a look of disbelief on our faces. We couldn't believe what we were seeing. I kept thinking, what if somebody sees us and sounds an alarm. After about five minutes, Johnson signaled for us to head out the way we came in. We climbed up and out of the crater and headed back to where the rest of the guys were waiting. I still could not believe that we had found an underground hospital.

Johnson called in the coordinates of the hospital to his Special Forces Outpost. Ray asked him if he was going to call in an artillery strike and he replied, "no, we don't shoot hospitals, we just want to know where they are located." On the march back to the Vietnam border, we passed by the location where the old papa San had been killed the night before. His body was still lying in the grass and his face looked gray and chalky. His stomach had started bloating, making him look like he was six months pregnant.

We walked another half a klick and set up our ambush site for the night. It was an exact redo of the night before. The yards set up mosquito netting for each of us to sleep under and then set booby traps all around us. Johnson told us it should be a quiet night and that he did not expect anything unusual to happen.

I remember laying there staring up at the stars and remembering when I was a young child laying in my backyard on a blanket, thinking the stars were close enough to reach up and grab. As soon as the sun came up, the yards broke out their pots and pans and started cooking their rice and fish. The yards had set fish traps in the nearby river and when they retrieved them, there were dozens of small fish inside of them. These yards definitely knew how to live off the land. I noticed that Johnson squatted with some of the yards and ate what they were cooking. He was scooping the food out of the bowls with his fingers while he talked and laughed with these little warriors. It must've taken a lot of trust for him to put his life in their hands.

Johnson was also responsible for paying the mercenaries each month when they returned to a Green Beret outpost. I wasn't sure what they would spend their money on but nonetheless, they were highly honored by the tribal people. We spent the rest of that day marching back towards the border and word came back that we would be at the exit point around 1700 hrs. Johnson and his mercenaries would wait at the jungle's edge as security. The choppers would arrive, and we would purple out of there and return to Tay Ninh. The term purple out came from throwing purple smoke grenades where you wanted the helicopters to land when picking you up.

It was common to hear one of the guys say, "let's purple out of this bad place." In order to accomplish the extraction, we had to move out of the jungle into a clearing and position ourselves in groups of five and wait for the helicopters to arrive. This always made us feel like we were sitting ducks. If Charlie was in

219

the area, he might decide to hit us while loading up on the Hueys. Today we were in luck and we all loaded up without incident. We lifted off and headed back to Tay Ninh.

When I looked back at the jungle's edge, I saw Johnson and his 12 mercenaries disappearing back into the jungle. I couldn't help but wonder if Johnson would survive his fourth tour in Vietnam. When we got back to our platoon area, we started telling the guys what we had seen. Most of the guys thought we were bull shitting them. The next morning the guys that had gone on the Cambodian expedition were told to meet at the company CP.

When we got there, the CO and a couple of the officers from Battalion in Cu Chi started asking us all kinds of questions about our mission. They were holding clipboards and making copious notes on everything we said. They told us they considered our mission to be a complete success and reminded us we should keep the details of our mission to ourselves. No letters home to tell of our escapades. I guess that's the way life is when you're a covert operator.

The CO And The Donut Dolly

Pound for pound crazy Larry Lamere was the best M-60 gunner in our unit and maybe the Army. His acts of bravery or craziness, (depending on who you talked to) were well renowned. No one ever questioned his ability and willingness to do his job under any and all circumstances. I personally witnessed several acts of courage that were beyond my understanding.

There was no telling how many lives he had saved since joining the platoon. In all of God's creation, personality has to be one of His greatest gifts. Larry had an unusual personality to those that did not know him well. Larry was a little anti-social and kept to himself and was a lover of science fiction books. While everyone else was reading a Playboy magazine, Larry had his nose stuck in the latest science fiction paperback.

I remember him reading authors like Arthur C. Clark, Philip Dick, Isaac Asimov, Robert Heinlein, Frank Herbert and HG Wells. As a matter of fact, Larry introduced me to science fiction by giving me a book titled "The Greks Bring Gifts" by Murray Leinster. I read that book three times and sent it home for safekeeping. I didn't become a sci-fi junkie, but I understood why Larry seemed way out in front of the rest of us.

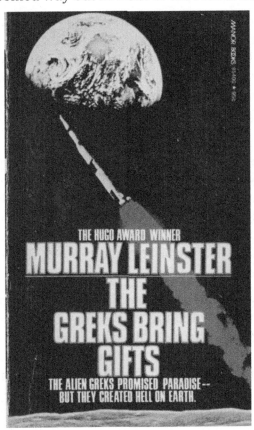

I remember sitting close enough to Larry with fondness to catch the fragrance of his cherry blend or borgam riff pipe tobacco burning in his pipe. He may have been one of the most well-adjusted men in my platoon! That being said, Larry also had a problem with authority, especially when it was doled out with impunity. Larry's nemesis was our CO Captain Sherwood.

The CO liked to pick on Larry because he was a loner. On several occasions, Larry would be chosen by the CO for some crap duty just to get his goat. This all came to a head the day the CO came out to Reed to promote Larry to E-5. Nobody deserved it more and nobody worked harder for it.

Sherwood walked up to Larry and held the new sergeant's stripes and orders up in the air and said, "Lamere, I want you to burn the shit cans in the latrine right after I pin these stripes on you." Lamere, without hesitation, said, "I'm not going to do that sir." Sherwood gave Lamere one more chance to comply before tearing up the orders and stuffing the chevrons back into his pocket.

Seething, Larry did an about-face and walked back to his bunker, saying something under his breath. Sherwood walked away with an evil grin on his face and started walking towards a donut dolly that had just arrived to mingle with the troops. I was taking pictures of some of the guys when I glanced over at Lamere and he had an M-16 pulled into his shoulder, getting ready to shoot.

I quickly looked in the direction of his aim and saw Captain Sherwood standing talking to the donut dolly with his back turned towards Larry. Holy shit, Lamere was going to assassinate the CO. Just before pulling the trigger, the donut dolly walked around behind the CO between him and Lamere. In an instant, Larry dropped the rifle and turned and put it back on the bunker. I quickly snapped a picture of Sherwood and the donut dolly and sent it home for safekeeping. Did I mention just another day in paradise?

Bob Hope Show, 1968

Joey Heatherton

Jerry Colonna & Bob Hope

Puddle Jumpers

Bob Segers Cobra Pilot

Rubber Plantation Tree

Chapter Thirteen
MY WORST NIGHTMARE
JANUARY 26, 1969

After new year's, we went to a place called Jackson FSB, and there was a new replacement there waiting to join our platoon. His name was John Boyle, and he told me his hometown was Boise. Idaho. I told him he would be joining my squad and that I was going to have him carry the M-79 grenade launcher left behind when Buck had gotten wounded in a bar brawl between Delta Company and Charlie Company back in Cu Chi.

Buck had sustained a million-dollar wound when he raised his hand to avoid being hit in the face with a beer bottle. The glass had sliced through a tendon, leaving him unfit for duty. Ray had commented, "some guys have all the luck; I wish I could get one of those and get the hell out of here." Boyle and I had a lot in common.

We lived with our dads when we both got drafted and dropped out of college, resulting in our landing in Vietnam. We both played in high school sports and we both liked to hunt. Our dads had taken us hunting since we were small boys and we both loved shooting guns. He was a bright kid that wanted to learn as much as he could as fast as he could.

I decided to take him under my wing. We spent a lot of time together and I told him about the firefights we had been in and about the guys killed and wounded. He caught on fast and realized he had joined a unit that had experienced a lot of combat. The first week he was with us he received a care package from his dad that included homemade elk jerky. It was some of the best I had ever tasted. I knew right then this was a kid I would grow fond of. When we went on day marches and ambush patrols, I kept Boyle close to me.

I was impressed when he found a tripwire attached to a booby trap his first week in the field. We had been on half a dozen ambush patrols without incident and the only real action he experienced was when a sniper pinned us down a klick outside the base. I was feeling pretty good about the lack of action and wondered if this was the beginning of a slowdown of VC activity in the area.

On January 25, Marquez told us we were going to do a day sweep outside Jackson about 2 klicks from the base. He said we would be going by a graveyard and that we would be returning there that evening to set up an ambush. The graveyard was located outside a large village surrounded by rice paddies. We really weren't expecting anything out of the normal but then again, what is normal? The day sweep went without incident.

When we got to the graveyard, we stopped, and Marquez told us to look around because this is where we would be setting up tonight. We stayed there and ate lunch and then proceeded into the village to have a look around. There was the usual hustle and bustle of village life with kids running up to us, pulling on our pant legs begging for candy.

One thing that did look out of place was a dozen young beautiful Vietnamese girls dressed up in fancy dresses and bonnets standing in the village square. I had never seen anything like this since being in Vietnam. I had our Kit Carson Scout Pete go over and ask them what they were doing.

He came back and said they were here for the NVA soldiers. The hair on the back of my neck stood straight up. This was one of those times the fight or flight reaction rattles around your skull. It took only a second to realize we had walked into an NVA R&R village.

I told Marquez what Pete had said and he immediately radioed to Battalion and they said they were sending an ARVN interpreter to our location ASAP. We were told to remain where we were and be prepared for contact. This put everyone on high alert. We took up positions sitting next to hooches that surrounded the village square. Pete had rounded up the ladies and had them waiting in the hooch where Boyle and I were sitting out front.

Doc came over and went into the hooch to see if the ladies would be willing to accommodate any of the GIs. Doc always had the guy's best interest at heart! After about 15 minutes, Doc emerged out of the hooch, pulling up his fly. Within 10 minutes of Marquez's radio call, a chopper set down right outside the village. An ARVN Ranger, along with his cadre, emerged in their skin-tight fatigues and chrome-plated 45 cal. pistols.

It seemed to me that we'd seen this movie before. They walked up to Marquez and Pete and exchanged pleasantries before they swooped down on the 12 ladies waiting in the hooch. I walked into the hooch with the Ranger and he immediately started yelling at the girls. Several of them started to cry and I had to assume they told him what they had told Pete.

226

The Ranger stormed out of the hooch and looked around until he spotted an old papa-san with a long white beard sitting under a palm tree, minding his own business. He marched straight away to the old man and when he got to him, he reached down and jerked him to his feet. We were stunned at what we were witnessing.

This was a really old man and the Ranger was screaming in his face and holding his pistol up to the old man's ear. At one point, he stuck the barrel of his pistol in the old man's mouth and jacked a round into the chamber. I could only imagine he was threatening to blow the old guy's brain out. The old man was whimpering with tears falling off his cheeks.

Several village women were spitting on the ground and crying for mercy for the old-timer. I asked Pete what was going on and he told me the Ranger wanted to know where the NVA were located. This went on for 10 minutes until suddenly the Ranger barked at one of his men to bring him a canteen.

The Ranger pushed the old man to the ground and made him lay face up in the scorching sun. He removed his bandanna that he wore around his neck and covered the old man's face with it. He took the canteen and poured water onto the bandanna. This created an airtight seal over the man's nose and mouth, suffocating him. The old man's body was flopping around like a fish out of water. Big Joe, right on cue, said, "isn't that against the Geneva Convention!" I thought I'd seen everything until now.

I knew this was downright cruel and unusual punishment for any human being. He removed the bandanna and let the old man regain his breath and proceeded with the interrogation. The papa-san had no information to offer so the Ranger repeated the process two more times before slapping the man silly, leaving him in the fetal position on the ground.

227

The Ranger talked to Marquez and returned to his chopper, where he and his merry men lifted off headed back to Saigon. Within minutes Marquez told us to saddle up and we hastily removed ourselves from the area. Boyle asked me if what we had seen was normal and I told him it was not. I said, usually the Ranger will throw the man out of a chopper at 500 ft. or electrocute his nuts off!

That was the end of that conversation. We walked about a quarter of a klick to the west and found a hedgerow where we could hide until dark. You would think this would be a good time to catch some zzzz's but that was impossible. You would sit or lie in the hedgerow and keep up a constant rhythm of slapping insects as they tried to devour your face. If that wasn't bad enough, you sat and stewed in your own sweat.

Marquez came to where Ray and I were sitting and told us the Ranger thought there was at least a Company of NVA or VC somewhere close to the village. He laughed and said, "those sonny beaches aren't going too far from da pussy!" We ate another box of C's just as the sun was going down and prepared to march back to our ambush sight. About halfway there, I felt my foot hang up in a tripwire. I jumped 3 feet in the air and 10 feet to my front when I heard a "pop."

Everyone behind me heard it and took a knee. I had hit a tripwire attached to an old dud chi com potato masher grenade. My heart didn't stop racing until we reached our destination. I had truly dodged a bullet, or should I say a booby trap. We set up an L-shaped ambush with rear security. My squad set up behind a dike facing the village across the rice paddies. Ray's squad was 90 degrees to our left. O'Grady and his RTO and one rifleman were our rear security.

My squad had the starlight scope. I placed Lamere and his machine gun right where the two dikes intercepted. If anyone came walking down the dike towards us, he would have a straight shot at them. His ammo bearer was next to him, then me, and then Boyle and Jack Slovey were on the far right. I told Boyle to give me his claymore and that I was going to set them on the dike to our front facing towards the village. I had to climb over the berm and walk in the water to where I was going to place the claymores.

They were about 75 ft. directly in front of Lamere. When I returned, I connected the magnetos and checked their conductivity and put them on safe. I took the LAWS rocket I was carrying and extended the tube until I heard the cocking mechanism engage, then I put on the safety. I laid it on the berm in front of me, along with two parachute flares. I turned to Boyle and told him to get a dozen buckshot rounds out of his rucksack and lay them on top of the berm in front of him. I said, "you better get a couple parachute flare rounds out just in case."

Within 15 minutes, we were ready to start our guard rotation. Lamere would be first and then pass the watch and starlight scope to his right. It felt really spooky setting up on the edge of a graveyard but at least it was dry ground. The old guys would tell the new guys stories about voices being heard and shadows moving around in the dark when they set up in graveyards.

It scared the hell out of me when I was a new guy! Willy told me that the platoon had set up in a graveyard and a bunch of VC walked into them. That night, our mess sergeant and one of his cooks came out on the chopper to serve hot chow and ended up staying with the platoon. Hill had mentioned to Willy that cooks rarely got the chance to kill VC.

The firefight that followed destroyed many of the grave markers. Willy said the markers were good to take cover behind. The last thing I said to Boyle was, "if we pop this ambush, get up and get your duper going as fast as you can." He said, "will do."

By this time in my tour, I couldn't really sleep on ambushes. I closed my eyes and saw stick men running across my mind.

However, my ears would be perked up like a Doberman Pinscher. You can't believe the strange sounds you hear or think you hear when you are lying out in a rice paddy in the dark. And oh yes, did I mention the mosquitoes? I was sitting with my back to the berm chasing little stick men around in my mind when Lamere's ammo bearer tapped me on the shoulder and said, "I think I see something." This happens at least a dozen times a night. I said, "give me the starlight." I put it up to my eye and looked in the direction of the village.

My whole body stiffened, and I tapped Boyle and said, "get everyone up and ready." What I saw made my blood turn to ice. There was a large group of VC soldiers standing at the end of the berm that led to our position. As I swung the scope to the left, I saw three VC point men walking down the berm about 100 ft. from our claymores. I whispered to Boyle, "get ready to shoot," then put the starlight scope on the ground, waited until the gooks were 10 feet from the claymores and then squeezed the two magnetos that I had grabbed off the top of the berm.

Within an instant, both claymores exploded and inside the flash, I saw 3 bodies flying in the air as if they were in slow motion. The front point man was flying upside down off the berm. A burst from his AK hit the top of the berm in front of me. The dirt hit me directly in the eyes, making it impossible to see. Lamere was shooting directly down the berm and Ray's squad was shooting with everything they had. I wiped the dirt from my eyes and immediately grabbed a parachute flare and popped it out in front of our position.

When the flare lit up, I could not see any of the VC that was walking point. I vaguely saw a lot of movement by the village but could not tell what they were doing. The noise from Lamere's machine gun was splitting my eardrums and when the first flare fizzled out, I popped the second flare out to our front. I noticed Boyle was slumped behind the berm next to me and I assumed he was scared to death in his first firefight. I reached over and grabbed his shoulder and shook him and I heard the distinct sound of a death rattle escaping his lungs.

Slovey heard it too and said, "oh Christ no" and when we pulled him away from the berm, I saw the bullet hole in his forehead. At that exact instant, an illumination flare delivered from a 155-artillery gun at Jackson popped out a way in front of us towards the village.

Slovey was dragging Boyle away from the berm behind me and I could see a large group of VC running back and forth at the end of the dike. I grabbed the LAWS rocket, took it off safety, and took the best aim I could and fired it towards them. I felt an instant shock in my legs like a thousand needles sticking me. Slovey let out a scream and I suddenly realized he was directly behind me in the backblast area when the LAWS went off. My legs had been stretched out behind me so I could get a three-point stance to shoot the LAWS.

My legs were caught in the backblast area as well. Neither one of us could make it to our feet. After the rocket exploded near the VC infantrymen, they disappeared into the village. I suspect they were deciding on whether to storm our position or not. I hoped the LAWS helped them make up their minds.

Everything got confusing after that. Ray came over and told me a medevac was on its way. I sat next to the berm and watched guys walking through the rice paddy to my front, looking for gook bodies. The lead point man that shot at me and killed Boyle was dragged up into the graveyard DOA.

When the medevac sat down, Ray came and got me and lifted me onto the floor of the chopper next to another soldier. As I lay on the floor, I remember the flashing red light on top of the ship. I remember the feeling of the chopper lifting off and wished I was with the rest of the guys. They were a bunch of brave men for sure.

On the way to Cu Chi, I turned my head to the side and was looking directly into the lifeless eyes of John Boyle. I started crying and realized the last thing I told him was "get up and start shooting when I pop the AP." In the pit of my stomach, I felt a horrible guilt and said, "I'm so sorry John."

I would never get the look in his eyes out of my head as long as I lived. The following day Ray visited me at the hospital and told me that they had taken a spent round out of Boyle's M-79. He had followed my orders exactly and now he was dead. A reporter from the Tropic Lightning news came to the hospital and asked me what had happened that night. His article showed up in the next week's issue.

The Fog Of War

. One of the guys who came into the platoon about the same time I did was a guy named Rickey Fowler. He was about 5 ft. 4 in. and weighed 99 pounds soaking wet. You could always find Rickey hanging out with Big Joe. New guys tended to hang out with guys that had been there for a while, hoping they could learn how to survive Vietnam.

One night we popped an ambush next to a Buddhist temple and during the firefight Fowler started screaming that he couldn't move his legs. We assumed he had been shot. His screaming was so loud that he was giving our position away. We took two incoming RPG rounds before Joe put his hand over Rickey's mouth. A medevac was called in and they flew Fowler to the 12th Evac hospital in Cu Chi.

The next morning when we arrived back at the fire support base, everybody was talking about how awful it was that Rickey had gotten wounded. The rest of the day, we sat around cleaning our weapons, writing letters to our girlfriends or family, and playing cards with our buddies.

Like clockwork, we saw the dust rising from the road where the supply truck was rumbling down from Cu Chi. This was the time of the day that everyone got excited because we knew the supply truck would be bringing beer and soda and a mailbag filled with letters and packages from home. Several of the guys started walking over to the CP bunker.

Much to our amazement Rickey Fowler jumped off the back of the deuce and a half and walked over to the platoon area. Ray looked at me and said, "didn't Fowler get dusted off last night?" I replied, "yeah I thought he was paralyzed after being shot." We looked at each other and shook our heads and said, "it don't mean nothin'." Fowler retrieved his weapon and his gear and returned to his bunker without saying a word.

A couple of the guys went over to Fowler's bunker to find out what had happened and Big Joe said, "give the guy a break, he got scared and froze up." A couple of weeks later, we made contact in the iron triangle and during the battle, Fowler started screaming his head off and tried to crawl under Big Joe. A medevac chopper came in and a couple of guys loaded Rickey up for another ride to Cu Chi.

The next morning a couple of the guys asked Big Joe if Fowler was wounded or if he just had another panic attack. Joe just shrugged his shoulders and said, "I don't know what the hell happened." It was like déjà vu when Rickey arrived back at the fire support base in a couple of days. He was acting really weird and stayed in his bunker and wouldn't come out to go to chow or talk to anybody.

Another incident occurred a couple of months later when Fowler jumped onto the medevac after Hannah was killed and two of our guys that were wounded were placed on board. Nobody knew whether Rickey was wounded or if he just broke down under pressure. A couple of days later, Fowler went on R&R to Bangkok.

While he was gone, several of us approached Glover and told him we were concerned that Fowler was not only a danger to himself, but to us as well. Glover agreed and said he was working on getting Rickey a job back in Cu Chi. When Rickey got back from R&R, he was very eager to show us his new tattoo. He rolled up his sleeve and on his upper arm, there was a bunch of red roses in a beautiful bouquet.

From that day forward, Fowler was known as, "Rosy Rickey." In a couple of weeks Rickey loaded up on the supply truck and went back to his new job in Cu Chi. Shortly after he arrived, we heard he had left a loaded 45 cal. pistol in the armory, and Lee, the armory Sgt., blew his thumb off when testing the pistol's safety

Spurill Jumps Ship

Our M-60 machine gunner Spurill had been out in the field for about 9 months. He had come to us from another unit and we suspected it was for disciplinary reasons. Spurill was a redneck from Oklahoma and we gave him the nickname of Okie. He kept to himself and rarely started a conversation. He was in my squad and always responded quickly whenever we would make contact. He was one of the better machine gunners we had. After being with us for a couple of months, he started telling me that he was getting short and wanted to get off the line.

234

Every day he would tell me how he had a bad feeling about getting killed before going home. I tried to tell him that was just superstition but as each day went by the more nervous, he got. He was on the verge of paranoia. He asked SFC Marquez to get him off-line and Marquez told him he would have to wait his turn. Lt. O'Grady told us we were scheduled for an eagle flight the following morning. He said we would be flying to a place called the Parrots Beak. He said there was a village there suspected of harboring NVA soldiers and their supplies.

Our mission was to sweep the village and see if we could roust out any enemy and confiscate or destroy any supplies they may be hoarding there. After O'Grady left, the grumbling began. Guys were saying how much they hated sweeping villages because you could never tell where the enemy might be hiding.

There was also the issue of accidentally shooting civilians if a firefight ensued. Several of the guys said they had heard that the 101st airborne had gotten hammered just a week before near this village. I looked over at Spurill as he sat motionless, looking towards the Cambodian border. We called this the thousand-yard stare. It happened to guys that had seen too much heavy combat. I was beginning to think that Spurill was losing it and could not be counted on to do his job.

The next morning at 0800 hrs., the platoon loaded up on Huey helicopters and flew straightaway to the beak. I was sitting in my usual spot behind the pilot on the floor with my feet hanging out touching the struts. Spurill was sitting directly to my right in the first web seat. The door gunner gave us the two-minute warning that we were about to touchdown in our landing zone.

We were about 30 feet off the ground and approaching our drop zone when suddenly Spurill went flying by me and out the helicopter door. It happened so fast I couldn't react. I watched as he fell and landed feet first in the middle of a rice paddy. From what I could tell he had sunk into the mud up to his armpits.

When we landed, O'Grady sent a couple of guys back to get him. They had a hell of a time trying to pull him out of the mud. Spurill told us that he had jumped in hopes of breaking his legs so he could get out of the field. I think the official report stated that he had tripped preparing to exit the aircraft. Sending someone in for discipline meant paperwork and none of the powers to be wanted that.

When we entered the village, we noticed there were no kids running around or coming up to us begging for candy. This is a sure sign that Charlie was in the area. We went from hooch to hooch looking inside, usually finding a mama-san and her kids squatting in the corner. We did find a cache containing 300 lbs. of bagged rice. We stacked the bags up, layering it with C-4 explosives and before leaving, we blew the rice to kingdom come.

I think there was rice scattered for a mile around the village. We were all relieved that we had not made any contact and O'Grady was able to report that we had destroyed resources hidden by the NVA. Big Joe, in his infinite wisdom, said, "that's what I call digging in Charlie's mess kit!" In reality, what we had done was destroy the village's source of food.

We returned to the fire support base and got ready to pull bunker duty and line up at the mess tent for a hot meal. On the menu that evening was spaghetti with meat sauce, sliced French bread and butter, and soggy broccoli. The mess Sgt. even put out cartons of white milk along with some chocolate pudding for dessert. Life was always good when we got a hot meal. Spurill stayed to himself and didn't speak to anybody about jumping out of the helicopter. He hadn't even sprained an ankle.

A week later, he paid another soldier a hundred bucks to break his arm with a 2 by 4. He finally got his wish to get offline along with an article 15 and a $100 fine for the destruction of government property. It's so comforting to realize that we are all at least worth a hundred bucks in the eyes of our government.

On January 15, 1969, Ed Rambo left our platoon to catch his freedom flight home. Ed was one of the guys that took me under his wing when I first arrived in the platoon. We went through a lot of battles together and I knew I was going to miss him. He was one of my best friends and he even gave me his cousin's name and address to write to. Her name was Rose, and she had a 1-year-old daughter born out of wedlock. For the last 6 months, she and I had exchanged many sizzling fantasy letters and promised we would get married if I made it home. I knew it was a bunch of bull shit, but it was fun getting those letters.

Writing to girls in the world and carrying on long-distance love affairs was very common in Nam. It helped to keep our minds off the misery at hand. On several occasions, one of the guys would get a Dear John letter and I would be asked to write the girl to see if things could be patched up. I had a reputation for writing the best letters, I guess. On one of these occasions, the girl I was trying to convince to stay with one of the guys would end up writing me instead!

At my high watermark, I was writing to 4 women at the same time. Two of them wanted to get married and two promised to save themselves for me until I got home. Another advantage to having so many pen pals is that they would send care packages from time to time. The serious Dear John letters were the ones when a guy's wife divorced him to marry his best friend. This process was called "being Jody'd." Jody was the asshole at home that stepped in to take care of a guy's wife or girlfriend in his absence.

Many a soldier would arrive home to find his wife pregnant with someone else's baby. I usually stayed out of those situations because I knew there was no hope to fix those relationships. Guys would lose their minds when their wives pulled that bullshit. We had to keep a close eye on them to make sure they didn't hurt themselves or get us hurt.

On a few of these occasions, guys would get a leave to go home to finalize divorces or shoot the bastard that stole their wife. There was only one time I ever saw a guy return from one of these leaves. Mess Sergeant Hill went home, got divorced, and returned to duty within 2 weeks. Turned out he didn't want to get married in the first place and she always complained about his cooking!

The Strongest And The Weakest

We had a new guy from New York come into the platoon to replace Rambo, whose name was Chris. I knew from the day I met him that he was going to be a problem. He was a loner and presented himself as a tough guy from a tough neighborhood in New York. He made it known that if anyone messed around with him, he would cut them. For the guys that had been in the platoon for a while, this was all just tough-talking. We had a saying in Nam, "you can talk the talk, but can you walk the walk?" Chris was always telling stories about how he was involved with the mob and how he hung around with the wise guys.

One day I told Chris I didn't give a shit what he had done back in the world but that I was only interested in whether he could do his job when the shit hit the fan. He tried to hang around a couple of other guys from New York, but they didn't want to have anything to do with him. It didn't take him long to buy dope from the village kids and he spent a lot of time smoking weed in his bunker.

SFC Marquez told Chris he would not tolerate smoking dope in the field. Chris started giving him a ration of crap and Marquez had him transferred into a different company. Nobody was sorry to see him go. He was one of the crazy braves and phony tough, and guys like that couldn't be relied on to pull their own weight. One night our platoon was pulling bunker duty at Jackson fire support base. At 0100 hrs., we heard Claymore mines exploding in the distance, followed by AK-47 and M-16 fire. One of Delta company's ambush patrols had opened up on a group of Viet Cong.

Over the noise level of the ensuing battle, we could hear a voice screaming at the top of their lungs, "I'm hit, I'm hit, somebody, please help me, O God please somebody help." As soon as it started, the screaming stopped. The firefight lasted another 20 minutes until Cobra helicopters showed up and the VC disappeared into the night. The next morning when Delta Company returned, their platoon sergeant told SFC Marquez that the asshole he had transferred to Delta almost got everybody killed.

In the initial ambush, he told Marquez that Chris had been shot in the shoulder and started screaming bloody murder. He went on to tell Marquez that he had to stuff a sock in Chris's mouth so that he would not give their position away. When Marquez told us the story, most of us broke out in laughter and Big Joe, in his infinite wisdom, said, "I guess he wasn't so tough after all, he's lucky he didn't get his head blown off." Chris was never heard of again.

February 1969

In the first week of February, I got a note from our company clerk Gary Hunt that he had an R&R to Hong Kong that I was eligible for. He said all I would have to do is request it and he would cut orders and send them out to the field. I told Bruns and Ray that I was going to take it and wrote a letter to my dad requesting that he send me money. I wanted to buy a camera and some stereo equipment, and I heard from some of the guys that the Army would ship the stuff home for free.

Bruns told me he was waiting for an R&R to Hawaii so that he could meet his wife, Becky. Ray told me he had just gotten a note from Hunt telling him he had an R&R to Hong Kong as well. Ray told me he was going to take that one but wasn't sure when he would be leaving. This would be the first time I had been away from the unit since arriving in August 1968.

I was very anxious to get the time off and looked forward to a new adventure. There were all kinds of stories going around about guys going on R&R and hooking up with beautiful girls. Joel Brown even gave me the name of a hotel in Hong Kong named the Merlin. When I got to the hotel, he said I should just ask the desk clerk where to go to meet prostitutes.

In Hong Kong, prostitution is completely legal and is looked upon as just another business. I was told that all the prostitutes were required to get regular medical checkups and had to carry a medical card stating they did not have any venereal diseases. Joel told me he had a great time in Hong Kong and that the ladies were very congenial.

On February 15, I jumped on a helicopter in Cu Chi and flew to Saigon, where I would board a plane that would take me to Hong Kong. I remember digging my khaki uniform out of my duffel bag and having a hooch girl run it down to the Vietnamese

240

laundry in Buckeye, just outside the gate. I told her I wanted it washed and ironed.

I remember thinking I looked pretty good in khakis and had one of the supply guys take a Polaroid picture of me that I sent home to my mother. The flight to Hong Kong was uneventful and I remember looking out the window and thinking how crowded it looked in the city. It was hard to believe that millions of Chinese lived in such a small area.

When we landed, I followed the signs to the military check-in area. There was USO personnel to help us convert our money from U.S. dollars to whatever the Chinese money was called. Yen, I believe. After that, I went to a taxi stand, got into a taxi and told the driver I wanted to go to the Merlin Hotel. The driver spoke broken English and told me we would be there right away. We weaved in and out of bumper-to-bumper traffic and eventually arrived at the hotel.

My first mission was to take a shower and go down to the restaurant and have a huge steak with all the trimmings. They had a display case that featured steaks from all over the world. There was Australian, Japanese, and Canadian and of course, good old Montana USA beef. It had been over six months since I had that steak at the Oakland reception station, and I was so hungry I could have eaten the southbound end out of a northbound mule. I ordered a 24 oz Porterhouse-cooked medium and proceeded to eat myself into oblivion.

After dinner, I went to the front desk and asked the clerk where I could go to hook up with a lady of the evening. The clerk had a smile on his face and said, "go out the front door, turn right and go two blocks to the Black Dragon bar." It was 6 PM when I left the hotel and walked down the sidewalk. I was amazed at how many people were out and about. It was shocking to see all the neon lights up and down the main street advertising all the

241

clubs and specialty stores. I was surprised to see the huge Coca-Cola and Pepsi signs as far as the eye could see.

There were several signs that displayed different beer brands that I had never heard of before. Hong Kong was turning out to be a very exciting place. As I walked past a jewelry store, I saw an open-air meat market right next door. There were plucked chickens cut in half hanging from hooks drying in the open air. There were flies covering them and it seemed to me very disgusting. I could only imagine the eggs those flies were laying in the carcasses. I passed many different shops, including Tailor shops that would make you a custom suit at very reasonable prices.

Since I was in Hong Kong, I had decided I would have a sharkskin suit custom-made and send it home. I finally saw the blinking neon sign that marked the location of the Black Dragon Bar. When I entered the bar, it was very dark and there was live music playing. The dance floor was crowded with people trying to dance and before I could take two steps inside the door, an older Chinese lady walked up to me and put her arm around my waist and said, "what are you looking for, soldier?"

I guess the short hair and my nerdy clothes were a dead giveaway that I was a GI. I told her a friend of mine had recommended this bar to meet a nice lady for some fun and relaxation. She smiled and said, "you have come to the right place." She guided me over to the bar and asked me what kind of girl I was interested in. I told her this was my first time doing this, so I had no preconceived notions about what kind of girl I was looking for. She set me down at a small table and asked me what I wanted to drink.

She told me girls would come and sit at my table and I could see what was available. She told me the rule was that I had to buy each girl a drink while we talked. I ordered a coke and within 30 seconds, a beautiful Chinese girl sat down at my table.

When the waiter brought me my drink, they also brought the girl what looked like iced tea on the rocks. The waiter smiled and said, "that will be 20 bucks." I handed him $20 in Yen, and he bowed and turned away. The girl smiled at me and started speaking in broken English.

She asked me if I was looking for a girl to have a good time with. I said yes, but I was unsure how to approach the subject of having her spend the night with me at the hotel. I was new at this and was definitely not on solid footing. She said, "no problem, you want me to show you a good time?" I told her, yes, but I wanted to know how much it was going to cost.

She immediately raised her hand and got the older woman's attention who had seated me and came straight away to my table. She bent over and put her face next to mine and asked me if I wanted to take this girl for the night. I asked her how much it would cost me and she said $50. She said that the girl would take real good care of me and I would be very happy. She held out her hand, indicating that I would be paying her the money.

I handed the old lady the $50 and she stuffed it into her bra, smiled, turned around and walked back to the bar. I looked across the table at my date, her head was tilted down with a very demure look on her face. As we got up to leave, I said to her, "by the way, what is your name?" She smiled and said, "my name is Nancy Ting." I said, "nice to meet you, Nancy, my name is John." As we walked back to the Merlin, I couldn't help but wonder what it was going to be like to spend the night with such a gorgeous girl.

Nancy was very petite, measuring 5 feet tall with a perfectly proportioned body. She had long black hair that was very shiny and bounced nicely on her shoulders as we walked down the sidewalk. We didn't have much conversation and I wasn't sure what we would talk about given the circumstances of our meeting. We arrived at the hotel and the doorman looked directly at Nancy and nodded his head with a smile. It made me wonder if he had seen her on a regular basis.

By the time we got to the room, it was about 8 PM and I was looking forward to a night filled with passion. Upon entering the room, Nancy politely excused herself and said she was going to the bathroom. I sat down on the bed and within two minutes, Nancy emerged wearing a red see-through nightgown that came down mid-thigh. I was taken aback by how fast this whole situation was developing. I don't know what I thought was supposed to happen, but I wasn't prepared for this.

I thought maybe we would sit and talk about who knows what before getting down to the business at hand. Without hesitation, Nancy walked over to the bed and turned down the covers and looked at me and said, "why do you have your clothes on?" She then proceeded to the light switch flipping it down, immersing the room into semi-darkness. Only the light from the neon signs outside coming through the window was reflecting off the walls, and like a dumb ass, I sat at the bottom of the bed and started taking my clothes off.

I don't know why I was embarrassed, but I left my boxers on. My eyes adjusted and I saw that Nancy had crawled under the covers and was waiting for me. I slid in beside her and thought it would be nice if we made out for a while to get things warmed up. I lightly brushed her breast with my hand and lowered my face to hers, expecting to begin with a kiss. She quickly turned her face away and, in a stern voice, said, "I don't kiss."

I was taken aback by this and it completely threw me off guard. Here I was getting ready to screw her brains out and she told me she doesn't kiss! Then she snapped at me, "get your pants off." Without hesitation, she grabbed my manhood that was already standing at attention and said, "get on."

Before I could say a word, she pulled me on top of her and slid me inside in one fluid motion and began thrusting her hips, almost throwing me out of the saddle. Before I could say what the hell, it was over. My inexperience had failed me.

All the thoughts of a long-lasting night of passion were over in a matter of seconds. I rolled off and laid there, embarrassed at what had just occurred. I was already planning on how I would control myself during our next coitus. It was like striking out at the plate and as you walked back to the dugout, you already knew you would hit a home run the next time up.

Before those thoughts had completely crossed my mind, Nancy had bounded out of bed and went straight to the bathroom. In my naive mind, I thought she was going to clean up and come back to bed. I heard the water running in the sink for a couple of minutes and then shut off. The bathroom door opened and as the light cascaded out into the room, she walked out completely dressed, looked at me, and said, "thanks for the nice evening." She proceeded to the door, opened it, and stepped out, closing it behind her as she left.

As I sat on the edge of the bed, it suddenly occurred to me that I had gotten screwed without even getting a kiss! So much for a night filled with passion. I made up my mind that I would go back to the bar the next day and ask the madam if this was normal procedure.

As it turned out, the madam told me there had been many complaints about this girl and she had been fired. Just my luck. What would Big Joe have to say about this? The madam also told me unfortunately, there were no refunds and no do-overs. The rest of my time in Hong Kong was spent going to places like Kowloon, where I spent quite a bit of time riding the ferry boats and visiting all the specialty shops around the harbor.

I did make it to the Navy store, and I purchased a nice Akai tape recorder and some other stuff that I sent home. I paid a cab driver to take me to the New Territories where I could look into communist China. There wasn't much to see out there, but I thought everyone should experience that at least once in their life. I ate some great Chinese food and it got my mind off Vietnam.

I went to a movie house where they were playing an army movie. It turned out that the film was a communist propaganda movie showing the NVA destroying U.S. forces in Vietnam and pictures of POWs being paraded down a city street in Hanoi. I could only sit through 10 minutes of that bullshit and got up and left. I was so mad in my face; I could have beaten any man half my heavy and twice my old!

Unfortunately, my seven-day R&R was coming to an end and I dreaded knowing that I had to go back to what would turn out to be my worst nightmare. It was February 20 when I boarded the plane that would take me back to Saigon. The plane landed at Tan Son Nhut airbase at 1500 hrs., and I hopped on a C-130 cargo plane headed to Cu Chi. I hated flying in those rattle traps. I had to sit in a web seat and listen to the loud whining of the dual prop plane as it pulled itself off the ground and into the sky.

I was always unsettled as I looked around the interior and could see daylight streaming through the many bullet holes that had riddled the plane. It was raining when we landed at Cu Chi and I hooked a ride in a Jeep headed to Charlie Company.

When I arrived, I went directly to the Company Quonset and signed back in. It was too late to catch a chopper ride out to Diamond, so I went to the company supply room and picked up my gear. I slept in the company hooch and felt sorry for myself that I was back in this sorry-assed place. That night I was brought back to reality when illumination flares popped overhead. This was a standard operating procedure to help the guys on perimeter duty see if any gooks were trying to breach the wire.

Later it was learned that Charlie had a complex tunnel system that ran under the base. In the morning, I went with Gary Hunt, the company clerk, to the mess hall and had breakfast. Much to my surprise, I saw Doug, my buddy from the second platoon, serving food in the line. I briefly asked him how he was doing, and he told me his back was peppered with shrapnel and it would take a while to heal. I told him I hoped he never had to come back to the field or, as we referred to it, "that bad place." He gave me a big smile and said, "not if I can help it." That would be the last time I would see him. There was a supply chopper getting ready to go to Diamond, so I hopped on it and dreaded having to go back there.

Chinook bringing supplies

Chapter Fourteen
RESCUING THE LRRPS
FEBRUARY 4, 1969

I t was February 4th and our platoon was sitting out on the helicopter pad waiting to be called out as a reactionary force. We were assigned to do this a week at a time and usually, all we did was sit out in the sun and cook our brains. The battalion started this procedure as a way to get American forces on the ground in a quick hurry in the event another unit got overwhelmed. The helicopter pad at Jackson was located about 500 feet from the wire and as we sat on the helicopter pad, we could look out and see Vietnamese farmers starting to harvest their rice.

It was interesting to see the method used by ancient cultures involving cutting the rice plant off at the ground and stacking them into bundles and tying them together with a piece of palm frond. When the bundles dried, the mama-sans would take the bundles and thrash the heads against a screen causing the rice to separate from the plant and fall on a tarp located under the screen. It was labor-intensive but very efficient.

Other workers loaded the rice into baskets and hauled them off in water buffalo-drawn carts. Even the carts were old-school, including wooden wheels. They reminded me of watching an old Viking movie. Rice was the number one crop being raised in

248

Vietnam and supplied the population with their main source of food. Lifer, our mongrel dog, hated Vietnamese people and occasionally would run out to the field and bark at the workers.

It was funny watching the old farmers cursing at him and sometimes throwing a rock or two to scare him away. We couldn't help but wonder if the farmers working the fields by day were VC trying to kill us at night. Only a couple of weeks ago, we were sweeping through an area next to a rice paddy when we saw a kid leading a huge water buffalo with a cord tied to the ring in the buffalo's nose. Water buffalo love Vietnamese kids and hate GIs.

One of the knot heads behind me shot his weapon and the water buffalo took off on the dead run across the rice paddy with the kid in tow. It looked like the kid was barefoot waterskiing behind the beast, trying to get it to stop. The kid dropped his horn made out of a buffalo horn and I quickly trotted out there and picked it up. As soon as we returned to base, I sent it home for safekeeping.

Four of us were just in the middle of a good game of pinochle when we saw several crew chiefs running towards the helicopters. This can only mean one thing: we were about to take a ride. The crew chiefs would jump into the co-pilot seat and get the jet engine started to warm it up before the pilots showed up. In doing this, the pilots could take off immediately and not waste any time.

Everybody threw in their cards and Bruns neatly put them back into a deck and shoved them in his fatigue jacket pocket. The crew chief on our helicopter told us that there was an LRRP (long-range reconnaissance patrol) team pinned down by some NVA and they had taken one casualty. We all looked at each other and knew that the shit was about to hit the fan.

249

Within a few minutes, the pilots came running out from their shack and yelled at us to saddle up. We immediately loaded up and took our positions, preparing to take off. Whenever we knew we were flying into a hot LZ, we would sit in silence, wondering what lay ahead of us?

One thing was for sure we knew it wasn't good and more than likely, some of us would get hurt or killed. I looked over at Bill Thompson and saw him bow his head and mouth a prayer or two. Bill came from a very religious family and his father was a preacher in the Antioch Baptist Church. Bill was a redhead with very little to say but was a hell of a good pinochle player. I guess it's all right if they play cards in the Baptist Church.

As the helicopter broke loose from the earth's gravity, I knew that every man on that helicopter was thinking of their dear/loved ones. It was just one of the things we did when we knew it might be our last eagle flight. Our objective was once we arrived at our designated landing zone, we would form up and fight our way into the overgrowth where the LRRP team was pinned down. We didn't know at the time that we would be going up against a company-sized unit of NVA regulars armed with RPGs and machine guns.

As we approached the landing zone, we flew over the firefight and could see smoke coming from where RPG rounds had exploded. As the helicopters banked sharply to the left, we started taking AK-47 fire directly below us. There's nothing like being shot at in a helicopter to cause your bunghole to get tighter than a Montana bull's ass at fly time! The helicopters lined up and swooped down parallel to the hedgerow. It was about 25 yards from where the main shooting was going on.

O'Grady told us to form up in two files and make our way into the undergrowth to where the LRRPs were pinned down. We didn't know that the NVA had completely surrounded the LRRPs and it was up to us to break their line and extract the team along with their dead and wounded. O'Grady told us that the 25th Aviation Battalion was assembling more choppers to get us the hell out of there as soon as a Special Forces helicopter came in to pick up the LRRPs. Moose took point and we started making our way towards the sound of the gunfire. About 75 yards after we entered the hedgerow, we started taking AK-47 gunfire.

O'Grady directed the second squad to move up and engage the two gooks that were pinning us down. Bruns was having trouble getting his 90 mm recoilless through the heavy vegetation. Joel Brown was walking in front of Bruns, chopping the tall grass and vines away to make a path for him to advance. The second squad was able to take out the two NVA shooters allowing us to penetrate the circle of NVA that were overtaking the beleaguered LRRPs. We were engaged with NVA to our right and to our left, but we were not taking any fire from our front. That meant we were close to our objective. We were in communication with the LRRPs and told them we were approaching them from the Southwest.

When we finally got to them, we saw seven guys lying in a tight circle trying to conceal themselves from the onslaught of their would-be killers. There was one dead soldier and five wounded and the only one not hit was the RTO.

We wasted no time in picking up the dead and wounded and we hauled ass out of there the same way we came in. It happened so quickly the NVA did not realize what had happened. The dense vegetation concealed our entry and our exit. Oggy, the Lt's RTO, told us that the Special Forces chopper was five minutes out and would meet us at our exit point.

When we broke into the clearing, we could hear chopper blades coming in low from the Northeast. There were still AK rounds cutting through the jungle to our rear. I didn't think the gooks knew exactly where we were located. Doc started

251

working on the wounded and did the best he could until the chopper landed. We loaded the team into the chopper, and it took off as quickly as it had landed. By this time, the NVA had figured out that we had gotten the LRRPs out they were moving up behind us. AK rounds were flying through the vegetation all around us. Lt.

O'Grady made the decision that we would move across the field and take up a defensive position on a small outcropping of laterite rock. This position would give us the advantage of being above the clearing and 50 yards from the hedgerow.

There was nothing up there that gave us any cover, so we had to form a defensive line and lay on our stomachs waiting for the NVA to break into the clearing. For some reason, the NVA did not pursue us. They may have thought that since they heard a helicopter come in that other gunships would be arriving.

Somebody yelled at SFC Marquez and asked him when the helicopters would be arriving to pick us up. He said he wasn't sure but thought they were on their way. Everybody breathed a sigh of relief, realizing that we had just pulled off a huge mission and no one got hurt or killed. I looked at my watch and it was 1630 hrs. I thought to myself that it was going to be getting dark soon and that we had better get our asses out of here as soon as possible.

There was an eerie silence surrounding us and the only thing you could hear were the guys opening their C rations. Some of the guys were smoking cigarettes and there was an overall sense of nervousness amongst the guys. We were still aware that there was NVA in the jungle to our front but at the moment, there was no movement from that direction.

O'Grady picked 2 guys to move down an ox cart path to a small hooch and set up a listening post. The hooch was halfway to the hedgerow. The two guys set up and concealed themselves as best as they could. Helicopter blades could be heard in the distance, but they were not the sound of Hueys coming to get us. It was the distinct sound of a Chinook supply helicopter. Within minutes we saw it approaching with a sling carrying a net full

Knife Throwing Contest

Huey Smoke Ship

John and Ray at DiamondFSB

Burning Shit Barrels

Danny Dietz swimming in bomb crater

Russ and Becky Bruns

Big John in Cu Chi for three-day standdown

Jack Slovey and Big John

254

Jimmy Langley at Waikiki East swimming pool

Phillips, SSGT Jim Calvert and Jim Marshall

Kid Lozon, George M.F.Kush, Greg Mannarelli, Dave Duininck

255

1st Row: Ray
2nd Row: Moose, Ed Rambo, Rick Galli, Bill Tennent, Hedgy Van Ark
3rd Row: Spurill, Joel Brown, Ed Frey, Big Joe, Lamere

Boys II Men

Vietnamese Brothel Advertisement

They hovered behind us and dropped the sling and then landed and unloaded a dozen men from another platoon. They immediately set up on the left flank. Within a minute, the Chinook lifted off and flew back the way it had come. We were looking at each other with dumbfounded faces.

Marquez yelled at the first squad to go retrieve the items in the sling. O'Grady walked by and told us our helicopters had been diverted to another unit and we had to dig in for the night and that no one was coming until tomorrow to pick us up. Brogan looked at me and said, "man, this is a giant shit sandwich!"

Guys were griping and cussing, and the sandbags had to be filled behind us, where dirt could be found. We had very little time to string a single strand of concertina wire and by the time it got dark, we found ourselves unprepared for combat.

At dusk, the two guys on the LP came running back and told us there were a hundred gooks or more just inside the hedgerow to our front, talking and laughing. They were scared shitless and said they thought we were going to get overrun. Guys were doing their best to dig fighting positions, but the hard rock made it almost impossible.

O'Grady was on the radio calling for artillery support but was told we were out of range. It was looking like we were in for the fight of our lives. The first rounds of RPGs came flying at 0130 hrs. Those first rounds were short, and we immediately opened up on the hedgerow with everything we had.

Bruns launched an HE round from his 90 recoilless and it hit the hedgerow with a huge explosion. In the light of the explosion, you could see gook bodies flying through the air. Moose was getting his dooper going as fast as he could. You could hear the sound of the grenades going off as they hit the hedgerow. Moose was a great shot with his M-79. John Boy, on his M-60 machine gun, was shooting in controlled bursts and every rifleman was shooting on semiautomatic.

It was getting hard to see and suddenly somebody popped a parachute flare to our front and we saw our worst nightmare. There were six gooks kneeling out in the clearing with RPG launchers on their shoulders. To our dismay, the flare enabled them to see us as well as we could see them. Within seconds six RPGs were sailing towards us. The first one hit in front of Moose. The second was in front of Bruns and a couple flew over our heads, exploding behind us.

O'Grady was screaming into the radio handset that we were under heavy fire and about to be overrun. Nobody responded. Bruns told Brogan, his ammo bearer, that he couldn't see, and Brogan looked at him and saw his face was covered in blood. Bruns had taken shrapnel in the face and was blind. The firefight went on for over an hour. One of the RPGs hit Bill Thompson in the head, decapitating him. Oggy got a piece of that RPG in his head and was knocked down. The gooks had zeroed in on our left flank and there was nothing that could be done about it.

Another blast covered Joel Brown's back with shrapnel. He lay on the ground moaning, "Oh momma, what I gonna do, help me momma help me." Doc said Moose was hurt bad and was incoherent. His face was also covered in blood. Nobody can explain why the NVA broke off their attack that night. We had killed and wounded a bunch of them and I'm sure they thought they should remove their buddies from the battlefield before the gunships arrived. O'Grady finally got in touch with a helicopter carrying illumination flares and they relayed our position and situation back to the battalion in Cu Chi.

It wasn't long before a medevac showed up and Moose, Bruns, and Brown were airlifted back to the hospital in Cu Chi. Thompson would be taken to graves and registration. At daybreak, Hueys came and extracted us off of the battlefield. Not a single man was talking. I kept thinking of Thompson saying prayers before we landed to extract the LRRPs and now I was wondering if God even showed up in this god-forsaken place.

Thompson was the son of a Baptist minister who never said a cuss word in his life. Why were all these good men getting killed? I think all of us were feeling forsaken. All I knew was I had just lost four of my best friends and didn't know if I'd ever see them again. We returned to fire support Jackson and were told we were assigned to perimeter duty that night. Business went on as usual. A couple of days later, word came from Captain Sherwood that the LRRP Company was putting us in for a unit citation. That was the last word we heard about that, and there was no citation.

There was no news about our wounded guys. All I could think was what Thompson's family was going to think when their son had been returned home in a sealed casket. Eventually, we heard Bruns and Moose had RPG fragments in their eyes and were blind. Brown was patched up and received a medical profile that would keep him out of the field. Somebody said they saw him serving food in the company mess hall in Cu Chi.

Recently our company had been working in the Tay Ninh area. There had been rumors that Ho Chi Minh was planning a big attack on some fire support bases close to the Cambodian border. There had been rumors in the past, but even the ARVNs were getting jumpy. There was also a rumor that Ho had asked the Chinese military to explode a small nuclear weapon near Saigon to end the war once and for all.

The rumor must have held some credence because we were all issued atropine injection devices. Now we had to worry about a nuclear bomb along with everything else. There had been increased NVA activity around the Ho Chi Minh Trail in the last month. Ho was pissed that we were digging in his shit on a regular basis and interrupting his supply lines into the south.

One ARVN interpreter told us Ho had promised he would wipe any base off the face of the earth that interfered with the supply route. Most of us who had been working the border knew the NVA had been amassing a huge amount of supplies and ordinance just inside the border for some time. As far as we were concerned, we believed the threats.

The 25th Infantry Division, in their infinite wisdom, however, decided to call Ho's bluff by building a fire support base just one klick from the Cambodian border and naming it Diamond. Charlie Company and Delta Company would be in charge of building it and manning it during the Tet offensive coming up in a couple of weeks.

Diamonds Are Forever

On February 21, 1969, an officer from the nearby ARVN compound dropped by to tell our CO that ARVN intelligence had gathered information that the NVA were amassing large numbers of troops just inside the Cambodian border. What we didn't know at the time but found out later was that our Battalion Commander and Glover had been told that this was the military's "greatest grand plan." We were to be the bait being dangled out there so close to the Cambodian border to lure the NVA into Vietnam, where the full might of the U.S. military was waiting to strike.

The jets and spooky were loaded, fueled and waiting to strike. Cobras were fueled and ready to go and the Battalion Artillery Officer had coordinated all the designated firing coordinates surrounding Diamond. They were waiting in the shadows, ready to strike. Once again, we were the bait. He said the communist government in Hanoi was determined to remove the constant interruption to the north's supply routes into South Vietnam.

Ho Chi Minh had put General Vo Nguyen Giap in charge of the operation. Giap was a believer in bringing big numbers of troops to the battle. He had commanded over 2000 NVA regulars at the battle of Ia Drang valley against Custer's infamous seventh Cavalry. The ARVN officer said he thought there would be 2, maybe 3, regiments of NVA involved. The Company RTO came over to our bunker and relayed the news to us. We all wondered why we were still sitting here! The rumor mill kicked into high gear and within an hour, the fire support base was buzzing with news that we were going to be hit by a thousand gooks or more.

Everyone knew this little base could not withstand that kind of onslaught. We were told to double the number of claymores and trip flares. A Chinook came in with several 55 gal barrels of foo gas that could be used to set up an improvised explosive device. To create the device, the barrel was tilted forward 45 degrees and secured by metal fence posts.

A shape charge was laid under the bottom of the barrel and when ignited, it would spray liquid fire out the front of the barrel. It was a devastating weapon that would stop an oncoming force trying to human wave the base. It was the poor soldier's version of napalm. Another Chinook arrived with four 105 howitzers from the 1/8 artillery battalion and the artillery crew to set them up and man them.

Our weapons platoon was setting up their mortar pit and guys were filling sandbags as fast as they could to fortify the bunkers on the perimeter. The second platoon had 3 bunkers on the southeast side of the perimeter facing the ARVN compound that was located 200 meters from our base. Sugar Bear brought over a brand-new recruit and introduced him as Private Carmichael. Marquez told Sugar Bear to put him in the first squad and show him where their bunker was located.

SFC Marquez was walking around barking orders to make sure our weapons were cleaned and every man had at least 20 magazines of ammo. He seemed very upset like he knew something horrible was coming. As the sun went down, we saw the first platoon getting ready to go out on an ambush patrol to the East. Delta Company would take their patrol out in the opposite direction.

As the sunset, the patrols made their way out of the wire and proceeded in their assigned direction. Ray was double-checking the claymore magnetos to make sure they were hooked up. Lt. O'Grady was in charge of the foo gas igniter. Guys were finishing up writing letters to their girlfriends or wives and some were eating the piece of cake they saved from that night's meal at the chow line. The night was eerily quiet.

So much so that you could hear the ARVNs laughing and joking in their heavily protected compound. They had the damn compound surrounded with land mines and booby traps! No human being could penetrate their defenses. First guard duty started at 2100 hrs. Each man stood guard for an hour and then woke up the next guy on the roster and gave him the watch.

Every half hour, you could hear the squawk on the radio speaker that reminded the man on guard to call in a sir rep (situation report). Marquez came by at 2200 hrs. and told everyone to be on extra readiness. We all knew what he meant, knowing that this was the night the NVA could storm across the border and try to run over the top of us. Everyone feared the worst.

During the night, there was a B-52 strike up by the Parrots Beak to our northeast. It was close enough that it lit up the sky and shook the ground beneath us. All of us enjoyed watching those bombing missions and secretly hoped they killed a thousand gooks. Everybody in the fire support base breathed a sigh of relief when the sun came up the next morning. The mess hall was serving bacon and scrambled eggs and toast with slices of cantaloupe and we were all glad we survived another night in hell.

February 22, 1969

SFC Marquez came around at about 1400 hours and told the platoon they were assigned the ambush patrol that night. He said the 1st and 2nd squad would be on ambush and 3rd squad would stay in the base and pull perimeter duty. We had a total of 24 men in the platoon at that time, so that put us at half strength. Nine guys would stay back, and the rest would go on ambush patrol. Pete, our Kit Carson Scout, would be going with the ambush patrol. There were guys sitting around playing cards and talking about what a suicide mission this could be.

A couple of guys suggested we refuse to leave the wire and others said we should leave the wire and go hide somewhere close by. We all knew neither of those alternative ideas would fly because both Lt. O'Grady and Flat Dick would be leading the ambush. The menu for supper was hamburgers and fried potatoes along with green beans and watermelon slices. The hamburgers were emptied out of large olive drab tin cans. The burgers looked precooked and swimming in yellow grease. The cooks just poured them out onto the grill and warmed them up. They weren't too bad when you dressed them up with lots of mustard and ketchup and a few pickle slices.

After chow, we assembled at the command bunker where O'Grady would give the final orders. Since we hadn't been outside the wire doing day sweeps, we had no idea where we would be going. When O'Grady told the 1st and 2nd squad they were pulling the ambush, the new guy Carmichael started crying and said he had a bad feeling about leaving the wire. He was really freaking out, so Crosby spoke up and said he would trade with him for bunker duty.

Marquez spoke up and told us we would be going East about a half a klick and setting up in an enclosed hedgerow facing the Cambodian border. Several guys whispered that at least we would be far away from the base. The ambush patrol was looking better every minute. Just after the sun went down, we bid our comrades that were staying behind good luck and told them we would see them in the morning.

Ambush Patrol Leaves Diamond FSB

Marquez, Ray and Crosby started out on point and headed straight East. The ambush sight was about a half a klick straight ahead. The platoon spacing was tight since it was so dark. O'Grady was located at the rear of the formation with his RTO Oggy. The terrain was flat, with the exception of a few ravines just outside the wire. It felt like we were going to run into some imaginary wall out in the middle of nowhere. Your senses play tricks on you in the dark. You think you hear something to your right, or you see a shadow walking next to you.

Walking around in the dark can really mess with a guy's mind. The patrol was moving at a brisk pace and I'm sure Ray wanted to get to the AP site as soon as possible. Usually, the patrol would stop several times when going out, but not tonight. After walking a quarter klick (1/4 mile), Ray veered right and headed North East. No one was sure why.

Did he get disoriented? After another couple of hundred yards, he veered back to the southeast and kept humping. We covered the distance to the AP site in about 20 minutes. That is damn fast at night. When Ray got about 100 ft. from the hedgerow, he stopped, and everyone took a knee.

Marquez and Ray walked into the hedgerow to check it out and determine where to set it up. They were gone for about 10 minutes which seemed like an hour when you're kneeling out in the dark, straining your eyes to detect anything moving. The word worked its way back through the file that we were going to set up inside the enclosed hedgerow to our front.

The hedgerow looked like it was about 250 ft. wide and 500 ft. long, located in the middle of a rice paddy field. Marquez placed the guys along the northernmost end of the hedgerow where it would be easy to see any troops approaching. Our machine gunner John Boy was placed in the middle along with his two ammo bearers. Guys carrying M-79s were next to them and riflemen were dispersed to the left and the right.

O'Grady and his RTO were setting up to the rear about 50 feet with one rifleman. They would act as rear security. Marquez settled down just behind Cook in the middle of the hedgerow. The only sound being heard was Marquez blowing up his air mattress. He had mentioned to a couple of guys he was getting too old to sleep on the ground. Nobody knew how old he was, but there was a rumor that he served in Korea and this was his third tour in Nam. His first and second tours were with the Big Red One.

Someone said he had been awarded a couple of silver stars and a bunch of bronze stars. He was a loner but kept us all in line. The guy on guard would take the starlight scope and lay on the edge of the hedgerow where they had an unobstructed view of the real estate between us and the Cambodian border.

Everything seemed calm until we heard O'Grady's radio squawk and him talking in a low tone. Ray looked at his watch and it was 2400 hours. O'Grady was on the radio with SSGT Glover, our old platoon sergeant who was sitting on top of the observation tower at Diamond looking through a crew-served starlight scope. He told O'Grady to get up and move to the alternative ambush site due west of where we were and away from the advancing NVA.

Another option was to stay where we were, do not fire and pray that we were not discovered. He told O'Grady he would not stay there if it were him. He said you guys better get the hell out of there and head west until sunup and pray that Diamond didn't get hit as Diamond would have their hands full and likely would not be able to support us if we made contact. The rifleman sitting next to O'Grady crawled up to where Marquez was laying on the ground and shook him out of a shallow sleep. "What in da god damn hell you tink you do, you sonny beach?"

Marquez sat straight up and listened intently to what was being said. He crawled forward to where the guy on guard was laying and took the starlight scope and tried to focus his eye on the green and black vision to his front. He let out a low "Oh shit" and crawled back and told everybody to get their gear on because we were going to move out quickly. There was chaos in the ranks as guys were waking up other guys and telling them to hurry up and put their gear on.

The sound of air being pushed out of Marquez's air mattress was easily heard. As soon as he had it rolled up, he gave the order to move to the opposite end of the hedgerow complex and set up exactly how we had been originally. O'Grady and Oggy had already moved out and were there when the rest of the patrol arrived. You could hear O'Grady on the radio trying to get in touch with the 105 artillery guns at Diamond. Nobody was responding. He was trying to hook up with Battalion TOC, but no one responded. No one knew that all these resources were being directed towards Diamond to support a possible human wave and that our radio was being jammed. A hasty ambush was set up in the bamboo facing north.

In what seemed like 5 minutes, the first group of NVA was breaking through the hedgerow to the front. The soldiers looked like a bunch of shadows and Marquez said, "nobody shoots, god dammit." This was one of those times that guys with any religious background would start praying. Every man present knew this was not going to turn out well. In the next minutes, about 100 soldiers made their way into the complex and they started dropping off gear about 100 feet to our front.

Marquez blurted out, "Oh shit, I left the starlight scope at the other hedgerow. He turned to John boy and said, "don't shoot me," and he jumped up and ran directly toward the shadows in front of us. He was gone only a few minutes running through the gooks, when we saw him returning to our position on the run holding the starlight scope. When all the gooks arrived in the hedgerow, they numbered 300.

Suddenly there were loud clanking sounds as the gooks were setting up rocket launchers and mortar plates and tubes. It only took a minute to figure out this was a huge weapons company preparing to hit Diamond. Looking through the starlight, Marquez could see most of the people milling around were not soldiers but rather civilian men being used as mules to haul all the equipment and rounds.

There was however plenty of regular soldiers carrying AKs and field packs. A 51 cal. a machine gun that was mounted on wheels was coming up from the opposite hedgerow. We would be no match for the 51 cal. and more than likely, everyone would be killed in the first five minutes. There were about 100 people milling around in front of us.

As more gooks entered the hedgerow, they dropped their loads and kept moving closer to our position. The gooks were talking and laughing and lighting up joints of marijuana. It took only seconds for the smell to waft overhead. It appeared the gooks thought they were out on a Sunday stroll. The NVA had no idea they were being watched. None of us knew what our plan was, but we all knew we couldn't just lay there and let these assholes rocket and mortar our guys inside the base.

A half an hour had passed and one of the gook mules walked up to the hedgerow where we were laying and stood in front of Ray and started pissing. Ray took his hunting knife and shoved it into the gook's stomach and as he fell, Ray slit his throat. All this happened in a matter of seconds and the gooks standing around didn't have a clue what had just happened.

O'Grady made the decision that we would pop our ambush at the exact moment the first 122 mm rocket was launched. Every man knew we were going to face unbelievable odds but hoped the element of surprise would give us some advantage. Marquez whispered to a couple of the guys next to him to kill as many gooks as you could.

Laying there, watching the gooks calibrate their sights with small flashlights gave us a pretty good idea of where we needed to concentrate our fire. Garcia whispered that he wished he would have brought a couple of LAWS rockets. O'Grady was still trying to get someone on the radio, but no one responded. You could hear him saying "shit" under his breath. The gooks walking around were almost on top of us and suddenly, we heard an NVA officer shouting out orders to his weapons squads. Everybody knew the game was on.

When the first rocket blasted off towards Diamond at 0115 hrs. on February 23, 1969, our platoon opened up. In the initial minutes there was so much confusion and yelling that the gooks didn't know what was happening. They started running around in circles as we kept our fire going towards the mortar tubes. The only reason we were not killed in the first two minutes was that the mules did not have any weapons. They were completely caught by surprise.

Gooks were diving into the hedgerows trying to escape the onslaught of our bullets. The NVA were still able to get some rockets off as well as some mortars and we could hear them exploding as they reached their targets in Diamond.

It didn't take long before the NVA figured out what was happening and they directed small arms fire into our position. One NVA soldier ran right up to us and Flat Dick stuck his M-16 into his gut and pulled the trigger. Keith had been hit in the face and was lying lifeless next to John Boy. Mora was hit in the chest and instinctively called out for a medic. Unfortunately, our medic, Doc Browning, had stayed back at Diamond.

When it looked like they were going to run over us, O'Grady started yelling for us to retreat. He realized we had no chance against these well-trained NVA. There was only one way for us to go and that was west away from the hedgerow. When we broke through the rear of the hedgerow, we were ambushed by NVA that had flanked our position during the firefight. They were running in the same direction as we were and did not realize we were GIs. Several gooks ran past us as we were carrying our dead and wounded away from the massacre behind us.

Everyone ran helter-skelter about 20 yards, and out in the middle of nowhere, there was a large square berm located to the front. It was like someone placed it there just for us. It was the only protection to get behind. It took about 5 minutes for all the guys to catch up. We were taking a lot of AK fire and the bullets were slicing into the front of the berm. A lot of the guys were hunkered down behind the berm, scared out of their minds. The sound of explosions going off in the direction of Diamond was nonstop.

We could only wonder what our guys were going through. Jackson, a big guy from Georgia, said he was getting the hell out of there. Ray told him he couldn't abandon the guys and told him to start shooting. Jackson dropped his weapon and jumped over the berm and ran away. He only got about 20 feet when a round hit him in the back of the head. He dropped like a wedge. One of the guys bringing up the rear was low, crawling towards our position. Rounds from our position strafed Burke's back across his kidneys. He laid out in front of us, moaning and crying for help.

Marquez jumped over the berm and lifted him off the ground and dove with his body back over the berm into our position. All that could be done to stop the bleeding was to stuff a towel into the wounds. He lay there the rest of the night softly moaning. Our Kit Carson Scout Pete told everyone to stop firing. He took off his fatigue jacket and pants and ran barefoot out in front of our position and grabbed an AK from one of the fallen NVA. He called out to the gooks and when they came up to him, he would shoot them dead. He started yelling at the gooks that all the GIs were dead and not to come over to where our guys were hunkered down behind the berm. It was the bravest thing

271

anyone had ever seen. He would be awarded a bronze star with a V device for valor.

When everyone thought nothing else could get worse, that 51 cal. machine gun on wheels had set up on the corner of the hedgerow and started shooting at us. The rounds were tearing the berm to pieces and it was only a matter of time before we would have no more cover. Crosby, our M-79 guy, stood straight up, bullets snapping past him and shot an HE round at the 51 cal. The round made a direct hit and knocked out the gun and killed the operator. This single act probably saved everybody's lives.

Lt. O'Grady tried without success to raise anyone on the radio. The two frequencies he used on the radio were being jammed up. He pulled a book out of his pocket that listed all the frequencies of all the available artillery units in the area. He was able to get the USS New Jersey on the line and was trying to get a fire mission going but it turned out they were out of shooting range. The rest of the night became a blur.

The direct shooting settled down to a couple of gook snipers trying to catch someone sticking their head above the berm. The rockets and mortars had completely stopped, and we assumed the weapons squads had packed up their weapons and dead and wounded and were hauling ass back to the sanctuary of Cambodia. The sky over Diamond was flickering orange from the explosions and fires inside the base.

0115 Hrs
February 23, 1969
Inside Diamond Fire Support Base

After the ambush patrol left the wire, the men of the second platoon had no idea what was about to happen that night. SSGT

Glover came by and warned the platoon to stay alert; his best guess was it would be a very busy night. Guys were playing cards inside the bunkers that were located on the southeast corner of the base. Carmichael told Brogan he was glad he had stayed back in the fire support base. Each bunker had one man standing guard outside the bunker, usually lying on top of the bunker looking out.

On this particular night, our guys had no starlight scope to help detect movement outside the wire. The ambush patrol had taken the scope with them. The sounds of muffled voices rose out of the bunkers as guys jazzed each other about who was going to shoot the moon or who was hiding the black bitch. Flashlights were used to cast a faint light across the bunker floor so everyone could see the hands being played.

From the top of a bunker, you could look back towards the northeast wire and see the aiming lights used by the artillery guys to aim their guns. At 0110 hrs., a lieutenant walked by, checking on the perimeter guards. The M-60 machine gun carried by Sneaker was sitting on top of one of the bunkers with 500 rounds of ammo clipped together, ready to rock and roll.

On the other bunker sat our 90 mm recoilless rifle with one round in the tube and a dozen flechette rounds sitting next to it. Sugar Bear had just returned from the latrine and ducked back into the bunker. Doc Browning was spending the night at the command bunker where the company aid station was located. Captain Sherwood had just been relieved of command and a new CO, Denton, was bedded down in the CP bunker with Brockway his RTO.

Brockway had recently been transferred from our platoon to the CP because he was getting really short. At exactly 0115 hrs., the distinct sound of mortars and rockets being launched could be heard in the distance. There is no scarier thing on earth than the whistling sound a rocket makes as it's coming down in

273

your direction. When the bunker guards heard the mortars, they immediately jumped down and dove into the bunkers.

After the first volley hit, more 122s and 81 mm mortars kept raining down inside the base. There was a huge explosion in front of second platoon's bunkers and Brogan was yelling for guys to set off the claymores. Every claymore failed to go off. The trip flares lay in the wire with pins inserted into their handles. The shape charge under the foo gas barrel lay silent not responding to the activated igniter. Its blasting cap had been removed. Diamond was being assaulted by the NVA's elite sapper squads with straw attached to their backs. They were simply the best at what they did.

When our guys inside the bunkers grabbed their weapons, they started firing out the firing ports built into the bunker. The initial explosion in front of the bunkers was Bamboo Bangalore torpedoes blasting huge holes in the concertina wire.

Now the NVA regulars carrying satchel charges were streaming in through the jagged openings and headed straight for the second platoon bunkers. The NVA had just successfully pulled off what the Army thought was impossible. SSGT Glover sitting in the tower thought it best to evacuate the tower when AK-47 tracers snapped past his head. The NVA was hitting the base with 3 Regiments of highly trained regulars, some of which were veterans of the I Drang Valley massacre. The north side of the base was being hit with withering fire from 51 cal. machine guns that were shooting from hastily dug out firing pits.

These pits made it hard for helicopter gunships to get a proper angle to take them out. RPG rounds were flying into the base by the dozens. Red tracers from AK-47s looked like ribbons of water being shot out of the end of a fire hose. Glover was headed to the company CP bunker when he saw the second platoon bunkers blown up by satchel charges full of dynamite. He knew if that hole in the wire wasn't plugged, there would be

274

no stopping a complete penetration by the human wave. The 105 howitzers from B Co 1/8 were shooting flechette rounds directly into the wire.

They were firing as fast as they could, but the gooks found a way to get close enough to lob grenades at the cannoneers. Several gooks trying to crawl through the wire were cut in half at the waist by the flechette rounds. Half of their body would be dangling in the wire with their intestines hanging grossly from the wire while the other half was lying on the ground behind them. It was like a scene from a macabre horror movie.

Meanwhile, one of the NVA sapper squads ran through the perimeter and threw a satchel charge into the opening of our command bunker. The explosion partially caved in the PCP and sandbags lying on top. Our buddy Paul Naso, our old RTO, who was also an RTO for the CP was knocked senseless.

The new CO Denton had light wounds to his legs and was huddled in the corner of the bunker sucking his thumb. He yelled at Brockway to go get Doc Browning at the aid station. Brock grabbed his M-16 and suffering from an ear drum puncture, ran across the base to get Doc Browning. Unbeknownst to Brock, Browning was headed to the CP bunker.

When they saw each other, they ran towards each other right in the face of AK fire. They were both cut down just as they reached each other. Neither survived. Glover saw what happened and ran to the ditch where the men were lying but it was too late. Denton meanwhile crawled out of the CP bunker and ran to the TOC leaving Naso behind. When he reached the TOC, he and a major laid on the floor holding hands the rest of the night.

Glover heard a voice yelling for help coming from a bunker. He saw a hand reaching up and he grabbed it and pulled John Vaughn out of the smoking rubble. Glover grabbed a PRC-25 radio and strapped it onto his back and fought his way through a dozen NVA to get to the Southeast corner of the perimeter. He could see that the second platoon bunkers were completely blown up. No soldier was there to return fire.

Glover hoped that the guys in those bunkers had gotten out before the charges were thrown into their bunkers. He had a gut wrenching feeling he was wrong. Glover was taking heavy fire and a couple of AK-47 rounds grazed the radio pack he was carrying. Two Cobra helicopters had just arrived on station and Glover thought he could get them on the radio and have them concentrate fire outside the wire where the gooks were pouring in.

Glover was able to get a Cobra pilot on the radio and asked if he could drop some ordinance near the southeast corner where the gooks had breached the wire. The Pilot, Bob Segers simply said, "Where do you want it?" Glover low crawled slowly as NVA were passing him on the left and right. They were anxious to get into the center of the perimeter and ignored him lying on the ground. He keyed the radio handset and said, "Diamondhead 36, Diamondhead 36 this is Charlie 2 over."

He waited for what seemed like a lifetime with his face pressed against the scorched earth. Glover's radio squawked and a crisp voice said, "Charlie 2 where do you want it?" Glover keyed the handset and said that he had a strobe light attached to the top of his radio and that anything in front of his position and the strobe light was fair game. Glover ended the transmission with, "Please don't drop it on me."

Glover was coordinating the Diamondhead Cobras and several sorties of Phantom jets carrying napalm and 250 lb. bombs. Once all the aircraft had cleared the area to rearm themselves, the artillery could be redirected to predetermined targets outside and inside the perimeter. That is when the order for "Broken Arrow" would be given. Between Glover directing the air attack and the Battalion AO directing the artillery fire support, they were successful in halting the NVA advancement into the perimeter.

With the perimeter cleared, the artillery batteries at Jackson could shoot at predetermined locations around the base. Glover quickly crawled back and took cover next to one of the blown-up bunkers. He thought he heard someone moaning but couldn't be sure with all the artillery going off. The situation at this time was dire and it looked like the NVA were going to take control of the base.

Glover looked around the perimeter and saw NVA soldiers tossing grenades into the bunkers. The first platoon was giving the NVA one hell of a flight. They were so close to the NVA that the Cobra pilots were unable to risk hitting our guys. More hell was about to be unleashed. Within minutes 155 arty rounds were landing on the edge of the perimeter.

The targets were away from the command bunkers but came very close to hitting the mess tent where cooks were fighting for their lives. These cooks, that hadn't fired their weapons since basic training, were standing toe to toe with seasoned war fighters. They acquitted themselves as America's finest fighting force.

There was a flare ship circling around dropping large illumination canisters. The scene of the battle was surreal as the dust and smoke from the artillery rounds hung close to the ground like a dense fog. There was a huge fire where the ammo dump had been hit by a rocket. Water was spilling out of the water trailer where AK rounds had hit it. There were screams of "Medic" echoing all over the base.

When the artillery started falling at the base perimeter the gooks formed up into small groups and looked for an exit back to the Cambodian border. Glover started walking towards the second platoon bunkers to see if there were any of the guys left. He passed the CP bunker that had taken a hit on the roof and caved in. He heard somebody yelling for help and removed timbers to find Paul Naso trapped in the bunker.

Paul had been injured and laid there all night thinking he was the lone survivor of this horrific attack. Paul had come close to losing his mind. When Glover carried him out and sat him on a sandbag, he gave him a 45 pistol. He told Paul "shoot any gook that comes running by." Glover turned and headed to the southeast section of the perimeter. The onslaught lasted until 0515 hrs.

The NVA had knocked out our three 105 howitzers and were able to drag one of the guns outside the base and pull it 50 yards towards the border. What the gooks didn't realize was that the gun crew had dumped a thermite grenade down the barrel welding the breech closed making the gun worthless. Those cannoneers fought hand to hand after they ran out of rounds to shoot. Some of those boys were killed and many wounded fighting for their lives.

The Cobra gun ships were continuing to shoot down NVA troops as they fled back to the border. There were so many NVA killed and wounded that the gooks didn't try to recover their bodies. O'Grady finally got Glover on the radio and said the ambush patrol was walking back in.

Ambush Patrol Returns To Diamond

The men of the second platoon, that fought so gallantly that night on the ambush patrol, could be seen walking in a staggered formation as it approached the destroyed fire support base. Each man had at least 2 AK-47 rifles slung across their shoulders that they had taken off dead NVA. The patrol looked beleaguered and disoriented. The looks on their faces was a mixture of shock and weariness. We called that look "The thousand-yard stare." None of the men were talking as they looked at a base that had been transformed into a burned-out smoldering hell hole.

When they reached the wire, or what was left of it, they had to step over dead gook bodies. Many of the bodies were torn to pieces; all of them had a pasty gray color on their faces. Some had their eyes opened some closed, some had no heads at all.

The first thing they wanted to do was hook up with the second platoon guys and see how they had fared during the battle. Marquez led the group to the southeast corner where the wire had been blown apart by bamboo Bangalore torpedoes. John Boy said, "where are our bunkers?" A sergeant from 1st platoon said they were over there, as he pointed to three holes in the ground.

None of us could comprehend that just 12 hours before there were three well-built bunkers manned by our 3rd squad. Ray asked the sergeant "where is the second platoon?" The sergeant turned and pointed to 9 ponchos laying on the ground lined up in a row. It still didn't sink in that we had not seen our guys when we returned.

I repeated the question and the sergeant said, "your guys are under those ponchos." I looked at the guy with disbelief and said, "No Way!" I turned to Ray and said, "what does that guy mean those are our guys?" I walked straight towards the ponchos and knelt down next to the first one on the left. I reached down and lifted the upper part of the poncho and there staring back at me was Sugar Bear Taylor. His skin was pale grey, and he had a blank expression on his face. I turned to the guys standing there and said, "Oh shit, it's Sugar Bear."

In an instant I flashed back to the many times he had showed us pictures of his twin baby boys that had been born just after he arrived in Nam. I bent at the waist and fought the urge to vomit. I was sick to my stomach. Just like doubting Thomas in the Bible, I refused to believe what lay before me.

I went to the next poncho and lifted the end and there was Robert Jones looking just like Sugar Bear. Sneaker was next then Doc Browning and Brock, next to him was the new guy Carmichael, Anderson, Keith and last in the row was Mora. I stood up and walked over to SFC Marquez and started to cry. Marquez broke down and wept along with every man standing there.

There is no way to describe the sadness and brokenness in our hearts. Then came the anger and the rage that welled up in my guts. The 1st platoon sergeant told us that the gooks had satchel charged the bunkers before the guys could get out of them. All the guys were blown up but one: Brogan.

When they dug the wreckage and bodies out of one of the bunkers Brogan was sitting in the back corner covered by two dead gook bodies he had shot while they tossed grenades into the bunker. Their bodies were the only thing that saved him. They medevaced him out just before we had returned. I looked at Garcia and said, "He will never be right again." In the next 10 minutes we carried our dead to waiting helicopters that had set down just outside the wire. It was a gruesome sight to see our guys stacked on the floor of the choppers like cord wood. Col. Odie's helicopter landed right in front of our blown-up bunkers.

When he disembarked a Major (the same one that Doc gave the gook ears to) that had been hiding in the CP bunker during the entire battle came walking towards Odie with SSGT Glover following close behind. The Major saluted Odie and started to tell him how he personally directed the battle that overcame the human wave. Glover heard what he said and got in his face and started yelling at him what a coward he was.

The major started to talk back and Glover grabbed him by his lapels and said, "I should shoot you dead right here you son of a bitch." Odie quickly broke up the altercation and told the major to go get in his helicopter. Odie knew the truth that Glover had called in the Cobras and artillery. He placed his hand on Glover's shoulder and said something that we couldn't hear.

Odie returned to his chopper and took off back to Cu Chi. Glover came over to us and told us how sorry he was that the second platoon had been decimated. He was visibly shook up and agitated. He always had a special spot in his heart for his old platoon.

He had taught most of us standing there how to survive in this hell hole. Marquez assembled us back where our bunkers were blown up and told us we had to rebuild the bunkers. I looked at Marquez and said, "Why would we do that?" He said, "because they have decided we are staying here tonight." In unison all the guys said, "You have got to be shitting us."

There was no way they would make us stay out there after what had just happened. Lt. O'Grady had walked to the command bunker as soon as the ambush patrol got back. He was made Company Commander on the spot due to the fact that the new CO was medevaced out crying hysterically. We never saw O'Grady again after he took command.

We continued digging the ruins out of our blown-up bunkers and John Boy stood up and held a jungle boot above his head. The bloody foot was still inside. Cook said, "Isn't this the shits." He tossed the boot out on the ground and returned to the job at hand. The guys were still mumbling about staying there another night and one guy suggested we go AWOL and try to make it to Tay Ninh.

Marquez heard the bitching and moaning and came over and made us stand before him and he said, "god damn you sonny beaches, what in da god damn hell you tink you do? We are staying here tonight and if we don't rebuild our fighting positions we will get killed just like the others." His voice was stern but not angry. He knew what we were going through. The platoon had just fought the biggest gun battle of their lives and killed over 40 gooks. It was starting to sink into our heads that these gooks were soldiers just like us.

There was no joy in what we did. All we could think of was the ARVN officers warning, "Ho will not stop until the base is wiped off the face of the earth." At 1400 hrs., a mosquito heavy lift helicopter, dropped a D-8 dozer in front of our position along with its operator. The operator dug a long deep trench and Marquez told us to go out and start dragging dead gooks over to the trench and dump them in the hole. The dead gooks had been lying out in the sun all day and their bodies were bloated and starting to smell.

Several guys tied a handkerchief over their noses but that didn't keep the stench from being sucked into their lungs. I saw a couple of the guys bent over at the waist vomiting up the C rations they had recently eaten. When I approached one of the dead bodies, I saw the back of his head was missing. One of his eyes was lying out on his cheek. For reasons unknown to me, I squatted next to the body and yelled, "hey Popeye, if you ever go to sleep on guard again, I'll kill you."

I then stood up and kicked the guy's head causing one of his teeth to fall out on the ground. I picked the tooth up and put it in my pocket and looked up to see Davis standing looking at me. He said, "that was the awesomest thing I had ever seen." The next time I wrote my dad, I enclosed the tooth and told him I'd explain when I got home.

This war was causing people to do irrational things and making monsters out of otherwise good men. My catholic upbringing had failed me. In total we dumped 127 NVA regulars from the 272-273 and 274 regiments of NVA into the pit. Engineers took bags of lime, broke them open, and scattered the contents over the dead bodies. After that, the dozer proceeded to push the dirt back into the pit.

When the dozer was done, the mosquito helicopter returned, hooked up to the dozer and headed back to Cu Chi. There had been a prisoner taken that night and SSGT Glover and an ARVN officer interrogated him. He had been one of many men forced to serve by the NVA. He was forced to carry satchel charges for the battle that night. He said after he dropped his load a NVA officer handed him a pair of wire cutters and told him he would crawl up to the wire and cut it. This man like so many other poor bastards was not trained in warfare.

They were victims like so many other North and South Vietnamese. He told the interpreter he didn't want to be there in the first place. By 1700 hrs., we were putting the final sandbags on top of the reconstructed bunkers. The holes in the Concertina wire had been repaired and claymore mines and trip flares had been put in place and ready to go. The only thing that was missing was the 55-gallon barrels of foo gas. Jimmy Marshall from the first platoon came over and told us what had happened the night before. His description of the rockets and mortars coming in was horrifying. He told us his squad almost ran out of ammunition and that he ran to the ammo dump and grabbed a case of M-16 ammo.

When he got about halfway back to his platoon a 122-rocket hit the ammo dump causing a huge explosion. With tears in his eyes Jimmy said, "if that rocket would've hit two minutes earlier, he would've died right there." Because of Jimmy's valor the first platoon was able to continue fighting off the NVA that had penetrated the perimeter.

As he was leaving, he said he had heard that hot chow was available at the mess tent. Charlie Company's cooks in Cu Chi had prepared roast beef, mashed potatoes and gravy, green beans, and even a large chocolate sheet cake with fudge frosting. We grabbed our mess kits and took turns going over to the mess tent grabbing what might be the last meal for some of us. We were all convinced that if the NVA human waved diamond again, it would not end with a good result. The images of our dead comrades were etched permanently in all of our minds. I saw SSGT Glover in the chow line and he looked beat. He hadn't gotten any sleep in the last 36 hrs.

I asked him how he was doing. He told me he had been coordinating fire missions with the 155 batteries at Jackson fire support base and the six-inch mechanized artillery in Trang Bang. He said spooky, known as Puff the Magic Dragon, would also be on call. Puff was a Douglas AC-47 cargo plane that had been modified into a gunship. The AC-47 was put into service during World War II. The 25th Aviation Cobras would be on alert and be able to respond in a moment's notice.

When I returned to the bunker line, I saw Garcia and Cook trying to dig foxholes on each side of the bunkers. The ground was so hard they were only able to get them deep enough to lie in. Marquez told us that as soon as the rockets and mortars started coming in everybody had to get out of the bunkers and be prepared to defend ourselves against another human wave. That plan goes against all logic. Who wants to get out of the bunker when rockets and mortars are exploding all around you?

These were not normal circumstances however, because the NVA regulars were trained to storm the wire as soon as the rockets and mortars were reaching their targets. I was convinced that the first wave of gooks were suicide troops. When we removed the dead gooks from the wire earlier in the day, we discovered some had baling wire wrapped tightly around their thighs and biceps. The purpose of the wire was to act as a tourniquet and reduce the flow of blood if they were shot in the legs or arms, thus allowing them to continue fighting.

We were fighting against a bunch of brainwashed lunatics. In final preparation for the night, which was rapidly approaching, we placed hand grenades along the outside of the bunkers. We also had a half a dozen LAWS rockets extended, cocked and ready to go.

We were determined not to go down without a fight. Just before dark a couple of Hueys landed outside the wire and dropped off several members of the Tiger Force. These guys were dressed in full camouflaged fatigues and had large black back packs filled with God knows what. I was happy to have all the help we could get.

February 24, 1969

At night fall we all gathered outside our three bunkers and sat around talking about our dead buddies and what we were going to do if or when we got human waved. We doubled the number of guys on guard and we had our starlight scope pointed out towards our front. Most of us couldn't sleep and only closed our eyes to get a cat nap. It's funny how you can be somewhere between resting and sleep and suddenly your entire body stiffens and your eyes fly open expecting to see a gook aiming his AK-47 at your head pulling the trigger.

Several times during the night an officer would walk by and ask how everyone was doing. I think they were coming around to make sure everybody hadn't fallen asleep. God it was hard to stay awake after working all day in hundred degrees plus temperatures.

Many times on ambush patrols the guy on guard duty would nod out and wake up two hours into his shift. The older guys in the platoon would threaten the new guys that they would cut their throats if they went to sleep on guard duty. Surprisingly, nothing happened that night. When daylight came Marquez told us to clean ourselves up and shave. Only a grizzled old professional soldier would come up with that idea.

Shaving was the last thing on everybody's mind. We were all relieved that we had all survived another night. At 0900 hrs., a Chinook supply helicopter dropped off a huge cargo net full of concertina wire, more metal fence posts, and thousands of sandbags. We spent most of the morning stretching wire around the perimeter. We used the new wire to create a new third row on top of the existing wire.

We thought it would slow down the gooks when they tried to run over the top of it. During a human wave, the lead NVA sapper would throw himself onto the concertina wire and his buddies behind him would run over the top of his back. These guys were committed. The sand bags would be used to reinforce our fighting positions.

We found the best place to fill sand bags was right out in front of our bunkers where the dozer had filled in the pit that was full of dead bodies. The dirt was nice and loose, and it made for easy shoveling. When we were through it looked like a hundred small bomb craters. I thought how sad it was that Bruns wasn't here to do some more grave digging! By midafternoon we noticed that the troops in the ARVN Compound were nowhere to be found.

This could only mean one thing: they knew something we didn't know and that's never a good thing. When Marquez returned from the Company briefing, he told us no ambush patrols were going out and that there was a good chance we would be hit that night. My first thought was if those bastards go back to the enclosed hedgerow where the platoon had popped the ambush, then pre-targeted artillery or Cobras could kick their asses. Marquez reminded us to clean our weapons and try to get some sleep.

Ray and I laid down in one of the bunkers and tried to sleep but lying in your own sweat doesn't help. We were both so tired that we were able to catch a couple of hours of sleep. We woke up just in time to run over to the chow line and get a bite to eat. As we went through the line the cooks kept asking us if we thought we were going to get hit tonight. The only response I could come up with was "keep your weapon clean and close by." These were the same cooks that had fought for their lives two nights ago. Eubanks our company barber had lost his life fighting next to them.

They all had very worried looks on their faces and none of them were anxious to go through hell a second time. Who knows maybe Ho would be satisfied with his troop's performance two nights ago and leave us alone.

When we got back to the bunkers, we were told which guard shift we would be taking. Ray had first guard and I would relieve him. As it turned out both of us would stay up the entire night. I checked and made sure we had an extra battery for the starlight scope and visually checked every claymore mine to make sure there was connectivity between the mine and the magneto.

We taped the blasting cap into the top of the claymore to make it near impossible to remove it. John Boy had gone out earlier and double-checked the trip flares. He pulled the pins as far out as possible making them a hair-trigger. Any sapper trying to mess with them would get a face full of white phosphorous. We even strung empty cans with rocks in them as early warning devices.

All that was left to do was wait and see what would happen. At 2400 hrs., I looked to the bunker to our left manned by first platoon and saw the bright orange glow of a lit cigarette. Some

287

asshole was smoking outside the bunker. Charlie could see the glow from a mile away. I took a can of lima beans and ham and threw it at the dumb ass's head. The can missed his head but hit him in the shoulder. He jumped five feet in the air. I whispered loud enough for him to hear "the next cigarette I see lit will be put out with a bullet." That was the last cigarette glow I saw all night.

I couldn't believe how ignorant some of these rubes could be. I looked at my watch at 1350 hrs. and thought, "If it's going to happen, it will be soon." Every swinging Richard had his weapon with him and was ready to fight. We didn't have to wait long.

At exactly 0355 hrs. February 24, 1969, the first rockets came screaming into the base. It hit on the opposite side of the base and I could not tell which direction they came from. The game was on and the rockets and mortars came in hot and heavy. They were hitting all over the base and several hit just behind our position. Luckily, we were out of shrapnel range and no one got hit. I wasn't going to wait for the gooks to come over the wire, so I popped a handheld parachute flare directly to our front. When the darkness was broken, our night vision went to hell, but not so bad that we couldn't see about 50 NVA lined up ready to blow the wire.

Oggy blew his claymores and Ray started to squeeze the magnetos connected to the claymores directly to our front. Claymores were going off all over the place. First platoon was reacting to our claymores and blew theirs as well. In the first minute we had knocked down half of the NVA lined up to our front. The remaining gooks opened up on us with everything they had. They tried throwing a satchel charge over the wire, but it hung up on the top strand and blew up only doing minimal damage.

I was glad we had put that third tier on. They were able to toss grenades over the wire but not getting close enough to do any damage. For every one they threw at us we returned two at them. Every man was firing his weapon. The M-79s were shooting double ott buckshot rounds directly through the wire. The 105 artillery guys were shooting killer junior rounds 50 yards to their front.

John Boy was putting a serious hurt on the gooks with his M-60 machine gun. The gooks were able to breach the perimeter on the north side of the base. They were able to blow two empty bunkers and were quickly killed by the men that had previously manned those bunkers. The gooks were not going to catch us off guard tonight. An illumination plane came on station in about five minutes and dropped large illumination flares above us. This allowed us to see a Company of NVA charging out of the ravine to our right and forming up to charge our position. Glover's prearranged artillery paid off and 155 rounds were landing all around the outside of the perimeter.

A Cobra helicopter flown by Greg Bucy flew over our head and hosed down the Company of NVA trying to form up to our right. This caused those troops to break ranks and skedaddle back into the ravine. Another Cobra pilot named Chuck Moore was also able to knock out 2 NVA 51 cal. machine guns wreaking havoc on the west side of the perimeter. What would we do without these brave pilots? I made up my mind I was going to locate them in Cu Chi and buy them a beer.

This was an entirely different picture than the one that played out on the 23rd. The Wolfhounds were kicking ass and taking body count. Nec Aspera Terrent... No Fear On Earth! Well that wasn't totally true, because we were all scared half to death. It's one thing to shoot at a gook in a hedgerow never knowing if you hit him or not, but we were seeing these boys eye to eye watching them get chewed up right in front of us, that's a different thing.

The battle lasted until 0500 hrs. At 0430 hrs., the NVA started picking up their wounded and high tailed it back to the Cambodian border. All three Cobras were having a field day picking off several of the retreating soldiers before they reached the sanctuary of the border. The dust and smoke in the base was so thick you could cut it with a bayonet. Everybody's lungs were burning and some of the guys had drenched their towels with water and covered their heads.

The Cobras were circling overhead and I saw SSGT Glover walking towards us. He wanted to check on us and see if everyone was ok? As impossible as it may seem not a single guy in our platoon was killed or wounded. Ray got a small piece of shrapnel in his hand that we put a band-aid on. No Purple Heart, no million-dollar wound! As the sun came up, we could see dead gooks scattered on the ground outside the wire.

You had to give them credit for being a bunch of tough bastards. I turned to Ray and asked him, "What's next?" He said, "I guess we get ready for another night of fun and games." At 0900 hrs., they brought us cases of C rations and told us there was not going to be any chow served at the mess tent. I thought maybe it had been blown up. As the guys were rifling through the C rations to get their favorite food, SFC Marquez came over and told us we were going to tear down the base and go back to Trang Bang. There was a simultaneous cheer amongst the troops, and we wolfed down our food so we could start to tear down the base.

Another D-8 dozer was brought in and Delta Company was assigned the task of dragging the dead bodies to the pit and tossing them into it. We found out later that Marquez had told O'Grady, the new CO, that his guys were not doing that duty again. Tear down consisted of slicing a hole in every sandbag and emptying the dirt out. The empty bags were thrown in a pile and burned. The PCP metal roofing along with metal fence posts and rolls of concertina wire was stacked in a central location in slings where a Chinook would come and pick them up.

For the first time since being in Nam not a single guy complained about working out in the baking sun. We only had one thought on our minds: GET THE HELL OUT OF HERE! Around 1600 hrs., flights of Huey helicopters came to pick up the troops. Marquez told us we had been assigned the duty of rear security and would be the last to leave. You could not believe the loud groaning that ensued. Marquez said we would only be alone for 15 minutes and we would get extracted without delay. I looked at Ray and said, "I can't believe we are drawing this crap detail." He looked at me and said, "It don't mean nothin."

The second platoon, all 10 of us, found ourselves standing alone in the middle of the torn-down base wondering how long the choppers would take to get us out. Garcia said in a sarcastic way, "they probably had to go back to Cu Chi to refuel." The ARVN Compound to the south had been re-inhabited and several South Vietnamese soldiers were standing on the roof looking at us. Soon we could hear the sound of choppers coming in the distance. We all felt like we might actually get out of here alive.

Two Hueys sat down in front of us and we scrambled to jump aboard. Just as we were taking off, we heard what sounded like artillery fire coming from Cambodia. Three 122 mm artillery shells exploded right in the center of the torn down base. The NVA were shooting Russian made D-74 towed artillery guns. I believe this was a final kiss off to us from uncle Ho. We all looked at each other and wondered why they didn't use those guns last night. That would have been a game changer. It was a short flight to Trang Bang and when we landed, we were told to go to the two bunkers located in front of the 8-inch mechanized artillery unit. If it wasn't for bad luck, we would have no luck at all.

February 26, 1969

While the second platoon sat in Trang Bang licking their wounds, the base camp in Cu Chi was about to be attacked. The men in Charlie Company working in Cu Chi had just finished their dinner at the mess hall and returned to the supply room to talk about the horrible events of February 23 and 24. One of the supply guys had bought a bottle of rice wine from a man in Buckeye and opened it up and passed it around for everyone to have a swig. The topic of discussion tonight was the devastation to the second platoon and Charlie Company CP at Diamond. The supply sergeant was grieving the fact that Brockway and Eubanks had been killed during the overrun of the fire support base. Hunt the company clerk knew all the men that had been killed that night. Lee the company armor had just been with these guys a couple of weeks before making sure every man's weapon was in top condition.

Besides a rocket or mortar dropping into the base once and awhile, life was considered fairly safe inside the Cu Chi base camp. They finished off the bottle of rice wine and at 2300 hrs. everybody decided to call it a night. As each man was looking forward to a good night's sleep, none of them could have known that VC sappers were crawling under their positions in tunnels that had been built in the 1940s. Miles of these tunnels stretched from Cu Chi all the way to the Cambodian border.

When all the men were visiting the land of Nod, the sappers emerged from the tunnels right behind the supply rooms. They set up in Bravo ammo bunker and started calling in fire missions. Additional sappers were carrying RPG launchers with many rounds to launch.

When the first explosion hit everyone thought it was just rockets. They had no idea the sappers were waiting outside their hooches. Jim Calvert was sleeping and was awakened by everything around him blowing up. He turned on his ceiling light and started to get dressed when a sapper tossed a concussion grenade at him through the firing port. Luckily, the grenade was stopped by the screen covering the opening.

When the grenade exploded it took out the window frame and one of the big beams holding up the roof. The entire room was covered in wood shrapnel and Calvert remained without a scratch. What are the chances? Calvert thought the sapper would come in and shoot him but instead the sapper blew up all the supply rooms and the Jeep sitting out front.

It was a miracle no one was killed or seriously wounded. Calvert and the rest of the men ran to a bunker behind the supply building and sat out the rest of the night. There were huge explosions in the direction of the muleskinners helicopter bunkers and when all the shooting stopped, 12 Chinook helicopters were taken out of commission. A total loss of 10 million dollars went up in smoke in less than 10 minutes. In addition, the sappers blew up an ammo dump and killed some of the men guarding the helicopters. The moral to this story is there was no safe place in Vietnam.

The Animals - We've Gotta Get Out of This Place

293

Chapter Fifteen
TRANG BANG MARCH 1969

When we arrived in Trang Bang we were told we would be standing down for a few days and that we could get new fatigues and boots if we needed them. A few of us still remembered when we were here in December pulling bridge duty. That was the best duty we ever had until Lamere tried to shoot the Colonel's helicopter out of the sky. After that everything seemed to get worse for us.

Lamere was just coming back from R&R to Australia having just missed the Diamond nightmare. He told us about going there with just $50 in his pocket and how he bought a huge sausage to eat and slept in hostels. He said Australia was an awesome place and that he would love to go back someday. We had taken over two bunkers that the 101st airborne had occupied just before we arrived. We stored our gear inside the bunkers and headed over to the mess hall for some hot chow.

It's hard to describe the hunger that a guy experiences when you are living on C rations. They came in different meals including spaghetti and meatballs, beans and franks, beefsteak, potatoes and gravy, ham and lima beans, meatballs and beans, boned chicken, chicken noodles, meatloaf, spiced beef, turkey loaf and ham and eggs chopped.

Each box also contained a plastic spoon, and accessory packet that contained cheese, crackers, cocoa, four cigarettes, toilet paper, coffee creamer, sugar, salt, matches, instant coffee, and Chiclets chewing gum. Some of the meals included fruit cocktail, peaches, apricots, chocolate nut roll, pound cake, and a chocolate energy bar. With every case of C rations there were also a handful of P-38s thrown in. A P-38 is a small hand operated can opener.

If we were lucky the chow hall would fly out hot meals while we were in the field. These meals were brought out in mermite insulated containers. Some of the meals included meatloaf, beef tips, chicken, mashed potatoes, veggies, cake or pie, ice cold lemonade and steaming hot coffee.

Once every couple of weeks we would receive a sundry pack that included writing paper, envelopes, blue ink pens, foot powder, toothbrushes and paste, chewing gum, M&Ms, Hershey bars, Almond Joy, Mounds, Three Musketeers, Snickers, and cartons of cigarettes. One of the highlights of our day is when the helicopter bringing us mail would also have a ration of beer and Coca-Cola.

Each man was allotted two beers and two sodas a day. I would always trade my beers to somebody that would rather drink beer than soda. Up to this point I didn't drink any liquor or beer. It wasn't a judgmental thing I just never acquired a taste for it. Toward the end of my tour the Army introduced us to LRRP rations. They were freeze-dried meals in a bag. They included beef stew, spaghetti and meatballs, and chili. The only downside to these new rations is that they required hot water to make them edible.

After we finished our meal at the mess hall, we returned to the bunkers to set up guard duty assignments. Garcia ask me if I had any playing cards and it suddenly hit me that Sugar Bear was the last guy to have the deck. Like a bolt of lightning I could see his vacant eyes staring at me when I pulled the poncho back at Diamond. My eyes filled with tears and my very soul ached knowing he and all the others that died that night would never return to play another hand of spades. I felt so sad. I had to grab my hand to make it stop shaking. I'll never forget the looks on those guys' faces.

We were settled in for the night and I thought we would get some much needed sleep. Everyone had been running on nervous energy and exhaustion had won the day. At 2400 hrs., we were ripped from sleep by the thunderous sound of the battery of 8-inch artillery guns going off behind us. The ground shook so severely that our weapons leaning up against the bunker had fallen into the dirt. Guys in the bunker were covered with dust that had fallen through the sandbags on top of the bunker.

The ringing in my ears was deafening. Several guys were cussing, and Ray threw a C ration can at one of the tanks. This was getting ridiculous and the shooting continued into the early morning hours. I used a couple of Salem cigarette filters to shove in my ears to dampen the sound. So much for catching up on our sleep, I guess it just wasn't in the cards. In the morning everyone was grumpy and even the quiet guys were bitching and moaning.

Marquez told us to go to the mess hall for breakfast and when we were through he wanted to have a platoon meeting. I could really get spoiled on eating hot food three times a day. When we returned Marquez told us he knew how tough the last few days had been. He informed us that we didn't have enough men to field an ambush so we would remain on bunker duty until our new replacements arrived.

We were assigned a new medic whose name was Doc Flores. He was a Mexican guy from San Diego, California. I knew from the first time I met him that he was going to be a loner. He did not have much to say to any of us and he kept pretty much to himself. He was carrying an M-16 without a clip in it and he wasn't carrying any extra ammunition. I asked him if he was a conscientious objector and he said, "no I'm here to keep you guys alive not to kill anybody."

He told me he would be glad to carry extra ammo for anybody that might run out. I asked him where he had done his basic and advanced training and he said Fort Sam Houston. I told him that he was joining a unit that had just been devastated just a week ago. He said he had heard all about Diamond while he was processing through the company in Cu Chi. I told him our last medic Doc Browning had been killed while running to the CP to help guys that had been crushed under a collapsed bunker.

As I turned to walk away, I looked back and said, "I hope you'll be around for a while." I was standing by our bunker with Ray when a new 1st lieutenant came walking up. He said, "is this the second platoon?" I said, "yeah are you lost!" Ray snickered behind my back and the Lieutenant said, "No, I'm your new platoon leader, my name is Joel Baker." I asked him where he was from and he said, "Wichita, Kansas."

I asked him where he took his training and he said, "I'm a National Guard Reservist." I was sure I had heard him wrong. I said, "did you say National Guard?" He nodded his head and said, "I was called up to active duty." Ray and I stood there with our jaws almost touching the ground in disbelief. We had never heard of any National Guard soldiers in Vietnam. I got a sick feeling in my guts thinking this guy knows next to nothing and he has just taken charge of our platoon.

Let's see, new troops, new lieutenant, definitely not good. He must have seen my face turning gray when he said, "I want you guys to know I don't know much about Vietnam but I'm willing to learn as fast as I can and try not to get anyone hurt." I looked at Ray and said, "that might be the smartest thing I've ever heard come out of an officer's mouth."

I asked Lt. Baker if he was trained to call in artillery and he said, "yes, but I only did it in training." I said, "we have a rule here: if in doubt call in a marking round." I told Baker that Ray and I would show him the ropes and begin by keeping him with us when we went on our next ambush patrol. He and Sgt. Marquez hooked up the next day and Marquez told him his version of what happened at Diamond. I think the last thing he said to the Lieutenant was, "Welcome to Vietnam, you sonny beach!"

Just as we thought we were going to get some time off the new replacements started to arrive. They would show up two and three at a time over a period of a week. They were quite a sight to see with their new fatigues and new combat boots. They approached us with worried looks on their faces not knowing what was in store for them. We had survived Diamond and the last thing we wanted was for a bunch of new guys to get us killed.

For the first week we shunned the new guys and refused to hang out with them. There was one little guy that refused to be put off. He kept hanging around me constantly asking me questions about what to expect when we went back out in the field. This little guy's name was Mike Lozon and he couldn't have been over 98 pounds soaking wet. He told me he was from Flint, Michigan and that he had worked at GM before being drafted. He informed me that his drill instructor in AIT told the trainees, "When you get to Vietnam attach yourself to an old guy."

The definition of an old guy was someone that had survived the bush for three or more months. I finally came to the conclusion that it would be better to keep him close and try to teach him the ropes as quickly as I could. I gave him the nickname "Kid" and that was what he would be known as the rest of his tour in Vietnam.

Another replacement was Ed Clennon, who was born and raised in Joliet, Illinois. He came from a family of catholic nuns and his brother Ray was a priest. Ed had started in the seminary but decided the calling was not for him. He dropped out and started furthering his education at the University of Illinois. While attending there, he met the love of his life, Marie. He told me they were planning to get married but then he got his draft notice and they decided to wait and get married when Ed returned from Vietnam.

Danny Dietz from Oregon came in with Clennon and stood 6 ft. 3 in. and weighed 155 lbs. There was another new guy Mannerelli that was also from Michigan. He was a short stocky young man that I decided would carry one of the M-60 machine guns. I decided a guy named Kush, who was 6 ft. 3 in., would be his ammo bearer. By the end of March, we had received 18 new recruits into our platoon. I couldn't remember half their names and really didn't care. The less I knew about them the less I would feel bad when they got killed or wounded.

One particular shake and bake sergeant struck me as having his shit together. His name was Jim Brandau from Iowa. From the time he arrived in the platoon he hung out with Ray and me. He wanted to learn the ropes and asked us if he could follow behind us for a couple of weeks. Jim turned out to be one of the best NCOs in our platoon. Ray and I were told we would be going to the Lightning Combat Leadership course so we could be promoted to E-5 Sergeant.

We were told to wait for the orders to come down. Hurry up and wait right? A new guy from Pennsylvania named Grimm showed up at the same time and I gave him the nickname Grimm Reaper. A guy named Duininck from Minnesota seemed like a solid troop, so I assigned him the M-79. Life wasn't so bad these days. Another shake and bake sergeant named Charlie Van Ark from Michigan showed up more than willing to take instruction on how to survive this hell hole. We were getting 3 hots and a cot, and we weren't being overrun or blasted by incoming mortars.

Now if we could just figure out how to get the 8-inch guns behind us to stop firing at night. I remember the first day sweep we took the new guys on outside the base. We were going to do a "walk around" a short distance from the base. Lt. Baker was leading the platoon, and Doc Flores was walking right next to him. Baker's RTO was following behind. Suddenly a shot rang out and Doc did a face plant onto the ground. Everyone hit the deck facing in the direction of the muzzle sound and I thought Doc had been head shot. Shit, so much for being with us for a while Doc.

Baker was kneeling next to Doc talking on the radio when Doc moved and got to his knees. He was holding his stomach and looked like he was going to chuck up his lunch. As it turned out the snipers bullet hit one of the M-16 magazines Doc was carrying in a bandoleer across his chest. The round knocked all the air out of his lungs rendering him temporally incapacitated. Lt. Baker was so taken aback by what had happened he asked Doc if he could have the magazine for a good luck souvenir.

Doc said sure and handed it to him. We never did locate the sniper and assumed it was some old VC who was hiding waiting for a chance to kill a GI. I had to give him credit for his excellent aim. If it wasn't for the magazine, we would be getting a new medic. The rest of the afternoon went without incident and we arrived back to our bunkers in time to go to the chow line.

They brought the mail around after supper and I hit the jackpot: 4 letters from 4 different girls and a care package from home. Mom had sent me several cans of Vienna sausages and a few cans of Hormel chili with beef. She also topped the box off with 2 dozen chocolate chip cookies that had turned into crumbs.

One of the guys received a care package with cookies surrounded by popcorn. I'll be damned if that didn't keep the cookies from falling apart and we had popcorn to boot. As March came to an end it occurred to me that nobody got killed or wounded in the last 30 days. Could this be a good omen? Were we finally out of the worst of it?

April 1969 April Fools

The answer to my question came on April 1. Lt. Baker and SFC Marquez had us meet together for a briefing. I knew something was wrong by the look on Marquez's face. He looked tired and drawn out. He informed us that Alpha and Bravo Companies were returning to the Cambodian Border to construct another fire support base. They were naming it Diamond 2 and it would be located a little closer to the border than Diamond 1. He said Charlie Company would be held in reserve if needed.

To the 10 guys that had survived Diamond 1, this was a terrible blow. We never in our wildest dreams thought the Army would send the Wolfhounds back there. The new guys only knew what we had told them about Diamond 1 and their instincts told them this was going to be their first shit show. They didn't know the half of it. Was this some kind of sick April fool's joke? Lt. Baker told us he was going to take the platoon on a shake-down mission first thing in the morning. This meant he was going to see how the new guys would handle their gear and start working as a unit.

The morning of the 4th we left the wire at Trang Bang knowing that tomorrow we might be headed back to the

Cambodian border. We headed to a nearby village and planned to eat our lunch there. Many ARVN families lived there, and it was considered a safe haven for American forces. The villagers were always friendly, and the little children would sit in your lap as you opened the C ration cans. I always shared my peaches or fruit cocktail with them, and they would say, "GI number 1, VC number 10."

Ray and I talked about Diamond 2 and he said, "maybe we should have re-upped and gotten out of this bad place." I agreed and said, "somebody has to show these new guys how to survive this shit hole." When we got ready to saddle up Marquez told Bill Tyron he was going to walk point with Alabama and Slovey. He wanted the new guys to get experience at all positions. We nicknamed Tyron "The old man" because when he got to Nam he was 33 yrs. old.

He was an RA with 6 years in the service. His rank was E-3 so I was anxious to hear his story. As soon as we were ready, we headed out the north end of Trang Bang. We headed straight away to the nearby village. It seemed unusually quiet, but I figured maybe everyone was taking a siesta. We spread out and sat next to the hooches and ate our lunch. So far so good.

A couple of the new guys pulled out a deck of cards and started playing hearts. Lt. Baker came by and said it was time to saddle up. We took a quick tour of the village looking inside the hooches and then headed back. The point element had just stepped through a hedgerow leading us to an open rice paddy when a single shot rang out. It sounded like an M-14 firing not an AK or M-16.

Everyone took a knee and waited for word to come back on what was happening. Somebody up front yelled for Doc Flores to come to the front of the column. We sat for 20 minutes or more when we heard the all too familiar sound of helicopter rotors whap whapping in the air. The chopper landed in the rice paddy to our front and it took off as quickly as it landed.

Slovey came walking back and told Ray and I that Tyron had been shot in the head by a sniper hiding in a spider hole. Jesus Christ, how the hell did that happen? I thought this was a friendly village. When the new guys heard what had happened, they were all speechless.

No one said a word. I knew they were scared to death and there wasn't a damn thing I could do about it. There was genuine terror on their faces. They were all looking at me to make sense of what just happened. I had nothing for them. That ugly dark dreaded feeling was creeping back into my mind and the only emotion I felt was anger. When we walked back into Trang Bang, we were met by the Company Commander. He wanted to know the details of the incident. Under my breath I said, "another one of our guys got wasted on some horseshit day sweep." Ray grabbed my shoulder and said, "Easy bro, it don't mean nothin."

None of the new guys knew Tyron so we didn't know much about him except he came from Kansas City, Missouri. Just another guy sent to graves and registration in a body bag.

Ray and I spent a good part of the night trying to prepare the new guys what to expect if we got called up to support Alpha and Bravo on the Cambodian border. The subject of Tyron never came up again. We told the guys that the first thing we had to do was fill sand bags as fast as we could to use in making fighting positions. Since Diamond 1 we learned that traditional bunkers were death traps if the NVA got inside the perimeter.

The new guys had already heard how our platoon was blown up when satchel charges were thrown into the bunkers full of our buddies. I wanted them to know how serious Diamond 2 would be. I prayed to God we wouldn't be called on to go. At 1700 hrs., Marquez came by our bunker and told us that second platoon would be going on the first flight to Diamond 2 to provide security. SSGT Glover stopped by and said he would be seeing us out there tomorrow.

As he was leaving, he turned and looked at us and said, "don't any of you assholes get killed out there or I will be seriously pissed." Some of the old guys got together and talked about what we could expect in the morning. We all agreed that we would have to keep an eye on the new guys and keep them focused on the job at hand. I doubted the NVA would be looking for us to return. They obviously didn't know how the U.S. Army thinks. Battalion had this idea that they were willing to give up 1 of us for 10 of theirs. They referred to it as acceptable losses. That's easy to say unless you are one of the losses!

We were being used as bait just like at Diamond 1. I made the rounds at midnight and found no one was sleeping. The new guys had very nervous looks on their faces and were not saying much. I told them, "If an old-timer tells you to do something just do it and don't ask why." I was beginning to have a bad feeling about tomorrow.

April 4, 1969

At 0700 hrs., our platoon started loading up on a Chinook helicopter. We were going to be the first troops to hit the ground and our mission was to secure the area where Diamond 2 would be located. Several Chinooks followed us carrying huge slings of building materials.

A mosquito cargo helicopter sat down a D-8 dozer and quickly lifted off to go back to Fire Support base Stuart to load up 105 cal. howitzers. Those cannon crankers were the same unit that supported us at Diamond 1. Like us, they had mostly new guys manning the guns. Sorties of Hueys would bring in Alpha and Bravo Companies.

Second platoon was assigned the north end of the proposed perimeter site and we spread out facing Cambodia. I wasn't worried about getting attacked in broad daylight, but I could feel the NVA looking at us through their fancy chi com binoculars. I imagined the officer in charge preparing reports that would be sent to their Regimental headquarters in Hanoi asking for orders concerning our arrival. I figured it would take a day or two for them to get organized and stage another attack.

The same regiments that overran us at Diamond 1 were still operating just inside Cambodia. The hair on the back of my neck was standing at attention again. It took the engineers about 2 hours to level out the perimeter. They took grade stakes and pounded them into the ground where the fighting positions would be located. The concertina wire would be stretched around the perimeter about 50 feet in front of the positions. This whole process had to be accomplished while the sun was still up.

The excess dirt was pushed into piles to be used to fill sandbags. I was hoping that when the perimeter was finished, they would get us the hell out of there. This would be Alpha and Bravo's fight, not ours. The good thing about pulling the security detail was we got to sit and watch everyone else do the work. Yeah, it was miserable sitting out in the scorching sun, but it beat the hell out of filling sand bags and stringing wire. I was impressed at how quickly Diamond 2 took shape. At 1300 hours a mosquito transport helicopter brought in a prefabricated tower. It looked huge, standing 3 stories above the ground. I wondered if SSGT Glover would be up there tonight with a crew-served starlight scope.

He had a lot more guts than I had. As far as I was concerned that tower was a direct target for RPGs. I noticed that the mess tents had been put up and guys with aprons were setting up tables and trash cans filled with water and immersion heaters. By 1400 hrs., the Howitzer crews had their guns setup and fighting positions completed.

I could see stacks of artillery round boxes stacked nearby, Alpha and Bravo's weapons platoons were putting the finishing touches on their mortar pits and fighting positions. A convoy arrived in midafternoon carrying the Headquarters Company and all their gear.

The artillery FO would be spending his time coordinating with Trang Bang and Jackson FSB for artillery support. Glover was busy coordinating with all the air assets. Marquez told us he was concerned because the radio chatter in the CP was all about the FSB being hit like Diamond 1. What a sick feeling knowing your leaders were setting you up for another bloodletting.

Good Lord willing, we would be sucking down a barley pop or soda in Trang Bang tonight. As it turned out the Good Lord was not so willing after all. A Captain from Headquarters Company came out at 1700 hrs. and told us our platoon would be manning three fighting positions on the north side of the perimeter tonight. Ray chimed in and said, "If it weren't for bad luck, we'd have no luck at all." I just said, "Fuck it." I was hoping the Army had its shit together better than they did at Diamond 1.

At 1750 hrs., our platoon marched back into the newly built Fire Support Base named Diamond 2. SFC Marquez assigned each of our three squads to a bunker and told us to prepare to defend ourselves. We took turns running to the chow line where we had meat loaf dropped into our mess kits. They were also serving mashed potatoes and gravy, mixed vegetables and cookies for dessert.

I grabbed a couple extra cartons of milk and walked back to the bunker line. Lt. Baker returned from the CP briefing and told us that the NVA had used artillery to drop CS gas into FSB Stewart. This was something new. He told us to have our gas masks close by in case the gooks tried this on us. There were stories being told about a marine base being gassed and overrun when the Viet Cong human waved them right through the gas.

I got my squad together and made them show me their gas masks and told them to wear them on their web belt. I had each man put his mask on and check to see if it sealed on their face. Remembering back to basic training and the gas chamber reminded me that CS gas will incapacitate a person and make them sitting ducks for enemy insurgents.

I warned them that there would be no one there to help them if they failed to get their mask on. I kept remembering the 3 artillery rounds fired at us as we left Diamond 1. The only difference was we were closer to the border and they didn't have to fire as far to hit us! Everyone had their weapons ready with plenty of magazines and we had hand grenades spread out at each man's fighting position.

Mannarelli had 500 rounds of M-60 ammo clipped together and was ready to rock and roll. My biggest fear was the RPGs that would be coming in. A direct hit to a fighting position from an RPG was a game changer. At 1950 hrs., the first artillery shell landed in front of the second platoon's bunkers. The rounds came from the Cambodian border and contained CS gas. I had been looking towards the border just minutes before and did not see any sign of movement. I did not expect a human wave but the way the breeze was blowing I knew we were going to get gassed.

Several guys were yelling, "GAS!" I looked to my left and Kid Lozon was donning his mask. It took me only seconds to get my mask on and adjust the straps and begin to breathe normally.

307

When the gas reached us, our exposed skin felt like it was on fire. The chemical was penetrating every exposed pore of my body. I yelled to the guys to get ready to shoot in case there was a human wave. The gas was so thick I couldn't see the wire. Just to be on the safe side I had Mannarelli shoot some M-60 machine gun rounds to our front.

Behind me, I saw a couple of guys from another squad writhing on the ground, wiping their crying eyes begging for someone to help. Those dumb asses had not followed directions and now they were paying for it. No sympathy from me! If we get humans waved, they are dead meat. The entire base was on high alert, waiting for incoming rockets and mortars, but nothing happened. The gas shells were the only thing that occurred. After the gas dissipated, guys were pouring water into their eyes and over their arms and necks.

What the hell had just happened? There was only one explanation: the NVA wanted us to know they knew we were there and what they had planned for us in the near future. What was it HO had said about wiping these nuisance bases off the face of the earth? At 2000 hrs., everything was quiet, and each position had their guards on duty. The night passed without incident except for some dumb ass tripping and falling on his face heading to the latrine in the dark.

April 5, 1969

The next morning was normal duty: get up, shave, wash your face, comb any hair you had left and go to the chow line. The mess sergeant was serving our favorite breakfast: SOS (shit on a shingle) and scrambled eggs. They had melons sliced up and leftover cookies from the previous night's meal. I was hoping they would pull the second platoon out of here and send us back to Trang Bang. So far all we have done is sit in the sun and get gassed. I hadn't had this much fun since I hit my thumb with a hammer.

When we got done with breakfast, we waited to hear from Lt. Baker about what they were going to do with us. Several guys were playing cards and Mannarelli was cleaning his M-60. I asked Kid Lozon if he wanted to play splits and he said he had never played before. "No problem Kid, I'll teach you." The game of splits has been an Army pastime since the revolutionary war. Two men stand facing each other about 5 feet apart. Both have their feet touching, like standing at attention. A knife or bayonet is used to throw to the right or left of the opponent's foot. The distance between knife and foot cannot exceed the length of the knife.

The opponent then moves his foot to where the knife is sticking in the ground. To be a legal throw, the knife must stick upright in the ground. Then that man throws the knife at his opponent's feet, etc. The object is to stretch your opponent's feet so far out that they lose balance and fall over. If the knife thrower is good, it only takes three or four throws to beat the other guy.

I was one of the best splits players in the platoon and very rarely lost. The only guy that could beat me was Big Joe because he had longer legs. After I had given Kid the directions, I suggested we give the game a whirl. I let Kid go first and his first throw failed to stick in the ground. My throw was just under the length of the knife, so Kid had to move his foot out. After a couple of throws I had Kid stretched out pretty good.

On my last throw the blade stuck in the top of Kid's boot. Kid looked at me like I'd just killed his favorite puppy then yelped, "shit Sarge you stuck my foot." I apologized profusely and told him this had never happened before. I couldn't help but laugh at the expression on his face and said, "I guess you win!" Lt. Baker came by and told us we would be staying at least one more day and night before returning to Trang Bang.

We could only pray that the NVA wouldn't hit the base any time soon. Most of us knew it wasn't if, but when they would do it. I looked down and noticed my hands were shaking again. I was getting that sick feeling in my guts and I could not get the picture out of my mind of Sugar Bear looking at me with those lifeless eyes.

The rest of the afternoon was uneventful. I went over to the observation tower and helped lift the large starlight scope up into the tower. We fastened the tripod to the floor and made sure it had a 180-degree swing facing the border. I saw SSGT Glover and he wanted to know where the second platoon was located. He told me to make sure the guys are out of the bunkers when the rockets and mortars start coming in. I asked him if he knew for sure when we would get hit. He said, "as soon as the NVA are ready."

As I stood in the tower looking over the vast area between our base and the Cambodian border, I thought about the Special Forces E-7 Igene Johnson and his gang of Montagnards and what they might be doing today. My mind drifted back to home and the old neighborhood I grew up in and all the guys I grew up with and what they were doing while I was in Nam.

I wondered why my sister never wrote me any letters and if my dad was going to move to Cody, Wyoming. I looked down on our bunkers and wondered how many of these new guys would be killed or maimed before their tour was over.

So many guys had died, and countless guys wounded and never heard of again. And I only have 172 days left until I get out of this bad place. When I came out of my daydream, I left the tower and returned to the second platoon bunkers. Mannarelli said he heard we were having hamburgers for dinner. He was all excited, but he hadn't seen where those precooked, floating in grease, burgers came from.

I was already planning to go to the mess hall and scrounge around for a case of C rations. At 1600 hrs., Lt. Baker had us gather up and he told us we needed to be ready for action tonight. One of the ARVN advisors reported that his intelligence officer indicated an immanent attack tonight. ARVN intelligence had been wrong before, but they had been right on February 23rd. Marquez reminded everyone how important it was for every man to defend himself and have his buddies back. He said, "there are no do over's in battle."

I knew in my heart we would be hit tonight, and it made me sick in my soul. It was knowing what was coming that made it worse. I spent the rest of the afternoon writing letters to my family and all my girlfriend pen pals. I could crank out a dozen letters in one sitting. I told one of my favorites how I looked forward to getting married and having kids. I think living in a fantasy world helped a lot of guys cope with the insanity that we lived in. It was getting dark when I dropped the letters in the mail bag, and I knew I had to help my guys make it through one more night.

Just like Diamond 1, the rockets and mortars started sailing in at 0130 hrs. I got all my guys out of the bunkers and hunkered down behind our fighting positions. It was black as the ace of spades and we could not see beyond the wire. I told the guys not to shoot until we could see the gooks trying to breach the perimeter.

I didn't realize it at the time, but the NVA had started moving their troops at sundown and the first troops to arrive were the 51 cal. machine gun crews. They had set up 25 yards to our front. Hundreds of NVA regulars ran past both our flanks and prepared to breach the perimeter on the southwest and southeast sides of the base. Several RPG rounds flew over our heads, missing us entirely but hitting the water trailer blowing it 15 feet into the air.

Almost immediately, tracers from the 51 cal. machine guns to our front were hitting the sandbags that made up our positions. I told Mannarelli to aim at the source of the tracers. He started working his magic with three and four-round controlled bursts. The rest of the guys were shooting single rounds on semiautomatic conserving their ammunition. Our two M-79 gunners were placing HE rounds as close to the targets as possible.

A twin-engine plane carrying illumination canisters could be heard overhead and suddenly flares were going off one right after another. The light from the flares allowed us to see what was going on in front of us. The 51 cal. crews had moved up to within 50 feet of the wire and several gooks were trying to feed bamboo Bangalore torpedoes into the concertina wire. I screamed for everyone to zero in on those bastards and within minutes, every one of those sappers had been killed or wounded.

Some of them were throwing hand grenades at us but we were just out of their range. Not to be outdone our M-79s were putting direct HE rounds into the wire. One of those rounds was a little high but ended up hitting one of the 51 cal. machine guns. While all this was going on, the entire perimeter was engaged in serious firefights. The NVA had breached the wire on the southeast side of the perimeter in front of the 105 cal. Howitzer emplacements.

The howitzers had lowered their barrels and were shooting flechette rounds and firecracker rounds into the mass of NVA soldiers maneuvering outside the wire. Two Cobra helicopters showed up and took out the 51 cal. machine gun that was keeping our heads down. Puff the Magic Dragon came on station and hosed down several groups of NVA hightailing it back to

Cambodia. At 0530, the fighting stopped and medevac ships were coming in to get our killed and wounded.

The second platoon, with all of its new guys had prevented an attempted overrun of the north side of the base. We had killed 19 NVA and an unknown number of wounded. We did all this without sustaining a single man killed and only two men slightly wounded. Uncle Ho certainly did not catch us off guard this time. I was never so proud of a group of guys as I was right then. I walked back towards the CP bunker and saw that it had taken a direct hit from a 122 mm rocket. It had partially caved in the roof and as I got closer, I saw a private first class sitting with his head between his legs holding a 45-cal. pistol.

When I got closer, I said, "what the hell happened here." He did not respond so I went over and knelt next to him and asked him if he was all right. He was covered with dirt and his face was covered with sticky blood. He looked at me with blank eyes and said, "somebody gave me this 45 and told me to shoot any gooks that might be running by." I could tell that the guy was in a state of shock so I yelled for a medic and told him everything would be okay. The last thing he said to me was, "have you seen SSGT Glover, he pulled me out of the bunker." I told him no, but I was sure he was around here somewhere.

When the company medic arrived, he told me that he had just come from treating SSGT Glover for a severe head wound. He said it could have been a bullet or piece of shrapnel from the ammo dump when it exploded. He said he had just put him on the medevac before coming back to the CP. He said Glover was really messed up. He said he might have been shot in the head. I heard what he said, but I could not comprehend that Glover had been fatally wounded on the front line doing what he always did: taking care of us.

When I returned to our bunkers, I told Ray about talking to the private first class and the news about Glover. We both got

313

tears in our eyes and Ray said, "not Glover." Of all the men we served with this man seemed invincible and surely would have made it home. He only had a very short time before going home but was asked by the brass to stay at Diamond before going home.

That night 15 U.S. soldiers lost their lives and another 32 wounded. The NVA body count was 109 not counting the bodies drug back to the border during the night. I would be returning to Trang Bang with a bunch of seasoned veterans, not new guys. The NVA had shot 350 RPGs, 150 82 mm mortars and an unknown number of 122 mm rockets at us.

When the fight is over and guys realize they are still in one piece, they begin to bullshit with the other guys on how many gooks they killed or thought they killed and how we really kicked their asses. There was a kind of jubilation and lots of high fives.

For just a moment the absolute fear and terror during a firefight gives way to celebrating life. Another pit was dozed out and 109 NVA KIAs were tossed into the hole without ceremony.

April 6, 1969

At 0800 hrs., the second platoon lined up outside Diamond 2, waiting for the choppers to take them back to Trang Bang. Alpha Company's CO came by and thanked us for our help. He said, "it's a miracle none of you guys got killed." I said, "Sir it was our turn for a miracle." When we loaded up, I took my usual seat on the floor, behind the pilot, with my feet dangling outside. I had a feeling of pride for all the new guys and how they stepped up when it counted. I felt like they had passed their trial by fire with flying colors.

Our future was unknown, but I knew they would have each other's backs. The pilots decided to give the new guys a thrill, so they descended to about 100 ft. and headed directly towards a massive hedgerow. We were traveling at about 90 knots when the ships swooped down to about 20 ft. off the ground.

When it looked like we were going to crash head-on into the hedgerow, the pilot yanked back on the stick and our hearts leapt into our throats as the chopper barely cleared the tops of the bamboo. We were so close the bamboo leaves touched my boots. After clearing the foliage, the ship took a sudden drop, almost touching the ground. There was a simultaneous roar of holy crap and gasps from the guys sitting onboard. The door gunner was laughing his ass off. This wasn't my first rodeo, but it always caught me off guard whenever they did it. Who said we never have fun in Vietnam?

Chuck Moore Cobra Pilot

I try with a little help from my friends

Little Bears Picking Us Up

Tunnel Entrance

316

Chapter Sixteen
I THINK WE NEED A WORD OF PRAYER

W e were working in an area around the Hobo Woods when we got the news that Charlie Company was going to be the Vanguard Company for a Battalion sized operation. The Battalion had been planning this mission for months. The NVA had gained such a foothold in the woods that they were able to operate bases out of there with impunity. They had tanks, artillery and several large trucks that they were bringing in from Cambodia using the Ho Chi Minh Trail.

They were building up forces to make a run at Saigon and the intelligence gurus were saying they planned to take out Cu Chi at the same time. The 25th Infantry Division took this personally and General Williamson said, "Not on my watch." This was going to be the biggest battle Charlie Company had ever been in. We were told the Army expected heavy losses but that the end justified the means. We were in a temporary lager just west of the woods two days before the proposed battle.

Every man was upset, knowing what was coming. We were told to write letters home and if we had any religious beliefs this would be a good time to pray. The evening before the battle a

317

Huey helicopter landed and a man in fresh fatigues jumped out carrying a briefcase.

The closer I looked, I could see a cross on one of his lapels and Captain bars on the other lapel. I had never seen a Chaplain before, but my guess was this man was one of them. He walked straight away to the Battalion Operations tent and disappeared inside. In about five minutes our First Sergeant walked out of the tent and headed towards us. He assembled the platoon sergeants in a huddle and in a few minutes the huddle broke up. SSGT Hannah came over to our area and told us to gather around. He told us that the

Army knew tomorrow could be a rough day and that a Chaplain was sent out to perform a service for anyone interested. The Chaplain set up a make-shift altar out of ammo boxes and opened his briefcase and took out a bible and other religious articles. Ray and I decided it couldn't hurt to go and see what the sky pilot had to say.

There were about 50 guys standing in a semicircle around the Chaplain. He introduced himself as Rabbi Goldmann. He said he had come to bring communion to the catholic boys, lay hands on the protestant boys and bestow a special blessing on the Jewish boys. He said any other denomination could join in wherever they pleased.

The first thing he said was, "Boys, there is no such thing as an atheist in a foxhole." He continued to say he had come to help each man, no matter what their faith, an opportunity to get squared away with God before we entered the woods tomorrow. He asked the catholic boys to raise their hands and come forward and he would give them the sacrament of communion. I turned to Ray and said, "I don't think a Rabbi can do that; it has to be an ordained priest." The Rabbi told us he had been given a special dispensation to minister to all faiths and that the communion had been blessed by the Catholic chaplain in Saigon.

318

At a time like this, I figured it wouldn't hurt to hedge my bet in the spiritual department. Ray and I went forward and received communion and the Rabbi placed his hand on our heads and said, "The body of Christ, God go with you."

When it was the Protestants turn, he laid his hand on their shoulders and prayed a prayer of strength and courage for each man. There were only two Jewish guys that went forward and the Rabbi prayed for them in Hebrew. After he was done, he packed up his gear and told us he would be praying for our safety and victory in battle. I felt a certain sense of peace and figured if I got killed tomorrow, I'd at least have a chance to go to Purgatory.

Riverboats on the Vam Co Dong River

319

VC Prisoners

John at Diamond

Doc Flores

John arming a claymore

Diamond Teardown

Chapter Seventeen
RIVERBOAT WARRIORS

No sooner than we got back to Trang Bang the Company Commander sent orders for the second platoon to report to the Navy Advanced Base in Go Dau Ha. Go Dau Ha was located on the Vam Co Dong River not far from Tay Ninh and Saigon. The Navy had PBRs (River Patrol Boat) and RAG (River Assault Group) boats operated by the Navy to support Army units interfering with NVA units headed towards Tay Ninh and Saigon.

These boats carried small groups of GIs up and down the river looking for enemy forces. The idea was to run slowly up the river and wait for the VC to open up on you, and then turn the boat towards the shore, jump off the boat and assault whoever was firing at the boat. Sounds simple doesn't it?

We had just been hung out as bait at the Diamonds and now we were literally being used as bait on suicide boats. They had barracks for us to sleep in with cots when we weren't river running. Now there are some advantages to working with the Navy. Their mess hall served steak and barbecue ribs at least 4 times a week.

There was always plenty of beer and soda and the meals were out of this world. I wish I had known about this because I would have joined the Navy! Besides being dead ducks sitting on the pond, this duty had potential. Our first river patrol ride was very interesting. The boat we were going to ride on they called a Tango. It was a LCM-6 landing craft. When we boarded, there were 7 sailors crewing the boat including the Captain.

The first thing I noticed was the armament onboard. There were 4-M1919 Browning Machine guns, 2-MK16 20 mm cannons and a MK-19 automatic grenade launcher. Each had enough ammunition to wage a 10-day war!

The Captain invited us to help ourselves to the soda cooler as well as a well-stocked snack locker. He gave us a brief orientation of the boat and told us where we would sit while cruising the river. He said if we had to beach the craft, we would have to un-ass the boat ASAP. Any stragglers would be thrown overboard. He said we would be hitting the shore guns blazing and should assume it would be a hot landing. Besides that, he said, "welcome aboard."

The Captain assumed his position behind the wheel and fired up the 2-Detroit 8V-71 Diesel engines. These babies had 460 hp sustained with twin shafts. The roar of the engines told us right away we would not be sneaking up on any enemy troops. We pulled away from the dock and headed up the river at 5 knots per hour. We passed by several Vietnamese junks and sampans carrying god only knows what.

The Captain told us the PBRs (River Patrol Boats) were responsible for inspecting their contents. Our job, he said, "was to find Charlie and blow him away." I was hoping these boat guns would do that before we had to land and assault. One of the sailors sat up front with a pair of binoculars, looking at the shoreline as we cruised by. His job was to notice any movement and tell the Captain.

322

Our first encounter was about 3 miles up the river. The lookout said he saw movement and the Captain immediately pushed the throttle full open and turned sharply left to turn around. I heard the sailors cocking two of the machine guns and one of the swabs jumped behind the 20 mm cannon. The Captain came full around and when we were parallel to the shore, all hell broke loose.

Most of us put our heads down and wondered what the hell was happening. The noise was deafening. The hot brass coming out of the machine guns burned anyone unlucky enough that it fell on. The firing lasted for about a minute then stopped as soon as it had started. We continued down the river as if nothing had happened.

The Captain told us that any movement seen on the shoreline was fair game. Sometimes it was just that: animals unlucky enough to have been drinking at the water's edge offered the gunners a chance to keep up their shooting skills and plus it broke up the monotony.

Now that everyone was wound up tighter than an eight-day clock, the Captain told us we would be approaching an area where they often took fire. He told us to get our gear ready and be prepared to jump. This was a completely different situation we found ourselves in. None of us knew what to expect and the idea of jumping out of a boat onto a shoreline didn't thrill anyone.

As we slowly made our way up the river, a PBR came along side us and shouted to the Captain that they had received a couple of hits from a sniper located just around the next corner. The Captain gave him the thumbs up and continued to move forward. The Captain told us we would be disembarking the ship as soon as we got around the next bend. He said we could do a recon and see if we could scare up the sniper.

As we cleared the bend the Captain turned the boat towards the shore and punched the throttle. The bow of the boat touched the shoreline and he yelled for us to jump! It turned out to be a major cluster. A couple of the guys tripped as soon as they hit the water and fell face-first into the mud.

Several of us made it to shore and spread out waiting for something to happen. When everybody was on shore we proceeded into the heavy vegetation. The captain dropped the transmission into reverse and backed away from the shore. It was an eerie feeling knowing that we could be walking into the snipers field of fire. We walked about 100 meters and turned around and walked back the way we came in.

I was glad we didn't see anything and looked forward to getting back to Go Dau Ha. Our boat was sitting 100 yards offshore and you could hear the engines idling. When the crew saw us, they put the boat in gear and came straightaway to our position. Upon arrival, we attempted to get back on board. That was another cluster as the gunwales of the boat were above our heads when we entered the water.

The crew had to pull the guys into the boat and as we cleared the side we tumbled to the deck. Who in the hell ever thought of this brilliant idea? We would be screwed if we had to leave in a hurry. After everyone was onboard and accounted for, the Captain put the transmission in reverse and slowly pulled away from shore.

He continued up river for another hour and then reversed our course and headed back to the naval base. The ride was uneventful, and we made it back in time to hit the chow hall. After dinner we went back to our barracks and played cards or wrote letters. Marquez told us it would take a few days for our mail to catch up to us. As we sat around, we could hear music coming from loud speakers located around the base.

The music was coming from AFVN American Forces Vietnam Network. They had a morning show and different public service announcements like caring for your feet, driving safely and a hundred other topics that had nothing to do with safety for the frontline combat veteran. You would have thought there would be one for us like: be careful and don't trip any booby traps or step on any land mines! Oh well, it didn't seem like the guys in Saigon related to us anyway.

On the night of the 13th, one of our guys returning from R&R told us he heard the 25th was building another base on the Cambodian border and they were calling it Diamond 3. I immediately felt numb. They wouldn't pull us out of here and put us there would they? We were told that Alpha and Delta Companies were the unlucky bastards chosen to build this third disaster ready to happen.

During our second week with the river boats we had our first real action. We were heading up river when suddenly the Captain turned the boat towards shore and slowly eased us up to the bank. He told us to be quiet and sweep the area out to 100 meters. We were getting better at disembarking and everyone got off without incident. We spread out in an assault on line formation and started walking slowly through the elephant grass. I hated walking through that stuff because it would cut your arms up like tiny razor blades. We had been walking for about 10 minutes when suddenly Mannarelli opened up with his machine gun.

Everybody hit the deck ready to shoot when Marquez yelled, "cease fire you sonny beach." As it turned out Mannarelli walked up face to face with an Indochinese Tiger. It scared him so bad he opened up on it firing over its head. The tiger bared its teeth, growled and disappeared into the tall grass. Mannarelli was visibly shook up and we decided that since we betrayed our position we should head back to the boat. As a result, we went back to the base without a body count: either human or animal!

Towards the end of the second week we were ditty bopping up the river when suddenly our boat was being pelted with AK-47 bullets. The two gunners opened up on the shoreline and the vegetation was being chopped up and flying helter skelter. The Captain yelled, "Let's go get those sons of bitches," and after making another run parallel to the shore guns blazing, he turned the nose of the boat towards shore and headed in.

By the time we got there the AK fire had stopped but we knew the gooks were still in there. I was praying they weren't sitting in spider holes where they could pick us off wholesale. When you know you are going into danger your mind shifts into a different gear. You are so focused that fear doesn't enter the equation. Some guys get pissed off and angry and others are super vigilant with all their senses on super sensitive. You are like a coiled spring waiting to suddenly unwind. We exited the boat post-haste and crawled into the tall grass.

Marquez gave the order to move out and we suddenly realized there were a number of ox cart trails leading down to the river. There must be a village close by. Garcia started down one of these trails when suddenly he jumped back and yelled, "Chu Hoi." In Vietnamese that stands for give up. Garcia had stumbled on to a young Vietnamese man sitting next to an AK-47. The man had his hands up and was saying Chu Hoi, Chu Hoi. Garcia picked up the AK and a couple of the guys tied the man's hands behind his back and led him back to the boat.

We figured we had stretched our luck and did not want to stick around to meet his other buddies. This guy was definitely VC, probably living in the nearby village. His job with a couple of his fellow VCs was to go to the river's edge and pop off a few rounds at riverboats cruising by. They weren't prepared for us to hit the beach and ran and hid in the tall grass. This dumb ass didn't get far enough off the trail.

When we got back to the boat the sailors put a sandbag over the man's head and had him squatting on the deck next to the helm. His head was bowed, and I could only imagine how scared he must have been. If he played his cards right, he could be reeducated and go to work for Uncle Sam.

Taking a prisoner in war is the highest prize a unit can get. A throng of swabs and non-military personnel at Go Dah Ha were waiting at the dock when we arrived. They were all there to see what a VC looked like. I'm sure they were expecting to see a ferocious-looking killer and surely must have been disappointed to see a young, skinny kid shaking in his Ho Chi Minh sandals.

We never underestimated these little warriors however, because they could kill you as fast as a seasoned NVA given the chance. Word came down that on April 14th Diamond 3 was hit by 2 battalions of NVA. The base was hit by 350 RPG rounds, one hundred and fifty 82 mm mortars and an untold number of 122 mm rockets. All soldiers on the LP were killed and our boys killed 228 NVA and inflicted another 200 casualties.

Artillery support from Jackson fired 2000 rounds and gunships from Cu Chi beat back the enemy denying them access to the base. Chills ran down my spine and I couldn't get the image of our lifeless guys lying under the ponchos. I was more convinced than ever that my chances of surviving this hell hole were next to none. I actually accepted the fact but was determined to take out as many VC as I could before I checked out. I had lost my appetite after hearing about Diamond 3, so I passed on going to the chow hall. We spent a total of two weeks with the River boaters.

All of us agreed it was not bad duty and the chow was the best we had ever had. I think all of us gained 5 pounds! In a soldier's life, all good things will surely come to an end. We were being sent back to Jackson FSB to join the rest of our company. They didn't say what we would be doing but we knew it wasn't going to be as good as the last two weeks.

SFC Marquez on Sunken Track

Chapter Eighteen
MAY 1969

As soon as we arrived back at Jackson FSB, they assigned us to a real shit detail. We were assigned to go up to the Cambodian border and find and detonate unexploded firecracker bombs. The firecracker bomb was an M449 artillery shell that at a designated height of burst, dropped 60 small bomblets. The bomblets had small fins that acted as rotors descending towards the ground. When the bomblets hit the ground, a wire sprang out, hurling the golf ball-sized bomblets five to six feet in the air where they armed themselves and then exploded. In the distance, the sound of the bomblets going off sounded like firecrackers.

As a bonus, we were going to be joined by a Monkey Track operator. The Army had come up with a small amphibious tracked vehicle that could seat 6 GIs and their equipment. These vehicles were supposed to take us to the bombing site, and we would look for the golf ball-sized bomblets.

When we located one, we would put a piece of C-4 plastic explosive next to it, insert a blasting cap and timed fuse and get away from it and let it go boom. This all looked good on paper but like so many other situations, we affectionately referred to this as FUBAR (fucked up beyond all recognition). When we got off the choppers, there were two of these experimental vehicles waiting with their drivers.

When 10 of us got seated and ready to go, neither of the vehicles would start. So here we are sitting in these miniature troop carriers and it's a no go. The operators messed around trying to start the damn things and finally gave up and radioed Jackson for a Chinook to retrieve both vehicles and drivers. SFC Marquez said to one of the operators, "What in da god damn hell you tink you do you sonny beach's?" The E-4 hung his head and had no response. Marquez decided we would walk to the bomb site and continue the mission.

We had been walking straight towards the Cambodian border and got about a quarter klick from it when we saw Cambodian peasants coming out of the hedgerows gawking at us. They just stood there looking at us as we continued towards them. Clennon and Slovey were walking point and brought us to a halt. They said they saw a few of the dud firecracker bombs lying in our path. Jimmy, an engineer from the 65th engineers had accompanied us to do the demolition.

He walked to the front and out to where the bomblets were sitting on the ground. A wire extending from the device was supposed to bounce the thing up into the air. These apparently did not work. It took Jimmy about 5 minutes to set both charges and we moved double-time away from the blast area. We continued this for the rest of the day. The peasants never left their positions and by the end of the day, we had exploded 67 bomblets.

Marquez told us we would come back tomorrow and take up where we left off. I said, "I wonder if those dumb ass monkey track jocks will try again tomorrow? The choppers came and we popped purple smoke and rode back to Jackson in time to hit the chow line. On this occasion we were a little late, so we got the leftover food. It didn't take too much spaghetti to fill our already shrunken guts.

There was plenty of bread and peanut butter and the mess sergeant saved us a pan of brownies. He surprised us and brought out a mermite full of cartons of chocolate milk on ice. All is well that ends well. The next day we choppered out to where we were the previous day and the two Monkey tracks and their operators were waiting for us with the machines idling.

Again 10 of us loaded up and away we went with the rest of the platoon following behind us. The machines were exceptionally loud and they only traveled at 8 mph. They were a novelty at best and a total waste of taxpayer dollars at worst. The second day went much like the first, except Jimmy let me set some of the charges. We exploded 75 bomblets before calling it a day. The monkey track operator told us he was going to take us out to a flooded crater and show us how well the vehicle operated as an amphibious craft.

When we arrived at the crater Sgt. Marquez sat in the rear with a couple of other guys in front. The operator eased the vehicle into the crater and when it got halfway across, it sank like a ton of bricks. All the guys, including the driver, with the exception of Marquez, baled and swam to the edge of the crater. Marquez rode the damn thing down until just the back end was above the waterline. He then stood up and looked at the driver and said, "What in da god damn hell you tink you do you sonny beach," and then proceeded to laugh his ass off. I took a picture of that scene and sent it home to show my dad how his tax dollars were being spent. That was the last time we saw the monkey tracks or the operator. Did I mention the total waste of taxpayer money?

When we got back to Jackson, we were told that we would be going into Cu Chi for a 3 day stand down. This was great news since we hadn't been allowed back in Cu Chi since the royal rumble with Delta Company in the EM club. That confrontation was a result of a Delta Company platoon popping an ambush on us while we were walking to our ambush site. It turned out that the Delta guys were set up in the wrong place.

We were walking on a berm headed south when all hell broke loose. Bob Noel was walking in front of me and an M-79 round hit the berm between us and I tumbled head first into the hole it made. Noel was knocked off the berm and wound up lying next to me. Red tracers were flying over our heads and Big Joe started yelling, "cease fire you assholes, we are GIs." You could hear the muffled voices coming from Delta's men and then somebody said, "sorry guys we thought you were VC."

Now that made no sense at all. GIs walking on a berm look a lot different than a bunch of VC ditty bopping around at night. For one thing, we were all wearing helmets. VC don't wear helmets! This was a case of some dumb ass shooting before he knew what he was shooting at. The rest of his platoon opened up, shooting wildly over our heads. We were so pissed off we felt like opening up on those morons.

It was a miracle that none of us were killed or wounded. That was the second time Delta had popped an ambush on us and we were fed up with them. The next time Delta and Charlie Companies were in Cu Chi for a stand down, we met those bastards at the EM club and a pier six brawl broke out. During the fight, Buck Buchanan got his hand and wrist cut open when he tried to deflect a beer bottle being thrown at his head. The breaking bottle severed a couple of tendons resulting in Buck getting a million-dollar wound. He was taken to the field hospital, never to return to the platoon.

The next day Ray was furious when he found out Buck got his ticket home. He lamented that he wished he had been injured during the fight. I had a black eye to show for my troubles. I did get in one good shot however, when I hit a guy over the head with a chair. Ray sustained a small cut above his right eye that was fixed with a band aid. That incident got both Delta and Charlie Companies banned from Cu Chi for the next 3 months. We all agreed it was worth it.

When we came into Cu Chi on this stand down, most of the old-timers were in need of new boots and fatigues and our machine guns needed new barrels and headspace adjustments. It would also mean that guys who received awards and citations would receive them in a formal company formation. A full bird Colonel would show up and say a few words that nobody cared about and then he would pin the ribbons on the men's shirt. It also meant we would get a steak dinner with several side dishes and all the beer and soda we could drink.

We were told to stay in the company area to avoid another debacle with Delta Company. The awards ceremony went on without a hitch. I received a Bronze star with a V device and a Purple Heart. Ray received his Bronze star with V, as well as the other guys that were at Diamond 1.

I remember receiving a bottle of Jack Daniels black label from a friend of mine at home and a couple of us polished it off the first night in camp. I also borrowed a small tape recorder from John Boy and taped a 15-minute message that I sent home. Because I wasn't a drinker, it didn't take much to get me stupid. In my stupor, I thought about all the guys that had been hurt and killed and I truly felt sorry for myself. The second day of our stand down included getting a haircut and going to the PX.

When I walked into the PX, I rubbed shoulders with a short black guy and as I turned to say something, I realized it was Byron from my AIT class. I couldn't believe it was him. What are the odds? He told me he was serving with the Americal Division and that things there were really messed up. He said there was no discipline and the troops did not respect the officers. He said he had been in a lot of combat and lost a lot of buddies. I replied, "Sgt. Kalice was right; Vietnam truly is a shit hole!"

We both had experienced way too much combat. I wished him luck and told him maybe we would see each other again someday. I bought a couple of packs of Polaroid film and headed back to the Company area. That night we were assigned bunker duty on the perimeter. There were six of us in a bunker which meant we would get some decent sleep. One of the guys had a bag of marijuana that he had bought from a village kid the week before. He said we should smoke it and get high. He said Salem cigarettes with the menthol filter worked the best. He emptied out the tobacco of a Salem and refilled it with the weed. I had never smoked dope before, but I thought what the hell I might as well try it.

We passed the joint around each of us taking our hits until it was gone. Another Salem was prepared, and we repeated the process again. As we got high on the dope, guys were becoming much more animated. We were laughing at jokes that weren't funny and one guy made up poetry that didn't rhyme. I lost all track of time until somebody said, "Big John, you are up for guard duty." I left the bunker and grabbed my M-16 and laid on top of the bunker looking out into the darkness. I felt relaxed and started day dreaming about what it would be like to go home.

I wondered what all the guys were up to. I knew my best friend Fred had gotten married to his high school sweetheart Cathy and was living in Pacific Beach. My sister had moved from San Diego to Fullerton not far from Disneyland. She had been working for the phone company as an operator since she was 18 yrs. old. My parents got divorced and my Dad was talking about moving to Cody, Wyoming to live with his girlfriend. My mom hooked up with an alcoholic and was becoming one herself. I thought of all my girlfriend pen pals and what it would be like to meet them all. I rolled on my back and looked up at the stars and thought to myself how unlikely it would be for me to survive another 106 days of this madness.

In my dream it was very quiet. There were no sounds of bombs dropping, no illumination flares, and no AKs shooting, just peaceful quiet. "Who's on guard here?" Did I just hear that or was I still dreaming? "Who's on guard here ?" I rolled over onto my stomach and realized there was a Captain standing next to the bunker. I had fallen asleep on guard duty and was about to be court marshaled. "Get down sir, get down." The VC can see your silhouette standing there. He squatted down and asked me if I'd seen any movement. I replied that all was clear. He stood up and walked off towards the next bunker. I knew I had dodged a huge bullet.

When I went into the bunker to get the next guy for guard duty all the guys were in a deep sleep. I looked at my watch and realized I had been on top of the bunker for 4 hours. I made a promise to myself that I would never smoke dope again. We were relieved of bunker duty at 0600 hrs. and we made our way to the mess hall. Everybody from my bunker had a serious case of the munchies! After breakfast, I went and took a shower that had hot running water. It felt so good that I sat down on the floor and just let the water roll over my head and shoulders.

On the third night of our stand down we went to the outdoor theatre and watched a movie titled Barbarella starring Jane Fonda. This was truly cruel and unusual punishment for troops that had been in the field for 3 months. The movie, although not having much of a plot, displayed Fonda in several soft porn scenes. Guys were going nuts and all kinds of lewd catcalls were being yelled out throughout the movie.

Not many guys would soon forget the images of Barbarella emblazoned permanently on their minds, including mine! All good things must come to an end and so it was for the second platoon. We gathered our gear and checked out our weapons from the armory and Lee wished us good luck. We loaded up on trucks and were transported back to Jackson FSB. A lot of guys were hungover and nobody was wisecracking or smarting off. The reality of where we were going and what new insanity we would face was sinking in.

May 4, 1969

We were running day sweeps and ambush patrols out of Jackson on a daily basis. There were a fair amount of VC and NVA in the area, but they had been keeping their heads down. We had not made contact in over a week.

I was sitting with a couple of my squad members Clennon and Dietz, writing letters and talking about what it was like before they got drafted. Clennon was from Illinois and came from a family of Catholic nuns and priests. He was the youngest of 7 children and after graduating high school his family assumed and expected he would go into the seminary. Clennon told us he really didn't feel the calling but said he didn't want to disappoint his parents. He entered the seminary and was immediately granted a college deferment keeping him out of the draft.

After a year, he decided the priesthood wasn't for him, so he dropped out and returned home. Unbeknownst to him, his deferment was withdrawn and the wheels of government were beginning to roll towards him. He signed up and attended college and met a girl named Marie and they hit it off from the very start.

They became inseparable and life could not have been better. They fell in love and were engaged to be married in a year. The selective service, albeit slow in Clennon's case, caught up with him when he least expected it. He had been caught in the same snare I had fallen into when I dropped out of college. Did I mention "Not so smart?"

Clennon told us he and Marie decided not to get married until he completed his military obligation. The discussion changed to the subject of when Clennon and Dietz were walking point and were ambushed by a bunch of NVA. A bullet had pierced Clennon's helmet and he went down face first like a ton of bricks. Dietz hit the deck and played dead. The rest of us set up a defensive position behind a rice paddy berm and laid down a withering response of fire. We were firing directly over the bodies of our fallen comrades. We assumed they were both dead as their bodies laid lifeless before us.

The firefight lasted for an hour and everyone was out of water and on the verge of dehydration. Marquez finally got the artillery battery at Jackson on the horn and requested a marking round where he knew the firing was coming from. Within a couple of minutes, we heard the sound of an artillery shell sailing towards us. The white phosphorus round exploded right over the heads of Clennon and Dietz.

Marquez requested add 50 yards and fire for effect. Within 30 seconds, 6 rounds of

337

high explosive hit the deck. Marquez had been spot on and the rounds hit the hedgerow where the gooks had been shooting from. Within a few seconds of impact Dietz and Clennon jumped up and ran straight to our position.

They both threw themselves head first over the berm. It shocked everybody and Ray said to Dietz, "We thought you guys were dead?" He told us they played dead and were whispering to each other the whole time. They told us they planned to make a run for it just before the artillery came in.

We passed Clennon's steel pot around and marveled at the hole located towards the top of his headgear. Both of those guys said they thought they were dead meat lying out on the ground. They both said they heard the snapping of bullets as we shot over their heads. They also saw some small shrapnel pieces falling around them. Slovey heard us talking about Clennon's close call and chimed in and said, "how about the time he got shot in the head while walking point with me and Alabama?" Clennon got a huge smile on his face and said, "that AK round blew my helmet clean off my head!" Clennon said, "I already knew the drill and lay on the ground and did not move."

The gooks shot a couple of RPGs at them and Slovey got hit with shrapnel in the right leg. We were able to call in a couple of gun ships and just as they arrived the gooks diddi mao'd (ran swiftly away) the area. A medevac came and picked up Slovey and Clennon and Alabama rejoined us for the walk back to Jackson.

Everyone was amazed that Clennon had missed death twice by a half an inch. Marquez told us we would have bunker guard duty that night and prepare to go out on a village sweep the following morning. He asked for a volunteer to carry his radio as his regular RTO was on R&R. Without hesitation, Clennon raised his hand and said, "I'll be your RTO tomorrow." I looked at Clennon and said, "didn't anybody ever tell you not to volunteer for anything in the Army?" He chuckled and said, "I always wanted to be an RTO."

May 25, 1969

After returning from breakfast, I got my squad together for a meeting before heading out for our walk into a nearby village. I told them the area around the village was dense vegetation surrounding rice paddies, with the village being located in the center. Marquez told me that we were going into the village to look for a man that made the majority of booby traps and land mines for the district. He said there was resident VC in the village as well.

Lt. Baker was in Cu Chi meeting with the Company Commander, so 1st platoon leader Lt. Ide volunteered to go with us. His platoon was scheduled to do a follow-up sweep tomorrow and he wanted to get the lay of the land. Tony Pieroni would be carrying the radio for Ide. It was just a short flight to the edge of the village. It seemed just like any other day as we proceeded to our objective. As soon as we entered the hedgerows around the rice paddies, we saw small "Tu Dia" markers next to the trail we were walking on.

These little markers were placed on trails and by hedgerows to alert the village people and especially the kids where the booby traps were placed. The kids knew where they should walk and where they shouldn't. In the entire time I'd been in Nam, I never saw a Vietnamese person or kid trip a booby trap.

We knew what the signs meant, and you would think we would take a different approach, but oh no, that's not the Army way. Marquez lined us up single file and I put Duininck out as our right flank. Ide, Pieroni, Marquez and Clennon would be front and rear security on our left flank. I lost sight of the two flanks shortly after entering the dense vegetation. Herrera was walking in front of me and Ray was in front of him.

We were taking it real slow when we changed directions and angled left towards the East side of the village. We had to climb over a 4-foot berm and walk across a wet rice paddy. Everyone ahead of us had made it across the berm and was waiting for us to catch up. Herrera turned around and looked at me and said, "hey sarge you doing ok?" I said, "yeah watch where you are walking."

He straddled the berm and slid his right foot down the side of the berm and as he was moving forward, a huge explosion went off. I saw Herrera flying up in the air and then found myself lying flat on my back. The blast had knocked me and Ray off our feet. I sat up and my ears were ringing so loud I couldn't understand what the other guys were yelling. They wanted to know if we were being ambushed or being hit by mortars.

I yelled for everyone to kneel where they were and stay put. I yelled to Duinick and he said he was ok. As I crawled forward, I saw Herrera lying in the crater that the land mine had created. He had stepped on a 105 mm artillery shell with a pressure device. The gooks were putting them in areas where they thought tanks or PCs would be operating. Herrera was awake and talking to me and I could see he was not in shock.

When I reached him, I realized no one but me saw what had happened and did not know Herrera had blown his leg off just below his nuts. Ray crawled up to where I was kneeling and said, "what the hell happened?" I yelled for Doc and told Ray that Herrera had stepped on a buried 105 mm artillery round. Doc jumped through the hole in the berm and told me to give Herrera a drink of water.

340

The bloody stump was not spurting blood like you would expect. The 2000-degree metal that cleaved off his leg had cauterized the blood vessels and arteries. Doc asked me if I got hit in the face with shrapnel and I said I didn't think so. He said, "you have blood on your face." I wiped my hand over my face and realized blood and small pieces of tissue from Herrera's leg had hit me in the face.

Doc started an IV bottle of albumin and asked Ray to hold the elevated bottle. From the time Herrera stepped on the mine until Doc got the IV running was about 5 minutes. Herrera kept telling me his leg was burning and felt on fire. I had no words to reply. I lifted my head and looked across the open field and saw Clennon and Marquez walking directly to our location.

Marquez had called for a medevac and was coming to assess the situation. Ide and Pieroni were walking towards us as well. One minute Clennon was walking and in an instant his body was being hurled upward under the blast of another land mine.

As I watched the scene unfold it was like watching a slow-motion movie: Clennon in the air and Marquez being blown off his feet. I looked right and saw Ide take his last step before he was blown up by another mine. Pieroni was flying through the air and landed face down in the water. I couldn't believe what was happening; my mind was about to snap, and I told Doc we had four guys down. I removed Herrera's belt and used it as a tourniquet on the oozing stump.

Doc grabbed his bag and jumped through the hole in the berm and ran straight away to Clennon's lifeless body. By the time he got to Clennon, Marquez was kneeling with his head bent forward shaking his head. Doc got up from Clennon and went to Lt. Ide. The shrapnel from the buried 105 round went up the inside of his leg and disemboweled him. His chest was reduced to jelly.

Marquez had seen Pieroni go face first in the water and knew if someone didn't get to him, he would drown. He grabbed the radio on Pieroni's back and lifted him straight out of the water. Marquez said, "you one lucky sonny beach." Doc was with Ide just a few seconds when he got up and moved to Pieroni. A piece of the shrapnel that killed Ide had gone through the radio and lodged in Pieroni's back. I knew Ide was dead and that the medevac was on the way.

My mind would not allow anymore comprehension to take place. I had gone so far past being scared that I was functioning on raw instinct. Time had come to a complete standstill. Marquez was yelling at me that when the medevac arrived, I would have to run out to the chopper and retrieve a stretcher to carry Herrera to the bird. My mind went haywire.

All I could think of was walking out in the clearing where Clennon just set off a mine. I was way north of terrorized and I couldn't get my hands to stop shaking. I told Ray what Marquez said and he got a horrible look on his face.

The next thought I had was that when the chopper landed it could cause more of the mines to go off. I was in a really bad place this time. I was convinced this would be my last day on earth. I had to resign myself to that fact before taking the first step towards the landed medevac. With every step I took I thought it would be my last. I walked by Clennon and there was no sign of the radio. It had been blown completely off his back. The crew chief was waiting and handed me the stretcher.

I turned around and walked back towards Herrera and Ray and I could not feel my feet. We loaded up Herrera and headed back to the chopper. It felt like Herrera weighed 300 lbs. pulling on my shoulders. By this time, they had loaded up Clennon's and Ide's lifeless bodies and when we lifted Herrera into the chopper, the medic on board said, "don't worry, we will take care of them."

Pieroni refused to get on the chopper with the dead bodies. We would take him back to Jackson with us. Ray and I knelt down so the helicopter could lift off. We watched it clear the hedgerow and knew we had to return to retrieve our gear. I was unusually calm on the walk back. My mind must have reached its maximum overload. Marquez was telling everybody to turn about-face and walk back the way we came in.

He said to walk in the footsteps of the man in front of you. Marquez's voice was breaking up and I had not seen that look on his face since Diamond. I yelled at Duininck to return to our location and walk back in with us. We went very slowly, and every man-made it out of there without tripping another land mine. I knew in my heart I would never be the same after today. I knew for sure I was losing my mind. The funny thing was it didn't bother me too much.

By the time we returned to Jackson, it was dinner time. The mess sergeant had heard what happened and made some special food for us. When it came time to hit the chow line, not a single man got up and got in line. I have never seen a more sullen bunch of guys.

I retrieved Clennon's duffel bag and pulled out a bunch of letters tied together with a bootlace. The letter on top was from his fiancée Marie. I had made up my mind that since I was his squad leader, I would write her a letter and explain what happened. I couldn't bring myself to open any of the letters; I was only looking for Marie's mailing address.

I already knew what was in the letters anyway. She had written him almost every day telling him how much she loved him and how excited she was to be his wife. She talked about having a family and all the other things young couples dream about. I was absolutely sick to my stomach about what happened.

343

Clennon was just too good a man to have been in Vietnam. He had served God his whole life and now he was rubbed out in the blink of an eye. No marriage, no kids, no job to support his family and especially no chance to reach his full potential in life. I damn sure knew this was not his potential.

By the way God, where were you when Clennon got blown up? I thought you were supposed to protect your faithful. Hell, the truth of the matter is you weren't there when it happened. I'm not sure you even exist. It would make more sense if I were killed instead of Clennon. He had everything to offer you and I have nothing. I suddenly realized I was talking to myself. As I put pen to paper the letter came out like this:

Dear Marie,

You don't know me but I am /was Ed's squad leader Big John, and I'm writing to tell you about a great loss that occurred today. Ed volunteered to carry the platoon sergeant's radio for the day, and we were sent into a village to capture a VC bomb maker. It started out just like any other day.

Before breakfast, Ed was reading his Bible as he did every day, and I was writing to my mom and dad. We went to the chow line together and had breakfast and returned to the platoon area to organize our equipment and get ready to head out. I remember teasing Ed about not getting shot in the helmet again and we all chuckled about that.

As we entered the hedgerow around the village, we saw signs warning the Vietnamese kids that there were booby traps present. As we got farther down the trail the man walking in front of me stepped on a mine which blew his leg off. We didn't realize it, but we had walked into the middle of a mine field. As soon as the platoon sergeant realized we had a man down he and Ed starting walking right to our location.

344

As I looked up, I saw Ed step on a mine causing his immediate death. I can assure you Ed felt no pain at all and did not suffer. The platoon sergeant was knocked off his feet but was not injured. We called in a medevac helicopter and our dead and wounded were flown back to Cu Chi. I wanted to write to you and tell you what happened because the telegram the Army sends will give no background information.

There are no words that I can say or think of that will lessen your grief and loss. Ed had told me many times about your plans when he returned and you two were married. I'm just sick in my heart that you and Ed will never realize your dreams. I know Ed was a very religious man and I have to believe God took him to heaven. Please extend my sincere condolences to Ed's family from me and all the guys that served with and respected Ed. Know in your heart Marie, that Ed loved you more than anything else on earth.

With abiding respect and affection, John "Big John" Quintrell. PS Please forgive the shaky writing. It seems like I can't get my hands to work right.

I folded the letter and put it in an envelope and addressed it to Marie in Illinois. I sent it the next day and never heard back from her. There wasn't a day from that point on I didn't think of Ed and Marie. It's not good for a combat soldier to overthink things after the battle. The less you dwell on things the better off you are. A man's mind has its limits but mine still had room to hate the VC that had built that mine. I was thinking of some heinous act I could perform on him.

When I finished the letter Kid Lozon came to tell me the mess sergeant had heard about what happened and brought hot chow to us. Well, I guess we shouldn't disappoint the mess sergeant!

May 28, 1969

Another day in paradise or so they say. A bunch of the Mexican guys came by and asked me what happened to Herrera. Garcia said he was from a town in Texas not far from where he lived. I told them what had happened, and they weren't shaken by the bizarre description of the quivering flesh that was left after the leg was cleaved off. I told them Herrera had asked me if he had lost any of his junk and I said, "another inch higher and you would have been a soprano!"

Everyone laughed at that as if nothing serious had happened. I couldn't get the picture of Clennon and Ide being blown up out of my mind. Marquez told us Pieroni had a piece of shrapnel removed from his back. The surgeon said if it had been a half-inch closer to his spine, he would have been paralyzed. Pieroni was put on a medical profile for two weeks. Ray made the comment that he wished he was the one to get a million-dollar wound. I was just glad we didn't get a piece of the 105 mines that blew Herrera's leg off.

A couple of us went over to the officer's tent to see if Captain Johnny Clack was around. We wanted to tell him what happened to his good friend Lt. Ide. Clack was our artillery FO (forward observer) who had just been promoted to Captain. We figured since he was promoted, he would be sent back to Cu Chi to head up the artillery batteries for the battalion.

He was not like most officers in the field. He would rather be out in the bush with us than sit back in the fire support base and wait for something to happen. He was never a prick to any of the enlisted but regularly would sit with us and teach us about calling in artillery. He always said we would never know if we would have to call in rounds if our platoon leader and platoon sergeant were killed or wounded.

Clack came from a military background. He was an Army brat that was born at Ft. McPherson. His dad had been an infantryman in WW2. He was eighth-generation Army. This was his second tour in Nam. His first tour was with II Field Forces.

He was an artillery liaison officer for the 9 provinces around Saigon. He had also married a colonel's daughter just before his first tour. He had an 8x10 glossy picture of her in a "Parlor Pose" wearing an almost see-through nightie. All of us agreed she was a blond bombshell and was definitely out of our league. We teased Clack constantly about how an ugly toad-like him could score such a gorgeous woman. His reply was always the same; he would grab his crotch with his hand and pull up with a huge smile on his face.

He would say, "some guys got it, some guys don't, ok." We found him sitting on his cot writing a letter and he looked up and said, "have you guys heard about our mission tomorrow?" We looked at each other and shrugged our shoulders and said, what mission? He proceeded to tell us he was in a briefing and the CO was sending us back into the village again to look for the VC bomb builder and VC.

He told us he volunteered to go with the second platoon to stretch his legs. He said Jimmy Langley would be his RTO for the day. This news caught us all by surprise as we had not heard anything about going back to the village where Clennon and Ide had gotten killed and Herrera and Pieroni injured. No sooner had we finished our kibitzing with Clack, that Marquez yelled for the second platoon to gather together for a briefing.

Marquez told us we would be going back into the same village to look for the bomb maker. There was an audible groan from every man present. Several of us bowed our heads and under our breath said, "you're shitting me"; another dreaded nightmare raising its ugly head again. I only remember bits and pieces of the briefing.

347

I remember the part where he told us we would be entering the village from the opposite side and that two tanks with flame throwers would be joining us. The 101st Airborne had a couple of M67 Flame thrower tanks also known as "Zippo" (named after popular brand of a cigarette lighter), sitting at Jackson. I couldn't imagine what the tanks were going to be used for. Maybe they would use them to find land mines! That night we spent sitting around talking shit about the Army. It seemed lately they were providing grist for the mill. Morale was at an all-time low.

Did anybody care that we were dropping off like flies out here? Garcia had a bottle of Tequila that was sent from his dad that he was passing around. Since I didn't drink alcohol, I passed the bottle to Alabama, who drank his share and my share! I honestly couldn't believe they were sending us back there.

It was Diamond all over again. Did the Army think that the VC would only booby-trap one side of the village? This was just another case of military insanity gone awry. There was a movie scheduled to be shown in the underground theater that night, so Ray and I decided to go to get our minds off of tomorrow's mission. The title was Change of Habit, starring Elvis Presley and Mary Tyler Moore. As it turned out, Elvis attempted to sweet talk a nun out of her habit! The Company mess hall even had popcorn for us to eat during the movie. We were definitely living the high life now. Did I mention another day in paradise?

May 29, 1969

The sun raised in the East way too early to suit me. I had recurring intrusive thoughts about Herrera, Clennon and Ide during the night. Sleep was a rare commodity these nights. None of the menu items at the mess hall appealed to me. Seemed like my appetite had abandoned me lately and I was relying on candy bars and Coca-Cola for energy.

At 0900 hrs., the second platoon was waiting to be picked up by the Little Bear's helicopter assault group. A smoke Ship (Smokey) was joining them to lay down a wall of smoke in front of the hedgerow that surrounded the village. That would stop any potential snipers from getting accurate shots at us upon landing.

It was only going to be a short ride, but I suspected that the Army wanted to make a grand entrance after what had happened on the 25th. Captain Clack and his RTO Jimmy Langley would join Ray, Doc Flores, Kid Lozon and I on the lead ship. Upon landing we would be the right flank entering the village.

As we loaded up on the chopper, I thought that riding helicopters was one of the few fun things we did these days including playing split. There is nothing like coming in hot with the door gunner shooting the hell out of everything to get your adrenaline flowing.

As we were about to touch down, I got a sick feeling that we were landing on top of a mine field. My intuition at this point was pretty spot on. Some would call it paranoia; I called it trying to survive hell in Vietnam. As soon as we un-assed the chopper we spread out and formed a line parallel to the hedgerow. The flame thrower tanks were already there waiting for us. Clack and Langley were positioned as our far-right flank and I, Ray, Doc and the Kid spread out to the left of them. We were spaced about 20 ft. from each other.

After all 10 ships unloaded, the pilots took off directly over our heads headed back to Cu Chi for another load of soldiers. Several of the door gunners gave us the thumbs up and one hippie from California flashed us the peace sign. Ray returned the gesture by giving the guy the finger and yelling, "screw off you dirty bastard."

As soon as all platoons were on line the order was given to move out towards the village. I guess my feeling that we landed in the middle of a mine field was unfounded. We reached the hedgerow without incident. To the left of us the tank was crushing bamboo down as it forced its way through to the other side.

On the other side of the hedgerow there were rice paddies that looked exactly like the ones we walked through on the opposite side of the village. The village would be located about 100 yards ahead. We climbed over the first berm and slowly walked forward on with caution. I was looking at the ground every time I took a step. We had walked about 75 yards when all hell broke loose. The hedgerow to our front opened up on us with withering AK fire. We dove onto the ground and returned fire.

I looked to my right and Langley was handing Clack the radio handset, Clack had his map out and was talking to someone at Jackson. The two tanks opened up with 50 cal. fire tearing the hedgerow to smithereens. An RPG round came out of the hedgerow landing in front of the tanks. That pissed the tankers off and they shot liquid fire into the hedgerow. I had never witnessed anything like it. The smell was a little like napalm. The hedgerow burst into flames and the sound of VC screaming was blood curdling.

All AK fire stopped and we were told we would take a break while the CO figured out what his next move was. Since the firing had stopped, I figured it was safe to open a can of peaches and sit back and relax for a few minutes. Ray and the Kid came over and we discussed what had just transpired. Kid's eyes were as big as saucers and said several AK rounds snapped next to his head.

I could see he was scared, so I gave him my chocolate energy bar to calm him down. We could see the two tanks moving forward with a half a dozen GIs walking behind them. I looked at Ray and said, "I wish we weren't here." Several guys were snacking on cheese and crackers and washing it down with a Coca-Cola. I took a couple of pulls off my canteen and wondered how Marie would react when she received my letter.

My mind was flying in all different directions when Ray touched my shoulder and told me we were heading out. "Shit Ray, you scared the hell out of me." He asked me if I was daydreaming and I said, "it don't mean nothin." I had just put my back pack on and adjusted the straps when I looked to my right and saw Jimmy putting his radio on.

Clack was already moving forward walking about 15 feet in front of the rest of us. Without warning there was a tremendous explosion that knocked Langley, myself and Ray off our feet. The radio had been blown off Langley's back. The dust and black smoke was so thick I could not see Clack. Someone yelled incoming but I knew immediately it wasn't incoming mortars or RPGs; it was another land mine.

I knew the explosion had occurred where I last saw Captain Clack. I was coughing up black smoke and my lungs felt like they were on fire. My brain went into auto mode and I crawled through the dust and smoke until I saw what looked like someone lying in a hole. I knew this was Clack and that he had stepped on a 105 mm land mine.

When I got to him and I looked at his face it was covered in black residue. The only thing I saw was the whites of his eyes. His right eye was partially out of its socket tilted downward. He looked at me and said, "I'm lying on my arm; can you get me off it?" What I saw before me was much worse that the goriest movie I'd ever seen. Both of Clack's legs were blown off; one just

351

below the knee the other mid-thigh. Just like Herrera the bloody ragged stumps were not spurting blood.

The arteries and veins had been cauterized by the extreme heat from the shrapnel. I started yelling for Doc. Ray and Jimmy crawled up to where Clack and I were located. When Ray saw Clack he said, "Holy Jesus not again!" The arm that Clack said he was lying on was gone as well as the shoulder it had been attached to.

When Doc arrived, he immediately told Ray and I to put tourniquets on the stumps. Doc got out a bottle of albumin and started an IV in Clack's remaining arm. Someone had called for a medevac and we could hear it in the distance. Clack never said another word. Ray and I took a poncho and put what was left of Clack on it and got ready to carry him to the chopper. I was concerned that Langley was in shock.

As we carried Clack to the waiting medevac, Doc carried the IV bottle and handed it to the onboard medic and turned and walked away. We placed the poncho with Clack in it on the floor of the chopper and the medic on board said, "we will take care of him from here." Ray and I knelt on the ground and waved at the pilot to take off. We covered our faces to avoid getting hit with debris from the rotor blades.

I said a prayer right then and there: "If there is a God, please don't let this man survive this, he is just too torn up." I could only imagine his wife coming to see him at the hospital and when she saw his injuries would turn and walk away forever. No man deserved to have this happen. When Ray and I stood up I told him what I prayed and he said, "I prayed the same prayer."

Both of us were too numb to cry as we walked back to retrieve our gear. We stayed there for another hour without moving. The order came that we were going back to Jackson. The Little Bears showed up and as we were loading up, we looked at each other and the empty seat where Clack's burned map and twisted M-16 were lying. He had been sitting there just hours before. My mind started to wander to another place and time. It was another illusion I chose to create.

It was summer and I was in my backyard in San Diego lying on my back looking up at the clouds floating by. I imagined seeing things like faces and dragons and even the stay puff marshmallow man as they slowly made their way towards the Laguna Mountains.

I think I was about 10 years old at the time. My biggest concern in life was going back to school and having old lady Stephens as a teacher. She was an old blister that rivaled the meanness of any nun teaching there. I suddenly heard, "Big John, get ready to bail buddy." Kid Lozon had interrupted my Walter Middy moment as the chopper was coming in for a landing. We got off the chopper and walked into the fire support base where there was an artillery officer waiting for us. He wanted to know what happened to Clack. I told him he stepped on a 105 mm artillery round land mine. How ironic that an artillery officer would be killed by a U.S. Army artillery round.

I told the officer I assumed Clack would not make it to the hospital in Cu Chi. He was just too torn up. I did not mention my prayer that supported that outcome. Later that afternoon Marquez came by and told us Clack had not survived. I breathed a sigh of relief. I could not add the thought of his wife seeing him in that condition to the long list of nightmares being catalogued in that dark place in my mind.

For some reason in the back of my mind I could hear Joel Brown moaning, "Oh momma what I gonna do." I had found myself in a quagmire of death and destruction and I wasn't smart enough to figure out how to cope with it much longer. I didn't think my mother could save me from this mess.

I sent a note to Gary Hunt our company clerk and asked him if there were any R&Rs available. I had to get out of this place. Rumors were flying that we were going back to the Cambodian border to the Vam Co Dong River. It was getting so bad that Ray and I didn't talk about what happened. Our minds were in the fetal position and we were trying to insulate ourselves from reality.

June 1, 1969

I received a note from our company clerk that the R&R that Lt. Ide was scheduled to take was now available. It was another opportunity to go back to Hong Kong. The R&R was scheduled for June 14, so I had to act fast. I replied and told Hunt I would take the R&R and immediately wrote my dad and asked him to send me $500 in traveler's checks.

He would draw the money out of a joint account we had set up where my Army pay was deposited each month. As an NCO I was making $307.20 per month which included $16 overseas pay and $65 hazardous duty pay. It beat the hell out of the $90 bucks a month I got paid in basic training.

The first week of June was fairly uneventful. We received word that Herrera had been cared for at the field hospital in Cu Chi and then flown to Japan for further treatment. We never heard another word about Captain Clack which confirmed our suspicions that he was KIA.

Things at home were changing rapidly. My Dad retired from the University of California at San Diego and moved to Cody, Wyoming to be with his girlfriend. He was retired for two weeks when he took a position as the head purchasing agent for Husky Oil Co. whose corporate home office was in Cody.

He sent me some pictures and said he thought I would like it there. He thought it would be a great place for me to get my head screwed on straight when I returned from the war. I wasn't sure there was a wrench capable of fixing my head! My Mom started selling Avon products and she was going steady with the man that had been dating my Dad's girlfriend before she dumped him for my Dad.

It seemed like there was plenty of drama to go around both in Nam and at home. My sister had been promoted with the phone company and seemed to be doing very well. I was still waiting for her to write me. Being a telephone operator must be a very busy job.

The rumors about going back to the Vam Co Dong River never came to fruition. Delta Company wound up with that duty and Charlie Company was heading up to the Parrots Beak. From what we were told the Parrots Beak was a base and rest area for the People's Army of Vietnam and the Viet Cong. It was also the terminus points of the Ho Chi Minh Trail / Sihanouk Trail. There were two known base camps there: area 367 and 706. This was mind blowing to all of us.

Why would we go to the Cambodian border and take a chance of walking into a VC R&R center. I thought there was an unwritten agreement between us and the VC that stated: you don't mess with our R&R center in Vung Tau and we won't mess with yours. This really sounded bat shit crazy to all of us. We had not been told what kind of an operation it would be, but it included the whole Company.

I was so strung out mentally that I popped off to the lieutenant about the Army trying to get us all killed, and he wasn't in the mood to hear about it. He said since I was such an expert on Army strategy, I would be leading a 4-man ambush patrol that night with 3 of the new guys in my squad. I said, "are you nuts," he scowled and said, "I'm going to be watching you the whole time with the crew served starlight scope, so don't try to hide out there." Great, I had just found myself in another world of shit. I felt horrible that because of my big mouth I was being forced to take 3 new guys out on an insane venture. I wasn't worried about myself, but I had no idea how the new guys would react if we made contact.

I chose 3 of my best guys and gave them the bad news. Kid Lozon looked at me and said, "don't worry about it sarge we trust you." I was already figuring out in my mind how to make sure nobody got hurt or killed. Marquez came by and showed me on the map where the Lt. wanted me to set up for the night. It was almost 3/4 of a klick from the base. The location was close to where Delta Company had popped an ambush just last week. Their new platoon leader unfortunately set up in the wrong place and a complete disaster occurred.

Bill Vaught a good soldier that had been in our platoon, had been reassigned to Delta Company. Most of us suspected it was for disciplinary reasons but weren't sure. Bill's platoon leader told him to go to the end of the hedgerow and act as a one-man listening post. This was not the way it is done. Bill told the new Lt. that it wasn't a good idea for him to be alone without a radio and the Lt. snapped back that he was in charge.

Bill went by himself while the rest of the platoon set their ambush. A half-hour after dark Bill thought he saw shadows moving towards him. He raised his weapon and waited until he could clearly see what it was. His eyes focused on the point man that was clearly a VC. Bill pulled the trigger and killed the point man instantly. The shadows started running and Bill moved his operating button to full auto and sprayed the rest of his magazine into the shadows.

When the shooting stopped, he heard American voices calling for a medic. Bill could not believe what he was hearing. By this time, the new Lt. came running up and he discovered that

356

Bill had killed a Kit Carson Scout walking point and wounded 12 other GIs. To say the shit hit the fan is an understatement. The next day there was an investigation and Bill's new Lt. threw him under the bus accepting no responsibility for what had happened.

As a result of the investigation, it was determined that the new Lt. set his platoon up in the wrong location. Bill was busted from E-4 to E-1 and sent to Cu Chi to burn shit barrels. Trying to learn from their mistake, I went over to the mortar platoon and sat down with a couple of the guys and Phil Iserino and coordinated mortar support with where we would be set up. We talked about how unfortunate it was that his cousin Paul Naso was wounded at Diamond. Phil and I were getting short and both of us were suffering from short timer's anxiety.

When I returned to my squad, I began to lay out our plan for the AP. First and foremost, I told them we were not going out there to get in a gunfight. With only 4 guys we were going to play this out like we were a listening post. I told them we would travel light with M-16s and 20 clips of ammo each. I wanted each man to carry 3 hand grenades and one claymore. I would be carrying the starlight scope and walk point with the radio and a LAWS rocket. Our canteens and poncho liners would be the only extra equipment we would carry. We were going to travel fast and straight to the AP site.

I spent the rest of the afternoon with Ray and he and I looked at the map to determine the quickest and safest way to get to the destination. He was pissed off that the Lieutenant would punish me just for a flippant remark. He said the Lt. deserved to be fragged and I laughed and said it would be his luck the grenade would go off prematurely and he would blow himself up. His reply was "if it just wounded me and I got to go home, it would be worth it." Rick o shay has spoken!

Letters and care packages arrived just before evening chow. I received a letter from Alan "Claymore" Larson that was sent from the hospital at Ft. Dix. He sent pictures of himself lying in a hospital bed smiling like a Cheshire cat. He told me he hoped I would make it home and maybe we could get together again. By the smell of the next letter, I was about to open I knew it was a letter from Becky Bruns, Russ's wife. She always put a dab of perfume on the letter to drive me out of what little mind I had left. Russ and Becky were living at Fitzsimmons Army Hospital in Denver, Colorado. He and Moose were being treated for blindness caused by fragments from an RPG that exploded in front of them.

I got a letter almost every week from Becky keeping me informed about Russ's and Moose's eye surgeries. She told me she would send a care package as soon as possible. In my return letter I told Becky if I got back to the world in one piece I would drive to Denver and see them.

The next letter was from my faux girlfriend Rose who was introduced to me by my buddy Ed Rambo. She was already planning our wedding and how it would be so exciting to finally be together. I had to start thinking about how I was going to end all these extracurricular pen pal relationships. It sure was fun getting all the letters and gave me something to do when we were sitting around doing nothing. At 1600 hrs., I gathered up my newbies and checked them out to see if they had the gear I requested.

Every man had listened carefully and complied with my orders. The Lt. came by just before we left the wire and asked me if I was ready to go. I said, "yes sir." He said, "I'll be over there behind the crew-served starlight scope to keep my eye on you." "Yes sir." Under my breath I said, "you sorry prick." He turned towards me and said, "what did you say?" I said, "see you in the morning sir." Since being in Vietnam, I had never heard of anyone being punished by sending them out on an AP with a couple of newbies. I had to focus and make sure I didn't get any of these guys killed. When we left the wire, I headed straight south for about a half a klick.

There was a half-moon shining so the starlight scope allowed me to see a long way out in front of us. I figured the Lt. had long since left his position on the scope and went back to his bunker. Ray and I figured I could take a short cut that varied from the usual route, so I headed southeast at a brisk walk. We arrived at our AP location in record time. I would wait to call in any sit rep for at least 20 minutes to make up for the time we saved by taking the shortcut.

We set up behind a rice paddy berm and prepared for a long night. I had the guys set up their claymores and I reminded them we would not shoot unless a gook walked up on us. I told them to get their knives out and lay it on the berm just in case. I took the first watch and scanned the area with the starlight scope. I could see a village about a quarter a klick away and several rice paddies to our front. There were several berms and a hooch not far from where we were set up. I was hoping no VC or NVA felt compelled to take a walk under the moonlight tonight. I passed the watch and radio handset to the Kid and told him what I had observed. I leaned back on the berm and closed my eyes hoping to get a few zzzz's.

My mind was fixated on our upcoming mission to Parrots Beak. I hated being on the Cambodian border with a passion. There were triple canopy jungles that prevented us from seeing 20 feet in any direction. If we got on a trail, we were sure to run into booby traps. The gooks always had the advantage no matter how you looked at it. If we got into contact no support would be available. The artillery saw the Parrots Beak as a no-fire zone and wouldn't shoot there. The Cobra guys would love to work there but were threatened with their rank if they were caught shooting there.

We would be on our own. I only had 13 days to go before I would be on R&R. I was hoping I would have better luck in Hong Kong this time than I did on the first R&R. I heard the Kid key the radio handset and whisper, "AP 1 negative sit rep (situation report)," then a squawk, then silence.

We were required to call in a situation report every half hour. The reports were received by our platoon leaders RTO and the Company command post. I guess to them no news is good news. If we did see anything or got into contact, we would radio in and the guys at the fire support base could get in touch with our mortar platoon and have them ready to rock and roll.

Kid passed the watch and handset to Kelly and promptly went to sleep. I couldn't get my mind shut down enough to sleep but kept worrying about one of the new guys going to sleep on guard and all of us getting our throats cut. I had been operating on nervous energy for the last three weeks and I knew I was getting edgy and paranoid, but I had to stay focused. I must have dozed off for a while when Norris shook me and said it was my turn to stand guard. I had slept through Kelly and Norris's time slots.

Two hours' sleep was enough to keep me going for the rest of the night. It was midnight and I could see the reflection of bombs exploding several miles away as they were being dropped on some unsuspecting souls. I loved to see the B-52 strikes and hoped they were killing beaucoup VC or NVA. The mosquitoes were especially bad, and I had to reapply the insect repellent three times already. No wonder there was so much malaria in this god forsaken place. It was a constant battle trying to keep from being eaten alive.

Between leeches and mosquitoes sucking your blood and Sir Charles trying to kill you, life in Vietnam was just peachy. I took another look through the starlight scope and did a 180-degree recon. Nothing moving as far as the eye could see. When I scoped out the area behind us there was nothing but rice paddies. The only thing that had changed was I could see a faint light flickering in a hooch nearby. Maybe they were making tea or changing a baby's soiled diaper.

Sitting in the dark is boring as hell and the longer you stare into the darkness the more you think you see something moving. I have seen what I thought was a line of VC walking in the distance only to find out when looking through the starlight scope they turned out to be some bushes or rice sheaves. I called in a sit rep and shook the Kid telling him it was his turn for guard duty. On an ambush patrol this second round of guard duty is the most dangerous. When a guy is awakened from sleep, his body tends to want to go back to sleep. In Nam it was referred to as nodding off. Wolfhounds are pushed really hard and very rarely get a chance to get good sleep.

We run day sweeps and hump 1 or 2 klicks and then turn around and pull an AP that night. Most of us were in the best physical condition of our lives but our brains were susceptible to burn out over time. I know a lot of guys that can sleep anytime, anywhere. If we stop marching for a 15-minute break, these guys are out like a light. Ketchum was one of those guys. I envied him a lot and would do anything for 8 hours of uninterrupted sleep. I caught the Kid nodding and told him I would take his time slot. He was fast asleep before I could key the handset to call in a sit rep.

Over the next 3 hours I caught myself nodding off several times. I was always yanked back to consciousness by some imagined noise in my head or someone turning over. I would have bright metallic flashes go off in my mind that would jerk me back to reality after a shot of adrenaline hit my chest. It was almost 0430 hrs., so I thought I'd take one last look with the starlight scope. As I was panning to the left, I noticed the flickering light in the hooch suddenly disappeared. I almost looked away when I thought I saw something move in front of the hooch.

I adjusted the focus on the scope and I'll be damned if it wasn't three VC standing out in front. They had their gear on and I could see they had AKs and each had RPG launchers. They headed out walking in the opposite direction from our location, like they didn't have a care in the world. I bumped the Kid and told him to look past the hooch. After a few seconds he mumbled, "Jesus Christ, those are VC!" I said, "yes they are, and we will tell the Lt. about them when we get back in the morning."

I woke the others up and told them we were going to move out in 15. I had them retrieve their claymores and double-check the area for any candy wrappers. I wanted to walk back to the Fire Support base the same way we came out. I wanted to get within 500 yards from the wire and lay low until daylight then we would get up and walk in.

As soon as we got back to our platoon bunkers I checked in with the Lt. and told him about the VC. I told him they were too far away to engage and that we should tell the Command Post about the location of the hooch. He agreed and told me to go straightaway to the CP and report my information. I did an about face and headed towards the CP bunker when the Lt. yelled at me.

When I turned to see what he wanted he said, "good job Sergeant, I'm sure your new guys learned a lot." I said, "yes sir," and continued to the CP bunker. I met up with Ray at the chow line for breakfast.

I had a huge appetite for some reason and ate everything they would put on my tray. Ray wanted to know how everything went and I told him about the VC and how there was no way in hell I was going to get in a gunfight with 3 new guys by my side. He agreed and said, "I still think we should mess up the Lt." I said, "it don't mean nothin."

June 3, 1969

This afternoon SFC Marquez had the platoon huddle up for a briefing. We would not be going on any AP tonight but instead we had to prepare ourselves for a seven-day sweep up at the Parrots Beak. Crap, that was the last thing I wanted to hear so close to going on R&R. After seven days up at the Beak I would only have 4 days to get my stuff together to go to Hong Kong.

Hunt always sent our orders a couple days before we left on R&R so we could get into Cu Chi and get cleaned up and turn in our weapons. I had already made up my mind I was going to find a chopper headed to Cu Chi and not ride in the back of a deuce and a half in the dust and heat. I figured I'd earned that bit of consideration.

The following morning, we loaded up on choppers and headed to the Parrots Beak on the Cambodian border. We were still not sure what we would be doing for the next 7 days and nights. Some of the guys thought we were going to move from the Parrots Beak down to Fish Hook not far from where we got ambushed going across the Vam Co Dong River. I still have nightmares about that day.

It was Monday, December 9, 1968 just 16 days until Christmas and we were assigned to act as a blocking force for Delta Company When we unloaded from the choppers, we were about 100 yards from the river. The Company Commander decided we should go across the river to set up our positions.

As soon as we got to the river, we realized it was too deep to cross. O'Grady called Cu Chi and requested a rubber raft be sent out to help in the crossing. Moose surveyed the situation and loaded a grappling hook round (designed to shoot a grappling hook attached to a thin cord) into his M-79.

He shot the hook 50 feet across the river into a stand of bamboo and it hung up allowing Ray to pull himself across the river with a rope tied around his waist. When he reached the other side, he climbed out of the water and pulled himself up onto the steep bank. He tied the rope to the bamboo stand and sugar bear pulled the rope taunt and secured it to a post that Moose had driven into the ground.

Ray came back using the hand-over-hand technique we were taught in basic training. He told us the river had a pretty good current and that there wasn't much room on the river bank. Just beyond the bank was a hedgerow of bamboo. My squad was the first to enter the water and cross the river.

Just as we began crossing, a loach helicopter hovered over the river bank and dropped an inflatable raft onto the ground. Bobby Noel, O'Grady's RTO, unfolded the raft and pulled a cord that operated a CO_2 cylinder which immediately inflated the raft. The plan was to put Bobby in the raft with the radio and have him pull himself and the raft across to the other side. Best laid plans somehow go awry. My squad climbed out of the river and I turned to the left and walked on the narrow strip of bank to spread out. Moose was the last man in the squad to arrive.

As soon as he reached the bank, they put Noel and the raft in the water, and he started pulling himself across. O'Grady and first squad followed behind. As soon as the raft reached the center of the river all hell broke loose. There were NVA soldiers inside the hedgerow and they opened up on us. Bullets were going everywhere including between our legs. There was no time to react, so I jumped backwards into the river with my M-16 blasting on full auto; the last 3 shells in my magazine were shot under water.

It was a miracle no one was killed in the first 30 seconds. My guys clung to the bank and held their rifles above the banks edge and opened up on the hedgerow. I was changing clips out when I saw a strafe of AK bullets skip across the river and hit the rubber raft. Within an instant I saw Bobby roll out of the sinking raft and go straight down. I had no idea if he was hit or not.

I did know with the weight of the radio on his back he would sink to the bottom and drown. O'Grady and the first squad were hastily retreating back to the other side of the river. Without hesitation, I pulled myself up on the bank and ran down in front of the hedgerow. I suddenly realized I was running across the NVA kill zone. When I reached Moose, I dove off the bank over his head and swam down to where I thought Noel went down. The water was murky and the visibility was next to nothing.

As I swam along the bottom, I kept reaching out in front of me hoping I would run into my beleaguered comrade. I knew Noel had been down 2 maybe 3 minutes and if I didn't find him, he would be screwed. I was just about to go up for air when my hand ran into the ruck sack attached to Bobby's back and he was still in it. He was sitting on the bottom of the river trying to hold his breath. I planted my feet on the river bottom and jerked him up and pushed him towards the surface. As luck would have it, he came out of the water under the rope. In a desperate grab, while sucking for air, Bobby grabbed the rope. I surfaced right next to him and pushed him to the shore.

I turned around and pulled myself back to where my squad was shooting the hell out of the hedgerow. We were in serious trouble. The guys on the opposite shore were pinned down and would not shoot over our heads (good thinking). We were too close to the NVA to call in any kind of support. The NVA had us dead to rights and there wasn't anything we could do about it. Hand grenades were out of the question because when they hit the hedgerow to our front they would bounce back into our laps.

Moose was using his M-79 like a mortar tube lobbing HE rounds over the hedgerow. There was no margin for error otherwise the round could fall back in his lap. When I got back to my gear lying on the bank, I thought our gooses were completely cooked. I saw Lamere stand up and drape several rounds of M-60 ammo over his shoulder and pick up his M-60 machine gun and walk down the river bank to our left. The NVA were trying to hit him and their rounds were landing around his feet.

There was a small mound of dirt about three feet high that he laid his gun on. He clipped together a couple of the belts of the 60 ammo and loaded up his smoke wagon and prepared to go to work. He started shooting across the river to the left of our position. He had them in a crossfire and suddenly the shooting to our front stopped. I will never forget seeing him kneeling behind his 60 with a cigarette in his mouth shooting controlled bursts of 4 rounds bringing hell down on the enemy. The AK rounds hitting in front of his position did not faze him a bit. Was Lamere gutsy or crazy; Hero or lunatic? I guess the jury was still out on that one. Lamere's heroic action gave us a chance to pull ourselves across the river back to our platoon.

Now that we were safely back across the river, we would have a front row seat to see the overwhelming power of the Air Force. O'Grady had the F-4 Phantom Jets on station within 10 minutes. When they flew over us, we noticed they were carrying 500 lb. bunker buster bombs. They were so low to the ground we could wave at them and see them give us a thumbs up. The

NVA had several men trying to shoot the phantoms out of the sky.

Tracers were above, below, in front and in back but never touched the plane. The enemy was going to pay for that! The planes made one dry run just across the river then banked sharply and returned and dropped their ordinance behind the hedgerow. The explosions were deafening. The ground shook like an earthquake. Huge clods of earth were being hurled into the sky.

One of those clods came over our heads and landed on the legs of one of our new guys. He was medevaced out and we never heard of him again. The air assault lasted for 30 minutes. It was getting dark and we knew we would be spending the night. The next morning, we would cross the river again and see what was on the other side of the blown-up hedgerow.

That night Delta Company set up a company-sized ambush and around midnight we heard several claymores exploding and hundreds of rounds of gunfire. I knew that the retreating NVA from the bunker complex to our front had walked into Delta's ambush. I hoped our guys killed every one of those bastards. During the night I dreaded the thought of crossing that river again. My 9 lives were about accounted for and I knew we were pressing our luck.

The firefight Delta had going on lasted about an hour then it was dead quiet. I closed my eyes and had no worries about the NVA coming across the river. I was almost certain the F-4 Phantoms had neutralized their assets. Tomorrow would be another day to survive. At daybreak we broke out a carton of C rations and ate what you would call breakfast. Unfortunately, instead of bacon and eggs and hash browns we had to settle for turkey loaf, beanie weenies or ham and lima beans.

As we started crossing the river, two Cobra helicopters showed up in case the NVA were still able to fight. I led my squad just like yesterday and the rest of the platoon followed. Noel held the radio above his head the best he could and was able to safely reach the other side. We positioned ourselves on line and moved forward through the torn-up hedgerow.

When we broke through to the other side it was like walking into a place hit by a tornado. There were bunkers that had the tops blown off of them and blood evidence that told the story of the crushing blow they had taken by the 500 pounders. My first thought was where are the bodies? The bunkers were littered with empty shell casings and several belts of machine gun ammo. In the second bunker there was an arm still in the uniform sleeve. As we moved further ahead, we realized we were in the middle of a bunker complex. Bunkers were located all around the open field.

The Air Force had done a number on these guys and I'm assuming they got the hell out of there even though it meant leaving guns and ammo behind. It was shocking to see how tough these bunkers were. They constructed the roofs with cut sections of bamboo and tied them together with jungle reeds.

There were several layers that made it impossible for a mortar shell to penetrate. There were several cooking pots and cooking utensils scattered around as well as bags of rice. The NVA had been here for a while and hadn't planned on moving anytime soon. I picked up an NVA flag and put it in my pack. I would send that home as a souvenir along with the NVA officer's belt I removed from its dead owner. This complex was not set up to fight out of but rather a place for the NVA to hide and recoup after a battle. We spent the better part of the day picking up weapons, ammo, grenades, RPG launchers and rounds and piled them up for the engineers to blow in place.

After all was said and done, we only had one battlefield injury and that was the new guy that had his legs crushed by a flying clod of earth. I wonder how they would categorize that wound; hit by a flying object? Delta was credited with 36 confirmed killed and estimated 25 casualties.

After unloading the choppers at Parrots Beak, we quickly organized ourselves into two files and headed into the jungle. Our objective was to find evidence that the NVA were preparing for another major offensive against Tay Ninh. I had mentioned to Ray that I thought this kind of work should be done by an LRRP team.

A platoon-sized element is slow and makes lots of noise that makes for a perfect combination to get ambushed. At this point my mind was on getting out of here and going on R&R. The first days search and destroy mission went without a hitch. I was getting tired of getting nicked by elephant grass and scrub brush and must have been doping off when I suddenly stepped into a hole and nearly broke my leg.

When I looked up, Mannarelli and Kush were looking at me with huge grins on their faces. They had seen the hole, stepped over it, and didn't give me a heads up. Those two bastards did this on purpose. I looked at Kush with an evil sneer and said, "you motherfucker!" From that day forward he was referred to as MF. I never heard him referred to as Kush again. That was one time I didn't intentionally give a guy a nickname, but it stuck.

We ended up 2 klicks from where we originally entered the jungle. Lt. Baker decided we would be safer setting up our ambush away from the jungle and into the open field. This brought good news and bad news. The good news was we wouldn't be eaten alive by those malaria-carrying mosquitoes. The bad news was we would have absolutely no cover to separate us from any oncoming enemy.

Either way it was just another opportunity to kill more NVA or get killed ourselves. Only 81 days and a wake up until I would be climbing on board that freedom bird back to the world. What were my chances? We decided on an AP out in the open with a straight line facing the jungle and a rear security element in case some VC moron got lost and accidentally walked into our position on his way back to Cambodia. I was feeling better about the new guys in my squad.

They were maturing very quickly and had acquitted themselves well in the fire fights we had been in. Kid Lozon was a scrappy little warrior and he packed as much if not more M-60 ammo than anyone else. He had begun to grow on me. We sat at the edge of the jungle and ate our evening C rations. We wouldn't be seeing a resupply helicopter for another day, so rationing was important. Water wasn't a problem because the triple canopy jungles had natural watering holes where monsoon rain would collect. When we were through, everyone dug a hole and buried all the trash. The most important thing was to camouflage the disturbed earth.

When a guy had to take a dump, he would move off the trail about 10 yards, dig a hole and when he had done his business cover the hole and camouflage it. The NVA had tracker dogs that could pick up our scent as we made our way through the jungle. There was no need to give the dogs anything more to smell than necessary. One thing we learned was that if you squirted a little insect repellent around the hole the dog wouldn't alert their handler.

It was dusk and time for us to head out to our AP site. We always started out walking in the opposite direction of where we would be setting up. We knew there were eyes watching us constantly and we did not want the NVA to guess where we would be. We would move 200 yards and take a knee for 10 minutes.

As soon as it was pitch dark, we would get up and alter our course towards the direction of the AP site. Sometimes it was so dark you had to hold onto the web gear of the guy in front of you. On those nights, the starlight scope was useless. Our point men were taught to count paces. One pace equaled 2 natural steps starting with the right foot. The average distance of a pace is 5 feet.

When the point man counted 100 paces, he knew he had gone 500 feet. Setting up that night went without any complications. I did catch a couple of guys nodding out on guard duty and warned them the next time I would cut their throats. On the third day we located what looked like a soldier's camp. There were about 10 hammocks set up in sleeping shelters and an area where a fire had been burning and still smoldering.

There was a lister bag full of water hanging off a bamboo rod they had tied up in the hedgerow. We had just rousted Victor Charlie out of his siesta! We all turned outward in a defensive position. Charlie was here alright, and it looked like a platoon-sized group. These guys were definitely on R&R and had no desire to get into a fight. Marquez said we should move on and report the location to Headquarters and let them decide what to do. It was definitely not a good idea to get in a gunfight in the jungle. We moved out and kept walking along the border parallel to the Ho Chi Minh Trail.

We were so close to the NVA supply route that we could see headlights moving along the trail at night from our ambush site. We continued doing day sweeps and pulling ambush patrols for the next 3 days and nights. We had one more day and night to go and I figured there was a good chance I might make it back in one piece to go on R&R. The last day was uneventful besides the three booby traps we found and blew in place.

We threw some grenades into three tunnel entrances knowing that they were old and probably uninhabited. It was good to blow off steam sometimes and nothing does it like blowing stuff up. On our last night we set up our AP location 300 yards south of the border half way between Parrots Beak and Fish Hook. There was absolutely no moon light or starlight showing through the overcast sky.

It was so black we had to hold on to one another's back pack so we didn't get separated from the rest of the platoon. This night reminded me of when we pulled APs at the sugar factory under triple canopy jungle. We set up a simple on-line formation with rear security. Everything was going fine until 0200 hrs. when a VC soldier showed up and stopped right in front of Marquez who happened to be on guard. The only thing that could be seen was a slight metallic glint from the shiny side of his AK.

Marquez reached out and grabbed the AK and drug the guy onto the ground. The little VC was a tough son of a bitch and damn near got the better of Marquez until Lamere saw a chance to shoot and zipped the guy with his machine gun. One more notch in Lamere's gun stock! Needless to say, we picked up our gear and beat feet out of there as quickly as possible. Marquez was concerned that this guy may have been walking point for a platoon of VC. Everyone was thoroughly jacked up and when we reset our AP nobody went to sleep.

I couldn't wait for the sun to rise so we could purple out of this bad place. Purpling out was when we would throw a purple smoke grenade out to indicate the location, we wanted the helicopters to land to pick us up. Every man was required to carry at least one purple smoke grenade. When we got back to Jackson, I told Ray I was going to take a shower and get ready to go to Cu Chi. I was able to get a confirmed seat on the resupply helicopter the next morning.

After getting cleaned up I met Ray and Kush and Mannarelli in the chow line. The new guys razzed me about getting a second

R&R before they got their first one. I told them, "You survive 9 months and you'll get a second one as well." Ray told us he just got orders for an R&R to Hong Kong. Our platoon had the night off so a bunch of us spent the time playing cards and playing fetch with our mascot mongrel pup Lifer.

One of the guys had bought him from a village kid for $1 MPC. Since arriving in Vietnam in August of 68 I had seen several of these pups come and go. Sheila the monkey recently went back to Cu Chi with Big Joe. He was going to give her to the supply guys to take care of. I had thought a lot about my first R&R and the disastrous experience I'd had in the romance department. I decided I would confer with one of the brothers and get there take on R&R protocol.

Percy Allen had already been on two R&Rs, both to Hong Kong, so I figured he could give me the straight dope on how to be more successful. When I approached him, he said, "what it is Big John?" I told him about my upcoming R&R and asked him for a few tips. He said, "the first thing you do is go straight to the bar and tell the madam you are interested in a companion for the night." I had already been this route before, so I waited with bated breath for the rest of the advice. He told me to pick out the girl I wanted and tell her you are interested in a long-term relationship.

Long Term was code for an entire week. Most girls preferred this arrangement because they could make more money from the guy if he lived at her place instead of the Merlin Hotel. Most of these hookers lived in multi-storied tenement buildings where the rooms included one room, kitchenette and bathroom. He also explained that the girl would ask for all my money up front and that she would pay all my expenses for the week. Percy got a huge grin on his face and said, "there is no limit on the number of times these girls will make love." This would surely work out better for a rookie like me!" Before I left, he said be sure you hide a hundred bucks in your sock in case of an emergency.

I arrived in Cu Chi three days before my flight to Hong Kong. I went to supply to turn in my weapon and pick up my duffel bag containing my Khaki uniform. Sgt. Calvert was there and asked me if I knew of any guys with AK trophies. He had a guy in Saigon that would trade an AK for a Jeep load of beer. That's where a lot of the beer came from for our stand-downs. The first thing I needed to do was to get Sergeant stripes sewn on my khakis and update my ribbons.

When I removed them from the bag they were wrinkled and smelled musty. I asked Fowler to run them down to the Vietnamese seamstress and have her sew the new stripes on and get the uniform laundered and pressed. I told him it was a rush job and he told me he would make sure it was done.

The mail clerk handed me a bunch of mail and I thumbed through it looking for the letter from my dad that included the traveler's checks I requested. Bingo, there it was. It was almost dinner time, so I decided to run over to the mess hall and grab a quick bite to eat. When I got in line, I noticed Bobby Noel standing two guys in front of me.

I called out his name and he turned to see who was calling. He got a big smile on his face and said, "hey Big John what's up?" I told him that I was in Cu Chi getting ready to go on R&R. I asked him what he had been doing and he said he was an instructor at the combat leadership school. He asked me if I could come over after dinner to catch up on what had been happening since he left the platoon. I said sure and we proceeded through the line filling our trays with the menu items of the day.

After dinner, we walked over to his hooch and sat on his cot and I proceeded to tell him about the horrible things that had happened since he had left. He sat there with a sad look on his face and when I was done talking, he said he had heard about the land mine incidence and that he had struggled knowing that he should have been there. He felt that somehow, he had let the guys down. I told him that a big part of surviving Vietnam was timing and that he should not blame himself for something he had no control over.

My words were of little consolation and in a few minutes, I told Bobby I had to get back to the company area to get ready to go on R&R. I never saw or spoke to him again the rest of my tour. I went to the company hooch area and picked out a cot to sleep on. I was already feeling nervous about not having my weapon with me. It's one thing to dodge rockets and mortars but it's another thing if you have gooks running around shooting at you with their AKs.

The only protection we had in Cu Chi were several bunkers that were built behind the supply building and the company sleeping quarters. I was tempted to go get some grenades and put them in the bunker directly behind where I was sleeping. Instead, I took out my writing gear and proceeded to write letters to my mom and dad. The letters contained the same old story that I included in most of my letters.

Everything was going great, I was excited about going to Hong Kong, and that I only had 77 days until I got on the freedom bird and came back to the world. I was officially a double-digit midget. I was so short I could sit on a dime and dangle my feet! I couldn't believe that I had actually made it this long. The chances of me completing another two months in the field were getting slimmer by the day, but I could hope. Maybe Sir Charles would give me a break and refrain from dropping mortars on us tonight. The following day I caught up with Fowler and he had my Khaki uniform ready to go. I gave him an AK clip I had picked up on the border for his trouble.

The guys in the rear with the gear always appreciated any trophies we shared with them. Some of the guys in base camp that acted tough and told war stories we called POGs. That meant personnel other than grunts. I spent the rest of the day hanging around the supply room watching the new guys coming into the company picking up their gear like I had done so many months before.

I didn't have the heart to tell them what they were getting into. Several of them looked at me out of the corner of their eye as if to say, "why is that guy staring at us?" Little did they know some of them would be assigned to my squad. I couldn't think of that now, I had to get out of this bad place.

John headed to Hong Kong

Big John Writing Home

Michelin Rubber Plantation

Annie

Nui Ba Din the Black Virgin Mountain

Vietnamese Graveyard

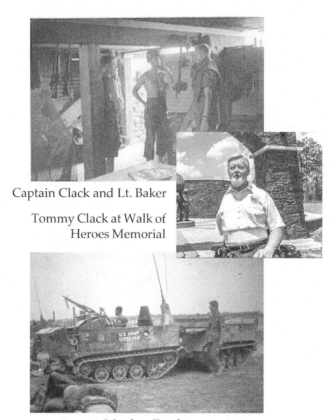

Captain Clack and Lt. Baker

Tommy Clack at Walk of Heroes Memorial

Monkey Tracks

Little Bears Pick Us Up

Chapter Nineteen
R&R OR AWOL

I arrived in Saigon on the morning of the 14th and checked into the R&R processing center to get my airline tickets for Hong Kong. I would be flying on Flying Tiger airlines that had been hauling freight and military personnel to Southeast Asia for years. They were considered to be the largest mail carriers in the world.

The flight would be about two and a half hours and I would get to Hong Kong by noon. This trip I would not be an accidental tourist. I had my game plan securely lined out in my mind and wouldn't make the same mistakes I made on my first R&R.

While waiting for the plane, I had another grunt take a few pictures of me to send home with my next letter. I would be incognito until I returned to Vietnam. Even before getting on the plane to leave, I dreaded returning to this hell hole that was so anxious to claim my life. So much had happened, and my mind was at the breaking point. I was seriously considering going AWOL and saying to hell with all of it. The plane to Hong Kong was ready to board and I grabbed my carry-on bag and climbed up the stairs to the door.

I was greeted by a beautiful Asian woman with a huge smile and perfect white teeth. I immediately thought it would be nice to take her to Hong Kong for a week. The flight to Hong Kong was uneventful and I tried to close my eyes and take a nap, but my mind would have none of that. My thoughts returned to the night John Boyle had gotten killed.

I could see clearly the exploding claymores and the bodies flying through the air. The muzzle flash from the point man's AK-47 was like flames shooting out of a blast furnace. I felt the dirt hitting me in the face and thinking that I'd been hit. I had played it over in my mind a thousand times; why did Boyle get killed and not me? If I hadn't told him to get up and shoot, he would still be alive.

I knew I would always feel responsible for his death. I planned on going to Idaho and meet his dad if I ever got back to the world. How would I explain to him what happened? Would I ask him to forgive me? All I could see were Boyle's lifeless eyes looking at me on the medevac ride to Cu Chi. Suddenly it is pitch black and I'm convinced I have wound up in hell for Boyle's death.

I feel a deep loneliness and sense of terror and at the same time I feel relieved that I will finally get to pay for what had happened. It feels like I am in the middle of an earthquake when suddenly I am awakened by the stewardess telling me we were about to land in Hong Kong. She handed me a couple of napkins to wipe the sweat dripping from my forehead and proceeded down the aisle. I was not the first GI she has seen coming out of a nightmare. I just can't go back to that bad place. I am in a world of shit for sure.

I looked out the window and noticed we were only a hundred feet off the water then without warning the runway came up under us and the plane touched down at Kai Tak airport and taxied down the runway to the arrival gate. With a numbness that is hard to describe, I walked off the plane and headed to the baggage claim area. I went to the nearest money exchange booth and turned my U.S. dollars into Chinese Yen. I hailed a cab and told him to take me straight away to the Black Dragon Bar located on Nathan Ave.

When we arrived, I paid the driver, grabbed my bag, and entered the establishment's front door. The bar was dimly lighted, and it took me a minute to adjust my eyes to the darkness. Sitting at the bar was the old madam I had dealt with on my previous R&R. I put down my bag next to an empty two-place round table and walked over to her to let her know my intentions. She got a toothy smile on her face and said, "hey GI you looking for nice girl for the night?" I smiled back and told her I was looking for a nice girl that would be able to spend the entire night with me. She said, "no problem, you know the drill go sit down and the bar girl will bring you a drink."

After I sat down, I noticed the old madam talking to some old Chinese guy who turned on his heel and promptly walked towards the rear of the bar. A sexy little Asian girl in a skimpy costume came to the table and asked me what I'd like to drink. I told her a Coca- Cola and she said that will be ten bucks. In about five minutes a beautiful woman approached my table and said, "would you like to buy me a drink?" I said it depended on whether she was available to be my date for the week. She smiled and waved the bar girl over and sat across from me at the small table. She told the bar girl that she would take her usual that was no doubt tea over ice.

When the bar girl returned with the drink, she said that will be ten bucks. Man, what a racket, I gave her a $20 and said I want my change. She gave me a dirty look as if to say you cheap skate! The lady sitting across from me introduced herself as Mai Lin. She spoke excellent English and I was immediately drawn to her beautiful eyes. She was drop-dead gorgeous and she asked me what I had said to the old madam. I told her I had indicated that I wanted a date for the entire night.

Mai Lin smiled and told me to finish my drink and leave the bar. She would meet me a block down the street in front of the Ming tea house. She said we would discuss our options then. She downed what was left of her drink and got up and walked to the back of the bar. I finished my drink and got up and headed for the front door. The old Madam cut me off before I could get to the door and hooked her arm around my waist. She asked me why I was leaving, and I told her I was going to check into the Merlin and come back later.

She cackled and said, "no worries I fix you up good." I walked the block towards the tea house weaving in and out of hundreds of people going and coming. Everyone seemed in a big hurry. I looked up at the 20-story tenement buildings and saw laundry hanging out of windows on make-shift clothes lines.

People here were literally living on top of each other. I walked past an open-air meat shop that had all kinds of butchered animals and birds hanging from hooks attached to the overhang of their shop. The flies were intense and crawling all over the bare meat.

I couldn't help but imagine all the eggs those filthy flies were laying in those carcasses. When I got to the Tea Shop, Mai Lin was standing out front in a beautiful full-length coat. She was very petite and stood at 5 feet 1 inch tall. When she came up to me, she reached out and took my hand and led me into the tea house. We sat in a secluded booth towards the back where we could enjoy some privacy. She started our discussion by asking me where I was from in the states.

She asked me how old I was and if I was a soldier in Vietnam. It seemed like I had GI tattooed on my forehead. It was probably the short military haircut and khaki uniform I was wearing that gave me away. Mai Lin told me about herself and that she was born and raised in Hong Kong and attended university for one year when her father died and she had to go to work to support her mother and younger brother. She told me her dream was to go to the United States and become a citizen.

I told her this was my second trip to Hong Kong and that my first experience was not good. She laughed and told me she hears that a lot from guys on their second R&R. She told me she would be willing to be my companion for the time I was in Hong Kong. She said there were a few conditions that I would have to abide by that included living with her in her apartment and giving her all my money up front. She said she would be responsible for all my needs including sex, meals, entertainment and sightseeing.

This sounded exactly what Percy Allen had told me about back in Cu Chi. I told her I thought the arrangement would be fine and reached into my pocket and handed her $400 in Chinese cash. I still had $100 hidden in my sock! She said if I decided to end our arrangement prematurely, she would not be obligated to give me any money back.

I agreed to her terms and she paid for our drinks and we headed to her apartment. Mai Lin lived in a very large tenement building in downtown Hong Kong. When we entered the building, she walked to the elevator and we entered it and she pushed the button for the 15th floor. When the elevator opened, she walked out and told me to follow her. We walked about 100 feet and arrived at her apartment. All wording and numbers in the building were in Chinese so I had no clue what they meant.

When we entered her apartment, I was pleasantly surprised at how neat and modern it looked. She told me Chinese apartments are empty when rented and the tenant can use their own money to decorate it and furnish it. The first thing I saw was a large queen-sized bed with a beautiful black enameled chest of drawers and matching vanity. The bed was a traditional Chinese platform bed with a woven mat for sitting or sleeping. To me it would be like sleeping on the ground. The wooden slats had spaces between them for air circulation that helped prevent mold. Mae told me to take my clothes out of my bag and she would hang them up.

She had a beautiful wardrobe closet full of beautiful clothes and a large selection of shoes. I was thinking how much different this week was going to be compared to my last regrettable rest and recuperation disaster. It was about 5 pm and Mai said she was going to take me out to dinner to one of her favorite restaurants after I took a shower. When

I emerged from the bathroom Mai had laid out my clothes and said we would leave as soon as I got dressed. She mentioned buying me a new set of clothes. We left the apartment and Mai hailed a cab and told the driver to take us to the Kowloon Shangri-la restaurant. It took about 20 minutes to get there by cab and Mai sat very close to me holding my hand for the entire ride.

When we arrived, Mai paid the driver and a valet opened the car door and stood there as we got out of the back seat. He closed the door and walked with us the short distance to the front door of the restaurant and opened it for us. Mai spoke to him in Chinese and handed him a tip. The hostess guided us to a booth towards the rear of the restaurant. Mai pointed to the restrooms and told me to go and wash my hands.

When I returned the waiter had brought complete set ups for two. I looked at the menu and it was written in Chinese. Mai chuckled and told me to tell her what I wanted, and she would order it. I assumed we were in a Cantonese restaurant, so I told her I liked sweet and sour pork and chicken chow mein. When the waiter returned, she told him our order and he bowed and left the table.

Mai asked me how long I had been in Vietnam and I told her a little more than 9 months. She wanted to know what kind of job I had, and I told her I was in the infantry. She nodded her head and said, "that's the worst job in the Army!" She told me her father served in the Chinese Army as a foot soldier. I had a feeling Mai had a pretty good handle on what guys did in Vietnam since she had met so many of them. Our dinner was served within 10 minutes and the presentation was outstanding.

Each selection was served in sterling silver bowls and plates with matching chargers. Mai ordered a hot pot full of everything but the kitchen sink. There were clams, snails, fish pieces, and an octopus arm with suction cups trying to crawl out of the pot. The waiter dished out my food and put a bowl of rice in front of my plate. Mai wasted no time digging into the pot. I sat there like a hick looking for the silverware. They only supplied chop sticks and I had never used them. I picked them up and tried to get them to fit in my hand with no luck. I was putting on quite a clown show.

When she noticed, she laughed and called the waiter over and requested silverware for me. Others sitting by us were laughing as well avoiding looking me in the eye. When the silverware arrived, I wasted no time in diving into the banquet that lay before me. The food was out of this world.

I had eaten plenty of Chinese food before, but this was far better than I'd ever experienced. We sat there for the next hour quietly enjoying our food. There were only a few times that we exchanged conversation. It occurred to me that this was a very upscale restaurant and that the cost for the food would be very expensive. I kept remembering Mai telling me that she would take care of all my needs including a place to live and food to eat. When we were finished eating the waiter brought each of us a fortune cookie and scraped the leftover food into cardboard containers for us to take back to the apartment.

The bill was placed in the center of the table and Mai quickly looked at it and opened her purse to get money to pay for it. While she was doing that, I had cracked open my fortune cookie and much to my dismay the fortune was written in Chinese. Mai reached across the table and took the small piece of paper out of my hand, looked at it, and got a big smile on her face. I asked her what my fortune was, and she read aloud in a low voice, "looks like you might get lucky tonight!" When we got in the cab to return to her apartment, she told the driver to take us around and show us the sites.

Every street was lined with neon signs advertising businesses and clubs. There was every color of the rainbow and I never saw two signs that looked alike. At every major intersection there was a traffic pagoda with a smartly dressed officer directing traffic. There were no traffic lights anywhere in Hong Kong. Mai told me to look out the window as we passed the TST Clock Tower. You could see the British Empire's influence in a lot of the architecture and even the names of the streets. The driver eventually wound up at the Macau Ferry Pier. Mai told me that sometime during the week we would come back and spend some time riding the ferry.

By the time we got back to the apartment, I was exhausted. Mai asked me if I had brought any pajamas and I told her the only thing I had to sleep in was a pair of olive drab military-issued underwear. She laughed and said, "no problem you won't need them anyway! She lit a stick of incense next to the bed and then went into the bathroom to get ready for bed.

I sat on the edge of the platform bed and realized how hard the surface was. There were several pillows leaning up against the headboard and a silk sheet covering the entire bed. Mai was truly a lady with class, and it made me feel special and glad we had met. When the bathroom door opened, I saw Mai standing there with the bathroom light cascading through the see-

386

through baby doll outfit she was wearing including a lace robe and g-string.

The whole outfit was pure white. I was already rising for the occasion. She glided over to the bed and stood before me and took my head in her hands and pressed my face to her stomach. Her smell was intoxicating, and for a brief moment, I thought I'd died and went to heaven.

Her touch was so gentle and caring as she ran her fingers through my hair. It reminded me of when I was a little child and my mother would hold me close to comfort me when I hurt myself. Mai told me to lie down on my stomach and she would give me a massage. Her hands were warm and very therapeutic.

She was finding knots in my muscles and firmly but gently working each one out. I became so relaxed I felt like I was levitating above the bed. In my mind I could feel the warmth of the sun as I lay on the beach next to crystal pier in San Diego. I could smell the salt air and the biggest concern in my life was graduating High School.

Life was so uncomplicated, and my buddy Packman and I had several girlfriends that liked hanging around watching us surf. We had bonfires on the beach almost every night and snuggling with one or two of the girls was always fun. I fell asleep on the beach and when I woke, I was lying on top of a platform bed covered by a silk sheet. I could smell coffee brewing and I felt disoriented.

I sat up and saw a beautiful Chinese girl standing at the sink slicing up fresh fruit. I realized then that I was in Hong Kong, in Mai's apartment, and that I had been sleeping for the past 8 hours. I had not slept like that for the past year! Was I still dreaming?

Mai saw me sitting on the edge of the bed and said, "good morning sleepy head." She told me breakfast would be ready in a couple of minutes and asked how did I like my coffee. Breakfast included pancakes, link sausage and fresh fruit. We sat at the small kitchen table and ate and chatted about what we would be doing that day. Mai said she wanted to show me Tiger Balm Gardens and the Kowloon Wharf.

After breakfast Mai cleared the table and said we should get ready to go see the city. As she walked by me, she bent down and gave me a light kiss on my lips. I wasn't expecting that and as I watched her walking towards the bathroom my mind kicked into overdrive about the romance that was to come. The day went by quickly and Mai bought us lunch at an outdoor restaurant at the wharf.

From time to time my mind would return to Vietnam and I would get a sick feeling deep down in my soul. I had a bad feeling about returning to the place that would eventually take my life. I did not want to go back and began planning a way to avoid returning there. Of course, that would include going AWOL, and if I was ever caught, I would face a court marshal and prison. I would worry about that later.

That night Mai and I made love and it was not what I expected. There were no frantic movements or sense of urgency to get it over with. Mai was a very sensual being and guided me through the most passionate experiences of my life. For the rest of the week Mai took care of all my needs including going to the Peak Tram, the Globe Cinema, the Roxie Movie House and several Tea Houses where several hundred people were served lunch at the same time.

It was a whirlwind of experiences and one day Mai took me to a tailor and bought me a new casual outfit and shoes. I'm not sure if I had ever been in love with a girl before but I was feeling something with Mai that felt like love. I felt she might have those same feelings for me. That same day Mai told me she had a young daughter from a previous marriage, and she wanted me to meet her. We took a taxi to Victoria Park and Mai's mother was there waiting with Mai's four-year-old daughter whose name was Jia Li (meaning good and beautiful).

Jia was dressed in a very fancy dress with lacy socks and black shoes. She was as cute as a porcelain doll. We spent the afternoon with her at the park where she could swing and go down the slide. Mai told me she had dreams of her daughter having a better life than she had. She asked me if I thought I could take her and Jia to the United States and have a life with them. She got tears in her eyes and I reached out and pulled her into my arms. At that second, I could see us living happily ever after but how would I get myself back to the States let along her and Jia.

All I had to my name was the clothes I brought from Vietnam, a hundred dollars hidden in my sock and a one-way ticket back to Vietnam. Mai continued to pay for everything, and she treated me like a king. As hard as I tried, I could not figure out how to make my plan a reality and on the sixth day I told Mai I would have to return to Vietnam and finish my tour of duty. I told her I would try to figure a way to get her and Jia to the states when I returned home.

It all sounded so easy at the time. Mai said she wanted to ride with me to the airport the following morning and see me off. We were both very sad that last night. We exchanged addresses and phone numbers and she said she would write to me in Vietnam. Parting was such a bitter-sweet affair. I was going to miss this woman who helped me forget about the horrors of war and treated me with love and affection. She was a remarkable person that I would never forget.

Returning To Hell

On the morning of my departure, I gave Mai the hundred dollars I had hidden in my sock. She smiled and said, "I saw that the first night you were with me."

We took a taxi to the airport and we kissed one last time with tears in our eyes. I boarded the plane that would take me back to hell. The plane landed at Saigon airport. I retrieved my bag and went to the transportation pool to see about getting a ride to Cu Chi. The distance to Cu Chi was 75 miles and I was hoping to catch a chopper instead of riding in a Jeep or deuce and a half. As luck would have it there was a mail chopper headed to Cu Chi that I could jump on.

I would have to sit in the middle of several mail bags full of letters and care packages, but it beat a long dusty ride in a Jeep or truck. We took off at noon and it only took 20 minutes to arrive at Cu Chi airstrip. I got off the chopper and started my trek to the Charlie Company Quonset. It was hot as hell and my khakis were already being soaked with sweat. I really hated Vietnam.

When I got to within 100 feet of the front door, I saw Gary Hunt walk out and skip down the steps. He was headed towards the supply room and when he saw me coming, he stopped and yelled, "Big John, welcome back." He then asked me if I got laid on R&R. Did I mention welcome back to Vietnam? I walked with Hunt to the supply room where I retrieved my duffel bag and picked up my M-16.

I was going to hitch a ride with the resupply truck to Jackson FSB. I had no idea where the platoon was located so I figured if they weren't there I'd hide out for a few days. Lee was going to Jackson to conduct a weapons inspection for the company. It

390

was sad to say but we were trying to fight a war with weapons that jammed up and broke.

The M-16 butt stock, hand guard and pistol grip were made of plastic. The rifle weighed in at 7.9 lbs. loaded with a full magazine. There was always a shortage of replacement barrels for our M-60 machine guns and the feed tray and the cover and chamber had to be cleaned daily. The gun including the permanently attached bipod weighed 23 lbs.

The 45 cal. pistols they issued us were completely worn out. The bullets never went straight because there were no riflings left in the barrels. When I carried one, I knew the only way it would be effective was to put the barrel in the VC's mouth.

The ride to Jackson was dusty, hot and miserable. We passed through small villages that housed Buddhist shrines and monasteries. It was common to see the monks sitting around in their saffron orange robes. I had read in the Army times that Buddhist monks were setting themselves on fire to protest the Vietnam War. That seemed a little extreme to me. I never had any issues with the monks and they stayed to themselves. They did however appreciate a donation to their cause when offered.

There were also Catholic churches run by local priests and nuns. Their primary purpose was to educate Vietnamese children and take care of their health needs. Many of the kids attending the schools were orphaned because they were Amerasian. These kids were the byproducts of American GIs screwing the Vietnamese whores. These kids stuck out like sore thumbs because their skin color was dark and some had afro hair. Others had blue eyes and had a European look. The Vietnamese people wanted nothing to do with these children and they associated them with a war that was destroying their country.

God only knows how many Amerasian kids were in Vietnam. I'm guessing tens of thousands. Prostitution is one of the biggest industries in Nam and you can find boom boom girls in every small village in the country. They stand outside the fire support bases every day hoping some horny GI will come out and partake in what they have to offer. As we approached the front gate of Jackson, I saw three boom boom girls dressed in colorful dresses holding parasols. When the truck came to a stop, I grabbed my gear and headed for the second platoon bunkers.

The first guy I saw was Ray sitting on our bunker. He was writing a letter and smoking a cigarette. When he saw me, he said, "where have you been you dirty bastard?" I threw my gear up on the bunker roof and sat next to Ray with a huge grin on my face. I said it's a long story and said I'd tell him all about it later. He told me I had missed out on a week filled with new guys stepping on booby traps including a medic that was covering for Doc Flores while he was on R&R.

I asked him why he didn't find one and get his million-dollar wound. He laughed and said, "it wasn't because I didn't try!" He said Flat Dick had gone on R&R just after I did and was going to Hawaii to see his wife. She would be flying in from Ft. Benning, Georgia where they have lived since Marquez joined the Army over 15 years ago. He was scheduled to return tomorrow, and I was glad he was coming back.

Marquez had been a thorn in our side since he took over as platoon sergeant, but he knew what he was doing and for the most part kept us alive. The new guys coming into the platoon were a lot less disciplined and were always complaining that Marquez wouldn't tolerate them wearing hippie beads and peace signs on their helmets. I wondered if the protests against the war back home had anything to do with it.

I remember Rocky painted FTA on the side of his bunker on wooden slats he scrounged from the artillery guys. Marquez hit the roof when he saw it and said, "what in da god damn hell you tink you do you sonny beach?" He threatened Rocky with an article 15 if he didn't get rid of it immediately. Smitty from the Company CP brought us our mail and care packages and I had quite a stack since being gone for a week.

In one of my dad's letters, he told me he had spotted a 20-acre piece of property in Cody, Wyoming up the south fork of the Shoshone River that had a trailer house and all utilities included. He said the price was only $4,000 and if I was interested, he would use my money and buy it. He said it was out of town and it would be a perfect place to have horses. I thought the property would be a good investment, so I told him to buy it.

My mind was so screwed up lately I couldn't keep two thoughts straight at the same time. Mannarelli and Kid Lozon came over and said they were glad I was back. The kid said he was worried something had happened to me on R&R. I told him something did happen: "I think I fell in love!" They all laughed loudly and Mannarelli said, "who would love an old cob like you?" I pulled out Mai's picture and said, "she does assholes, so go screw yourselves."

They gazed at Mai's picture like drooling dogs looking at a T-bone steak. The kid said she was gorgeous and Mannarelli said, "I'd sure love to get into that." No class and no respect. Ray said, "you're not serious about her, are you?" I just shrugged my shoulders and put the picture back into my waterproof baggy. I was brought back to reality when the 155 mm howitzers cranked their guns in a fire mission.

Some poor GIs had found themselves pinned down by a bunch of NVA. Hopefully, the artillery would be effective, and I prayed we would not be called up to go pull their asses out of the fire. For a brief minute, I had forgotten how scared I'd become when we left the base camp. It hit me that I only had 64 days left until DEROS (date estimated return from overseas).

I still have this feeling that I wasn't going to make it. We pulled perimeter bunker duty for the night and I thought it would be a good time to get to know my new guys better. I wanted to stress upon them how serious it was in Vietnam and the necessity for disciplined behavior outside the wire. Sometimes being inside the fire support base gave a guy a false sense of security. Besides the occasional mortar round coming into the base, not much happened during the day.

It was at night when we were outside the wire that we had to be on our best game. Two weeks ago, Delta Company had men on an ambush patrol go to sleep and Charlie took advantage of the situation and snuck up on them and slit their throats. When the sun came up the platoon sergeant was horrified to see four of his men dead without a shot being fired. I would use this story tonight to impress upon the new guys that it never pays to go to sleep on guard duty. Hell, Sergeant Hannah had threatened us with slitting our throats if he caught anyone going to sleep on guard.

When I was a new guy Hannah had kept his promise and cut Lemere's skin around his throat. It oozed blood but not fatal. Everyone got the point. That afternoon Ray and I decided to have a knife-throwing contest with the new guys. We took some wooden artillery rounds cases and made a backstop. Someone had a poster of Ho Chi Minh's face in the middle of a bull's eye, so we tacked it up and made it our target. The bull's eye was between Ho's eyes and in order to win that's where you had to hit.

I had the new guys line up and brandish their favorite knife that would be used in the contest. There were a variety of weapons ranging from k-bars to bayonets to hunting knives that had been sent from home. I would be throwing a 10-inch skinning knife that I took off the first gook I killed. There were many stories about GIs being scalped and given a Columbian necktie after being captured. Another favorite of the VC was to cut a GI's penis and balls off and shove it in his mouth while he was still alive. They would leave the man to bleed to death. I could not imagine what that would be like.

Unthinkable Horror

When I first arrived in the platoon, they were telling us new guys about first platoon getting into an all-day firefight. The VC had captured the two-point guys and the platoon sergeant didn't know if they were alive or dead. The shooting stopped as the sun went down and the platoon was told they would set up right there for the night. Sometime around 0100 hrs., the screaming began. They said it was horrendous and everyone knew their buddy was being tortured. The screaming went on for an hour and then dead silence.

There were a couple of guys who wanted to crawl out to where the screaming was, but it was too dangerous. When the sun rose the platoon sergeant and two other guys crawled out to see if they could locate the two men. When they cleared the high grass, they saw one of the men sitting tied up with a gag in his mouth. Lying next to him was the other point man. He had been stripped and skinned alive. When they asked the man sitting there why they didn't kill him, he said they left him alive to tell the others what would happen to them if they ever came back. Guys from that platoon came back to Crockett in total shock. These men had witnessed the worst that humanity had to offer.

My thoughts always return to the guy who wasn't killed. He would never be right. My guess is he was declared section 8. These were not just scary stories to be told around a camp fire, these were things that actually happened. The knife-throwing match went on for about an hour with Ray and I being the last two contestants. Both of us threw 3 bulls' eyes in a row and called it a tie. The new guys were totally impressed. Marquez told us we were going to be air lifted into the Michelin rubber plantation in the morning to do a mop up after a gun battle between the VC and the First Cavalry. Michelin Rubber Company established the Michelin Rubber Plantation in 1925. It was 31,000 acres in size and was located 72 km northwest of Saigon. The plantation served as a major staging area for VC and PAVN forces.

It was no secret that Michelin had been paying the VC off for years to keep the plantation operating. The U.S. government even had an agreement with Michelin that the Army would pay for any trees damaged as a result of conflicts with the VC. I hated these missions because there was always a chance a VC would be hiding in a hole amongst the trees. This was their backyard, not ours. Many times, the hair on the back of my neck would stand up with the feeling a VC had me in his cross hairs. We were no strangers to the Plantation.

When I arrived in the platoon in August 1968, the platoon was sent into the Rubber trees to do battle with a hardened VC regiment. The operation was named Diamond Head and lasted through September. This battle was Phase Three of the Army's offensive. In March 1969, we were sent in to mop up a huge battle between the 1st Infantry Division and the 11th Cavalry and the 1/4th Cavalry and VC regulars. That operation was called Atlas Wedge. The Army paid beaucoup bucks for damaged trees after that battle!

The Army was never able to run the VC out of the Plantation and we took our lives into our own hands whenever we went in there. This was just another case of SNAFU. I had a bad feeling in my guts about going out tomorrow. I asked SFC Marquez if he had heard about any jobs off line I could get. He looked at me with sad eyes and said, "Sergeant, I'm doing the best I can, but you know we have so many new guys it's hard to send in a seasoned veteran like yourself." I told him thank you and went to my bunker to sulk.

There is an interesting phenomenon that occurs when a combat soldier gets short. The men around him know that being short puts a guy on edge and they tend to avoid hanging around him. Guys will start wondering if the old-timer still has what it takes under fire. I was starting to notice this with the guys in my squad. It was a lonely feeling. Ray and I were almost inseparable and spent most of our time together.

We would talk about what it would be like to be back in the world. I told him I wanted to meet his dad Louis, who had faithfully written to me for the past six months. We promised each other we would stay in close touch the rest of our lives if we got out of here. Now I had to plan a way to let all my girl pen pals know we probably would not be getting married and spending our lives happily ever after. I thought about just not writing them and let them think I'd been killed but that would be heartless.

Maybe I could have Ray write them a letter and tell them I had taken a blow to the head and had amnesia. Oh well, I would wait a little longer and enjoy the letters I was receiving. That night Sir Charles decided to mess with our minds by launching a half a dozen mortar rounds into the fire support base. Lucky for us the mortars did not hit any bunkers but did make a direct hit on the latrine located behind the mortar platoon pit. Phil told me the smell was a horrendous mixture of cordite and human waste.

By morning, the dust and smoke had settled, and first platoon was being sent out to see where the mortars had come from. Good luck with that. Charlie could clean up after himself better than any soldier on the face of the earth. They would also scrounge anything a numb-minded GI would discard while outside the wire. Without exception Charlie would use his findings against us at a later time.

Most of the booby traps GIs tripped were made from U.S. hand grenades and Coca-Cola cans. It's amazing how many knuckle heads would ditch their ammo and grenades to lighten their load during a brutal march in the 120-degree heat.

Heat exhaustion was common, and our medics were constantly giving us salt tabs and trying to prevent us from stroking out. Many a scout dog was medevaced out of the field with heat exhaustion. Charlie was smarter than that. He stayed cool underground during the heat of the day and walked around at night like he owned the joint.

Shamrock Hard Spot

Doc Flores and Dave Grimm

Purple Out

Chapter Twenty
CLOSE TO THE END

The following morning we lined up outside the fire support base and waited for our airlift ride to the Rubber Plantation. The Little Bears would be showing up shortly and I would pop a purple smoke grenade to mark where we wanted the lead ship to land. As soon as I heard the distinct sound of the rotor blades, I pulled the pin let the handle fly and tossed the grenade out to my front.

There were 10 helicopters in the formation and second platoon would be first in and last out as usual. I was starting to get a funny feeling again about getting killed before I got out of this bad place. The nightmares were occurring on a regular basis now and my nerves were shot. I knew I had a job to do and a bunch of newbies that looked to me to keep them alive.

Hannah had the same feeling the night he went out with us and died. As we lifted off the ground I sang "Up, Up, and Away" by the Fifth Dimension in my mind. I had started the habit shortly after my first chopper ride. That seemed like such a long time ago. I thought the song was like a good luck charm. It had worked so far and although we had been hit by AK fire we never got shot down! God bless these brave pilots.

It was a clear day and I could see for miles and the first thing that caught my attention was Nui Ba Din also known as the Black Virgin Mountain. The vacated volcano reached 3268 ft. into the sky. It was the tallest landmark in an otherwise flat terrain. The Special Forces took control of the top of the mountain in May 1964. The area around the mountain was very active as the Ho Chi Minh Trail ended a few kilometers west across the Cambodian border.

The 25th Infantry Division took over guarding the radio stations on top of the mountain in November 1967. The stations were highly sophisticated listening posts that intercepted Viet Cong and NVA radio transmissions. Just before I got to Vietnam, the Viet Cong assaulted the mountain top killing 24 Americans and taking 2 POWs. The Viet Cong gave up 24 lives in the attack. The mountain itself had many honeycomb caves dug into it. They were so large that they served to house troops and equipment. These tunnels were impervious to bombing and artillery barrages.

The U.S. Army controlled the top and the Viet Cong controlled the bottom and sides of the mountain. We had operated day missions around the bottom of the mountain but knew there was no way we were going to make a dent in the enemy defenses. Going to Nui Ba Din or the rubber plantation were equally dangerous. I was glad we were going where both sides wanted to preserve the rubber trees. It might mean less shooting and there were all kinds of cover afforded by the large trees.

I wasn't sure why we were coming to the plantation and it seemed like it was just another snoop and poop mission. Before landing, a smoke ship flew parallel to the tree line dumping smoke in front of the trees. This gave us a better chance of not getting sniped right off the bat. The company lined up parallel to the tree line and each man was separated from the man to his left and right by 20 ft. Upon command, we started walking slowly into the plantation trying to stay on line with the rest of the company.

I noticed there were several carvings in the trees bark left by previous GIs. Lots of FTA and fuck you Charlie along with a few uncomplimentary political statements about President Johnson. He was definitely not one of the GI's favorite people right now. He and McNamara had plenty of blood on their hands and Johnson announced he would not run again for President. I wondered if his conscience was bothering him about all the men who had been killed up to that point in the war. Nixon was promising to get us out of Vietnam with an early withdrawal.

I told my mother, a lifelong democrat, to vote for Nixon so I could get out of Vietnam. She did, and it was the first and last time she ever voted Republican. As it turned out Nixon did accelerate the number of troops going home but the men leaving were guys in the rear with the gear and administration types. The Infantry would be staying until the last dog was hung.

The Company was halted after entering the plantation about 300 yards. Someone spotted a booby trap and it would take a few minutes to blow it. This gave me a chance to drink some water and break out the cheese spread and crackers I had thrown in my backpack. Overall, the day was turning out pretty good. I suspected that if Charlie wanted to jump in our backpacks he would have done so by now. The break turned out to be about a half-hour when the silence was broken by the sound of the C-4 plastic explosive going off destroying the booby trap. That served as a signal that we were going to get up and move out.

The Company Commander decided we had seen enough and called battalion and arranged for our extraction. On the ride back to the support base I pulled out my short-timers calendar and filled in another square with the number 59 in it. Less than

2 months and a wake-up and I would be getting on the freedom bird headed to the world. Not many men in the field broke those odds and made it the whole 365 days and I was getting more nervous by the minute. When we returned to Jackson there was a package waiting for me along with some mail.

My mom had sent me another care package and she included some canned Vienna sausages, several packets of presweetened kool-aid and a couple dozen homemade chocolate chip cookies. She took my advice and filled the box with popcorn and that kept the cookies from completely disintegrating. I sent Ray over to the mess tent and had him scrounge a large empty tin can and some ice.

We would mix up a packet of kool-aid and sit and eat cookies and popcorn until it was time to head to the mess hall for dinner. Ray said they were serving chicken and mashed potatoes with gravy and vegetables with dinner rolls. A couple of the guys in the squad joined us and we sat around and bull shitted with each other. Some of them asked me what to expect when they went on their R&R next month.

I gave them the best advice I could and recommended they get back to the company on time and not take any extra days causing an AWOL. Hunt was training a new company clerk and I wasn't sure the new clerk would be as generous as Hunt had been with the guys. We had a new Company Commander that seemed to be more by the book and less tolerant of guys pushing the rules and regulations. "Leaving on a jet plane, don't know when I'll be back again."

I kept wondering if Marquez had found me a job off line yet. I couldn't keep asking him about it and figured what would be, would be. Lamere had just left the field and I felt insecure without him covering my back. So many old guys had left and so many new guys were arriving every week. I couldn't keep up with it all. It seemed I was avoiding getting close to any of the new guys these days. I didn't want to know about their families or if they were married with kids or if they had a sweetheart.

I had already lost so many good friends and so many good men had been broken and sent home. I requested that Grimm Reaper be transferred to my squad. He was a solid troop and would work well with Mannarelli and Kush. Marquez came by and said our platoon was staying inside the base tonight and pull perimeter duty. He told me tomorrow we would be leaving for another 7-day sweep north of Tay Ninh up on the Cambodian border. He said the Army suspected another buildup of NVA troops that were planning another assault on Tay Ninh.

We were supposed to act as eyes and ears on the ground and act as an early warning. That meant we would try to stay alive long enough to avoid getting run over. I couldn't believe this is how I was going to spend my last days in the field.

That night I wrote letters to my mom and dad and told them I would be off the grid for a while and not worry if they didn't hear from me. I reminded them that no news was good news. That night I spent checking out my squad's gear and made sure they had plenty of magazines of ammo and grenades.

I insisted that each man carry at least two smoke grenades and an extra canteen of water. I double-checked that Butler my M-79 guy, had plenty of HE rounds and several parachute flares along with a couple CS gas grenades just in case we got close enough to use them. I was trying to be extra careful and I could hear the guys grumbling about the extra weight I was making them carry.

None of them had experienced being down to their last magazine and being forced under fire to crawl to a wounded buddy grabbing his ammo bag to keep fighting. Running out of ammo at this point in my tour was not an option. I loaded up my backpack with six hand-held parachute flares in case we had to pop an ambush.

Just that minute of illumination can make the difference on getting a shot at a retreating enemy. I suddenly felt a hot flash in my face and poured some water over my head from my canteen. My hands were shaking again, and I felt tightness in my chest. I had to hold it together and took several deep breaths before standing up and walking to the latrine.

Last Combat Flight

After breakfast Marquez talked to us about what our mission was going to be for the next week. In addition to throwing out several cases of C rations we were also given some new dehydrated packets of food called MREs (meals ready to eat). These meals were designed to be easier to carry and much less weight. They came in a variety of menu items like spaghetti and beef in sauce, beef and beans, chili and beans, beef shredded in barbecue sauce, chicken with egg noodles and veggies in sauce and chicken chunks in sauce.

The problem with these rations is that you had to re-hydrate the contents with hot water. The only way to accomplish this in the field is with a piece of C-4 explosive. An empty tin can was filled with water and held over the burning C-4. It was similar to using a Bunsen burner. If that wasn't bad enough, the meals had a tendency to exacerbate an ever-present case of diarrhea. These along with malaria pills kept a GI loose in the bowels most of the time. After everyone had a chance to pick out their meals, we started making our way to the exit point in the wire.

The Little Bears would be here shortly, and we would once again fly off into the wild blue yonder. Pete, our Kit Carson Scout, asked me if he could ride with me on the eagle flight. I told him sure and he looked at me with a toothy grin. Pete had been a surgeon in Hanoi when he was impressed into the North Vietnamese Army. His real name was Trung Van Than. He was a highly educated man that spoke four languages including pretty good English. The communists threatened to kill his wife and daughter if he didn't agree to serve.

They sent him to a large underground hospital located on the Cambodian border. It could have been the same hospital we had discovered when we joined the Special Forces Sergeant and his merry band of Montagnards. After being there for a year he received word that his wife and daughter had been sent to a re-education camp. He knew he would never see them again and decided to desert the hospital and give himself up to the U.S. Army under the Cu Hoi program.

This program allowed enemy soldiers to come over to our side and pledge their allegiance to America and serve as scouts for Army Infantry units. It was a perfect fit because the scouts could act as interpreters in the field. Most of the time the Cu Hoi's were grateful to have three meals a day and good boots on their feet. Sometimes however the allure of returning to the old VC unit was too strong and when this happened, we would simply hasten their way to the big Buddhist temple in the sky.

Pete had turned out to be an exceptional asset. He had obtained the rank of E-5 and had received several medals for valor. I always looked at Pete as my bell-weather. If he didn't get hurt or killed, I probably wouldn't either. Pete also acted as our backup medic. He carried a medic's bag along with his M-16 and the rest of his gear.

I knew he was going to be a good troop when he volunteered to crawl down into tunnels to check for any VC or caches. He would take a 45-cal. pistol and a flashlight and go headfirst into the hole chattering nonstop in Vietnamese

405

undoubtedly telling the occupants he was a friend coming to visit. I am happy to say that he never ran into any VC, but we did get credit for finding caches of rice and ammunition.

A few months before we were working in the Iron Triangle, Duininck shouted that he had found a tunnel roof located in the underbrush. I told Pete to go check it out and he uncovered the hole and went head first straight down. Within a few seconds he reemerged and said, "this is a tank!" I thought he was kidding so I went over and looked down the hole to see Pete grinning at me and sitting in the driver's seat.

This was an old French Panther tank that had been captured and buried by the PAVN troops fighting the French. No doubt they planned to come back and retrieve it for a future battle. Instead, it had been swallowed whole by the Vietnamese jungle. We marked the location of the tank on the map and would report its location to Battalion when we got back to base camp.

When we loaded up, Pete waited until everyone else had boarded then jumped on sitting next to me in the chopper's door opening. He did something unusual and draped his arm around my shoulder. I got the feeling he thought we might not be together much longer. I had been telling him I was going home in less than two months and he seemed sad that I was leaving.

I would miss this man that had saved my life more than a few times and showed me what bravery looked like in real-time. He told me he would never go back to North Vietnam even after the war. I was hoping the Army had a program to bring the Kit Carsons back to the U.S. when the war ended. God knows they deserved it. The flight to the border was business as usual. There was nothing to see on the ground except open fields and rice paddies.

The peasant population had gotten so used to Army helicopters flying over them they seldom looked up to see what we were up to. The door gunner signaled that we were landing in two minutes, so I looked over my shoulder and gave the guys thumbs up. I was praying this would be my last week in the field and wondered if I would really make it.

Thoughts of Spurill jumping out of the chopper raced across my mind. He had reached his breaking point and thought that was his only ticket out of the field. He no doubt thought it was worth the article 15 he received. Our ship landed about 100 yards from the border and as soon as we jumped off the choppers, we set up a defensive posture facing the jungle to our front. Our objective was to get out of the open as fast as possible and secure a position just inside the jungle.

The heat was blistering as we quickly made our way to the border. I have never gotten used to 120-degree heat with 90% humidity. It seemed like we were going to make it without incident and proceeded to set up a temporary position inside the jungle. We were not far from the Ho Chi Minh Trail and I expected to see signs of human life in the area. The NVA were in the habit of grabbing villagers and making them repair the trail after B-52s chewed them up during a bombing raid.

It seemed there was always a lot of activity around the border. After fifteen minutes the platoon got up and started to move to the east to see who might be hanging around. When we came in contact with the enemy our goal was to draw them out to the border where Cobras and artillery could do a number on them. I hated this tactic because more than once we took friendly fire as we ran out of the area.

Goats And Ghosts

Today was uneventful and by 1600 hrs., SFC Marquez was getting us close to our ambush site for the night. We would set up next to an ox cart path that was parallel to the Ho Chi Minh Trail. I told Mannarelli that we would find a good hiding place and stay there for the entire week if it were up to me. It just never made sense to me to send a platoon-sized unit into an area where there were company-sized units of NVA.

Somebody at Battalion was trying to get their ticket punched and the way to do it was through body count. I wondered what the acceptable loss rate would be today. In theory we were not supposed to shoot outside Vietnam so why were we being sent into Cambodia? My stomach started growling and I regretted not eating a few more pancakes for breakfast. We pulled into our ambush site just after dark and set up parallel to the path with the Lt., his RTO and a rifleman in rear security. I had my squad set their claymores aiming them down the path pointing away from our position.

I double checked to make sure no one had their claymore pointed towards our position and asked them to show me their field of fire. I set up the order of guard duty and reminded the guys that if anyone went to sleep on guard, I would personally cut their throats. They knew I was just crazy enough to do it too. I took the first watch and after two hours I woke up the Kid and handed him the watch. I laid down and put my head on my back pack and covered myself with my poncho liner. All was well with the world until I heard a rattling sound coming down the path.

I bolted upright and squinted to adjust my eyes and I saw a damn goat walking down the path towards our position. The goat walked right over our claymores and proceeded to walk off into the darkness. Only in Vietnam could a guy experience such outrageous events. I resumed my supine position and was just dozing off when I had one of my recurring nightmares. I sat upright drenched in sweat realizing it was just an hour before sunrise. I told Kush to give me the watch and get some sleep. I wasn't going to be able to sleep now being wound up tighter than a two-dollar watch!

I hated how adrenaline hits made me feel after one of these episodes. All I could do was look forward to eating my lima beans and ham for breakfast. One day down, six more to go. The rest of the week went without incident. We had run into several civilians and Pete asked them what they were doing. Most of the civilians were peasant farmers moving from one growing field to another. Most of these people had a hard life and looked way older than their actual years.

I guessed a male in Vietnam would live an average of 45 years before the parasites ate him up from inside his guts. The older women were wrinkled old hags with horrible teeth. They all suffered from gingivitis and periodontitis and their gums were black as tar. They routinely chewed betle nut leaves or roots rubbing it on their gums to deaden the pain. The Betel palm provided this holistic narcotic. You could tell the old women by how black their teeth were. We never saw males between the ages of 12 and 18 because they were already serving in the Army.

Overall, dealing with the civilians was uneventful. We always had a treat for the little kids and some of their first words were: GI number 1, VC number 10. We had regular coke kids that would show up with cans of coke in a little box with ice. Our favorite coke kid was Tong. He showed up at the darndest times and the darndest places. He would spin the coke can on a small piece of ice making it so cold it would burn your throat.

By the way where did those kids get the ice in the middle of nowhere? On our fifth day in the field Pete told me that one of the peasant farmers told him there was a large group of NVA soldiers camped not far from our position. The Lt. radioed the Company commander and asked him what he wanted us to do. The CO told him to set up an ambush site next to the trail and be prepared to make contact.

He said he would have the Cobras on alert and the artillery guns would be aimed around our location. Now things really began to suck. Everyone was dead tired from humping in the jungle all week and now we were close to making contact.

Everyone was on nervous as hell mode when we set up that night and I think I told God I would be a better man if He let me make it out of this mess. I was on edge as I reminded my squad that no one could go to sleep on guard tonight. Our lives depended on it and it was imperative that everyone did their job. I took first guard again and stayed up for two hours before waking up the Kid and handing him the watch.

The rest of the squad was sound asleep and I had to throw a rock at a new guy to stop his snoring. He sounded like a love-sick wart hog. I asked Kid if he was awake and he said he was fine. I closed my eyes and nodded off. I was half asleep when I heard a weird hissing sound. My eyes flew open and I thought a ghost was standing behind me. I lay completely still not wanting to give my position away. I was so terrified I could not reach for my rifle afraid the ghost would see my movement.

This was the end and I was going to die lying on the ground. I heard the hissing sound again and strained my ears to see where it was coming from. My eyes adjusted and I saw the new guy Detmire sound asleep next to the radio with the handset sitting on top of his shoulder. The hissing sound was coming from the Lt's RTO, keying his radio handset asking for a sit rep. I came off the ground like a spring and in one leap I was on top of Detmire with my hands around his neck. I was choking the life out of him and I didn't realize what I was doing. I was beyond rational thinking and it was like having an out of body experience. I was looking down at myself digging my thumbs into this man's windpipe.

He had no chance to offer any resistance and suddenly I was snapped back to my senses when the Kid grabbed me, pulling me off and saying, "sarge you're killing him." I let go of the death lock I had on his throat and sat down cross-legged wondering what had just happened. By this time, the rest of the squad was awake and wondering what was going on. The new guy was coughing and gasping for air and when he tried to talk his voice squeaked. I was numb and realized I had finally lost my mind. I was terrified, I was finished. A mind is a terrible thing to lose, especially when it's lost in front of your men.

The next morning, I noticed guys looking at me askance and whispering to each other behind my back. The Kid asked me if I was alright and told me I had messed up the new guy's voice box. I had nothing more to say and turned away and opened up a can of peaches. I felt no remorse or sorrow for what had happened. I told these guys what would happen if they went to sleep on guard and now it happened. The story of the night's event spread around the platoon like wildfire.

It was everyone's opinion that I had snapped, and they were right. Pete came walking by me and stepped across the path to take a leak when a booby trap went off injuring his foot. He let out a cry and fell to the ground. Someone yelled medic. As I lay on the ground in the fetal position covering my head, I knew I had no more hope. That booby trap was only 10 feet from where I was lying, and I had walked over it when I set up my claymore. I was going to be lost with Pete gone. I sat and watched as our medic worked on Pete's foot. Ray came over and sat next to me and said, "you look like shit." He didn't know the half of it.

411

Big John and John Close

Pete with Wife

Agent Orange

John and Pete

John's Vietnam Uniform

John's Vietnam Trophies

412

Chapter Twenty-One
LEAVING THE FIELD

FC Marquez came over to me and told me to get my gear together and get ready to jump on the resupply helicopter that was coming. I don't think I fully understood what he was saying. He put his hand on my shoulder and said, "you have done a good job Big John, now it's time for you to get out of here." He had never touched me the whole time we had served together, and his acknowledgment meant everything to me. I gathered up my gear and told the Kid I was going back to Cu Chi. He got a huge smile on his face and said, "I always knew you would make it Sarge."

When the resupply helicopter landed, they put Pete on a stretcher and loaded him up. I threw my gear under the web seat and sat in the doorway with my feet touching the struts. As the ship rose up into the air, I felt a horrible sense of abandoning my guys. How would they survive without me telling them what to do? I looked down and the Kid was brushing his teeth. He looked up at me and gave me a salute. I was overcome with emotion as I raised my hand to my brow and saluted him for the last time. I wondered what I would do when I got back to Cu Chi. Was Ray coming in a few days?

I was told to report to the First Sergeant when I arrived in Cu Chi and he would give me my assignment. Maybe I would work in the supply room or help out in the armory. I didn't really care because I was going to be off line. The first thing I wanted to do is take a shower and get clean fatigues. The hot water in the shower was glorious. In the field we only had a lister bag with a shower head under it that served as a shower. You would get a buddy to dump water into the bag and when you were done, you did the same for him. In Cu Chi they actually had plumbing that supplied unlimited water.

After showering, I went to the supply hooch and got clean fatigues and turned in my M-16 and web gear. There was a no-weapons rule in Cu Chi that assured no crazed GI would shoot some officer or other GI. After I finished at the supply hooch, I went straight away to the Company Quonset and asked to see the First Sergeant. I was shown into his office and told him Marquez had sent me to get a job off line. He looked at me with an odd sneer and said, "I have no jobs right now." I panicked thinking I would be sent back to the field.

The First Sergeant told me to take a seat and he would make a few calls to see if he could find me job. After two or three calls I heard him tell the person on the other end of the line that he would send me right over. He hung up the phone and wrote the name of another First Sergeant on a slip of paper. He handed it to me, and it said, "First Sergeant Bishop, 65th Engineers." I asked the First Sergeant where to find Bishop and he told me he was located in a Quonset building behind the EM club. I got up and headed back to the supply hooch to grab my gear and report to First Sergeant Bishop.

When I walked past the EM club, I saw a Quonset building in the distance. It had a sign out front that said 65th Engineers Battalion Company E. It showed the unit crest with the words First in Last Out painted in red, white, and blue. I would later find out that this unit arrived in Vietnam in 1966 and was given the job of building the base camp at Cu Chi that would be the headquarters for the 25th Infantry Division. The unit specialized in building bridges, but they never saw much bridge-building duty.

When I entered the front door, I saw a black man sitting behind a desk at the end of the building. It turned out that man was First Sergeant Bishop. There were other empty desks located around, but no other personnel were present. I walked up to the First Sergeant and told him that First Sergeant Romanski sent me to see him for reassignment. Bishop told me to take a seat and asked me what I had been doing since I arrived in Vietnam. I told him I was a Wolfhound and that I'd been in the bush for over 10 months.

He was very familiar with the Wolfhounds because his engineers were embedded with us to blow up bunkers and tunnels. I had made a couple of good friends that served in the 65th. He told me Romanski wanted him to find me a job and carry me on his unit morning report until I left in August. He said he had a couple of options and proceeded to tell me about the jobs he had available.

One job was to do daily mine sweeping of the Highway outside the base. The VC and their sympathizers were constantly setting land mines in the road to disrupt convoys and sometimes inflict injury to soldiers traveling by truck or Jeep. I started to feel sick to my stomach. I didn't want a job that required me to leave the base looking for mines to blow up. The next option was to carry C-4 explosive and blasting caps for the engineers going out to the field to blow things up. He must have seen the sullen look on my face when he asked me which of those jobs I wanted.

In a low almost whispered voice I said, "I just can't go back out there Top." He got a sad look on his face realizing I'd seen too much combat and said, "maybe I can have you help my guys build the new swimming pool and recreation area."

Waikiki East

First Sergeant Bishop told me they were naming the new project Waikiki East. My head snapped up and I blurted out, "I can do that." He got a huge smile on his face and told me he had two rules I had to follow: number one was that I better show up the day before my DEROS so I could process out of the company. Number two was that I stay out of trouble and not bring any shame to his unit or him personally. I told him I could certainly do that, and I would not do anything to reflect negatively on him.

A private came into the office and the First Sergeant told him to take me to my assigned hooch located not far from the perimeter. I could not believe my ears. I was actually going to have my own hooch to live in. Man, things were looking up. I would not see First Sergeant Bishop again until the day before I left Vietnam. The private took me to a small hooch and told me this is where I would live. He informed me that I had a hooch buddy and that I would be expected to pay half the charges for a hooch girl to clean the hooch every day.

When I walked into the hooch, I saw a guy sitting on a cot writing a letter. He looked up and said, "that's your cot over there." I introduced myself and asked him what his duties were. He was another short-timer that had been assigned to the 65th to get him out of the field. He served with the 1/12th white warriors. He had 30 days until he boarded the freedom bird. He was also working on the swimming pool project. His name was Jason Fulligar and he was from Cincinnati, Ohio.

It was almost lunchtime and he offered to show me where the chow hall was. He also told me the NCO club did not open until 1700 hrs. He mentioned that they sold great cheese burgers and fries and had a couple of pool tables and cold beer. After lunch, I returned to the hooch and pulled out my writing

416

gear and penned a note to my mom and dad about getting off line. My next letter was to Russ and Becky, who were still living at Fitzsimmons hospital in Denver, Colorado. I wrote a quick note to the Kid telling him my new assignment and new mailing address. As it turned out the Kid wrote me faithfully even after I got home.

I wrote Ray a short letter telling him where I was and that I would speak to First Sergeant Bishop about getting him a job. I was worried sick that something was going to happen to Ray now that I wasn't there. The first night in the hooch was different than I was used to. First and foremost, I was sleeping on a cot off the ground. Secondly, I lay looking up at a thatched roof not the stars hanging in the night sky. The first night I could not sleep and felt claustrophobic. I got up and took my poncho liner outside and lay down next to the hooch.

Tomorrow would be my first day to report to the swimming pool project and I was looking forward to doing something different. After breakfast, I showed up to the construction site where the pool was being built. There were several guys working dressed only in shorts and combat boots. The dress code was definitely different in the engineers than in the infantry. I asked around to find out who was in charge and was directed to a guy sitting in a beach chair writing something on a clipboard. His name was Sergeant Bailey and he was a lifer engineer. I told him I was supposed to start working on the pool and he looked at me and said, "where did you come from?" I told him the Wolfhounds and he said, "great, another short-timer with problems." I had no idea what he meant by that and asked him what I should do.

He told me to check with his foreman and I would be assigned to a job. The foreman asked me if I could pound nails and I said sure. He had me join a couple of other grunts that were starting to build lifeguard towers.

417

The pool construction was about half done and looked like it was going to be very big. It was a concrete structure that would hold hundreds of thousands of gallons of water. It would have a filter system that was designed with diatomaceous earth filters. There was no need for a heating system because the 120-degree days provided all the solar heat needed to keep the pool at 90 degrees. It would be like swimming in a rice paddy. The lifeguards would be drafted from grunts like me waiting in Cu Chi to go home. Many would-be guys that had received two or three Purple Hearts that were exempt from returning to the field.

One of those guys was a Wolfhound named Vladimer. He served in Charlie Company the same time I did and had been wounded three times by booby traps. One of those injuries occurred while he was carrying radio for my friend Sergeant Jim Brandau. His injuries were not serious enough to send him back to the states, so he was in Cu Chi working various jobs for the battalion.

The lifeguard gig would turn out to be a sweet assignment and allowed Vladimer the chance to unwind from the 9 months he had spent in the bush. After we finished the towers, we painted them white with red trim. One of the guys was artistically inclined and volunteered to paint a 3 feet by 6 feet sign that identified the area as the Waikiki East Resort.

After that was completed, we started building a fence that completely enclosed the pool and barbecue area. The battalion commander did not want any Vietnamese kids sneaking into the pool and causing trouble. The workday ended at 1630 hrs. each day and most of the guys would go take a shower and head over to the mess hall. I returned to my hooch and noticed the dirt floor had been swept and my poncho liner was neatly folded and placed at the bottom of the cot.

418

There was an olive drab laundry bag hanging on the wall at the head of my bed and a military handkerchief lay out on the ammo boxes being used as a night stand. I asked my hooch mate where all the stuff came from and he told me Lin our hooch girl had brought it with her that morning.

The laundry bag was for any clothes I wanted washed. Lin would take it to the laundry in Buckeye on her way home and bring it back the next morning. He said it was customary to tip the girls for extra duties they performed. I was anxious to meet Lin and see how she looked. My hooch mate asked me if I was going to go to the NCO club and get a cheese burger and fries. I said that sounded good and decided to go around 1730 hrs.

Crying In My Cups

The walk to the NCO club was just a short 500 feet from my front door. I arrived at the club at 1745 hours and was looking forward to a good meal. When I entered the club only one soldier was sitting at the bar. The rest of the club was empty. I walked up to the bar and was about to ask the bartender about the burgers when this man sitting at the bar looked at me with vacant eyes and said, "pull up a seat."

He told the bartender to get me what he was having and introduced himself as Sergeant John Close. He had served in a mechanized artillery unit and was waiting to go home. He said he had 39 days and a wake-up. I sat down next to him and the bartender sat a stovepipe style glass in front of me filled with ice and the contents he called a gin Collins. It was dressed up with some fruit floating on the top and a straw pointing at the ceiling. I was not a drinker and very rarely drank a beer, so I had no clue what to expect.

When I took my first pull on the straw, my mouth was filled with a citrus-tasting drink. It was like drinking soda pop. My new friend and I ordered cheese burgers and fries and sat back and started our conversation with the usual questions like what unit did you serve in, what is your home town, non-important stuff like that. Close was from Illinois and had gotten married just before coming to Nam. By the time he got to the part about being a newlywed, we had finished our first drink and ordered a second round. My hooch mate was right about the cheeseburgers; they were outstanding.

They were ½ lb. of fresh ground round, hand patted into a perfect round burger topped with two slices of cheddar cheese sitting on a sesame seed bun. There was lettuce, tomato, pickles and a thick slice of red onion on the side. The French fries came in a basket and looked like about a pound of potatoes. This might have been the best meal I'd had since arriving 322 days ago. The gin Collins drinks went down real smooth and didn't taste like liquor to me at all. After the fourth Collins, Close looked at me and said, "do you want to hear the worst thing that happened to me out in the field?" I said, "Sure, what happened?" He proceeded to tell me about his mechanized artillery unit driving down an oxcart path heading to their night lager position.

The lead tank that was just ahead of his tank had a tank commander beside the turret behind a 50 cal. machine gun. Close's tank was 10 yards behind. All of a sudden there was an explosion and the lead tank came to an abrupt halt. The tank Commander that had just been standing there was not to be seen. Maybe he ducked down inside the tank just before the explosion. The entire column came to a halt and everyone was at high alert. Charlie hung a claymore mine in the bamboo next to the path and trip wired it across the path.

The claymore was strategically positioned so that when it went off, the explosion was aimed just above a top of the tracks.

The explosion had vaporized the commander's top half and pieces of him were stuck to the bamboo on the opposite side of the path. His lower half had crumpled down onto the tank floor draining his remaining blood onto the floor.

On another occasion the mech battery was set up on a night lager when they came under a mortar attack. John's best friend was sleeping in the tank directly under the open hatch. A mortar shell entered the tank through the open hatch hitting his buddy. The result was horrific. The next morning the CO told Close he had to clean the tank out and put his buddy's remains into a body bag. With a strained look on his face and tears in his eyes, he recounted the rust smell from the blood inside the tank. The inside of the tank was covered in blood and tissue.

Trying to grab hold of the intestines was almost impossible. He said he vomited as he scraped what was left of his best friend into the black bag. He said he has nightmares about it often. He asked me if I had any horror stories and I told him about the night Boyle got killed. By the time we were into our sixth drink we both had tears running down our faces.

At 2200 hrs., we called it quits and headed back to our hooches. I was having trouble walking straight and halfway to my hooch, I doubled over and vomited the contents of my stomach onto the ammo box sidewalk I was walking on. I guess those drinks packed a punch after all. When I walked into my hooch, I fell onto my cot and didn't remember going to sleep. At 0700 hrs., my hooch mate Jason was shaking me and telling me to get up. I felt disoriented and my stomach ached. Lin had already arrived and was sweeping the floor.

She looked like she was about 13 years old with a cute smile and her hair was pulled back in a ponytail. She looked at me and said, "chao anh" (hello). I nodded my head which caused a sharp pain in my temples. I was already sorry I had drunk those damn Collins drinks. I didn't feel good, so I skipped breakfast and headed straight to work at the pool. By noon I was feeling much better and was starving to death.

A couple of us went to the mess hall and had lunch. The rest of the day was filled with building fence. The foreman told us to slow down and make the job last. He said when this project is finished, we wouldn't know where we would wind up. Good advice indeed, no use getting in any hurry. I kept thinking Ray would be showing up any day, but he seemed to be stuck out in the field. A couple of months ago, Ray's dad Louis, had written a letter to his senator about the complaints Ray was sharing with his dad about conditions in the field.

The Senator wrote a scathing letter to the Battalion Commander and threatened him with his rank. The Battalion Commander was so infuriated he called Ray into Cu Chi and locked his heels before two generals. They tore Ray a new asshole and asked him if he was crazy. Ray made the mistake of telling the generals what was actually happening in the field. As a result, Ray was sent to see the Battalion Psychiatrist for a complete mental evaluation. After sitting for 4 hours being asked question after question, the shrink said he was perfectly sane and sent him back to the field. This sealed Ray's chance of getting off line early.

Shamrock Hardspot

Marquez was a good man and protected Ray by keeping him inside the wire for the rest of his tour. He wrote me several times, keeping me informed about Shamrock hard spot. Shamrock didn't turn out to be lucky, however. Our buddy Sgt. Jim Brandau had been assigned to take over first platoon to cover their platoon sergeant Don Grissom who was leaving on R&R. Jim had been running the platoon without incident until

July 16 when he tripped a booby trap on the way back to the base.

His RTO Vladimer was also injured along with Ricardo Zamora. Jim's injuries were substantial, and he would eventually lose his leg below the knee. I felt terrible and recalled it was Jim who had pinned on my sergeant's stripes at a time. Marquez and I were looking cross-eyed at each other over a comment I had made at Diamond. The CO had the Wolfhounds lay the perimeter wire right up against a bunch of bamboo at Shamrock. The whole area was loaded with booby traps designed to blow a soldier's foot off.

The night of July 19, the NVA barraged the hard spot with RPG rockets and B-40 rockets. The rounds hit the bamboo and exploded like a height of burst artillery shell. The shrapnel rained down on the guys sleeping on the ground and in the bunkers. In the initial attack, Mack Mitchell, William Bass and Michael Scott were killed outright. Doc Flores was in that bunker and got seriously wounded, resulting in getting him sent back to the world. Lanny Ross, Leroy Crabtree, The Kid, and many more were wounded and medevaced out.

Once again, the Army had placed guys in harm's way, and because of poor design and fore thought men lost their lives. This had nothing to do with fighting communism.

The next evening, I found myself sitting next to John Close at the NCO club. I must have had a short memory because I started drinking more Gin Collins drinks. Our discussion was much the same as the night before; one horror story after another followed by crying and staggering back to the hooch and falling passed out on my cot. This went on for two straight weeks except the amount of booze we were consuming increased.

During that time, the pool project had ended, and we were supposed to show up at the First Sergeant's office every morning for our assignments. I had not showed up since the pool job. I basically stayed hidden during the day and drank myself into imbecility at night. It got to the point that when I rolled off my cot in the morning, I couldn't remember walking back to the hooch. Maybe some guardian angel helped me back each night. I kept Lin busy getting my laundry done when I started throwing up on myself during the night. The acid from my stomach would burn my skin and vomit filled up my belly button, galling my skin. I was in misery with the acid burns. Lin complained about how I smelled and by that time, Jason had gone home and I was occupying the hooch alone.

Every morning I would go to the shower and turn on the water and sit on the floor, letting the cascading water wash the dried vomit off my neck and stomach. Close was no better off and we both ended up being sorry asses crying in our cups night after night. By the time my DEROS date was approaching, I had craved gin Collins drinks morning, noon and night. Close and I exchanged home addresses and promised to stay in touch after we got home.

The day before my DEROS date, I showed up at First Sergeant Bishop's office to pick up my DEROS paperwork. He had me sit down at his desk and told me he was glad to see I had made it. He handed me my orders and stood up and stuck out his hand. I grabbed it and he shook my hand vigorously saying, "Good Luck Wolfhound, keep your nose clean." I thanked him for letting me work with the engineers and told him I hoped he made it home safe and sound. I left his office and went to Charlie Company to look for Ray.

That night the guys in the supply room gave us a going away party. It seemed like there were not many guys that made it the whole 365 days and we were looked upon as some kind of heroes.

Getting The Hell Out Of This Bad Place

The next morning, we caught a ride on the supply truck headed to Long Binh. We laughed as we rumbled down the road recalling this is just how we had arrived a year before. By 1300 hours we were standing in line at the processing out center having our paperwork processed. They threatened all of us that if we had any weapons or war trophies in our duffel bags, we better get rid of them. If we were caught with contraband, it could mean we would be staying in Vietnam a while longer.

My bag was full of trophies, including an AK-47 bayonet and several banana clips. I had worked hard and risked my life for this stuff and wasn't going to give it up now. I decided to take the risk. They gave us ID tags to put on our bags and sent us down the line without looking in our bags. Damn, I wished I'd have stuffed an AK in that bag now! They had us get in two lines when approaching the gate. I was in the left line and Ray was in the right line.

There were two large airplanes sitting on the tarmac. One was a United Airlines plane and the other was a large Air Force transport plane. When it was our turn to walk out to the plane, I was told to go to the United Plane and Ray was sent to the Transport Plane. We looked at each other with guarded smiles and gave each other the thumbs up. I yelled at him, "see you in Barstow." When I got to the bottom of the stairs, an airman took our bags and put them on a wheeled luggage cart. My heart was pounding a hundred beats a minute as I climbed the stairs to board the plane. A fleeting thought passed my mind about planes being shot down or hit by mortars.

425

Well, it was too late to worry about that now; what will be will be. There was a beautiful middle-aged stewardess with gorgeous blue eyes waiting just inside the plane when I walked through the door. She smiled and said, "Welcome aboard, pick any seat you want." I walked to the middle of the plane and sat down in a window seat. I didn't want to miss seeing Vietnam disappear behind me if the plane got off the ground.

A guy from First Cav took the seat next to me and nodded his head to acknowledge my presence. The plane was quickly boarded, and the captain got on the intercom and said we would be taking off shortly. He said we would not stop at the end of the runway to wait to take off. Once the plane started moving, he would get us on the runway and go. He said a moving target is tougher to hit. Just what we needed a freaking comedian. My mind drifted back to the platoon and the guys in my squad.

I had a sharp pang of guilt, thinking I had left them behind. How would I know who made it home? I didn't have anyone's addresses and half the guys went by nicknames. I knew most of their hometowns but that was about it. I thought about Russ and Moose at Fitzsimmons Hospital and how I planned to see them when I got to the states. I wondered where I would spend my last six months in the Army. Maybe they would send me back to Ft. Ord or give me an early out like Nixon was promising.

My thoughts were suddenly jolted back to the moment when the plane started taxiing down the side of the runway. I looked out the window and could see Vietnamese women cutting down weeds next to the runway. As I looked behind the plane, I saw the processing center getting farther away. The guy sitting next to me had his eyes shut.

I wondered if he was sleeping or afraid something was going to go wrong. When we got to the end of the runway, the captain steered the plane hard left and as he was turning onto the runway, he ran the throttles full forward and I was pushed back into my seat. The ground beneath the plane was going by faster and faster and a rumbling sound broke through the whine of the jet engines. The plane was rolling over potholes at high speed and suddenly the nose came up and it was silent.

The wheels retracted and the wheel hatches thumped close. The captain pulled the plane into a steep climb and peeled off left over the jungles surrounding Long Binh. I watched as Long Binh got smaller and smaller. Almost in unison, the men in the plane broke out into cheering and hollering and whistling. Hats were flying everywhere and some guy sitting 6 seats in front of me had his hat land in my lap. I peeled the headband back and saw it belonged to SPEC 4 Roosevelt Jackson.

I took my first breath since the plane left the ground. I finally dared to imagine I had made it out of Vietnam on my 365th day. As soon as the plane leveled off at 35,000 ft., the stewardesses came down the aisle throwing bags of peanuts at everyone. They were smiling and telling everyone we were going home. One guy held up a $50 bill and offered it to one of the stewardesses for a kiss. On Ray's Transport plane however, a much different scenario was playing out.

There were cheers and hoopla but instead of round-eyed stewardesses walking down the aisle they had airmen first-class walking down the center of the aircraft checking that everyone had their safety harness attached to the web seat they were sitting in hanging from the ceiling. They announced that bag lunches and water would be handed out in an hour. Those poor bastards. I could only imagine Ray was frothing at the mouth. Meanwhile, our stewardesses were rolling a cart down the aisle passing out cold soda pop of all varieties. I hadn't seen or drank a cream soda since I was home over a year ago. We were told we would be served a variety of sandwiches and bags of chips shortly.

Somebody asked what was for dinner and the stewardess said, "steak, baked potato, green beans and salad with your choice of dressing." I was beginning to like this flight already. I started to imagine what it would be like to step foot on the good old USA again. I already planned on kissing the ground at the bottom of the steps. I leaned my head back on the headrest and closed my eyes. I felt totally exhausted and wondered if I could sleep during the flight home.

Wow, home, I can't believe I'm going home. The next thing I remember is being nudged and asked what kind of sandwich I wanted. They had ham and cheese, turkey and cheese, roast beef and cheese and pastrami on rye. The sandwiches came with all the condiments like pickles, onions, lettuce and tomato as well as packets of mustard and mayonnaise. I chose the ham and cheese on whole wheat. I was surprised how fresh everything tasted. I was so hungry I could have eaten the southbound end out of a northbound mule!

The next 12 hours were spent dozing off and thinking about the last 12 months. I went to Vietnam to serve my country, albeit not willingly at first, but nonetheless, I would do my patriotic duty. I believed in my heart I was going to fight communism. Now I was coming home a disillusioned, broken man who had lost his faith in God and his country. I had left behind any self-confidence I had in myself. I tried to make sense of it all and try to figure out what I had done in Vietnam.

It suddenly came to me that all I had was the man on my right and the man on my left. I would die for them and some of them died for me. How would I ever repay these heroes? I will be seeing my family soon. Would I look different to them? Had things changed in the year I was gone? The Captain announced that we would be landing in Hawaii and that there might be some required maintenance on the plane. I had never been to Hawaii before, so this would be a first for me.

When we landed, the Captain said there was something wrong with one of the engines and that it could take several hours to fix. We were instructed to stay in the airport and not leave the area. He said when the time came to board the airplane, if you weren't there, you would get left behind and would have to get home on your own. The first place everyone went was the airport bar. It was a huge room with several bars and several waitresses running back and forth, taking and delivering orders. I saw a large round table with several GIs sitting there and sat down in one of the empty seats.

Most of the guys had been on my plane and were marking time until our departure was announced. The waitress came by and asked what I wanted to drink, and I said, "Gin Collins please." In the next eight hours the occupants of that table got shit-faced drunk. I started drinking Mai Tais then switched to Blue Hawaiians. The Blue Hawaiians had an orchid, umbrella, a slice of pineapple and extra cherries. That drink went down smooth but kicked like a mule.

I vaguely remember drinking Hawaiian Margaritas and an interesting drink called the Lava Flow. I remember that there was lots of food brought to the table, but I have no recollection of who paid for everything. By the time they announced our departure, I could not stand on my own two feet. Two GIs that I had never seen before stood me up and put my arms around their shoulders and walked me across the ramp to board the plane. I don't remember how I got to my seat and could not tell you when we took off.

Somewhere between Hawaii and Travis Air Force base I woke up. I felt like a midget had walked across my tongue with muddy feet! The guy sitting next to me said I had gotten up and went to the bathroom a couple of times, but I could not dredge that memory from my foggy brain. The thought came to mind the lyrics to a country song, "let's get drunk and be somebody."

429

Well, I was somebody alright, a dumb-ass grunt who had lost any semblance of self-control. I was lucky I hadn't thrown up all over myself like I did in Cu Chi.

Montanard Trooper

Chapter Twenty-Two
ARRIVING BACK IN THE USA

I wondered if John Close made it home. I still had his address in my duffel bag and would try to contact him when I got home. I felt very grungy and smelled like hell, but I was going home, I wasn't sure what awaited me, but I was guessing my mom would plan a nice dinner for me. I must have slept the remaining leg of the trip and missed a couple of great meals. I was awakened by a nudge from the guy next to me telling me we were close to Travis. I was finally going to land where I had taken off 366 days before.

The stewardesses made their final pass down the aisle collecting any trash and within minutes, we heard the roar of the wind as the landing gears dropped into place. I could see the ground and knew it would only be minutes until I would step foot in California. The Captain told us that after landing, an Air Force officer would board the plane and give us our instructions on what to do when we got off the plane.

The landing was near perfect and again there was a throng of cheers and whistles as we taxied down the runway. I smiled, feeling thankful that we wouldn't have to worry about being hit by a mortar or RPG round. The plane came to a stop and the engines wound down until they stopped spinning. I asked the guy next to me what day it was, and he said it was Friday. The main cabin door opened, and I could feel a blast of California air enter the cabin.

An officer walked on board and told us there were buses waiting to take us to the in-processing center on the other side of the base. He said our bags would be brought there and we could pick them up after processing in was completed. When I reached the bottom of the stairs there was a Salvation Army lady greeting each GI and handing them a small bag of goodies.

I thought it was ironic that the only person seeing us off when we went to Vietnam was a Salvation Army lady and now it was another Salvation Army lady welcoming us home. I made up my mind that I would never pass by a Salvation Army volunteer ringing the bell for Christmas, without dropping some cash in the kettle. When I cleared the last step, I knelt down and kissed the ground. I was not the only man on bended knee that day. At the rear of the plane, I saw flag-covered caskets rolling down the cargo ramp being placed in a covered trailer. I hadn't realized some of my dead brothers had caught the freedom bird home with the rest of us.

How sad that those brave men would never realize their dreams. Maybe in some small way, if I could make a difference for the good, it would be honoring their memory. We boarded the buses and took a 10-minute ride to the opposite side of the base. On our way we passed the guys waiting to board their plane to Vietnam. I tried to remember what I had felt that day when I left for war but could not summon those feelings. I only knew I felt sorry for those poor bastards and knew that a bunch of them would be coming home in coffins.

We headed to a huge aircraft hangar that had been converted to a processing center. We unloaded and walked into the hangar through a set of double doors. The hangar was filled with Army issue cots and there were tables and chairs set up to accommodate a couple hundred men. My first thought was why are there cots here? An Air Force Captain's voice came over the PA system directing us to find a chair and sit down.

I looked at my watch and it was 1600 hrs. We were told that processing in could take as long as eight hours and since it was Friday, we would have to wait until Monday to complete the process. A tumultuous grown filled the hangar as we all contemplated staying the weekend in the hangar. We were so close to getting home and now this. Just another SNAFU but why should it be any different than it was in Nam?

The Captain waited until the rumbling settled down and then he told us that since we had just arrived from Nam, he would bypass the normal requirements and only require that we sign out in a registration book before leaving. He said our duffel bags were outside the hanger and the buses would take us to the front gate. His last comment caught me completely off guard. He said, "I recommend that you don't wear your uniform when you leave the base. Jane Fonda has a bunch of her Vietnam War protesters sitting outside the gate and they love to harass returning Vietnam Vets." I thought, what the hell is that all about? I suddenly had a flashback to Barbarella!

I thought there would be people welcoming us home as heroes. It took the better part of an hour for everyone to sign out in the registry book and find their duffel bags. I quickly took out my civilian clothes and along with most of the guys, changed out of my uniform. We loaded up on the buses and were driven to the front gate, where lines of yellow cab taxis were waiting to take us to our destination.

What happened next, I could not be prepared for. As we walked through the front gate, we were stormed by a bunch of hippie-looking girls and a few long-haired guys. It reminded me of when I was in Haight Asbury and the hippies were giving us the bums rush asking for change. This group was a bunch of angry people on a mission. The first thing that happened was a young girl spit on me and said, "you filthy baby killer." Others were throwing rotten produce, no doubt retrieved from the dumpsters behind a local Safeway store.

My first reaction was to reach out and grab the little bitch by the throat and choke her to death, but she read the look on my face and ran away like a coward. I was getting very worked up when a GI grabbed my shoulder and said, "cool it man, it means nothin." Four of us shared a cab and asked the driver to take us to the nearest greyhound bus station. My first thought was to find a payphone and call my sister and mom to inform them I had arrived back to the states.

By the time we arrived, it was 1800 hrs. and I wondered if I could even get a bus to Fullerton where my sister lived. There was a bank of payphones just inside the bus terminal and I grabbed one and started feeding quarters into the slot. There was a sudden bang just 20 feet from where I was standing, and I found myself lying face down on the ground. Several people stared at me as if I was some kind of nut. It was a car backfiring. I broke out in a sweat and wondered if I would ever fully get out of Vietnam.

After four bells, I got a dial tone and dialed my mom's number. I stood there my hands still shaking and the instant mom heard my voice, she started crying and said, "are you really back?" I told her I was calling from the bus station in Vacaville and that I was going to try to catch a bus to Joanne's house in Fullerton. I told her I would see her in a few days and that I loved her. Next, I called my sister and told her where I was and that I didn't know how soon I would make it to her house. She told me to call her as soon as I arrived, and she would come and pick me up no matter what time it was.

The bus ride would take about 6 hours and I was prepared to sleep in the bus station until morning to catch the next bus. I approached the ticket counter and asked when the next bus to Fullerton would be and the agent said, "it leaves in 20 minutes." I asked if there were any available seats and he said yes, so I bought a ticket and went to the vending machines to get some snacks and a coke. I had not been on a Greyhound bus since I traveled from San Diego to LA for my induction physical.

I wasn't looking forward to it, but I was exhausted and hoped I could catch some sleep on the way. When we boarded the bus, they took my duffel bag and put it in the luggage storage area under the bus. There was no assigned seating and the driver told us to pick any seat we wanted. Before leaving the terminal, he told us where the bathroom (that was smaller than a porta-potty) was located in the back of the bus.

He said we would be stopping at different towns to unload and pick up new passengers. This particular bus was heading to Anaheim, the home of Walt Disney and Disneyland. The bus ride was uncomfortable, and it was almost impossible to go to sleep. The old man sitting next to me snored like a wounded hound dog. I dozed off a few times and mostly thought about the guys in my squad I'd left behind.

I wondered how Jim Brandau was doing after blowing his leg off on a booby trap on June 16. Ray and I had nudged him off the back of an armored personnel carrier rumbling down the road into Trang Bang as a joke. He cracked his ankle and ended up in Cu Chi on a medical profile. That's when Ray and I nicknamed him "shammer." Who needs friends when you have Big John and Rick o Shay? Did they send Pete back out to the field after his foot healed?

Just before I left, the platoon was attacked at a hard spot they named Shamrock; that certainly didn't turn out to be lucky in any way. How did those wounded guys make out? The carnage just wouldn't end until we either bombed Hanoi off the map or the U.S. got the hell out of there. I arrived at the Anaheim terminal at 0100 hrs. and decided to take a cab to my sister's house instead of waking her up. It was only 4 miles away and I could ring the doorbell and surprise her when I arrived.

When the cab driver, a young black man, opened the trunk and pulled my duffel bag out, he looked at me and said, "you coming back from Nam?" I said, "Yeah, why do you ask?" He said his brother was a marine killed in Nam on April 1, 1968, at a place called Khe San. I told him I had heard about it and was sorry he lost his brother.

I stood there starring into the distance remembering the 45 men that had given their lives while serving with them. Forty-five families, wives, brothers, sisters, children would be destroyed because of this damn war. "Are you ok, man?" I snapped back to the moment and said, "yeah just thinking of some of my buddies." I pulled out my wallet and asked the driver how much I owed, and he said, "this ride is on me, glad you made it home." I thanked him and handed him a ten-dollar bill as a tip, and he smiled and put it in his pocket.

As the cab pulled away from the curb, I walked up to my sister's apartment and reached out to push the doorbell when suddenly the door flew open and my sister, with her roommate Marie, were standing there in their nightgowns reaching out to hug me. My sister had tears in her eyes and grabbed my duffel bag and dragged it into the apartment with Marie pulling me behind her. My sister hugged me and kissed me on the cheek and asked me if I was hungry. I told her no, that I was just tired and wanted to get some sleep. My sister had prepared the couch for me to sleep on and showed me where the bathroom was and told me we would have breakfast in the morning and go see mom.

The girls went back to bed and I pulled my poncho liner out of my duffel bag and laid down on the floor and drifted off to sleep. Sometime during the night, I had a nightmare and when I woke up, my sister was standing over me with a horrified look on her face. I was drenched in sweat and shaking like a leaf. She asked me who Boyle was and I told her it was a long story; one that I did not intend to tell her about. I came to the realization that I had left Vietnam, but Vietnam had not left me and never would.

My mother called and asked me if there was anything special, I wanted when I got to her house. I assume she was thinking of some dessert or special treat, but all I could think of was a bottle of Beefeater Gin. She hesitated for a second and said, "that's it?" I said, yeah that will do.

Before leaving, I put on my dress greens and my sister said I looked very handsome. Mom wanted me to show up in uniform so she could get a picture of me and her. After having breakfast at the neighborhood IHOP, we loaded up my sister's Volkswagen Bug and headed down the old Pacific coast highway. It hugged the coastline and went through all the towns I had hung out at as a young man. We passed through Huntington Beach and continued down to Laguna Beach then San Clemente.

When we got close to Mission Beach, I knew I was close to home. I had surfed this part of the coast when I was in high school. We passed La Jolla, where my dad worked for 10 years at the Scripps Institute and then passed by crystal pier at Pacific Beach. I had to smile when we passed the amusement park at Mission Beach. It brought back many happy childhood memories. What I wouldn't do to go back to those carefree days.

I wondered if I would ever be happy again. Joanne headed east on Hwy. 8 and headed towards Mom's house. She asked me if I was happy to be home and I simply nodded my head. What was it going to be like to be home? Would I fit back in? I guess I

437

would deal with that later because now I was about to see my mom, who was waiting for me on her front porch, standing next to the American flag she had flown every day since I arrived in Vietnam.

When Joanne turned onto Stewart Street, a chill ran up my spine. A thousand memories flooded my mind all at once and I felt overwhelmed. We pulled up to mom's house and I got out of the car and walked up to my mother and gave her a big hug. Tears were running down her face and she kept kissing me on the cheek. Mom's friend, Bill Smith, was standing behind her and tears were running down his face as well.

I stood there stone-faced with a lack of emotions. My sister snapped our picture and mom ushered me into the house and my senses were overloaded with the smell of turkey, dressing, mashed potatoes and all the things mom used to make for Thanksgiving. The table was set with mom's best china and silverware and she seated me at the head of the table.

Bill said the grace and ended the prayer with "good God, let's eat." As the food was being passed around the table, my mind went back to the Thanksgiving I had spent in Nam on the Cambodian border. It felt like I was still in Vietnam and couldn't get out of there. I looked down the table and said, "will someone please pass the fuckin' butter." My mom's face turned pale and she turned to Bill and whispered, "this isn't the same boy that went to Vietnam," and she was right.

Big John and Bob Noel getting ready to leave Vietnam

Colonel Hamilton, Big John and SFC Linehan. Col Hamilton is promoting John to E-6 at Ft. Campbell, Ky

CIB Patch

John and his mother Eleanor

439

John standing in front of flag his mom flew the entire time John was in Vietnam

5-4-69

Mom,

HAPPY MOTHERS DAY

Sorry it's not a card but it's my own original. Things are about the same here - The weather is hot - no rain yet - I expect it any day - We went through the swamp today - it was up to our necks - God I got three damn leeches too - Hows my Mom? Did you get another job - I pray you do - St. Anthony has never let up town yet - I've only got 100 days left - It's great to reach that mark -

Have you heard from Linda lately? I never have heard from JoAnn - I guess she has the wrong address or something?????? Thanks for letting her out anyway.

Well gotta go now - thanks for being such a great mom - Again I want to say Happy Mothers Day

Love You always
Your Son

Letter Home

Crossing Vam Co Dong River

Wolfhounds Forever!

AUTHOR'S NOTES

When I got home from Vietnam, I was assigned to complete my military obligation at Ft. Campbell, Kentucky. When I showed up for duty, I was told I had 3 choices of MOS. This distinctly sounded like something I had heard in Vietnam! The clerk told me I could be assigned to the engineers who go out on 7-day training exercises and blows stuff up. I could not imagine being around explosives again. The next choice was to be assigned to the 82nd airborne. Jumping out of perfectly good airplanes did not appeal to me either. I was getting worried that I might get stuck picking up cigarette butts outside the Post Commander's office.

The third choice was to join the Committee Group and teach basic trainees one of the required classes to prepare them for Vietnam. My mind immediately went back to my training at Ft. Ord and the returning Vietnam Vets that taught us. They had made a difference and helped us understand the seriousness of learning as much as we could before being thrown into a real war. I told the clerk I would take that assignment and within 10 minutes I was leaving the office with a new set of orders.

I reported to the Committee Group office the following morning and was assigned a place to live and an assignment to assist at the rifle range. I would be sharing a room with another Vietnam Vet that had been a cook in Saigon. He returned to the states as a PFC. Unfortunately, that arrangement did not last long after he complained to the First Sergeant that I screamed in my sleep. I would continue to have flashbacks and nightmares the rest of my life.

The requirements to be an instructor were that you break starch at least twice a week and have spit-shined combat boots.

They issued me a black enameled helmet liner that was to be worn at all times and had to be so shiny you could see your face in it. When I reported to the rifle range, I reported to Sergeant First Class Linahan.

He was a lifer that had been to Vietnam twice and was not interested in doing anymore that he had to. The officer in charge of the range was a young man straight out of OCS marking time until he got his orders for Vietnam. The purpose of the range was to teach new trainees how to shoot the M-16 rifle. Linahan told me right up front that I was going to teach the classes. He handed me a three-ring binder and said learn this tonight, you'll be teaching tomorrow.

When I reviewed the Army manual it seemed like a bunch of gobble gook to me. I made up my mind I would spend the hour and a half I was allotted to teach these newbies about surviving Vietnam. How long would it take to tell these youngsters to keep their weapons clean and oozing with LSA. I created my own lesson plan that included 20 minutes of jokes and the rest of the time begging them to pay attention and not to go to sleep in the bleachers.

Just like my instructors in Basic and AIT I would get very emotional and tears would often run down my cheeks. Linahan was so busy doing crossword puzzles in the tower he didn't have a clue what I was teaching. Many of my trainees achieved expert and sharp shooter badges. Somehow word got to the Post Commander about my unorthodox style of teaching. He and three other officers did a surprise visit to my range and stood behind the bleachers and listened to my presentation.

I was unaware of their presence, until Linahan told me they were there. The following day I was told to show up at the Post Commander's office. I figured my goose was cooked and there were plenty of police calls in my future. Colonel Hamilton invited me to sit down in front of his desk and proceeded to congratulate me on being an outstanding instructor. He told me the Army needed more men like me preparing men for Vietnam.

Hamilton had served in Vietnam three tours all in the infantry. He offered me a direct commission and said he would send me to OCS. I asked him where I would wind up and he said back in Vietnam. I politely declined and he asked me to stand up and he presented me with Staff Sergeant Stripes. He had a photographer take a picture of the event. He also told me I was being assigned as the NCOIC of the rifle range. I guess Linahan would have to do his puzzles somewhere else.

Those six months at Ft. Campbell was a bitter-sweet experience. I had an alcohol addiction that I took care of every night at the NCO club. Being young comes with great resiliency so I didn't have a problem with doing my job. I did make it to Fitzsimmons Hospital to see Russ and Becky but missed Moose because he was getting debridement care while I was there. I kept in touch with Ray and Russ and exchanged Christmas cards with Hedgy Van Ark for several years.

Alan Claymore Larsen wrote the first year I was home but not after that. Ray would become my first sons godfather and we lost track of each other for 20 years after that. There wasn't a day that I didn't think of him and the guys I served with and the heroes that died while I was in Nam.

You might recall the naive girl I met on the boardwalk at Santa Cruz. She and my sister planned our wedding that I was required to show up at shortly after I got out of the service. We moved to Cody, Wyoming where I worked for Safeway and drove 18 wheelers. I met a man named Bud Williams at the Buffalo Bill bar on main street Cody. I noticed him nursing seltzer water with a slice of lime on top.

Our eyes met and we nodded at each other and Bud got up and sat beside me at the bar. He told me he was a recovering alcoholic and a minister at a local non- denominational church. He asked me about myself and I told him the usual blather. Over the next two years this man loved me for who I was and led me back to my religious roots. I had shared with him a few things about Nam but not the part where I stopped believing in God altogether. One Sunday morning as he was approaching the pulpit, he handed me a card. On it was written the following words:

Footprints in the Sand

One night a man had a dream. He dreamed he was walking along a beach with the Lord. Across the sky flashed scenes from his life. For each scene, he noticed two sets of footprints in the sand; one belonged to him and one to the Lord.

When the last scene of his life flashed before him, he looked back at the foot prints in the sand, He noticed that many times along the path of his life there was only one set of footprints. He also noticed that it happened at the very lowest and saddest times in his life.

This really bothered him, and he questioned the Lord about it. Lord, you said that once I decided to follow You, You'd walk with me all the way. But I have noticed that during the most troublesome times in my life, there is only one set of footprints. I don't understand why, when I needed You most, You would leave me.

The Lord replied, "My precious, precious child, I love you and would never leave you. During your times of trial and suffering, when you saw only one set of footprints, it was then that I carried you."

Author unknown

When the pastor invited people to come forward and give their heart to the Lord, I approached the altar as a broken vessel realizing that the Lord had been with me the whole time I was in Vietnam. I now realized that He carried the men who lost their lives in Vietnam across the finish line of their lives. That very day I gave my heart to Jesus and He has always walked by my side no matter the problems life has brought me.

I eventually moved to Billings, Montana where I earned a bachelor's degree in education and began a teaching career. I have three wonderful children from my first marriage Tim, Tom and Tammy. Like so many Vietnam combat vets, unfortunately, I didn't do too well in the marriage department. My first marriage suffered because of my flashbacks, nightmares and PTSD I did not know I had.

I got married a second time and have a wonderful daughter Laura Louise from that marriage. They say the third time is the charm and in 1992 I married the true love of my life Laura Anne. As of this writing I have 12 grandchildren and three great-grandchildren. I have had several careers and finally settled down as an Allstate Insurance Agent in Great Falls, Montana. I retired from that position after 25 years of service.

In 1990, my boyhood best friend Fred Pease wrote me a letter and said he would be leading his squadron of F-15 fighter jets into Saudi Arabia in advance of Desert Storm. That letter reawakened something inside me and I began thinking about my time in Vietnam. I got my Bronze Star and Purple Heart out of the box and framed them and put them on my office wall.

I began writing him letters and sending him care packages. In return he sent me pieces of scud missiles that had fallen around his bunker. I felt such pride in what my friend was doing, and our government finally let the military win a war with no holds barred. The Generals running that war were all Vietnam

Vets and vowed not to get us into a war that we wouldn't be given permission to win.

Fred told me the nation had the Vietnam Veteran to thank for this because of the shameful way we were treated when we came home. I realized at that time that I was proud of my service but never expressed it. That would all change in the years to come.

In 2003, I retrieved the two boxes in the attic that contained my Vietnam letters and memorabilia. The boxes were water-stained and looked like they were about to fall apart. When I opened them, I pulled out the water Buffalo horn the Vietnamese boy had dropped while being drug across the rice paddy. Next were the NVA belts, flags and several AK-47 banana clips I had recovered while in Nam. All the letters I'd received were there as well as the letters I wrote to my Mom that she gave me when I got home.

There were envelopes full of Polaroid pictures I had taken as well of photos of me taken by other guys. My mind was going into sensory overload. I called Ray and Russ and told them I wanted to find the guys we had served with. Ray suggested if I found enough of them, we could have a reunion of some kind.

This was before military reunions were popular. My wife Laura had just purchased our first computer and I used it to track down as many guys as possible. I also located the families of our fallen brothers including Marie in Illinois. If it weren't for my buddies, I would never have been able to find as many as I did. Amazingly, I would find out that the men I served with came home with many injuries, both seen and unseen.

They tackled life with the same survivalist attitude as we had in Vietnam. Some became doctors, lawyers, stockbrokers, insurance professionals and salesmen of all kind. They worked as civil servants, and some made the military their career. Our group included choir directors, deacons, and ministers. A couple of the men served veterans as veteran's representatives. Others worked in the postal service and others in the food industry.

Our guys worked in all kinds of trades including welding, electrical, plumbing, and general contracting. We have a chiropractor, CPA, auto workers and musicians. Some became mechanics others long-haul truck drivers. Many started successful businesses and became involved in the emerging tech industries. We represent the best part of the American fabric and are not ashamed to show our patriotism.

In June 2004, 20 Wolfhounds and their wives met in Washington, D.C. for our first reunion. It was truly an event to remember. The guys that were quiet in Nam were still quiet and the smart asses in Nam were still smart asses. Conversations picked up right where they ended in Nam. In those three days together we all experienced a healing beginning in our souls. We pledged to meet every two years at a different venue.

Over the next 16 years, I found over a hundred men and our reunions grew bigger every year. In 2019, I decided to get live interviews from all the guys. This would be a historic record of our service and our lives. Generations to come would be able to hear the stories firsthand. My son Tim and I headed out on a cross-country excursion and taped 77 interviews.

We went coast to coast and created a place on our Wolfhound website to save them for the next 100 years. Schools are using these interviews as a resource to study the Vietnam War. It seems like it has been a whirlwind these past years but looking back it has been worth it all.

I am now looking forward to interviewing the remaining Wolfhounds from Charlie Company and securing a place for us in American Military History. Wolfhounds Forever! I want to end with a saying my pastor friend Bud Williams always said,

"May the good Lord bless and keep you and all the good things come to you, until we meet again."

AFTERWORD TIMOTHY QUINTRELL

When I was 8 years old, I remember looking out the window and watching my dad work through the night on his old 1948 Chris Craft boat. I remember he would often wear a green field jacket on our hunting and fishing trips. Back then, I had no idea the impact his service would have on his life and the lives of many others.

Growing up, I wasn't aware of dad's service, the nightmares, the cold sweats, or the loaded pistol only a reach away. When I was 12, my dad took us kids on a camping trip to sunlight basin in Wyoming. I'll never forget that second night when we were taught what words like ambush patrol and walking point was.

Many years went by and one day he phoned me and asked me about some sound gear and projector for a veteran reunion he was planning. Having no idea about his service, I was quickly taken aback and in a state of shock and awe, when he sent the videos of the reunion for me to watch. I watched and cried and thanked God that somehow, I knew he was helping grown men who had been paralyzed by fear and other haunting aspects of their services.

I watched as grown men opened their hearts and wept and talked with their brothers about the memories of their service. It was then I made a life promise to dad that I would do everything in my power to help reach and serve this great brotherhood of heroes. Getting to serve by his side for over 15 years now, loving and serving veterans has changed my life forever.

451

I never thought things like maintaining a website, or providing Audio Visual Services for reunions, or recording the many stories from the unit's history would have such an impact on me. The first time I showed up to help the vets, I was overwhelmed with emotion. To meet the men who bravely served and have an opportunity to serve them, was too much to comprehend.

Over the years, I have watched my pop age and deal with the effects of growing old and begin to fall apart. Diabetes, kidney issues, knees, back, and shoulder issues, some from the gift of agent orange. Yet, through the chapters of his life, I've never heard him complain; he just continues to put one foot in front of the other.

The years he has spent "finding the guys," reuniting, and cultivating has been so productive. No one except for Laura Anne, his wife, will ever know how much time, money, tears, sweat, and effort Dad has poured into the journey of reuniting the brotherhood of the Wolfhounds.

I hope as you read and enjoy this excellent book, you will never forget the great sacrifice many young men and women made to fight and serve our great nation. And I hope you know this book was just the beginning of a tremendous life well lived. Pop you're my hero, confidant, father, mentor, and best friend! I'm proud of you and it's an honor to walk all the way to the finish line with you!!

Tim Quintrell is the Senior Pastor of Light House Church where he has served for over 20 years. Tim has been married to his wife Dawn for over 27 years and has 2 children Jared and Britney and 2 grandchildren Audrey and Truett.

GLOSSARY AND ABBREVIATIONS

AIT: Advanced Infantry Training

Article #15: Uniform Code of Military Justice provides commanders with a non-judicial, administrative tool to maintain discipline for relatively minor infractions involving enlisted soldiers. For officers, it is often a career-ending punishment.

ARVN: Army Republic of Vietnam AWOL: Absent without leave

Boom Boom Girl: A Vietnamese prostitute.

Boonie hat: Hat worn by soldiers while operating in jungle warfare.

Bouncing Betty: A mine with two charges: one to propel the explosive charge upward and the other set to explode at about waist level.

Booby Trap: An improvised explosive devise hidden with the purpose of killing or injuring soldiers.

DI: Drill Instructor

Charlie: Slang for Viet Cong.

Chinook: The official name of the CH – 47 tandem rotor transport helicopter. Also known as a "hook."

Chop Chop: Vietnamese slang for food.

Chopper: Helicopter.

CO: Commanding officer.

CS Gas: Known by the name "Tear gas." it is a chemical substance that temporally incapacitates the person it comes in contact with.

DEROS: Date of estimated return from overseas. Diddi Mau: To run away. Get the hell out of the area.

Dust-off: Radio call sign for medical evacuation helicopters; the term refers to the great amount of dust thrown up by the rotors as the medevacs come into land.

Fire Base: An artillery battery set up to give fire support to surrounding units.

GI: Government issue. Often a reference to men drafted for military service and called a "GI"

Gook: Slang word used to describe Viet Cong soldiers.

Green Beret: Popular name for the special forces, taken from the color of their distinctive headgear.

Grunt: A non-offensive term used to designate the guys on the ground. Originally slang for a Marine fighting on the battlegrounds of Vietnam, but later applied to any infantryman fighting there.

Hedgerow: A stand of bamboo plants and heavy brush. Used as a wind break and hiding place for snipers and bunkers.

Hooch: The living quarters for Vietnamese peasants and their families also a building housing military personnel in the combat theater.

Huey: HU-1, the utility helicopter that was the workhorse of Vietnam.

KIA: Killed in action.

Kit Carson Scout: Viet Cong soldier who surrenders to the U.S. and pledges allegiance to South Vietnam, who voluntarily works for the U.S. military, usually with combat infantry units.

Klick: 1 kilometer or 0.6214 miles.

LZ: Landing zone.

LOH: Pronounced "loach" – light observation helicopter. MOS: Military occupation specialty.

M-16: American 5.56 mm infantry rifle. M-60: Machine gun

M-79: A weapon that shoots grenades

Mama-San: Term used in Vietnam to describe an older woman. Medevac: Term used for aerial medical evacuation.

Medic: Medical aid service man or woman on the battlefield or in a hospital unit.

Mermite Can: Insulated container used to keep food hot or cold. NCO: Non Commissioned Officer

NCOIC: Non Commissioned Officer in charge. Napalm: Jellied gasoline used in air strikes.

NVA: North Vietnamese Army or generic term for any soldier or group of soldiers from the north.

Point: The lead man in a patrol. PT: Physical Training

Quonset hut: A multi-use light weight prefabricated structure of corrugated galvanized steel having a semicircular cross- section. Used in Vietnam for hospital wards storage and buildings.

R&R: Rest and recuperation: reference to time off for military personnel.

RPG: Rocket propelled grenade

Sapper: Enemy soldier trained to attack fortifications.

SNAFU: Situation Normal All Fucked Up

TOC: Tactical Operations Center.

Viet Cong: Also known as the national liberation front – a mass political organization in South Vietnam and Cambodia with its own army that fought against the United States and South Vietnamese governments. Abbreviated as VC; also known as "Victor Charlie."

WIA: Wounded in action.

Made in the USA
Monee, IL
18 July 2022